Prayer and Play in Late Tokugawa Japan

Harvard East Asian Monographs 185

Prayer and Play in Late Tokugawa Japan

Asakusa Sensōji and Edo Society

Nam-lin Hur

Published by the Harvard University Asia Center
and distributed by Harvard University Press
Cambridge (Massachusetts) and London, 2000

Printed in the United States of America

The Harvard University Asia Center publishes a monograph series and, in coordination with the Fairbank Center for East Asian Research, the Korea Institute, the Reischauer Institute of Japanese Studies, and other faculties and institutes, administers research projects designed to further scholarly understanding of China, Japan, Vietnam, Korea, and other Asian countries. The Center also sponsors projects addressing multidisciplinary and regional issues in Asia.

Library of Congress Cataloging-in-Publication Data

Hur, Nam-lin

Prayer and play in late Tokugawa Japan : Asakusa Sensoji and Edo society / Nam-lin Hur.

p. cm.--(Harvard East Asian monographs ; 185)

Includes bibliographical references and index.

ISBN 0-674-00240-7 (cl : alk. paper)

1. Sensōji (Tokyo, Japan). 2. Recreation--Religious aspects--Buddhism. 3. Amusement--Religious aspects--Buddhism. 4. Buddhism--Social aspects--Japan. I. Series.

BQ 6353.T6492 S465 2000

306.6'943'0952135--dc 21

99-04499

Index by the author

Printed on acid-free paper

Last figure below indicates year of this printing

09 08 07 06 05 04 03 02 01 00

In memory of my mother

Acknowledgments

About a decade ago I was looking for "raw" materials at Princeton's Gest Library for my yet-to-be-defined dissertation. What occupied my mind were two words that my advisor, Professor Helen Hardacre, had emphasized to the point of rendering them into mantras: primary and original. Even though these two conditions were expected for any Ph.D. dissertation, the problem was that there was already a vast literature on Tokugawa society and religions. After ransacking promising-looking materials in the stacks housing the Japanese collection, I found that no one seemed to have touched (at least at Princeton) the ten-plus, thick, fresh-looking volumes of the *Sensōji nikki* (Sensōji diaries). I therefore decided to check out these volumes, even though I had not the slightest idea what they might be about.

Some years later I passed along the bustling pathway of Sensōji Nakamise and finally stood before the Main Hall, where the Asakusa Kannon was supposed to be enshrined. It was an exciting moment. I marveled at the crowds of visitors and was amazed at the interesting combination of religion and non-religion. Upon returning to Tsukuba, where I was guided by Professor Miyata Noboru, I found myself puzzling over how to relate the scene at Sensōji to the Buddhism I knew through Buddhist scriptures. The *muen teki* (untied-to-anything) scholarship of folk religion and folklore to which I was exposed at Tsukuba was of great help to me not only in understanding the complexity of Sensōji Buddhism but also in discarding the narrow academic focus of my thinking. I am grateful to the Japan Foundation for funding my stay at Tsukuba.

Within the next few years, I went back to the "primary" materials in search of an "original" discovery concerning Sensōji Buddhism. My reading of the Sensōji diaries progressed smoothly, thanks to the training I had received from Professors Tamamuro Fumio and Martin Collcutt. It was a long but rewarding process. Nevertheless, the task of deciphering the seemingly hidden information on Sensōji and the task of understanding Sensōji Buddhist culture were not necessarily the same. In my attempt to contextualize Sensōji Buddhism within Edo society as well as within Japanese religion in general, Professors Marius B. Jansen and Jacqueline Stone were particularly helpful. In my attempt to locate it within the larger context of East Asian Buddhist culture, Professor Stephen F. Teiser enlightened me in many ways.

I was fortunate to have post-doctoral training at Harvard with the generous financial support of the Edwin O. Reischauer Institute of Japanese Studies. During this period, I had an opportunity to expand the scope of my studies on Japan and to reflect on the Sensōji project in a larger context. At Tokyo University the following year, realizing that my knowledge about Japanese history and culture was still too *hazukashii* (shameful), I paid further attention to diverse subjects beyond Tokugawa Buddhism. During these years, Professors Harold Bolitho and Shimazono Susumu, as well as my old teachers, were great sources of encouragement and inspiration.

Along with developing and creating teaching materials and new research topics at the University of British Columbia, I revisited the Sensōji project and began to revise older chapters while writing new ones for publication. Vancouver has proved to be a wonderful place for research and writing. During this period I was energized by the encouragement of Professors Yunshik Chang and Daniel L. Overmyer, and I was greatly helped by Mr. Tsuneharu Gonnami and Ms. Linda Joe at the Asian Library. I express my deep thanks to all of them. In editing the manuscript, Ms. Brittani Faulkes and Dr. Joanne Richardson were of great help to me. The financial support of the University of British Columbia, through a startup grant and UBC-HSS grants, was indispensable.

The critical comments of the anonymous reviewers of the manuscript were especially helpful in revising it into a better shape. The current form of the book reflects their insightful suggestions. I am grateful to John R. Ziemer of Harvard University Asia Center for treating this manuscript with professional care and respect throughout the publication process. Finally, without the endurance and love of my family, both in Korea and in Canada, this book would not have been possible. My deepest thanks and love go to my father, parents-in-law, brothers and sisters, and to Jin and Erin.

N.-L.H.

Contents

Reference Matter

Figures and Tables

Figures

Tables

Abbreviation

The following abbreviation is used in the text and notes:

SN Sensōji hinamiki kenkyūkai, *Sensōji nikki*, 18 vols. (Tokyo: Kinryūsan Sensōji, 1978–96).

Prayer and Play in Late Tokugawa Japan

INTRODUCTION

The Rise of Sensōji Buddhism

Religion was a shield for the political ambitions of Tokugawa Ieyasu (1542–1616). Ieyasu's advisors, particularly Tenkai (1536–1643), a Tendai monk, insisted that military strength could be enhanced through divine protection. Thus, when Ieyasu took over control of Edo, the heart of the Kantō region, from the Later Hōjō in 1590, he swiftly selected two religious institutions to protect his family: Zōjōji, in southwestern Edo, as a site to honor his ancestral deities, and Sensōji,* in northeastern Edo, as a prayer hall to ensure the prosperity of his family.[1]

A decade later, Ieyasu came to appreciate the protective power of Sensōji even more. At the Battle of Sekigahara in 1600, which would determine his entire political fate, an anxious Ieyasu sent for Zon'ō (1544–1620), the head monk of Zōjōji, and asked him to lay a curse on the opposing forces. Zon'ō, a highly respected Pure Land Buddhist monk, believed that especial protection could be obtained from two deities in Kantō: Kashima Daimyōjin in Kazusa (who offered Shintō protection) and the Asakusa Kannon of Sensōji (who would provide Buddhist protection).[2] Zon'ō singled Sensōji out as having the most prominent Buddhist deity in Kantō. Sensōji officials responded to Ieyasu's summons and quickly came up with a prayer ritual alleged to have been

* The native Japanese reading of the Chinese characters with the sinitic pronunciation "sensō" is "asakusa," and the main deity of this temple is familiarly known as the "Asakusa Kannon" and the area surrounding the temple is referred to as "Asakusa."

conducted for Minamoto no Yoritomo when he had charged a Taira force at Fujikawa in 1180. They promptly sent Ieyasu talismans bearing the protective power of their deity, the Asakusa Kannon.[3] Proof of the divine might of the Asakusa Kannon came as Ieyasu emerged the decisive winner of the Battle of Sekigahara and started a new chapter in Japanese history—the Tokugawa shōgunate. After this episode, Sensōji's status as a leading prayer hall of the Tokugawa family was secure.

The prosperity of religious institutions in premodern Japan was guaranteed by affiliation with political leaders such as Ieyasu. The past glory of such prominent institutions as the Ise Shrine and the Tōdaiji, Enryakuji, Kōfukuji, and Gozan temples, to name but a few, illustrates the benefits of linking religion and political power. Sensōji could not afford to miss the opportunity of associating itself with Tokugawa Ieyasu, particularly since Sensōji, which was located on the periphery of Edo, did not, at this time, enjoy the same prestige as the great Buddhist institutions in the Kansai region.

When Tokugawa Ieyasu entered Edo Castle in 1590, Edo was still an isolated town in the wild plains of Kantō. Despite its strategic importance, Edo, which then contained approximately 100 households and a population of less than 1,000, was of little importance compared with the bustling urban centers of central Japan.[4] Sensōji was located on the rural outskirts of shabby Edo. In the eyes of people from the Kansai region (hitherto the nation's political center), who were acquainted with the glorious traditions of influential religious institutions, Sensōji would have appeared negligible. However, at this critical juncture, Tokugawa Ieyasu, whose power was based in Kantō, paid special attention to Sensōji in anticipation of the divine protection that its main deity, the Asakusa Kannon, would provide him. His patronage marked a watershed in Sensōji's prosperity.

As soon as it was designated a prayer hall for Ieyasu and his family, Sensōji emerged on the national stage, and its long dormancy drew to an end. Before it became associated with the Tokugawa family, Sensōji, which belonged to the Tendai sect, had been in institutional disarray. As Tokugawa chroniclers of Sensōji would lament, prior to its affiliation with the shōgunate, Sensōji monks had ignored even the most basic precepts of their sectarian tradition, "mingled with women," and adulterated

Tendai Buddhist rituals and ceremonies by adding to them Shugendō and shamanic elements. Shugenja (practitioners of Shugendō) had been a perennial component of Sensōji. In the mid-sixteenth century, an abbot named Chūkai had expelled married monks and shugenja and tried to reorganize the remaining, "clean" monks into a Tendai Buddhist order, but his reform efforts were short-lived.[5]

Despite the rather dilapidated state of Sensōji in the late sixteenth century, Sensōji chroniclers of later years depicted Ieyasu's choice as a natural one. They claimed that Sensōji was the oldest Tendai temple in the Kantō to have preserved the solemn Tendai tradition of "pacifying and protecting the nation" (*chingo kokka*). That was why, they added, Sensōji had served the two preceding medieval shōgunal houses, the Minamoto and the Ashikaga.[6] Moreover, its chroniclers emphasized that Ieyasu chose Sensōji as the major prayer hall for his family because, as the oldest Tendai temple in the Kantō, it reminded him of Enryakuji in Kyoto, the head temple of Tendai Buddhism, which provided the imperial family with divine protection.

For the new ruler of the realm, Sensōji, as the *Tokugawa jikki* notes, did, in addition to being an old Tendai prayer temple decorated in the *chingo kokka* tradition, seem to be endowed with an auspicious aura of divine guardianship. Located on the northeastern boundaries of Edo, Sensōji was perfectly situated to be the "demon gate" (*kimon*).[7] As the name indicates, the Japanese believed that a capital city was vulnerable, particularly at first, to outside intruders. According to Yin-Yang cosmology, invaders—the "demons"—are most likely to penetrate the capital from the northeast (front demon gate) or the southwest (rear demon gate). Throughout Japanese history, the defense and stability of the political center were major concerns for any new regime. Previous political centers, whether Nara, Heian, Kamakura, or Kyoto, all had had physical and spiritual defenses, and Edo was no exception. When Ieyasu was appointed the "barbarian-subduing generalissimo" (*seii tai shōgun*) in 1603, the demon gate became a matter of some political urgency. For the shōgunate, the barbarians were, traditionally, the Ainu people, who had been forced into the far northeastern corner of the realm. The Ainu "barbarians" were positioned so that, in theory, they could advance on Edo along the Ōshū highway. Fortuitously, Sensōji was situated at the beginning of this highway to the northeast. Like Zōjōji, which was located at the southwestern boundaries of Edo astride the rear demon gate, Sensōji was an ideal choice for Ieyasu.[8] When a five-storied pagoda was rebuilt at Sensōji in 1649, a demonic gargoyle, which served to fend off intruders and misfortune, was carefully attached to the ridge of the third roof, visually reinforcing the demon gate's strength as a defensive position.[9]

The administrators of Sensōji moved quickly to reform the institution in order to establish it as an exemplary shōgunal prayer temple that would also serve as the "demon gate" of Edo. First, they removed all married monks and then organized the remaining celibate priests into two groups: seniors and juniors. Each member of the two groups formed a subtemple residential unit outside the inner precinct. In total, twelve seniors and twenty-two juniors were established.[10] All these subtemple units were put under the supervision of an abbot (*bettō*), who served as the chief executive officer of Sensōji. The abbot, who resided in his own residential unit (named the Denbō-in and located in the corner of the inner precinct), was also in charge of the operation of the Main Hall (Hondō), which housed the Asakusa Kannon. Sensōji successfully restructured itself as a "clean" Buddhist institution, containing a headquarters and thirty-four subtemples.

Having straightened up the organizational mess, the Sensōji administrators proceeded to elevate the religious prestige of the Asakusa Kannon, the principal deity of the temple, in an effort to promote Sensōji Buddhism among the general public beyond the shōgunal family. This was a natural course of action, since the Asakusa Kannon was considered to be the religious lifeline of Sensōji Buddhism.

What was the Asakusa Kannon? And why was it so important to Sensōji Buddhism? The name referred to a tiny statue, allegedly made of gold, of the Buddhist deity Avalokiteśvara (Kannon in Japanese) enshrined in a sealed receptacle in the Main Hall of Sensōji. As the major object of worship, it was the focal point of religious veneration at Sensōji. The centrality of the Asakusa Kannon image in Sensōji Buddhism was based on the Japanese conception of a deity's epiphanic ability. In the traditional understanding, a deity exerted its salvational power more directly when it was invited to a temporary lodging place (*yorishiro*) and was worshipped at that spot. Most religious rituals in Japan, therefore, involved a tripartite procedure: inviting a deity to a lodging place, worshipping it, and sending it back to its permanent residence.[11] When anthropomorphic Buddhist statues were introduced, the Japanese understood them less as visual representations of Buddhist deities and more as the lodging places of those deities, around which local elements such as miraculous stories, geographical symbolism, political authority, and cosmology could be woven.[12] The Asakusa Kannon statue was none other than a *yorishiro* of the Avalokiteśvara Bodhisattva (Kannon Bosatsu). But it was not a usual *yorishiro*. The mysterious aura surrounding it gave it a potential for growth in religious reputation. In order to understand Sensōji Buddhism, we need to examine the historical background of the Asakusa Kannon statue.

According to Sensōji chronicles, the Asakusa Kannon statue was found by two fishermen—the brothers Hinokuma Hamanari and Hinokuma Takenari—on the eighteenth day of the third month of 628.[13] In the quiet morning of that day, the two brothers were casting nets in the Sumida River in the Asakusa area. They tried in seven different places to catch fish, but, to their disappointment, every time they drew up their net it contained the same small statue. Upon closer examination, the brothers saw that the statue glittered (see Fig. 1). Realizing that this was an unusual statue, they carefully placed it under a Japanese pagoda tree and bowed to it in a pious manner. After that, their nets were always full of fish. The morning after the fishermen set up the statue, ten youngsters from the village of Asakusa built a temporary shelter for it and offered it flowers (see Fig. 2). In the meantime, the Hinokuma brothers reported the wondrous happening to their village head, Haji no Nakatomo. Haji immediately realized that the unusual statue was an incarnation of Avalokiteśvara and full of supernatural virtue. He soon converted his house into a Buddhist temple, became a self-ordained priest, and devoted his whole life to worshipping the statue. Such was the historical genesis of Sensōji and the Asakusa Kannon.

Twenty years after the Asakusa Kannon statue had been discovered, the monk Shōkai stayed at Sensōji for several days. One day he found that all his possessions, consisting of three priestly robes and a bowl for food, were missing without a trace. Moreover, he was suddenly afflicted with an eye disease. In grief, he prayed to the Kannon of Sensōji. A while

Fig. 1. Fishermen draw up a glittering, small statue caught in their nets (from Saitō Gesshin, *Edo meisho zue*).

浅草寺観音大士
の出現ありしハ
推古天皇三十六年
戊子三月十八日なり
土師臣中知をよひ
檜前濱成武成等
の主従三人その宮
戸川に網を下して
此本尊を得たり
しよし縁記
の中に詳なり

Fig. 2. Fishermen install the statue under a Japanese pagoda tree, and youngsters from Asakusa village offer homage to it (from Saitō Gesshin, *Edo meisho zue*).

later, Avalokiteśvara appeared before him and said, "If you keep looking at my face while praying, you will be punished. The property you lost is a warning signal." Then it hinted at the whereabouts of the monk's missing belongings and restored his eyesight. After this ominous occurrence, Shōkai sealed the Asakusa Kannon in a receptacle so that its numinous face could no longer be exposed.[14] Thus the Asakusa Kannon was effectively made into a "secret" deity (*hi*-Butsu) and removed from public sight.

Some two centuries later, the Asakusa Kannon was further mystified by an eminent Tendai monk, Ennin (794–864).[15] Sensōji chronicles say that Ennin, while staying at Sensōji, noticed that the original "gold" statue was vulnerable to corrosion. To reduce this danger, he carved a wooden statue of the same size and shape as the Asakusa Kannon and substituted it for the original. To imbue the Asakusa Kannon with additional mystique, Ennin put the copy into a sealed receptacle and placed it in front of the original one. Thus even this wooden statue, which was named "the main statue standing before" (*omaetate no honzon*), was made a secret deity. It was displayed only on occasions of *kaichō*—the special, public exhibition of a secret Buddhist deity.[16] In the long run, Ennin's concern effected a lasting and double-edged benefit to Sensōji: (1) the creation of a wooden Kannon endowed with a religious aura comparable to that of the original and suitable for public exhibition (kaichō Buddha) and (2) the elevation of the original Asakusa Kannon to the status of ultimate mystery. The "gold" statue of the Asakusa Kannon permanently vanished from the public gaze and dwells behind the curtain of myth.

Through these legends, from 1600 on Sensōji officials aggressively popularized the mysterious genesis of the Asakusa Kannon. Yet, due to its permanent enclosure, no member of the general public could hope to see the original Kannon deity. This increased the level of curiosity concerning the Asakusa Kannon. Endowed with wonder and mystery, the Asakusa Kannon was well positioned to be received by a wide audience.

On top of this, the Tokugawa connection enabled Sensōji, through generous government support, to establish a stable source of income. In 1613 the Tokugawa bakufu granted a sizable tract of land in the surrounding area to Sensōji.[17] The estimated yield of rice from this temple land (*jiryō*), which included fields, was, according to the bakufu registry,

500 *koku*—an endowment of land that could certainly be regarded as special. This was roughly equivalent to the amount of land granted lower-ranking shōgunal bannermen (*hatamoto*) and about half the average size of a land grant to the traditionally prestigious *monzeki* (imperial abbacy) temples, in which sons and daughters of the emperor and high-ranking courtiers were installed as head monks.[18] The sudden rise of Sensōji in status from a local temple to a generously supported "public" temple was certainly an unwonted blessing.

Along with the "black seal" document issued to Sensōji in 1613 regarding the land grant, the bakufu specified that (1) half the rice yield (250 koku) was to be allocated to the head monk, and any costs associated with the repair of temple buildings were to be paid by the shōgunate; (2) monks in the temple, as members of a shōgunal prayer hall, were to observe the regulations of the Buddhist order; and (3) the temple precinct and its *monzen* (front districts or streets) were exempted from taxation.[19] Although the granting of land carried with it the obligation to maintain a "clean" temple, under extraterritorial possession, Sensōji was able to secure a steady tax income from its 500-koku land grant. Regular income from the land, which varied according to the annual harvest and Sensōji-imposed tax rates, met basic institutional operating expenses.[20] In addition, the bakufu provided special funds for rebuilding the Main Hall and carrying out other forms of physical maintenance, for performing grand rituals to commemorate Tokugawa Ieyasu (who died in 1616), and/or for performing special services for the welfare of the bakufu (e.g., when the abbot Chūson accompanied Shōgun Iemitsu as a member of his retinue during visits to the emperor in Kyoto in 1623 and 1634, all his expenses were paid by the bakufu).

Ironically, although Sensōji secured a steady income from the 1613 shōgunal land grant, in the long run the static nature of its income structure, which was sealed off from the sprawling early modern economy of Edo, was not always advantageous. Sensōji soon began to experience financial shortages because of its inability to diversify its sources of income. Part of the reason for this was its affiliation with the Tokugawa family: Sensōji was not able to overcome its lofty image as a shōgunal temple existing apart from the ordinary people. Not surprisingly, this special status discouraged members of the general public from expressing their veneration for the Asakusa Kannon freely. In the early seventeenth century, Sensōji Buddhism had not yet integrated itself fully into the rapidly growing urban culture of Edo. In spite of its promising start, it was clear that Sensōji had to undergo another major transformation before attaining acceptance among the general populace. As it turned out, Sensōji eventually succeeded in transforming itself into a popular Buddhist temple.

About two centuries later, in the early nineteenth century, Terakado Seiken (1796–1868) opened his *Edo hanjōki* (A record of Edo's prosperity), a series of essays describing the hustle and bustle of Edo, with a comment about Sensōji: "Sensōji is first among the places for burning incense in the city. Hubs of carts knock against other hubs, and shoulders rub against shoulders. Worshippers do not stop coming to the temple even for a moment."[21] In Seiken's depiction, Sensōji is crowded and thriving. Crowds mill about; visitors flow in and out along the paths to the Main Hall. Seiken paid particular attention to the various actions and gestures of the throngs of worshippers heading to the Main Hall—worshippers burn incense, join their hands and bow in prayer, make small offerings (usually a few copper coins are dropped into the offertory box), utter a few words to the Asakusa Kannon, attend rituals presided over by priests, and buy amulets and talismans. Not only the Main Hall but also other less prominent shrines, scattered throughout the inner precinct, attract crowds of worshippers, as different deities, be they Buddhist or Shintō, compete with each other for religious customers. The actions of visitors seeking divine compassion are largely informal, casual, peaceful, and individual.

Religious activities were not the only things that attracted Seiken's attention. In addition to stops of religious significance, visitors gather in and around storytelling halls, vendor stalls, teahouses, archery halls, and street circuses. Businesses that do not seem to bear directly on Buddhism, or any religion for that matter, are ubiquitous throughout the precincts of Sensōji and attract large crowds. Leisure activities are so intermingled with religious activities that it is almost impossible to distinguish one from the other. People who have just paid homage to the Asakusa Kannon or some other deity easily became fun-seekers, spectators, game players, travelers, or shoppers. To Seiken, the fascination of Sensōji lay not only in the world of Buddhist worship but also in its recreational attractions.[22]

Between the early seventeenth century and the early nineteenth century, Sensōji underwent a remarkable metamorphosis from a Tokugawa prayer hall, deeply imbued with religio-political privilege, to a popular gathering place, liberated from Tokugawa influence and open to the general public. Data on the temple's income provide a tangible indicator to help us gauge the extent to which the religious and cultural fabric of Sensōji Buddhism was transformed over this period. The early seventeenth-century Sensōji did not have to rely on the financial contributions of commoners, for it had a steady income from shōgunal land. In contrast, when Terakado Seiken observed it two centuries later, despite the fact that Sensōji still retained its 500-koku land tract, it was much more dependent on the common folk for just about everything—including its income. In other words, in terms of income ratio, the contribution guaranteed by the black seal document became minuscule compared with the offerings and donations of ordinary worshippers and visitors. This was the result of the slow but steady growth of popular Sensōji Buddhism, which had already begun in 1625 when Sensōji ceased to be the prayer hall for the shōgunal family. In an attempt to establish an eastern center of Tendai Buddhism, the bakufu erected a grand Buddhist hall (Kan'eiji) on Mount Tōei in Ueno and arranged for this new eastern Tendai center to serve the shōgunal house just as Enryakuji (the western Tendai center) on Mount Hiei did the imperial family.[23] At the time, this seemed a fatal blow to Sensōji, but in the long run the move transformed Sensōji into a popular urban Buddhist temple with a wide base of lay support. After being disconnected from the Tokugawa house, Sensōji was reborn as a people's (*minshū*) Buddhist institution.

This evolution can be seen in the development of the Sensōji land over time. When Sensōji received the grant of temple land from the bakufu early in the seventeenth century, about two-thirds of the agricultural fields in the area of the grant were located in Senzoku Village northwest of the temple and the rest were in the surrounding monzen area. Even though the latter had pockets of paddy and dry fields here and there, most of it was still virgin land. This environment helped situate Sensōji in a quiet and isolated setting. But with the expansion of Edo, these tranquil surroundings as well as the original farmland were soon subject to speedy development.[24] By the time of Terakado Seiken, the wild plains of the Sensōji land were transformed into a busy temple complex and bustling front districts. The serene landscape of the past could hardly be imagined.

As Figure 3 illustrates, encircling the Main Hall (Kannon-dō) were dozens of minor Buddhist halls and Shintō shrines. Most conspicuous among them were a five-story pagoda, a bell tower, and Sanja Daigongen (later referred to as Sensō Shrine). In addition, Sensōji hosted all kinds of Buddhist deities, including Jizō, Fudō, Yakushi, Fugen, Benzaiten, Enma, and Seishi as well as Shintō branch deities invited from the Fushimi Inari, Kumano, Atago, and Tenmangū shrines. All these deities were housed in permanent shelters of various sizes and shapes.

In addition to the religious structures, both the inner and the outer precincts were packed with commercial enterprises. Particularly spectacular was the rear of the Main Hall, known as Okuyama, which was home to a wide array of business booths and commercial attractions. Outside the inner precincts were numerous souvenir shops, street vending stalls, teahouses, and restaurants, along with a total of thirty-four subtemples in four groups. Further out were areas that had been covered with wild grasses and brush but that were now thriving front districts. Thousands of new urban residents settled in these districts and established a sort of business center, milking the prospering "religious" culture of Sensōji.

The physical metamorphosis of the Sensōji area was directly reflected in its changed income structure: it had been transformed from a shōgunal prayer temple whose major source of income was a land grant into a popular urban temple with highly diversified sources of income. In the late Tokugawa period, the earnings from Sensōji's 500-koku landholdings no longer made a meaningful contribution to its coffers.

In 1800, for example, according to financial records in the Sensōji diary, the largest source of income was *saisen* (offertory coins)—coins that ordinary worshippers tossed into the box in front of the altar. The saisen income in 1800 amounted to approximately 1,609 gold pieces—48 percent of the total income of 3,322 gold pieces. The approximate income from the bakufu-granted paddy and dry fields, in contrast, was 177 gold pieces—a bit more than 5 percent of the total income—even though rice harvests were unusually good that year. The remaining income of 1,536 gold pieces, or 46 percent of the total, came from various sources that had been virtually unknown in the past, such as the sale of amulets and talismans, annual land taxes paid by monzen residents, and rents paid by merchants and entertainers who engaged in business at Sensōji.[25]

The diversification of the temple's income clearly suggests that the nature of Sensōji Buddhism had changed considerably over time. Sensōji's financial dependence on agricultural land was a thing of the past. In its stead, Sensōji reached out to a wide range of new income sources, from casual offerings of copper coins by commoner-visitors to rents and the sale of religious products. Needless to say, these new income sources would not have existed had Sensōji not been involved in the activities of visitors and entrepreneurs. This leads us to the next questions. What kinds of activities were taking place at Sensōji? Was there any pattern to them in the late Tokugawa period?

The financial records in the Sensōji diaries offer the most specific and most tangible evidence for what was happening at this time. Table 1 compares the temple's income at five-year intervals between 1790 and 1830. This period corresponds to the years during which Edo firmly established itself as the nation's cultural center. Dubbing the era *Kasei bunka* (the culture of the Bunka and Bunsei eras), historians often compare the culture of this period to that of the Genroku period at the turn of the seventeenth century. Based on the more or less standardized entries in the diaries, Table 1 divides income into three categories: saisen, a combined income from rents and sales of religious goods, and the rice tax.

Although Sensōji treasurers usually lumped rental income and sales of religious goods together in their records, there were rare occasions in which these two seemingly unrelated income sources were kept separate. The accounts for 1814 disaggregate income from rent and religious goods for the first, second, sixth, and twelfth months. Table 2 shows that income from rental lands (most of which were on yearly contracts) was heavily concentrated in the twelfth month. Rental income included the regular annual rent collected from monzen residents once at the end of the year and leasing fees imposed on commercial sites. In contrast, income from sales of religious goods was largest in the first month,

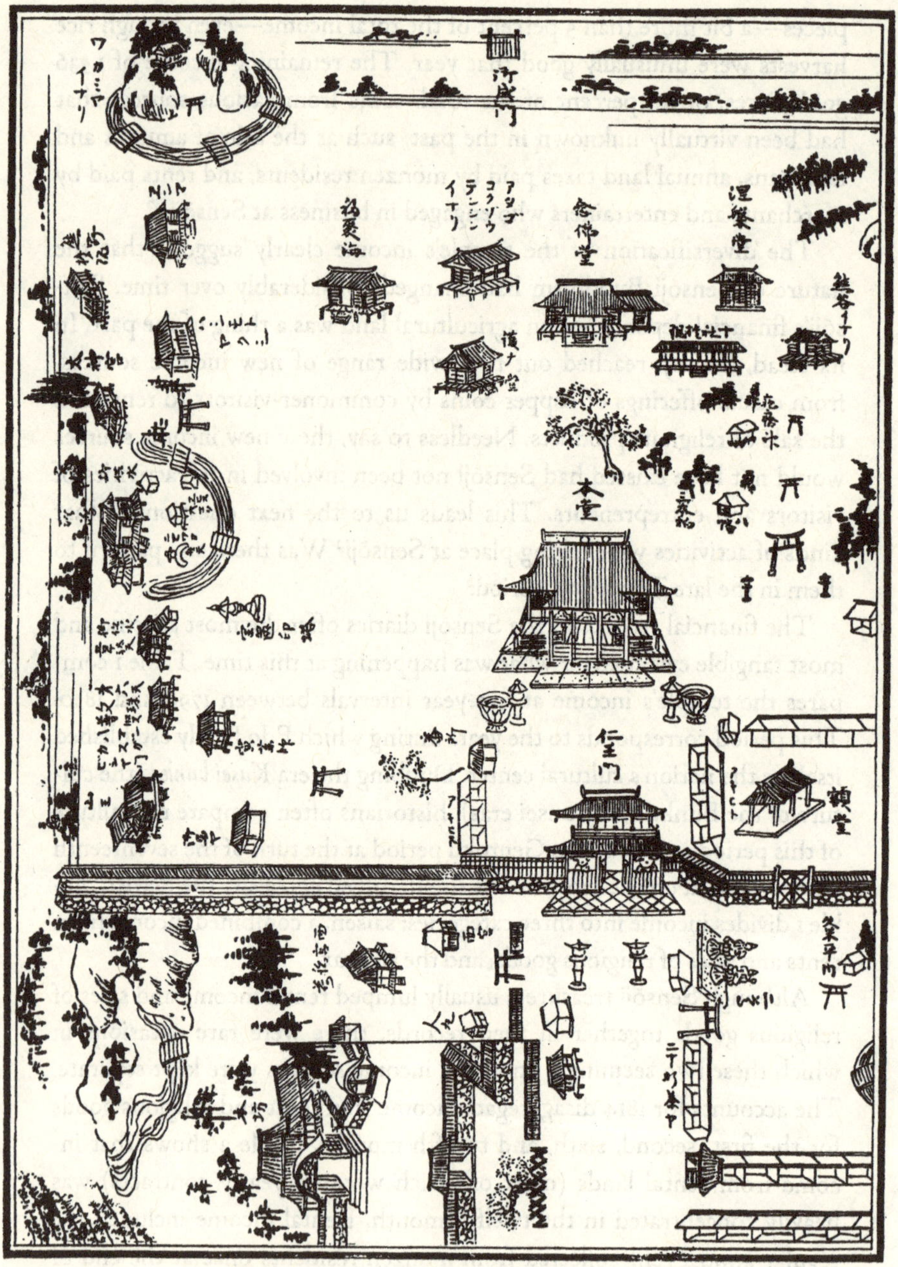

Fig. 3. The inner precincts (*keidai*) of Sensōji and its western districts (from Matsudaira Kanzan, *Sensōji shi*). Reproduced by permission of Meicho Shuppan Publishing Co., Ltd.

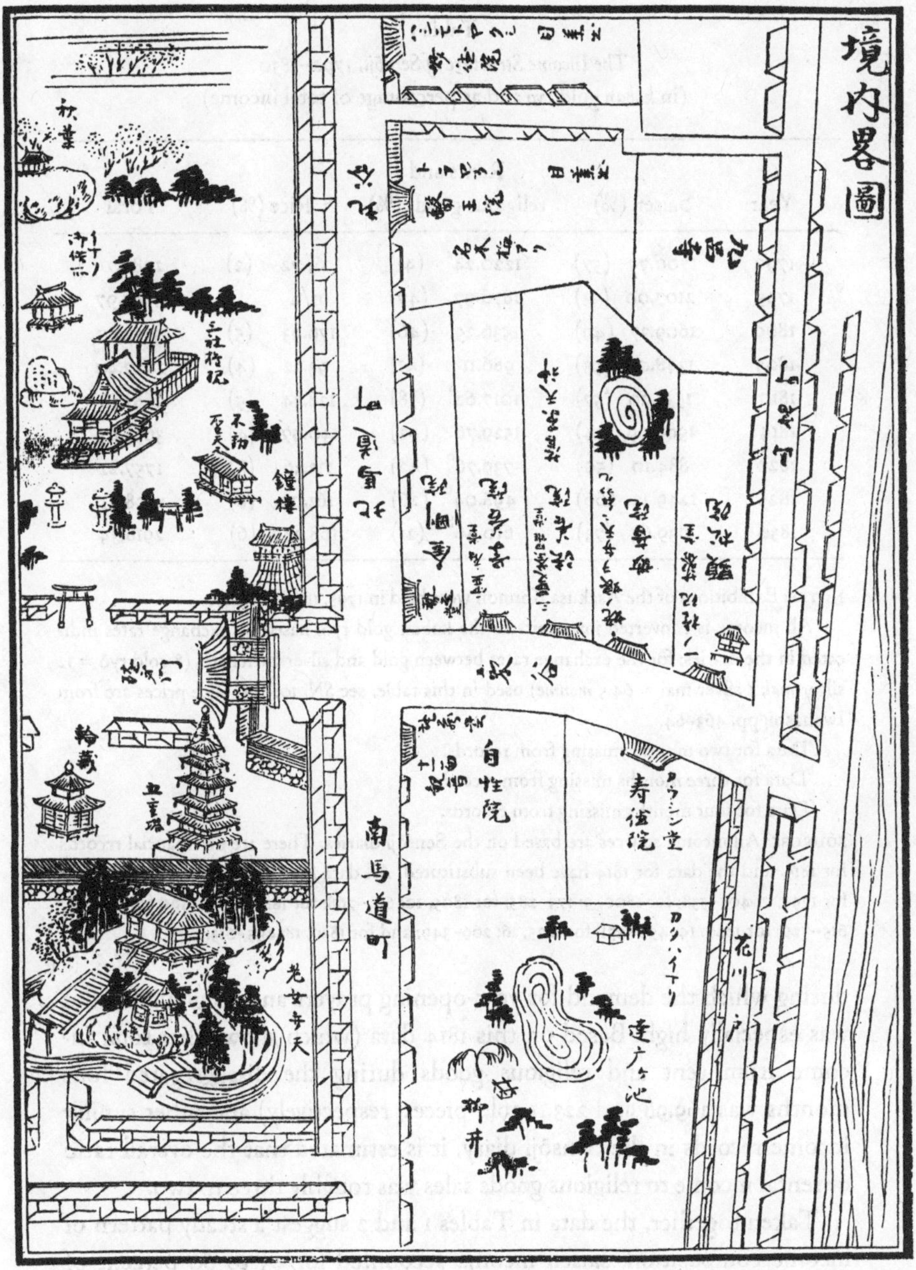
境内畧圖
南馬道町
花川戸
鐘楼
輪蔵
五重塔
自性院

Table 1
The Income Structure of Sensōji, 1790–1830
(in *koban* gold *ryō* and as percentage of total income)

Year	Saisen (%)		Rents and religious goods (%)		Rice (%)		Total
1790	1700.75	(57)	1220.24[a]	(41)	61.72	(2)	2982.71
1795	2107.00	(53)	1878.97	(47)	n/a		3985.97
1800	1609.37	(49)	1536.25	(46)	176.93	(5)	3322.55
1805	1348.01	(55)	986.11	(41)	93.32	(4)	2427.44
1810	1537.20	(57)	1017.62[a]	(38)	128.34	(5)	2683.16
1814	1968.09	(54)	1529.76	(42)	140.97	(4)	3638.82
1820	884.10	(50)	739.76[b]	(42)	133.36	(8)	1757.22
1825	1249.32	(66)	498.04[c]	(26)	161.05	(8)	1908.41
1830	2139.64	(73)	610.46[b]	(21)	168.24	(6)	2918.34

NOTES: Exhibitions of the Asakusa Kannon were held in 1795, 1814, and 1830.

All income is converted into units of the koban gold ryō, based on exchange rates indicated in the diaries; for the exchange rates between gold and silver currencies (8 gold ryō = 12 silver *mai*, 1 silver mai = 64.5 *monme*) used in this table, see *SN*, 10: 745. Rice prices are from Iwahashi, pp. 463–64.

[a]Data for two months missing from records.

[b]Data for three months missing from records.

[c]Data for four months missing from records.

SOURCES: All income sources are based on the Sensōji diaries. There are no financial records for 1815, and the data for 1814 have been substituted. All data from *SN*: for 1790, 6: 368–458; for 1795, 7: 405–538; for 1800, 9: 173–285; for 1805, 10: 691–768; for 1810, 12: 90–191; for 1814, 12: 615–726; for 1820, 14: 496–571; for 1825, 16: 269–349; and for 1830, 18: 495–613.

during which the demand for year-opening prayers and religious fetishes was especially high. Based on this 1814 data (which shows that total income from rent and religious goods during the disaggregated four months was 369.98 and 223.11 gold pieces, respectively) and other similar income records in the Sensōji diary, it is estimated that the overall ratio of rental income to religious goods sales was roughly three to two.

Taken together, the data in Tables 1 and 2 suggest a steady pattern of income composition: saisen income accounted for 45 to 60 percent of total income, rental income 25 to 30 percent, income from the sale of re-

Table 2
The Monthly Income Structure of Sensōji, 1814
(koban gold ryō)

<table>
<tr><th>Month</th><th>Saisen</th><th>Rent</th><th>Religious goods</th><th>Rice</th><th>Total</th></tr>
<tr><td>1st</td><td>105.57</td><td>25.29</td><td>114.96</td><td></td><td>245.82</td></tr>
<tr><td>2nd</td><td>118.9</td><td>24.36</td><td>42.01</td><td></td><td>185.27</td></tr>
<tr><td>3rd</td><td>241.29</td><td colspan="2">(129.2)</td><td></td><td>370.49</td></tr>
<tr><td>4th</td><td>312.18</td><td colspan="2">(160.06)</td><td></td><td>472.24</td></tr>
<tr><td>5th</td><td>311.41</td><td colspan="2">(236.88)</td><td></td><td>548.29</td></tr>
<tr><td>6th</td><td>186.95</td><td>17.46</td><td>32.92</td><td></td><td>237.33</td></tr>
<tr><td>7th</td><td>155.20</td><td colspan="2">(155.18)</td><td></td><td>310.38</td></tr>
<tr><td>8th</td><td>118.18</td><td colspan="2">(50.53)</td><td></td><td>168.71</td></tr>
<tr><td>9th</td><td>104.91</td><td colspan="2">(112.93)</td><td></td><td>217.84</td></tr>
<tr><td>10th</td><td>95.73</td><td colspan="2">(46.15)</td><td>140.97</td><td>282.85</td></tr>
<tr><td>11th</td><td>65.98</td><td colspan="2">(45.74)</td><td></td><td>111.72</td></tr>
<tr><td>12th</td><td>151.79</td><td>302.87</td><td>33.22</td><td></td><td>487.88</td></tr>
<tr><td>TOTAL</td><td>1968.09</td><td colspan="2">(1529.76)</td><td>140.97</td><td>3638.82</td></tr>
</table>

SOURCES: See Table 1.

ligious goods 15 to 20 percent, and income from the rice tax 3 to 8 percent. Sensōji raised most of its revenue from saisen offerings and commercial sources. Not surprisingly, the income from the 500-koku land base was significantly reduced. Moreover, one of the major income sources for the vast majority of Buddhist temples in the Tokugawa period—funerary patron houses—was not present in the Sensōji case at all (except in some subtemples, which independently maintained small numbers of their own funerary patrons).

The leading income source, saisen, consisted of copper coins, the lowest-value currency, which visitors to Sensōji threw into wooden boxes as a small offering. Every Buddhist hall and Shintō shrine on the Sensōji ground had offertory boxes in front of the altars of divine statues. Long and perpendicular with an opening at the top formed by parallel crossbars, these boxes were designed to enable visitors to deposit their coins without being hampered by formality, time, or congestion.[26] Whatever their reason for visiting, it was assumed that visitors would first toss a small offering into these boxes. Even those who visited Sensōji just for fun usually dropped some coins into the offertory boxes to express their veneration for the Asakusa Kannon. For worshippers, this form of offering, which became popular in the late Tokugawa period, was the most convenient, the simplest, and the easiest to bear. Traditionally, the Japanese had offered such items as cloth, paper, jewels, rice, weapons, and horses at temples or shrines. But in the remarkably well developed monetary economy of the late Tokugawa period, coins gradually replaced these traditional offertory items, particularly in urban areas.[27]

There were dozens of offertory boxes at Sensōji in the late Tokugawa period, all visible and carefully maintained. Once a month, Sensōji officials collected the coins from these boxes, exchanged them for currencies of higher value, and then deposited the money in the treasury of Kan'eiji, the temple that headed the group of Eastern Tendai temples to which the Sensōji belonged. In the months when special events were held and more visitors and donations were expected, the collecting and tallying of offertory coins took place more frequently—every week or every other week. The seventh and twelfth months were particularly important because of the annual events of special worship and the market fair (discussed in Chapter 1). In any case, throughout the late Tokugawa period, saisen was the largest source of Sensōji income.

The second largest source of income was non-agricultural land. Through deputy administrators (*daikan*), monzen residents living on Sensōji land were obliged to pay an annual rent, usually in the twelfth month. Similarly, those who leased a space and ran a business in the temple precincts paid rent according to the terms of their contracts with Sensōji. Rent collection was not always problem-free for the temple. The leaseholders frequently presented petitions to Sensōji for rent reductions or exemptions because of depressed business, fires, floods, or other disasters. With regard to the payment of rent, there was room for negotiation, compromise, and even resistance.[28] But, on the whole, Sensōji's income from non-agricultural land held quite steady at 25 to 30 percent of its total income.

The third largest source of income was the religious/commercial operations of the Main Hall (the Asakusa Kannon Hall), which included the sale of charms and talismans, prayer fees, and various donations from lay confraternities (*kō*). This category contributed about 15 to 20 percent of the total income. The growing fashion for possessing Asakusa Kannon amulets or talismans among Edo residents boosted sales of these goods enormously. In addition, the Main Hall had five prayer patron families of daimyō rank, and the income earned from prayer services conducted for these patron families added about 20 to 30 gold pieces to the Sensōji coffers annually, in addition to the prestige they brought to Sensōji. Donations from lay confraternities, which ranged from cash and ritual items to volunteer services, were also a valuable component of the finances of Sensōji.

On the whole, Sensōji's income in the late Tokugawa period was made up of previously unknown sources. By this time, Sensōji Buddhist culture had become considerably diversified, popularized, and commercialized. Visitors to Sensōji could no longer sense the institution's past religious/political attachment to the Tokugawa family—an attachment that had once distinguished it from other Buddhist institutions. Instead of receiving messengers from Edo Castle, Sensōji now hosted ordinary people who swarmed into the complex for a multitude of reasons: to pray to the Asakusa Kannon, to attend a religious event, to watch a spectacle, to play a game, to shop for souvenirs, to meet friends, or to conduct business. These seemingly disorderly activities were reflected in the highly variegated but stable sources of income—saisen, rents, sales of talismans, ritual fees, casual donations, and so on.

As noted above, missing from among these activities was something considered to be a major religious function of Tokugawa Buddhist temples—funerary or memorial services. The lack of death-related ritual activities at Sensōji is exceptional, especially given the fact that, during the Tokugawa period, the vast majority of Buddhist temples were financially dependent on local families who were registered as their funerary patrons (*danna*). Although, as has been said, some of the independently run subtemples offered funerary or memorial services, at the headquarters level Sensōji was completely detached from such functions; rather, it concentrated on the other major religious functions of Tokugawa Buddhist temples—those related to prayer (*kitō*). More important, the kitō function of Sensōji was not limited to a select group of patrons but was wide open to the general public. By the late Tokugawa period, Sensōji had been transformed into a people's temple that specialized in kitō.

Contemporary Japanese-English dictionaries invariably render "kitō" as "prayer." However, within Tokugawa Buddhism, the term signified more than its contemporary usage might lead one to believe. The *Oxford English Dictionary* defines "prayer" as "(1) a solemn and humble request to God, or to an object of worship; a supplication, petition, or thanksgiving, usually in words; (2) a formula appointed for or used in praying; e.g. the Lord's Prayer; (3) a religious observance, public or private, of which prayer to God forms a principal part; (4) an entreaty made to a person; and (5) the matter of a petition, the thing prayed for or entreated." Similarly, *The Encyclopedia of Religions* defines "prayer" as "human communication with divine and spiritual entities" in the form of "petition, invocation, thanksgiving, dedication, supplication, intercession, confession, penitence, and benediction," or as "an act of speech" that may involve performance elements such as "certain body postures and orientations, ritual actions and objects, designated architectural structures or physical environments, particular times of the day of calendar dates, specified moods, attitudes, or intentions."[29]

However, within Tokugawa Buddhism, "kitō" referred to more than human-spiritual communication. The *Bukkyō bunka jiten* (The encyclopedia of Buddhist culture; 1989) categorizes what were known within Tokugawa Buddhism as "gatherings for the [Buddhist] dharma" (*hōe*) into three rites: (1) self-disciplinary rites (*shudō girei*) for professional monks and nuns (e.g., ordination ceremonies, disciplinary training, meditation, mountain retreats, fasting, daily worship, devotion); (2) merit-transfer rites (*ekō girei* or *tsuizen kuyō*), or funerary and memorial services for the deceased and ancestors; and (3) prayer rites (*kitō girei*), a catchall term that includes almost all other Buddhist rituals and events conducted for the purpose of supplication, petition, invocation, celebration, repentance, dedication, worship, and so on. The category of kitō in the context of Tokugawa Buddhism encompassed not only personal devotional acts but also collective seasonal ceremonies and annual observances in aid of good harvests and national peace and prosperity. Similarly, the *Bukkyō-go daijiten* (Comprehensive dictionary of Buddhist terms; 1975) gives *kigan*, *kinen*, and *kishō* as synonyms of "kitō" and defines it as: "(1) to wish, supplicate, or invoke; (2) to request Buddhas or Bodhisattvas to remove misfortune and/or bring good fortune with their divine power." It is, therefore, no wonder that Japanese historians often classify Buddhist temples in Tokugawa society as either *dannaji* (funerary temples) or *kitōji* (prayer temples). The term "prayer," as used in this book, carries with it the connotations of "kitō" in *kitō girei* and/or *kitōji*.

The term "prayer" thus covers a wide range of religious activities that flourished at Sensōji in the late Tokugawa period: bowing before sacred objects; making offerings of such items as flowers, incense, lamps, food, or coins; wafting incense smoke over one's body; chanting sutras or uttering mantric spells; making ritual gestures; undertaking pilgrimages; purchasing amulets or talismans; participating in rituals or ceremonies; and/or attending seasonal events and annual observances. As we have seen, such prayer activities provided more than half of Sensōji's income. In this sense, prayer was certainly a major aspect of Sensōji Buddhism in the late Tokugawa period.

The statistical dominance of income from prayer activities, however, does not necessarily reflect the whole of Sensōji Buddhist culture. The rents paid by residents of the front districts and by entrepreneurs in the temple precincts may have accounted for only 25 to 30 percent of the Sensōji income, but these sums do not reflect the entirety of the economy in the Sensōji area. The economic activities that generated roughly a quarter of Sensōji's income must necessarily have been larger than the rental income that found its way into Sensōji's coffers. On this assumption, we can estimate that the magnitude and vitality of non-prayer activities in the Sensōji area were almost equivalent to the magnitude and vitality of prayer activities.

Can we lump the various non-prayer activities into one category? This would seem to be quite a challenge, since the category should include such diverse activities as shopping for souvenirs and local staples; watching street spectacles, theaters, or circuses; visiting teahouses; participating in archery or other games; going to storytelling halls; taking a day off; and/or just strolling around crowded streets. The traditional Japanese concept of *asobi* will help us here.

According to the *Kadokawa kogo dai-jiten* (The Kadokawa comprehensive dictionary of old terms; 1982), "asobi" means: "(1) playing, amusement, or pleasure; (2) to play music; (3) hunting; (4) gambling; (5) 'play girls' (*asobime*); and (6) prostitutes, as a slang term used in the brothel quarters." *Kenkyusha's New Japanese-English Dictionary* adds the following meanings: a pastime, a game, a sport, a pleasure trip, an outing, a jaunt, merrymaking, and debauchery. When we combine all these definitions, we find that the non-religious, cultural activities taking place in the Sensōji area are almost all contained within the concept of "asobi," which is commonly rendered as "play" in Japanese-English dictionaries.

Despite our immediate tendency to think of the word "play" as referring to children's play, in cultural studies it is defined to include activities that occupy a threshold between reality and unreality (e.g., games, sports, festivals, gambling, and children's activities); that are not always subject to the rules of ordinary life; or that are engaged in for amusement, pleasure, or recreation.[30] Brian Sutton-Smith, an expert in the field of play, breaks the forms and experiences of play into nine subcategories, within which almost all the non-religious activities practiced at Sensōji in the late Tokugawa period have a place.[31] Indeed, the concept of "play" as it is used in cultural studies is the same as the concept of asobi as it relates to Sensōji culture.

Bearing in mind the definitions of kitō and asobi discussed above, we can characterize Sensōji Buddhism in late Tokugawa Japan as a culture of "prayer" and "play." As Terakado Seiken observed early in the nineteenth century, these two cultural components were intermingled within Sensōji Buddhism. Moreover, this composite Buddhist culture was tied neither to the shōgunal family nor to the upper strata of Edo society. It was a culture produced and consumed by Edo commoners, who projected on to it their everyday concerns, habits, beliefs, and tastes. Sensōji Buddhist culture was, in this sense, a collectively authored popular culture.

The popular Sensōji Buddhist culture of prayer and play was not, however, something that Tokugawa elites eagerly embraced. As far as the

Tokugawa bakufu was concerned, Buddhism, which had caused much of the sociopolitical havoc in the medieval period, was to be contained within the feudal system of control and utility. In order to bind Buddhism to the new political system, the Tokugawa bakufu confiscated all temple lands and then restructured the economic base of Buddhist institutions. It allocated lands to temples in the name of providing "expenses for public duty" (*yakuryō*) and, in return, obligated these now publicly "supported" temples to carry out their "public duty" (*yaku*) for the well-being of the nation.[32] More specifically, the bakufu controlled individual sects and priests by implementing the head-branch system (*honmatsu seido*) along with regional administrative networks (*furegashira*). Laypeople were forced to affiliate themselves with these networks through the system of temple registry (*terauke*). All these measures were directed at establishing the so-called *bakuhan* system of Tokugawa Buddhism.[33] When the bakufu granted 500 koku of land to Sensōji and subjected it to the supervision of Kan'eiji in the early seventeenth century, the Tokugawa authorities saw Sensōji as being firmly situated within the framework of the Buddhist bakuhan system.

In fact, in imposing a public duty on Sensōji, the bakufu made its expectations clear through the role model of the head temple of Eastern Tendai, the Kan'eiji. The Mount Hiei Regulations (*Hieizan hatto*), which the bakufu issued to Kan'eiji in 1654, stipulated the terms of its 5,600-koku land grant: "Do not neglect [to do your public] duty of conducting the assigned annual [prayer] rites." While emphasizing the temple's prayer duties, these regulations strongly prohibited women, drinking, and dancing within the temple.[34] Thirteen years later, in 1667, the bakufu specified its desires even more clearly in the Regulations for All Temples (*Sho-jiin jōmoku*): "Neither fighting nor disorderly deeds will be tolerated in the precincts, because temples are places for praying for the peace of the nation."[35] With these decrees, the bakufu set the tone for what it considered to be the ideal conduct of Buddhist temples in Tokugawa society. As far as the authorities were concerned, Buddhist rituals and ceremonies were to form the spiritual foundation for protecting the nation and benefiting the people, and therefore monks should strictly adhere to Buddhist precepts. Activities that were deemed injurious to the solemn duty of Buddhism were condemned and punished.[36] These shōgunal regulations, though addressed primarily to Buddhist priests and the sangha (the collective body of monks), clearly implied what the shōgunate expected from Tokugawa Buddhism in general: "prayer" (good) was not to be muddled up with "play" (evil).

Despite the ideological impositions of the bakufu, Sensōji in the late Tokugawa period turned out to be a nurturing ground for a composite culture of prayer and play. It would be naïve, however, to attribute the emergence of such a culture to a relaxation of bakufu policies toward Buddhist temples. In fact, the bakufu often wielded its administrative power in order to prevent Buddhist institutions from deviating from the bakuhan Buddhist system. For example, when, in 1685, the Sensōji head monk Chūun challenged the checks and controls that were being imposed, the bakufu expelled him from office.[37] After this incident, Kan'eiji tightened its grip over Sensōji by unilaterally appointing its head administrator from without. Decades later, in 1740, the bakufu abolished the position of head monk at Sensōji and installed a deputy head monk chosen from among officials at Kan'eiji. The bakufu even deprived Sensōji of its own budgetary powers and turned them over to Kan'eiji-appointed treasurers.[38] With the imposition of these regulatory measures, the bakufu hoped to contain Sensōji within the ideological framework of Tokugawa Buddhism.

Nevertheless, the bakufu's willingness to tame Buddhism was limited, since Buddhist institutions functioned as quasi-state agents for hunting down Christians and keeping the populace under surveillance. Because of this, the bakufu found it quite difficult to crack down arbitrarily on Buddhist temples. Early bakufu leaders, including eminent Buddhist advisors such as Tenkai and Sūden (1549–1633), were aware of what had happened to such ill-fated leaders of the Sengoku period as Oda Nobunaga (1534–82) and Toyotomi Hideyoshi (1536–98), who had been relentless in harassing and even destroying major Buddhist establishments.[39] The Tokugawa bakufu was cautious in dealing with Buddhist institutions, for it could not afford a repetition of the Sengoku turmoil, which might well have occurred had it ignited Buddhist revolts. For the new Tokugawa regime, which subscribed to the Confucian concept of "benevolent rule" (*jinsei*), political power certainly had its limits when it came to attempting to manipulate early modern Buddhist culture.

Of course, Tokugawa leaders hardly regarded the thriving of an indiscreet popular culture at a Buddhist institution with pleasure. To them, the popular Buddhist culture typified by Sensōji was nothing less than a symptom of Buddhist corruption. Some Confucian critics vehemently charged that popular Buddhist culture seriously harmed the morality of Tokugawa society, which was based on the order of discrete status. Kaibara Ekken (1630–1714), an eminent Confucian scholar, for example, lamented that "even though Buddhist temples were prospering, the Law of the Buddha had already decayed and the Way of the Buddha was becoming more and more dilapidated."[40] In his view, a temple in which people were free to unleash their unfettered desire to mix prayer and play was no longer a fit place for the Way of the Buddha. As far as the Tokugawa system was concerned, the goings-on at Sensōji in the late Tokugawa period were certainly a menacing omen. Irritated and frustrated critics angrily condemned popular Buddhist culture as "degenerate Buddhism" (*daraku Bukkyō*).

No matter how frequent the rebukes, however, Sensōji's cultural transformation from a shōgunal prayer hall to a popular cultural center combining prayer and play represented the trend of urban Buddhism in late Tokugawa Japan. Not only that, Sensōji far surpassed every other Buddhist temple in Edo in terms of popularity and prosperity. By the mid-eighteenth century, Sensōji was Edo's foremost center of prayer and play. Its Asakusa Kannon ranked high as a favorite object of folk piety and worship, and its precincts and front districts were crowded with all kinds of playful enterprises. Within Sensōji Buddhism, prayer and play were two sides of the same coin—inseparable and interdependent.

What caused Sensōji to prosper as a popular cultural center of prayer and play? How was it able to expand its cultural arena beyond the ideological framework of Tokugawa Buddhism? What was the nature of the cultural amalgam of prayer and play at Sensōji? Was it not antithetical to Buddhist teachings and the bakuhan system? How did bakufu leaders deal with it? Despite discouragement by the bakufu, why were Edo residents so fascinated with the Sensōji culture of prayer and play? Was there a built-in socioeconomic structure that sustained Sensōji culture? If so, how did it work? If Sensōji culture was a product of the natural evolution of Edo Buddhism, then how should we evaluate it within the context of Edo society? Was Edo's moral economy affected by this Buddhist culture of prayer and play? Whatever the answers to these questions, Sensōji was a prosperous cultural hub that responded to the popular demand for prayer and play. By the same token, Edo society, which nourished Sensōji culture, was not easily contained within the neat design of feudal order.

Bearing the above questions in mind, I aim to explore the contextual dimensions and significance of Sensōji culture, which reflected as well as projected changes in Edo society in late Tokugawa Japan. In Chapter 1, I provide a detailed description of the two core ingredients of Sensōji culture—prayer and play—relying on anecdotes, observations, and records derived from Sensōji diaries, chronicles, and other sources. As we will see, Sensōji truly emerged both as a mecca of popular worship and as one of Edo's major amusement centers—a combination that the bakufu did not appreciate. Nevertheless, the cultural union of prayer and play was not a transitory phenomenon but, rather, a union based on and perpetuated by tradition.

Chapter 2 addresses the coupling of prayer and play at Sensōji and traces its roots within the tradition of Japanese religious culture. After examining the union of prayer and play from cultural, socio-geographical, and institutional angles, I propose that prayer (religion) and play (entertainment) within Sensōji culture constitute a natural, perhaps even an inevitable, union. Furthermore, the combination of prayer and play in Sensōji Buddhism had strong socioeconomic support.

In order to identify this support, in Chapter 3, I relate the rise of popular prayer and play to the gradual decline of the traditional *machi* ([townspeople] ward) community in Edo and to the thickening layers of commoner cultural consumers. The resulting social change produced lonely urban dwellers and helped nurture the spirit and values of individualism in Edo society; this, in turn, contributed to expanding the social base for popular prayer and play. During this process, commoners gradually replaced the debt-ridden samurai as the new driving force behind Sensōji culture, which offered job opportunities for the newly emerging urban lower classes.

Beyond these socioeconomic factors, Edo commoners found within the popular culture of prayer and play an expression of cultural vitality and new spiritual authority. In Chapter 4, I discuss the creation of new divinities and the expansion of new arenas of play, both of which seemed to defy the Tokugawa status system. As the case of Sensōji culture demonstrates, Edo commoners incorporated cultural politics into their daily lives through their pursuit of prayer and play.

In the Conclusion, I show that understanding the Sensōji culture of prayer and play debunks the myth of "degenerate Buddhism." The reappraisal of prayer and play and their inherent interconnectedness provides a cultural critique of conventional scholarship, which has been mired in the trap of the historiography promoted by the Tokugawa ruling class. Sensōji Buddhism was far more than a religious enterprise—for Edoites it was a sociopolitical attempt to resist the very fabric of Tokugawa feudal society. This does not, however, mean that Sensōji culture spearheaded anti-feudal sentiment or that it helped Edoites eliminate the ideological burden of Tokugawa politics. Sensōji culture was, in the final analysis, fashioned far from the reality of the Tokugawa system and, therefore, fell far short of coming to terms with the real problems of Edo society.

ONE

The Buddhist Culture of Prayer and Play

As the apt expression "be born Shintō and die Buddhist" indicates, Buddhists enjoy a monopoly over death rituals in the Japanese cultural tradition.[1] In contrast, Shintō priests are so hypersensitive to the slightest hint of pollution that they try to distance themselves from death-related religious services. Unlike their counterparts in China and Korea, Japanese Confucianists, even during the Tokugawa period when their influence was at its apex, avoided death rituals and ancestor worship and instead devoted themselves to political economy and social engineering. This vacuum left the field open to the Buddhists, who concentrated on matters relating to death rituals and the afterlife. For this reason, scholars often employ the term "funerary Buddhism" (*sōshiki Bukkyō*) to indicate the primary function of Japanese Buddhism.

In fact, during the Tokugawa period Buddhists were successful in making funerary rites and memorial services their exclusive domain. Mortuary rituals and memorial services became the major sources of livelihood for most Buddhist institutions and their priests, whatever their sectarian affiliation. This is partly attributed to the bakufu's policy on registration of the populace. By the mid-seventeenth century, on the pretext of hunting down Christians, the Tokugawa bakufu (which had no extensive administrative apparatus of its own) utilized the nationwide network of Buddhist temples as quasi-official agents to help it register and monitor the entire population. Under this surveillance system, each individual was required to register at a Buddhist funerary temple, which would then issue a certificate attesting that he or she was not a Christian; the temple would then submit its funerary patron registry to the government. This evolved into the danna house system, which further determined the functional scope of Tokugawa Buddhism. Taking advantage of their quasi-official status, the functionaries of the Buddhist temples sometimes abused the registry system to promote their private interests.[2]

Sensōji was, somewhat tangentially, part of this system. Sensōji's central administration, represented by the Main Hall of the Asakusa Kannon, did not conduct funerals and hence did not maintain a danna registry. But some of its thirty-four subtemples were deeply involved in the business of death rituals, claiming more than 800 households on their danna registers in total. Through these subtemples, Sensōji had a far greater number of such households than did the average Buddhist temple during the Tokugawa period. When Matsudaira Kanzan edited *Sensōji shi* in 1813, Enmei-in, one of Sensōji's subtemples, boasted as many as 256 danna households; Hōzen-in had 132; and Tokuō-in 123.[3] Funerary Buddhism was the major religious function of these subtemples and the source of their livelihood. Even though the Main Hall had no funerary patrons and did not conduct funerals, Sensōji's central administration had to collect the danna registries of the subtemples under its jurisdiction and submit them to the Kan'eiji for transmission to the bakufu once a year.

No matter how seriously some subtemples devoted themselves to death rituals and memorial services, funerary Buddhism at Sensōji was overshadowed by visitors heading for the Main Hall of the Asakusa Kannon in search of something else. As far as Sensōji Buddhist culture was concerned, the role of the Main Hall was so detached from funerary Buddhism that the funerary patrons of subtemples were hardly noticed. According to one estimate, in the late Tokugawa period Sensōji was visited by more than 10,000 people a day in fine weather and no fewer than 3,000 or 4,000 on rainy days.[4] Endowed with neither funeral danna patrons nor a cemetery behind it, the Main Hall and its precinct held no appeal as places for religious services for the deceased. If funerary Buddhism was not visitors' main concern, what then brought them to Sensōji? As I suggest in the Introduction, the attraction was the opportunity for prayer and play.

Takizawa Bakin (1767–1848), author of the popular novel *Nansō Satomi Hakken den* (A tale of Hakken [the samurai Hakken with eight Confucian virtues] of the Satomi House in Nansō [Kazusa]), was, throughout his life, a frequent visitor to Sensōji. Bakin had deep faith in the Asakusa Kannon and other deities and often turned to them for help when he encountered difficulties. The compassion and sympathy of the Sensōji deities was, indeed, the final court of appeal for his misfortune-stricken family. He also enjoyed many happy moments in the Sensōji precincts, eating with his family at the outdoor teahouses, strolling around the playgrounds, and shopping at the street markets. To Bakin, Sensōji was a place not only to placate sorrow but also to enjoy leisure time.[5] It is not hard to imagine thousands of other Bakins who appeased their misfortunes or sought moments of pleasure at Sensōji. Prayer and play, not bound to funerary Buddhism, were the driving forces behind the prosperity of Sensōji in the late Tokugawa period.

How did the culture of prayer and play prosper in Sensōji? What kinds of prayer activities did people conduct there? Was a regular annual or seasonal schedule of prayer rituals offered to the general public? Or did individual visitors perform prayer rites on their own? How did visitors engage in prayer? What about play? What kinds of play activities were available and popular at Sensōji? Did they have any particular characteristics? How did visitors spend their time at Sensōji? By focusing on these questions, I will attempt to describe the popular Buddhist culture of prayer and play at Sensōji.

Sensōji as a Prayer Temple

During the early Tokugawa period, when Sensōji was a prayer hall for the shōgunal house—the political entity that represented public authority (*kōgi*)—it was expected, through Buddhist prayers, to provide spiritual protection for the Tokugawa regime and to ameliorate the misfortunes of the nation. After the shōgunate gave it a 500-koku land grant, Sensōji immediately went about establishing itself as a dutiful public religious institution dedicated to protecting the nation and placating the spirits. It soon set up an annual schedule of religious events (*nenjū gyōji*) with a focus on promoting the public good. Once this annual schedule, which featured prayer rituals, was firmly established, Sensōji held to it even after its affiliation with the Tokugawa house was officially discontinued. Although Sensōji as a prayer temple devoted to public religious duty (a devotion that had abated considerably by the late Tokugawa period) is not the primary concern here, its annual public prayer rituals do provide a way of understanding the salvational mechanism of Sensōji Buddhism—a mechanism that conditioned its later popular prayer culture.

Sensōji's annual public prayer rituals were concentrated in the first month of the new year: the *shūshō* ritual (the New Year nation-protecting rite, which lasted from the final day of the twelfth month to the sixth day of the first month), the *Goō kaji* ritual (an invocation of the power of the Goō deities, on the fifth day of the first month), and the *onza darani* ritual (the "warm-seat" mantra recitation, from the twelfth to the eighteenth day of the first month). In addition, a series of prayer rituals was held throughout the year (for example, the *nehan* [nirvāṇa] ceremony to celebrate the Buddha's enlightenment on the fifteenth day of the second month, the *kan*-Butsu [bathing the Buddha] ceremony to celebrate the birth of the Buddha on the eighth day of the fourth month, the Dengyō memorial service to honor Dengyō Daishi Saichō, the founder of Tendai Buddhism, on the fourth day of the sixth month, the *seikai* ceremony to renew vows of adherence to Buddhist precepts on the twelfth day of the eighth month, and the Tendai ritual to perform a Tendai prayer for the public on the twenty-fourth day of the eleventh month).[6]

Among these, the shūshō prayer ritual was specifically designed to ensure the safety and peace of the nation at the beginning of a new year.[7] The Sensōji shūshō ritual focused, in its initial stage, on the recitation of the three nation-protecting sutras (*Hokekyō*, *Ninnōkyō*, and *Konkōmyōkyō*), followed by a question-and-answer ceremony. But with the rising popularity of the Asakusa Kannon among Edoites, Sensōji soon abandoned this conventional Tendai formula for Buddhist ritual and, instead, constructed a Kannon ritual of its own, the *Kannon-hō* (the dharma of Avalokiteśvara), in order to appeal to the Asakusa Kannon's power of salvation. At the same time, the question-and-answer ceremony was replaced by a dramatic ritual known as *tsuina*, which portrayed the expulsion of evil spirits from the nation.[8]

The revised shūshō ritual started around three o'clock in the afternoon of the last day of the year, with the first performance of the Kannon ritual. After that, eight monks repeated the same Kannon ritual once a day at the same time until the sixth day of the new year. The Kannon ritual, which was esoteric, took about an hour. Even though the public was never allowed to watch the ritual itself, people believed that its annual performance ensured the safety of the nation and their well-being for the new year.[9] The protection-oriented symbolism of the Kannon ritual was complemented by the purification-oriented tsuina ceremony, which was conducted in the middle of the first performance.[10] Against an ebullient background of monks chanting mantras, scattering paper flowers, and beating on gongs, drums, and wooden blocks, a monk donned the mask of a devil and ran around the altar while being chased by a monk holding the twig of a Japanese apricot tree. When the monks returned to their seats after completing three circuits of the altar, the ritual master completed the rite as other priests chanted in unison the twenty-fifth chapter of the *Lotus Sūtra*.[11] As this skit illustrates, tsuina was a purificatory ceremony designed to expel evil spirits and forces from the nation and, thereby, to ensure its safety for the new year.

The protective power of Sensōji deities was more graphically expressed to the general public through the Goō kaji ritual, which was performed on the fifth day of the first month—near the end of the shūshō ritual. Sensōji's Goō kaji was an esoteric prayer designed "to grasp" (*kaji*) the divine power of the Sensōji "Goō deities," represented by Sanja Daigongen (the "three great deities" of the Sensō Shrine) and the Asakusa Kannon.

Nine officiants performed the first stage of the ritual in the curtained inner sanctum of the Sanja (Sensō) Shrine around six o'clock in the morning. The ritual format was simple. One of the officiants conducted the secret Goō kaji ritual at the center of the sanctum, while other monks chanted mantras and scattered paper flowers around the altar. At the completion of the ritual, an assistant took nine flat bowls from the altar and distributed one to each of the nine participants. Another assistant filled those bowls with sacred sake, and the monks drank it. The ritual stage then moved to the Main Hall of the Asakusa Kannon, where the officiants, who were empowered by Sanja Daigongen, invested prepared talismans with the divine power of the Asakusa Kannon. After the presiding monk completed a Goō kaji prayer, a ritual assistant took the talismans from the altar and distributed one to each of the nine priests. Another assistant imprinted each talisman with the Sensōji Goō seal (*SN*, 2: 371–72; 12: 313). After the completion of the ritual procedure, the talismans were sold to the general public in the Main Hall until the eleventh day of the first month. Sensōji Goō talismans, which symbolized the embodiment of the combined power of the Asakusa Kannon and the Sanja Daigongen, were very popular with the public.

Unlike the shūshō and Goō kaji rituals, which incorporated a number of indigenous religious elements, the onza darani, the most renowned annual prayer ritual at Sensōji, is imbued with Buddhist esotericism. As the title onza darani (literally, "warm-seat dhāraṇī") indicates, the ritual was composed of the nonstop performance of 168 rounds of Kannon rituals, along with the continuous chanting of mantras over the space of 156 hours from the twelfth through to the eighteenth day of the first month.[12] The attending priests took turns occupying the presiding seat, keeping it "warm" day and night throughout the ritual period. In addition to the chief priest, who officiated at these around-the-clock Kannon rituals, about twenty assistant monks were assigned to chant the Senju dhāraṇī (mantras for praising the compassion of Sahasrabhuja or the Senju Kannon), which helped to maintain the ritual's esoteric aura. Because the massive labor required for such intensive mantra chanting exceeded what was available at the temple, Sensōji usually hired ritual monks from other temples. The religious efficacy of the onza darani was believed to increase in proportion to the magnitude and quantity of the repetitions of the Kannon ritual and of the recitation of esoteric spells. For this reason, after completion of the ritual, Sensōji posted the number of Kannon rituals that had been performed and the number of times the Senju dhāranī had been recited during the ritual period.[13]

Despite the esoteric foundations of the onza darani, the final round was concluded with a non-Buddhist, indigenous ritual formula known as *jinku okuri* (sending off divine offerings). While the chief priest conducted the last round of the Kannon ritual, two assistant priests collected rice cakes, incense, flowers, and other offerings at the altar and carried them to the backyard of the temple. There they dug a hole, threw the collected objects into it, scorched them with a pine torch, and then filled up the hole. Meanwhile, in the Main Hall ritual priests disassembled the onza darani altar, extinguished the 108 lanterns, and drew down the curtains of the sanctum. Then the chief priest offered blessings to the four directions and to the worshippers. The rite of jinku okuri dramatized the expulsion of negative forces that might bring misfortune upon the nation. In this case, the items offered at the onza darani and then buried symbolized grudge-bearing spirits and evil forces. By permanently burying these items at the intersection of the vertical and horizontal boundaries of their Buddhist sanctuary, Sensōji officials convinced the public that all the causes of misfortune had been removed and that national safety for the new year was ensured.

In addition to these regular annual prayer rituals for the well-being of the public and the state, Sensōji responded to the occasional national crisis with its own prayer formulas. Whenever bad crops or natural disasters hit the nation, Sensōji, as a beneficiary of public funding, offered religious countermeasures, sometimes urged on by shōgunal order. For example, when the nation suffered a series of disasters in 1787 and 1788 (a massive fire at Mount Fuji, famines and epidemics in the Dewa region, a flood in the Kantō area, and a big fire in Kyoto), the shōgunate ordered all temples and shrines to mobilize their spiritual power to overcome vengeful spirits that might be causing the misfortunes. It designated six temples, including Sensōji, to conduct special prayer rituals to placate these spirits (*SN*, 6: 117–18). When a wildfire destroyed the Great Image of Buddha at Mount Atago in Kyoto in 1801 and shortly thereafter lightning destroyed Shitennōji in Osaka, Sensōji was again ordered to perform a massive prayer ritual to prevent further disasters. On both occasions, Sensōji officials conducted the Kannon ritual and/or the Dai-Hannya (a ritual chanting of the *Mahāprajñāpāramitā Sūtra* [*Dai-Hannyakyō*]) (*SN*, 9: 455). Sensōji's role as a public prayer temple thus took various forms.

Whether annual or occasional, most of Sensōji's public prayer rituals appealed to the divine compassion of the Asakusa Kannon through the

Kannon ritual and possibly the recitation of the *Mahāprajñāpāramitā Sūtra* (which incorporated a number of indigenous ritual elements). The ritual formulas of Sensōji prayer were even more prominent during private prayer services for individual patrons. Compared with other Edo temples, Sensōji attracted a large number of prayer patrons (*kitō danna*) thanks to the fame of Asakusa Kannon. During most of the late Tokugawa period, five prayer patron households of daimyō rank (the Matsudaira of Echizen, the Hosokawa of Nagato, the Mōri of Suō, the Tsugaru of Etchū, and the Rokugō of Sado) and thirteen prayer confraternities composed of commoners were affiliated with the Main Hall of the temple. Its subtemples, according to a survey in the early 1810s, claimed more than 450 prayer patron households, mostly commoners.[14] Since the Main Hall of Sensōji did not solicit daimyō patrons and since daimyō households usually maintained their own Buddhist prayer halls in their Edo residences, Sensōji's special relationship with these five powerful daimyō households testifies to its religious prominence in Tokugawa Buddhism. Because of the privilege it bespoke, the private prayer service that Sensōji offered individual patrons attracted the keen interest of the general populace of Edo. Sensōji's private prayer services provide a glimpse into yet another dimension of Sensōji prayer culture.

Sensōji's prayer services for daimyō patrons were conducted on a contractual basis and assumed mutual obligations. Sensōji conducted prayer rituals designed to ensure the welfare of its daimyō patrons on a regular basis (usually three times a year), and its daimyō patrons paid prayer service fees (usually three to ten silver *chōgin*).[15] In addition to these regularly scheduled prayer rituals, the Main Hall of Sensōji dutifully responded to the special requests of patrons who sought divine help on the occasion of such mundane events as disease, childbirth, or an "ominous" year (*yakudoshi*). Sensōji officials usually performed their specialty, the Kannon ritual or the recitation of the *Mahāprajñāpāramitā Sūtra,* and then sent ritual products (talismans and votive offerings) to the daimyō family on its completion (along with such well-wishing gifts as *nori* [edible dried seaweed] and money). After receiving the ritual products and gifts, prayer patrons were expected to remit their prayer fees to Sensōji.[16]

For individual patrons, the privilege of receiving Sensōji's prayer service was available only so long as they fulfilled their contractual obligations. In times of financial strain, daimyō patrons sometimes suspended their contracts with Sensōji temporarily on the pretext of not violating sumptuary regulations. Bad crops in their home domains, natural disasters, and even the alternating attendance (*sankin kōtai*) system provided good excuses for such suspensions. Ironically, when religious help was most badly needed, the privilege of a Sensōji prayer service often turned out to be too expensive, even for daimyō households.[17] In such cases, Sensōji was never generous enough to confer free ritual services.

Within this framework, Sensōji promoted its specialty prayer rituals—the Kannon ritual and the recitation of the *Mahāprajñāpāramitā Sūtra*. These highly acclaimed rituals were beyond the means of ordinary Edoites. Nevertheless, commoners' veneration of Sensōji had much to do with their belief in the efficacy of the Kannon and *Mahāprajñāpāramitā Sūtra* rituals that they could not personally attend. Sensōji diaries and chronicles contain numerous stories of the miraculous qualities of these specialty rituals and attribute these qualities to an ever-rising folk piety, which took as its object the Asakusa Kannon. To judge from these stories, the religious interests of Edo commoners were closely tied to the fame of Sensōji. Did the Asakusa Kannon and *Mahāprajñāpāramitā Sūtra* rituals have special qualities that were particularly relevant to the religious concerns of the general populace? For Sensōji priests, the Kannon ritual, a ritual dedicated to the worship of their own main deity, would be a natural choice. For a major Tendai temple, the recitation of the *Mahāprajñāpāramitā Sūtra*, a sutra strongly associated with the *chingo kokka* tradition of Tendai Buddhism, would also be a natural choice.[18] But why did the general populace of Edo, which was not bound to the priestly role of Sensōji monks, display such a keen interest in these rituals? What really triggered their veneration of Sensōji? Here we need to examine how the Asakusa Kannon and *Mahāprajñāpāramitā Sūtra* rituals nurtured Edoite respect for Sensōji Buddhism.

The main body of the Kannon ritual basically followed the general format of a six-stage esoteric prayer ritual, despite its heavy incorporation of Sensōji's own formulas concerning mudra (*inzō* or *ingei*), mantra (*shin-*

gon), and meditation on the main image.[19] In any event, lay Buddhists had no way to comprehend in detail the entire procedure of the Kannon ritual as it was conducted at Sensōji in the late Tokugawa period. Sensōji priests emphasized secrecy, performing the ritual in the name of "secret dharma" (*hihō*). Prayer patrons were never expected to understand the seemingly unintelligible mystic spells and gestures of the Kannon ritual; instead, they were reminded that the mystic nature of the ritual was indicative of the salvational power of the secretive Asakusa Kannon.[20] On the other hand, the *Mahāprajñāpāramitā Sūtra* ritual was based on the doctrine that the merit acquired by reciting Buddhist scriptures could be transferred to prayer patrons. In theory, this ritual was to be conducted by an assembly of 100 or 600 monks, who would recite assigned chapter(s) of the *Mahāprajñāpāramitā Sūtra*, which consisted of 600 fascicles. But Sensōji practiced a markedly abridged form of recitation—a few monks read the cover page of the *Mahāprajñāpāramitā Sūtra* and then proceeded to a "skipped reading" of the rest, simply opening up and then folding back the accordion-style text.[21] The performance of the *Mahāprajñāpāramitā Sūtra* ritual was extremely formalistic and pedestrian, but this did not appear to matter to prayer patrons.[22]

Prayer patrons never bothered to attempt to understand the mechanisms of the prayer rituals that Sensōji offered them. What they wanted was material evidence—something that gave tangible proof of Sensōji's religious fame and efficacy. The Asakusa Kannon was meaningful to prayer patrons only when they could possess palpable objects that they believed embodied its mysterious power. Those objects, the end products of the Kannon ritual, were talismans (*fuda*) and votive offerings (*kumotsu*). Similarly, the merit derived from reciting the *Mahāprajñāpāramitā Sūtra* was obtainable only when prayer patrons received the ritual's material products. It was a common belief that these products embodied the supernatural power of Buddhist deities and that, when properly carried or placed, they protected their holders from misfortune and helped them to realize their wishes.[23] To Sensōji prayer patrons, talismans or votive offerings ensured the protective power of the Asakusa Kannon and, by extension, of other deities. Buddhist soteriology was effectively wrapped in material form. In satisfying the strong demand for these prayer products, Sensōji officials made sure that they were attractive. Sensōji usually used high-quality paper or flat pieces of wood to make a talisman, on which was written a Sanskrit letter along with information on the ritual and its patrons. The Sanskrit letter signified the manifestation of the Asakusa Kannon. Similarly, votive offerings such as silk cloth, colored yarn, goose figurines, paper fans, rice, and red and white rice cakes wrapped in oak leaves were also treated as religious fetishes.[24] Sensōji officials, aware of their patrons' overriding concern with prayer products, delivered them to their customers immediately upon the completion of a ritual; prayer patrons, aware of Sensōji officials' overriding concern with material compensation, unfailingly provided prayer fees upon receiving the prayer products.

The material exchange of sanctified religious fetishes for prayer fees formed the basic framework of Sensōji prayer culture, and it applied to the general populace as well as to a select group of prayer patrons. Visitors who could not afford Sensōji's costly religious services offered their own form of worship to the Asakusa Kannon. In this case, Sensōji officials neither played a priestly role nor collected prayer fees. But this did not mean that these casual worshippers enjoyed the benefits of Sensōji Buddhism without paying for them. As indicated in the Introduction, Sensōji relied on these lay visitors for much of its income. Before conducting their own prayers, they usually tossed a few coins into the offertory box, and on completing their prayers, they often bought talismans or amulets stamped with the emblem of the Asakusa Kannon. Thus there existed a voluntary but customary system of exchange between the Asakusa Kannon and lay worshippers.

The religious context within which lay worshippers conducted prayers at Sensōji did not differ from the one that underpinned the formal prayer rituals performed for the state or private patrons. Lay worshippers sought the esoteric power of the Asakusa Kannon but were indifferent to the esoteric modus operandi of its ritualization. They simply followed the framework of exchange, offering their coins and receiving ritual products. Popular prayer at Sensōji in the late Tokugawa period was a continuation (albeit in abbreviated form) of the specialty ritual formulas that had been promoted since the early seventeenth century. In other words, Sensōji owed its prosperity as a prayer temple to the religious exchange between the prestigious Asakusa Kannon and lay Buddhists. Through the system of monetary offerings (saisen) and the sale of talismans, Sensōji utilized people's reverence for the Asakusa Kannon for its own financial benefits.

In terms of the folk piety directed toward the Asakusa Kannon in the late Tokugawa period, there was really no distinction between daimyō and store clerks. Yanagisawa Nobutoki (1724–92), a retired daimyō, provides a good example of the populace's passionate veneration of the Asakusa Kannon. Nobutoki, who in 1773, at the age of fifty, retired as the lord of Kōriyama in Yamato province and returned to his Edo residence (Rikugien), was an ardent worshipper of the Asakusa Kannon. After his retirement, Nobutoki visited Sensōji on an average of once every other week and faithfully venerated the Asakusa Kannon until his death in 1792. According to a diary he began keeping in 1773, known as *Enyū nikki*, Nobutoki visited the Asakusa Kannon fourteen times in 1775, twenty times in 1776, twenty-four times in 1777, twenty-nine times in 1778, twenty-six times in 1779, twenty-five times in 1780, twenty-two times in 1781, nineteen times in 1782, twenty-one times in 1783, and thirty times in 1784—a total of 230 visits over a period of ten years.[25] Nobutoki's veneration of the Asakusa Kannon remained sincere and steady throughout his life. When he was unable to pay homage to the Asakusa Kannon for several weeks late in the sixth month of 1781, he found himself "kneeling toward the Kannon in his early morning dream."[26] Nobutoki frequently visited the deities housed in Gokokuji, Yushima Tenjin, Nezu Gongen, and other nearby temples and shrines, but, for him, none of these could match the miraculous power of the Asakusa Kannon.

Matsudaira Kanzan (Ikeda Sadatsune, 1767–1833), a retired daimyō of the Tottori domain, was also an ardent worshipper of the Asakusa Kannon. Kanzan's faith in the Asakusa Kannon is particularly well known thanks to his compilation of the two-volume *Sensōji shi* (Sensōji chronicles). In the preface of the book, he wrote: "There are a lot of Buddhist temples in Edo. But Sensōji is the only temple that has not changed its location for approximately 1,200 years. This is truly a sacred place."[27] As far as Kanzan was concerned, everything about Sensōji deserved to be recorded and made known to future generations. His devotion to the temple may have been extraordinary, but Kanzan was just one of Sensōji's innumerable celebrity visitors.

The Sensōji diaries contain countless mentions of visits by daimyō and other high bakufu officials throughout the Tokugawa period. Women from the shōgunal harem in the Edo Castle were also frequent visitors to the Asakusa Kannon. These *ōoku* ([dwellers] in the great deep) women, whose lives were otherwise strictly confined to the shōgunal castle, sought to alleviate the monotonous cycle of daily routines by conducting prayer rituals to the Sensōji deities.[28] As custom dictated, all these casual visitors first worshipped the Asakusa Kannon, next bought talismans bearing its emblem, and only then proceeded to do whatever else they had in mind.

By the mid-eighteenth century, Sensōji was the favorite destination in Kantō for Buddhist worshippers. The *Bandō Kannon reijō ki* (A record of the miraculous places of Kannon in the Kantō region), published in 1771, flatly declares: "Sensōji is a temple unrivaled by any other in the Bandō." The Asakusa Kannon Hall had been, to some extent, known to the populace in the past. For example, the *Kaikoku zakki* (Miscellanea of traveling about the country), written in 1486, remarks: "This is the temple called Sensōji that enshrines a miraculous Buddha that has no peer." Apparently, Sensōji had captured the attention of travelers by the early seventeenth century. The *Heishin kikō* (An account of a journey in the year *heishin*) of 1617 informs us: "There seem to be more crowds of men and women swarming [to Sensōji] than to Kiyomizu in Kyoto."[29] But Sensōji's reputation blossomed fully only in the late Tokugawa period, when it clearly outranked other Buddhist temples in Kantō in popularity. Edo's other famous deities (for example, Kameido Tenjin [Kameido Tenmangū], Shinobazu Benzaiten, and Meguro Fudō) were popular with Edo Buddhists, but none of them rivaled the Asakusa Kannon.

Miraculous stories of the Asakusa Kannon inundated the ears of the populace through rumors, tour guidebooks, storybooks, poems, religious chronicles (*engi*), temple leaflets, ukiyo paintings, and kabuki plays. Consequently, the Japanese of the late Tokugawa period were well acquainted with Sensōji as a national center of folk piety. Hokkei (d. 1850), a disciple of the renowned ukiyoe painter Katsushika Hokusai (1760–1849), created a bird's-eye view of the Sensōji area in the Tenpō era (1830–43; see Fig. 4). The crowds milling around Sensōji capture our immediate attention.[30] This would have been a typical scene during Hokkei's days at Sensōji.

Those innumerable folk on the streets were what nurtured and sustained Sensōji as a popular prayer center. Sutejirō, a shop assistant at Shiroki-ya in Nihonbashi, was one of those common folk. The Asakusa Kannon was the only god Sutejirō had known before his arrival in Edo. When, as a young teenager, he left his home village of Ōmi in Kansai to work at the Shiroki-ya, his anxious parents told him about the Asakusa Kannon and assured him of its divine compassion and protective power. Hundreds of miles from home (he would not be given time off to visit his parents until his ninth year of employment), Sutejirō, who was often exhausted from cleaning the shop, checking inventories, collecting outstanding bills, and running errands day and night, made it his daily habit to chant the name of the Asakusa Kannon in the hope of invoking its protection.[31] Edo became home to tens of thousands of such transplants at the lower end of the social scale. To them, tutelary deities like the Asakusa Kannon were a daily spiritual comfort.

Some commoners even worshipped daily at the site of the Asakusa Kannon. A story dating from 1834 about an Edo merchant and his religious companion (found in *Jijiroku* [A record of various happenings], compiled by an anonymous editor) provides a typical example. The merchant meets a faithful worshipper of the Asakusa Kannon at Sensōji. This man runs a drugstore called Kinokuni-ya, and he soon becomes the merchant's close friend. Both of them offer daily early-morning prayers to the Asakusa Kannon, even though the round-trip means a walk of seven to eight kilometers. One day they make an appointment to meet in front of the Main Hall to have a cup of tea and a chat after the usual morning service to the Asakusa Kannon. When the faithful friend does not show up, the merchant suspects that something unusual has happened. He calls at his friend's drugstore to see what is wrong. The friend is about to be poisoned by his shop assistant and his estranged wife, who have conspired to kill him and to take over the store. Just as the servant is

Fig. 4. A scene at the Sensōji complex. From Hokkei, *Tōto Kinryūsan Sensōji zu*, Tenpō era (1830–43) (from Henry Smith, *Ukiyoe ni miru Edo meisho*). Reproduced by permission of Iwanami Shoten.

poised to carry out this plan, the merchant walks in and rescues his friend. Thanks to this friendship, mediated by the daily worship of the Asakusa Kannon, the merchant is able to save his friend's life. Both men, of course, greatly appreciate the care of the Asakusa Kannon, and their faith becomes even deeper.[32]

There are many other stories of the miraculous powers of the Asakusa Kannon. Saitō Gesshin's *Bukō nenpyō* (Annual chronicles of Edo), edited in 1806, tells of an Osaka traveler named Akashiya Shinzō. Upon being accosted by a robber in Edo, the traveler prays to the Asakusa Kannon for help. Suddenly the robber becomes helpless, and the traveler is able to escape. Afterward, out of gratitude, the traveler donates to Sensōji a painting of Asakusa Kannon rescuing him from the robber.[33]

People's expectations of the Asakusa Kannon were literally limitless—from the curing of disease to rescue from disasters to the granting of wishes. Saitō Gesshin himself implored the Asakusa Kannon whenever he faced unyielding difficulties.[34] As mentioned above, for the celebrated novelist Takizawa Bakin and his family, the compassion of the Asakusa Kannon was their last hope. While he was struggling to restore his family's fallen status at the turn of the 1830s, Bakin endured, one after the other, the deaths of his only son, his son-in-law, and his wife. His only hope, his grandson Tarō, was too young and too sickly to be of any help. Until his death in 1848, the blind Bakin dictated his novels to his daughter-in-law in order to make a living; one of these novels was *Nansō Satomi Hakken den*. Bakin's diary tells us that, four days before his death, his two granddaughters, Otsugi and Osachi, "prayed to the Asakusa Kannon for the family one hundred times," while he himself, being enfeebled, bowed toward the four directions in lieu of visiting Sensōji. When Tarō became sick in 1849, his mother visited the Asakusa Kannon every month to pray for his quick recovery.[35]

As can be seen from these and other examples, the Asakusa Kannon was the focal point for the religious sentiments of Edo commoners. The prayers they directed toward the Asakusa Kannon are filled with a deep faith in its compassion and ability to provide divine help. Transcending the borders of wealth, power, gender, age, and social status, the Asakusa Kannon was a great source of hope and comfort to the Edo populace. No wonder that thousands of people visited Sensōji every day. As noted in the Introduction, the income from casual offerings accounted for over half of Sensōji's entire annual income of about 3,000 gold pieces. If, on average, a visitor tossed five copper coins into the offertory box (the price of a cup of tea at a teahouse),[36] then Sensōji had more than 1.2 million paying visitors per year during the late Tokugawa period. These visitors were also the major buyers of religious products, another important source of income. The demand for these products was so high that Sensōji consumed large amounts of paper. For example, in 1813 Sensōji spent about sixteen gold pieces on paper. This is a significant amount of money in light of the fact that one gold piece was enough to provide basic support for one adult for one year (*SN*, 12: 464). But these sixteen gold pieces, with the blessing of the Asakusa Kannon, would have been multiplied tens of times over upon the sale of these paper products.

Clearly, Sensōji owed much of its prosperity as a prayer temple to the fame of the Asakusa Kannon. Whether in formal organized prayer rituals or individual prayers, the Asakusa Kannon was a source of religious inspiration and hope for its worshippers. But the role of Sensōji was not limited to alleviating suffering. As the misfortune-ridden Bakin sometimes found when he and his family enjoyed happy outings at Sensōji, the blessing of the Asakusa Kannon stretched beyond the domain of prayer into the domain of play.

Sensōji as a Play Center

Sensōji administrators occasionally conducted land surveys (*kenchi*) and drew maps in order to verify the territorial boundaries of their highly urbanized territory. Internally, Sensōji land, which consisted of the inner precincts of the Main Hall, subtemples, front districts, agricultural fields, and other support facilities, was so disorderly and mixed up that it was sometimes not easy to locate all taxable sources. A 1798 land-survey map, which was perhaps drawn for taxation purposes, identifies all commercial business locations in the inner precincts (*SN*, 4: appendix).

This map delineates the density of Sensōji's business stations (*mise*). Among the commercial enterprises in Sensōji's inner precincts were approximately a hundred teahouses, four vegetable-rice teahouses, four dumpling teahouses, one sweet liquor store, ninety-three toothpick shops, nineteen papier-mâché stores, twelve archery booths, seven sundry goods shops, three candy shops, three painting paper shops, three florists, one tobacco shop, and a couple of *shibai* theaters and street-show places.[37] In a space of 9,166 *tsubo* (30,248 square meters), there were about 250 commercial spots in addition to numerous Buddhist and Shintō halls, stupas, and other religious facilities. By 1822, the number of street *mise* increased to as many as 292, of which 180 had attached kitchens (*SN*, 15: 55–58). The inner precincts of Sensōji would have been seen as a prosperous commercial district had visitors not been most impressed by such imposing religious structures as the Main Hall, a five-story pagoda, and the Sanja Daigongen Shrine.

In Japanese Buddhism, the inner precincts (*keidai*) of the temple, which were separated from the secular world, were a place where one could feel the sacred aura of intense solemnity. And indeed, Sensōji's inner precincts, which accommodated the Main Hall of the Asakusa Kannon and other major religious structures, were certainly its sanctum sanctorum. But this seemingly sacred space was also full of commercial booths and shops. Wherever space was available, profit-seeking merchants could be found. In particular, the rear ground of the Main Hall, known as Okuyama ("deep mountain"—in theory, a sacrosanct retreat for Buddhist monks), offered a spectacular scene of hustle and bustle, with entertainers, merchants, and crowds of customers. Without a doubt, in the late Tokugawa period commercialism prevailed in Sensōji's inner precincts.

Commercial activities at Sensōji were, however, not confined to the inner precincts. They spread out into the outer precincts (the *sannai*, or "inner mountain"), where subtemples were located, as well as into front districts (*monzen machi*). The major approach to the Main Hall, stretching approximately 130 meters in the buffer zone of outer precincts between the Kaminari Gate (the entrance to the sannai) and the Niō Gate (the entrance to the keidai), was particularly famous for the "inner stores" (*nakamise*) lining both sides of the street. This street formed a sort of shopping mall for Sensōji visitors, who had to traverse it to reach the Main Hall after passing through the Kaminari Gate, which separated the Sensōji Buddhist complex from the secular world. Unlike many temporary business setups in the inner precincts, this street boasted dozens of well-established permanent stores specializing in such goods as tobacco, tobacco pipes, sandals, products made of bamboo, eggplants, cookies, toys, umbrellas, artificial flowers, buckwheat noodles, soybean pastes, and other local staples.[38]

Well aware of the benefits that this kind of permanent market generated, some subtemples, such as Iō-in, Jissō-in, Konzō-in, and Chōju-in, encouraged merchants to develop market streets along their entrance paths. In fact, those subtemples able to lure shops and teahouses to their front streets usually attracted more visitors to their Buddhist halls and, at the same time, received sizable rental incomes from shop owners. Nichion-in, Kanchi-in, and Chōju-in even rented out small spaces within their precinct boundaries—spaces usable only for attached temporary "suspended shops" (*kakemise*).[39] All this effort to raise more income helped transform Sensōji's precincts into a prosperous commercial pocket of Edo. Some visitors even complained that the streets were too crowded with vendors and that commercial stalls blocked the pathway to the Main Hall (*SN*, 7: 736–37).

Outside the Kaminari Gate were twenty front districts under Sensōji's jurisdiction. Although this monzen area was primarily given over to housing for townspeople (*chōnin*), entrepreneurs could not pass up the commercial opportunities offered by the area. For example, Namiki Street, which had been a quiet neighborhood (as its name, Namiki [a row of trees], indicates), had become a busy commercial zone by the mid-eighteenth century.[40] Visitors could find a variety of stores, teahouses, and restaurants (more than 100 by the 1810s) along Namiki Street and other neighboring front districts.[41] As Matsudaira Kanzan noted in his Sensōji chronicles, visitors were delighted to find the well-known staples of the Sensōji area, such as Asakusa seaweed, Asakusa sake (called *morohaku* and famous for its pure taste), Asakusa rice cakes, and buckwheat noodles.[42]

By the late Tokugawa period, the Sensōji area had been transformed into a commercial center that boasted permanent as well as occasional markets. In particular, special fairs, held three times annually, amused visitors and shoppers: the *ennichi* (day for connection) fair held on the tenth day of the seventh month, the Bon fair held on the twelfth and thirteenth days of the seventh month, and a year-end fair called *toshi-no-ichi* (fair of the year) held on the seventeenth and eighteenth days of the twelfth month. Among these, the ennichi fair created a spectacular scene, with the display and sale of colorful Japanese ground cherries (*hōzuki*) on every corner of the temple precincts. According to a Sensōji chronicle, an Atago deity appeared in a dream to a man living in Shiba and told him that drinking ground-cherry tea on the tenth day of the seventh month would eradicate dysentery in adults and intestinal parasites in children. During the Meiwa era (1764–71), opportunistic merchants began to sell the plant (an antipyretic in Chinese medicine) in Sensōji on this "day for connection." The ground cherry soon came to represent the ennichi fair itself.[43] The Bon fair, held two days after the ennichi fair, was an occasion for Edo families to purchase ritual items to decorate their Bon altars and to prepare seasonal foods to offer to ancestral spirits during the Bon festival. The year-end fair was similar to the Bon fair, but its magnitude and popularity far exceeded that of other fairs.

The *Tōto saijiki* (A record of annual observance in the eastern capital) of Saitō Gesshin vividly describes the crowded scene at the toshi-no-ichi fair (see Fig. 5 for an illustration from his *Edo meisho zue* [Illustrations of famous places in Edo]):

> Not to mention the precinct, the fair stretches to the Komakata Hall in the South, to the Ueno area in the West, and even to a gravel yard in Yamanojukuchō in the East, filling the streets with stall shops that sell decorative items for the New Year, foods for sacrificial offering, worship service equipment, seasonal toys, and gifts. The noisy clamor of traders fills the streets throughout the day and night.[44]

In the late Tokugawa period, the fair was, by and large, driven by sheer commercialism. According to a Sensōji chronicle, this fair had originally been held in an Ebisu shrine (allegedly a branch of Ise Shrine) near Sensōji's Kaminari Gate on the ninth and tenth days of the twelfth month. But merchants, who were confident of greater commercial growth in Sensōji, moved the fair to Sensōji's inner precincts in the early eighteenth century. The Sensōji administration welcomed this relocation and even allowed merchants and shoppers to use the Niō Gate, the inner gate of Sensōji, until two o'clock in the morning (the usual closing time was at sunset).[45] In the long run, the commercial streets and special fairs established at Sensōji proved a powerful magnet for the general populace.

The Sensōji area also offered a variety of entertainments. As Yanagisawa Nobutoki noted, he was attracted by the fame of the Asakusa Kannon, but religion was not the sole reason for his frequent visits to Sensōji. When he stopped by Sensōji, Nobutoki often idled the time away, from morning to evening, or sometimes from late afternoon to the middle of the night, sipping tea at a teahouse, chatting with friends, or just strolling around Okuyama. There were plenty of circus shows, archery booths, street performances, and other pastimes, all of which occupied his leisure time to one degree or another. After enjoying Matsui Gensui's top-spinning tricks and ball-juggling demonstrations, Nobutoki would take a rest and sip a cup of tea at the Sakai-ya teahouse, while his companions shopped for toothpicks, hair strings, ornaments, combs, and candies. Sensōji was a pleasant place for Nobutoki's lighthearted outings. When he became bored with Sensōji, he sometimes ventured to the nearby Yoshiwara brothel area or to other teahouses rumored to have hired pretty servers. His adventurism and curiosity were not, however, always satisfied. An entry in his diary for the twenty-second day of the tenth month of 1783 expressed disappointment: "A girl at the Naniwa teahouse had been the talk of the town for her beauty. I soon checked that place out, only to find that she fell far short of the gossip."[46]

Saitō Gesshin's diary also regales us with stories of the amusements he enjoyed at Sensōji. The pursuit of recreation in the Sensōji area was apparently as meaningful to him as was the paying of homage to the Asakusa Kannon. Gesshin's enthusiasm for spending his leisure time at Sensōji resulted in the development of a warm friendship with Matsui Gensui, probably the most prominent street-art performer at Sensōji during the 1830s and 1840s.

As a place of leisure and entertainment, Sensōji was open to anyone. Saitō Gesshin's *Edo meisho zue* again provides us with vivid illustrations. Upon entering Sensōji's inner precincts through the Niō Gate, it was almost impossible for anyone to ignore the seemingly limitless opportunities for entertainment. Sensōji's inner precincts were a world of street asobi (play). The center of the right-hand panel of the drawing reproduced here as Figure 6 shows a shibai theater, a storytelling hall called *kōshaku* (preaching the Buddha), toothpick stalls, and a row of teahouses known as Nijikken chaya (twenty teahouses). In Figure 7, in the far left corner, a circus called Gensui (in honor of the main performer) attracts a crowd of onlookers circling Matsui Gensui's performance, as well as other business booths and stalls. Okuyama, the grounds behind the Main Hall, was far more prosperous, as is illustrated in Figure 8. Couched in the woody land behind the protective shield of the Asakusa Kannon and inside the walls that separated it from the agricultural fields to the north and from Yoshiwara, Okuyama seemed an ideal space for providing Edoites with moments of relief from their daily routines.

Because of the considerable contribution of commerce to Sensōji's revenues, it is not surprising that its land-survey registries paid a great deal of attention to the businesses located within its precincts. A 1778

(*text continues on p. 60*)

Fig. 5. A bustling scene at the year-end fair (from Saitō Gesshin, *Edo meisho zue*).

十二月十八日
年の市

Fig. 6. A scene at Sensōji centering around the Niō Gate and the five-story pagoda (from Saitō Gesshin, *Edo meisho zue*).

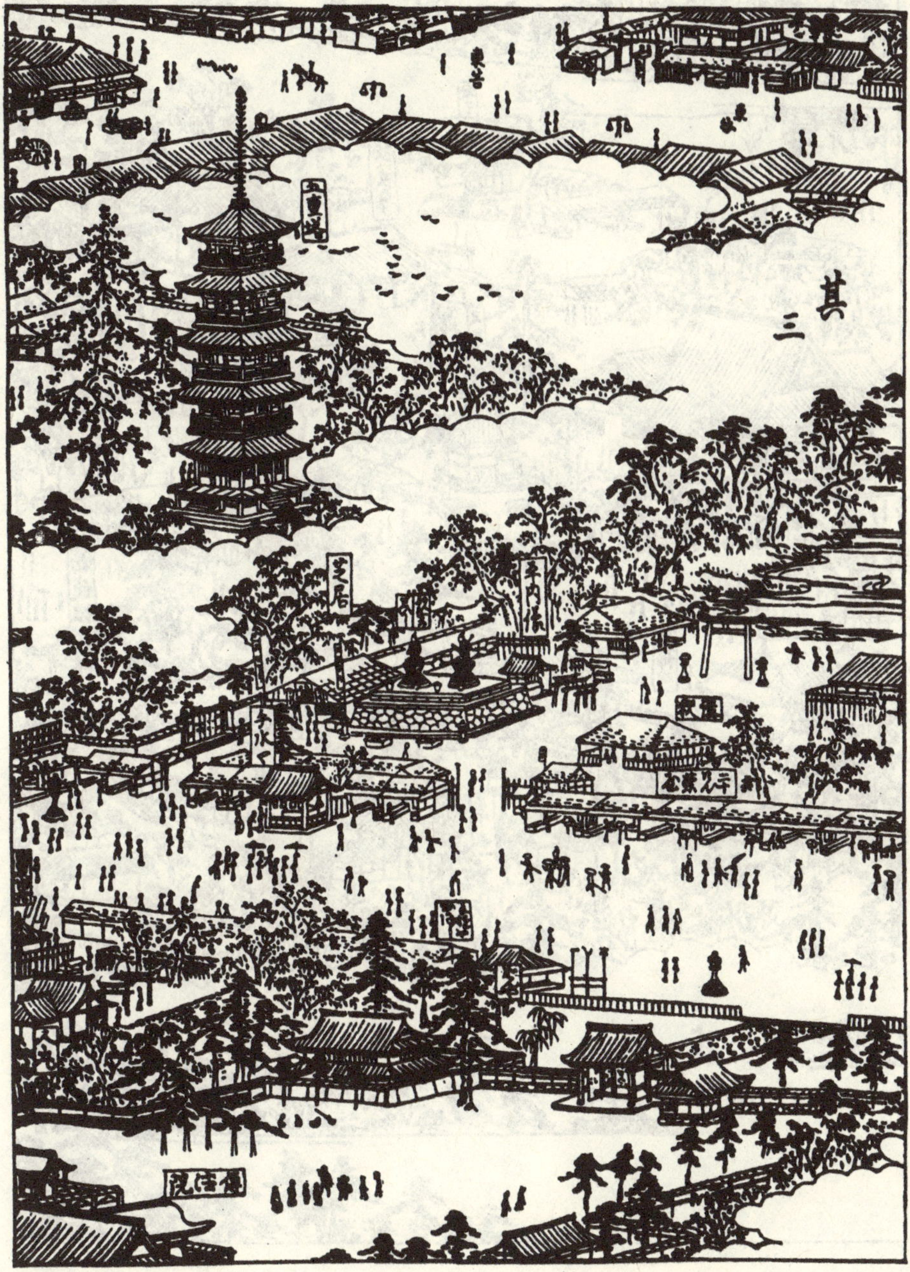
其三

Fig. 7. A scene at Sensōji centering around the Main Hall (from Saitō Gesshin, *Edo meisho zue*).

Fig. 8. A scene at Sensōji Okuyama (from Saitō Gesshin, *Edo meisho zue*).

其五

roster of renters called *Keidai sō mise unjō chō* (A rental list of all shops in the precinct) in the *Sensōji shi* indicates the magnitude of business activities at Sensōji.[47] This registry lists a total of 280 shops and their tenants, including 112 teahouses, ninety-one toothpick shops, sixteen toy shops, seven archery booths, six candy shops, and six storytelling halls (*Taiheiki*), as well as space for circuses, exotic exhibitions, and the sale of homemade medications. The convenient concentration of various commercial business and entertainment attractions must have been a tremendous draw not only for Asakusa Kannon worshippers but also for ordinary Edoites.

Among the wide range of entertainment opportunities at Sensōji, the *misemono* (display of things) spectacle was the perfect choice for those thirsty for the exotic. In the misemono booths, Sensōji visitors could view wonders that would otherwise have remained unknown to them. Misemono merchants, who set up exhibition booths called *yoshizubari* (loquat leaf enclosures) in the Sensōji precinct, competed with one another to lure customers. The following list of some notable misemono exhibitions at Sensōji in the late Tokugawa period gives some idea of the range of attractions available to Edoites.

1769 A girl with only two fingers, referred to as *kani musume* (crab girl); a giant toad

1813 A *karakuri ningyō* (contraption doll) installed in a pond near the Benten Hall and a spring-driven automaton that was capable of a limited range of repetitive motions

1814 A self-boiling pot

1816 A giant porcupine

1819 Bamboo-wicker replicas of birds, beasts, plants, and historical figures made by the renowned basketry artisan Ichide Shōshichirō and his disciples; *karakuri* that moved around in the water

1820 Scenic constructs depicting the secret lives of courtesans, climactic scenes from well-known novels, and legendary Japanese and Chinese figures—all positioned against a background of refined replicas of animals, plants, and landscapes

1829 Puppets jerking on their strings

1835 Lifelike dolls

1836 A "diamond ship" made of glass, featuring the T'ang emperor Hsüan-tsung and his eunuchs and entertainers at a party

1841 Grandiose tableaux of scenes from popular novels, kabuki favorites, legendary heroes and deities, and imaginary animals
1847 A "diamond ship" in subtle motion, featuring Dutch traders
1848 A four-season flower garden
1855 Breathing dolls with foreign faces; "living figures"; and a lifelike effigy of the kabuki actor Ichikawa Danjūrō (who committed suicide) on his way to Paradise[48]
1862 Models of an open womb showing the growth of a fetus[49]

The objects displayed in misemono exhibitions included any item, natural or artificial, that was wondrous, rare, fascinating, or sensational enough to attract a crowd and bring profit. Among the popular natural objects were exotic birds (parrots and peacocks), scary beasts (tigers, bears, porcupines, and wolves), tame wild animals, tropical fish and sea animals, exotic flowers, wondrous topiary and bonsai, and even human prodigies.[50] The exhibitions of human freaks and deformities, which were often touted as object lessons in the Buddhist principles of karmic reward and punishment, offered a graphic demonstration of Buddhist commercialism. Often displayed demonstrating odd skills, disabled humans were exploited to underscore one of the best-known Buddhist teachings—a sinful act in this life will result in deformity in the next. Such exhibitions of humans continued until the Meiji government banned them in 1873.[51]

On the other hand, handiworks offered misemono merchants great opportunities to create their own prolific worlds of wonder and exoticism. Using straw, bamboo, mother-of-pearl, ceramics, papier-mâché, and other materials, misemono entrepreneurs competed with one another to reproduce traditional cultural themes, popular actors and heroes, the world of Yoshiwara courtesans, and the daily lives of Edoites. No matter what subjects they chose, success depended on achieving a level of creativity and attraction that would capture the curiosity and imagination of the Edo populace. With the introduction of peep shows (*nozoki*) and contraption dolls in the mid-nineteenth century, the sophisticated misemono world of lively artifacts further elevated the popular taste for novel delights. Sometimes misemono wandered into depicting the pleasure quarters or sex scandals, and sometimes they were tainted by exaggeration and hoax.[52] But the challenge of the business lay in overcoming the relatively static nature of exhibitions as such. Anyone who came up with more animated diversions for pleasure-seeking patrons could dominate the world of Sensōji entertainment for some time. Among the many lively entertainments at late Tokugawa Sensōji, storytelling, which enjoyed a great popularity among Edoites, deserves our attention.

Storytellers, who conducted "lectures on the Buddha" (*kōshaku*), entertained members of their audience by making them burst into laughter, by saddening or exciting them, or by leading them into a wondrous imaginary world. In the mid-eighteenth century, Fukai Shidōken (1679–1765), who opened his "lecture" hall in front of Sanja Daigongen (Sensō Shrine), was without peer in the Edo storytelling world. Hiraga Gennai (1728–79), a disciple of Shidōken, left this description of the funny appearance and reputation of his master:

> He attracts crowds with stories of heroic soldiers. Holding a funny-looking wooden pointer resembling the shape of a phallic *matsutake* mushroom in his hand and moving it along the lines [of a storybook], he convulses an audience with laughter. . . . My master, who is slim and close to ninety years old, is superb in mimicking even the subtleties of gestures and voices of a female. . . . There used to be two popular characters. One was Ebizō (a kabuki actor), and the other Shidōken. After Ebizō died, there is only one left who deserves the moniker "Edo meibutsu" (famous person of Edo).[53]

Until 1765, when he died at the age of eighty-six in a shabby apartment in the Sensōji district, Shidōken pioneered the *yose* (vaudeville theater) business at Sensōji and nurtured the cultural spirit of "silly works" in Edo.

Other storytellers soon followed the path that Shidōken had paved. They rented space from Sensōji, set up their walled storytelling halls whose *kido* (wooden doors) opened to the outside, charged entrance fees, and competed with one another in displaying their lecturing talents. As we can determine from a typical placard (which read *Taiheiki*) erected to advertise the storytelling halls, storytellers usually took their topics from traditional military tales (*gunki monogatari*) and often related them to Buddhist didacticism. Some storytellers amused audiences with erotic material, and others ventured to touch on sensitive political gossip. Baba Bunkō (1718–58), another renowned storyteller in the mid-eighteenth century, sometimes satirized contemporary politics and poked fun at factional disorders (known as *oie sōdō* [household disturbances]) among certain daimyō houses. Bunkō had a critical turn of mind and could not come to terms with Shidōken's rather straightforward commercialism; he labeled the latter's art "an evil way." Baba's audience found his tone and wit so poignant and cathartic that it was as if "their dissatisfaction had been washed out."[54] But his courage cost him his life. He was eventually put to death by the bakufu, leaving behind laughter and cynicism.

In contrast to storytelling, which amused an audience with masterly words, street-art performances amused audiences with dexterous actions. As one of the most popular centers for circus performances in Edo, Sensōji had generated its own unique circus culture since the mid-eighteenth century. Sensōji visitors could easily find, here and there in the precinct, crowds surrounding oval enclosures, where acrobats and clowns presented a variety of entertainments known as *misemono-gei* (arts that show things). Some notable examples of the late Tokugawa period include:

1742 Acrobatic feats of a man-horse (performer: Kirinnosuke)
1769 Acrobatics (*karuwaza*), martial arts, and superhuman muscular skills (performers: Hayakawa Toraichi, Haruyama Utanosuke, and others)
1770s Juggling with beans and sake bottles (*tokuri*) (performer: Keshinosuke)
1773 An off-season sumō tournament (*hanazumō*) and equestrian feats
1780 A comic drama performed by children
1805 A comic drama performed by children to promote the sale of "wonder" drugs
1807 Sumō wrestling matches and acrobatics performed by a man of great strength
1808 Matsui Gensui's top spinning; a puppet show
1811 Sumō wrestling matches
1816 A ballad drama sung to the accompaniment of a samisen (*jōruri*); acrobatics by a boy (performer: Yamamoto Kojima)
1819 Equestrian feats
1820s Flying paper butterflies and an exhibition of sleights of hand performed while playing with ghostly puppets (performers: Yanagawa Itchōsai and Tanigawa Sadakichi)

1828 Power competition (*kakuryoku*) in the form of sumō
1829 Dance performances by children; a puppet play in Okuyama
1841 Nineteen ball-juggling tricks (*kyokumari*) (performer: Kikukawa Kunimaru)
1844 A composite show consisting of top-spinning tricks (*kyokugoma*) and dancing
1846 Acrobatics, tightrope walking, and falconry dancing (performers: Yamamoto Kojima and his group)
1847 Ise dance to the beat of samisen
1853 An equestrian circus
1855 An acrobatic variety show (performers: Masukagami and his group)
1857 Ten acrobatic feats (performers: Sakurazuna Komaju and Hayatake Torakichi)
1862 Eleven acrobatic feats (performer: Hayatake Torakichi)[55]

The misemono business in Sensōji exploited the popular taste for ephemeral and sometimes illusory stunts. Acrobatics, top-spinning tricks, and ball-juggling formed the core of this popular repertoire, often complemented by magic tricks, equestrian circuses, and demonstrations of sleights of hand, martial arts, swordsmanship, and muscular skills.[56] Visitors to Sensōji enjoyed watching displays of these skills, which were never in short supply. Circus performers, who entertained for free or charged an entrance fee of only a few copper coins, competed to lure customers into buying their "wonder" drugs after a prelude-performance.

Among the dozens of misemono performers who sold nostrums prepared according to secret family recipes, for generation after generation the members of the Matsui family ranked number one thanks to their superb top-spinning skills. In particular, the thirteenth heir, Matsui Gensui, was so adroit that he was often called to amuse the shōgun and other high officials.[57] In 1866, in Matsui Gensui's final days, he even undertook a two-year tour abroad with other popular entertainers.[58] Kikukawa Kunimaru, famed for his ball-juggling skills in the 1840s, attracted 5,000 to 6,000 spectators a day. His lavish spending in the neighboring Yoshiwara pleasure quarters, however, eventually cost him his career, when he was expelled from Edo by the bakufu. However, his legendary success long echoed in the world of Sensōji misemono arts.[59]

Not only individual performers, but also troupes were often the talk of the town. Comic dramas performed by child prodigies as a prelude to the selling of "cure-all" lotions attracted crowds, as did acrobatics and circus groups featuring feats of tumbling, illusionary tricks, dancing, and martial arts. Troupes of acrobats preferred to charge somewhat high entrance fees rather than to sell "magic" medications, for the income from entrance fees usually proved quite lucrative once a walled enclosure, surrounded by tiers of gallery benches (*sajiki*) and ground seats, was well established.[60] Puppet theaters also attracted a large number of spectators, as did monkey shows. This amalgam of performing artists transformed Sensōji into a sort of entertainment melting pot. Entertainers and misemono merchants never hesitated to display, adjust, transform, or even counterfeit their talents and skills in the pursuit of profits. As long as commercial interests were involved, Sensōji's play culture, whether in the form of performing arts or traditional sports, knew no restraints.

Sumō wrestling is a case in point. After the shōgunate recognized sumō as a leisure profession and a legitimate means of achieving a livelihood (*tosei*) in 1744, the Yoshida Zenzaemon family claimed licensing rights over sumō wrestlers and organized them into a professional association. Yoshida Oikaze, who was officially recognized as the *iemoto* (proprietor) of the sumō profession when he successfully staged a sumō show for Shōgun Ienari at Edo Castle in 1791, began to exercise tight control over the approximately 150 sumō wrestlers of Edo, Osaka, and Kyoto. Yoshida's sumō organization annually held "four seasons," or sumō competitions (*shiki kanjin sumō*): two in Edo and one each in Osaka and Kyoto.[61] For commercial reasons, Yoshida organizers favored Ryōgoku, a plaza beside the Sumida River, as the stage for the show when it was held in Edo, but sometimes, for a change, they chose temples or shrines (including Sensōji). Over time, the "four seasons" *kanjin* sumō show, which enjoyed an explosive popularity, evolved into a national pastime. Needless to say, the Yoshida family and its sumō wrestlers endeavored to tighten their monopolistic rights over sumō and the sizable income from this popular sport.

Entertainers and misemono merchants, however, could not resist the temptation of such a potentially lucrative source of income. In an attempt to evade the bakufu's regulations on sumō, some misemono merchants began to mimic sumō shows, often featuring theatrical matches consisting of "surprise" raw power or unusual physical skills at crowded intersections or at temples and shrines. These entrepreneurs, who could not mobilize "licensed" wrestlers, instead attempted to create an exoticized form of sumō, often in combination with sideshows involving singing, dancing, or dramatic performances. Thanks to its reputation as a prosperous amusement center, Sensōji naturally attracted many sumō entertainers in the late Tokugawa period, and visitors to Sensōji often encountered "peculiar" sumō matches involving female wrestlers with distinctive physical marks.

Beyond the sumō misemono, visitors to Sensōji could enjoy more participatory forms of asobi, such as archery (*yōkyū*). The 1778 Sensōji land survey listed seven archery booths within the temple precincts, and the Kansei map of 1798 shows twelve. Archery, which had originated in T'ang China and had become popular among Kyoto court nobles in the Muromachi period, had evolved into a popular leisure pastime by the late Tokugawa period and was easily available for a few coins. The format was simple: shoot a twenty- or thirty-centimeter-long arrow toward a ten-centimeter target at a distance of approximately thirteen and a half meters. Traditionally, arrow shooting was believed to drive away evil spirits or to aid in divination. Some people played archery for stakes.[62] The female attendants who served the mostly male patrons were an added attraction. Among the many archery booths in Edo, those at Sensōji were especially famous for the colorful views provided by the "young girls who pick up the arrows" (*yatori onna*).

The handful of archery booths at Sensōji were far outnumbered by toothpick shops. Ninety-one toothpick shops were in business in 1778, ninety-three in 1798, and an astonishing 220 in 1807. First-time visitors must have been surprised to encounter hundreds of similar shops scattered all around the grounds of Sensōji. As Figure 9 shows, a toothpick shop usually consisted of a vending stall formed of one or two wooden panels (portable and foldable) and sold toothpicks, dentifrice, beans for pigeons, toys, and other miscellaneous items. In a society in which tooth decay and toothaches were rampant and medical knowledge to prevent or lessen them almost nonexistent, dental care was a universal concern.

Fig. 9. Toothpick shops on the grounds of Sensōji (from Saitō Gesshin, *Edo meisho zue*).

Picking the teeth after a meal was common, and brushing with dentifrice or powered gallnuts was very fashionable, even though their sanitary effects rested largely in the verbal promises of toothpick merchants. Still, one wonders how so many toothpick shops could stay in business. The competition between them was understandably intense. Like those who ran archery stalls, the owners of these shops found that the major way to survive the heavy competition was to hire attractive salesgirls.[63] For many visitors to Sensōji, the voyeuristic enjoyment of watching these salesgirls and chatting with them was a form of asobi that was otherwise hard to come by in feudal society.

The teahouse business was neither less voyeuristic nor less oriented toward asobi than the toothpick business. As the Sensōji chronicles note, the precursor of the many teahouses found at Sensōji in the late Tokugawa period, referred to as the "Nara chaya" (Nara teahouse), which sold meals as well as tea, first appeared in Namiki-chō in the Tenna era (1681–83). But it was not until the Hōreki era (1751–63) that teahouses selling only tea began to spring up along the eastern side of the nakamise. At this early period, the famous Nijikken chaya (twenty teahouses), which would later move to the inner precincts, were most conspicuous.[64] The number of teahouses in the Sensōji precincts, both inner and outer, eventually increased to about a hundred (there were 111 in 1778 and 104 in 1798). These teahouses were temporary structures, walled and partitioned by reed screens, in which two or three tables were placed. Visitors to Sensōji were attracted to these teahouses by the lanterns or placards bearing such words as "a place for resting" (or the name of the shop) hung at the entrances. People patronized these shops for several reasons—to meet with friends or acquaintances, to drink a cup of tea, to hold business talks, or just to rest their sore feet. Sometimes sake was also available on special order.

Most teahouse customers were male, and most of these crowded teahouses hired young and attractive women, known as *chakumi onna* (women who scoop up tea), and "displayed" them in order to lure male clientele. These teahouse girls offered male Edoites the exotic pleasure of watching an attractive woman or talking with her. For the women, the teahouse was a place where they could display their personal beauty and dress while making money. Although the shōgunate stipulated that teahouse waitresses could wear only cotton cloth, these young women had no compunction about donning silk and black satin sashes. Colorful aprons were special accessories that added to their stylish appearance.[65] At the crossroads of commercialism and male voyeurism, the Sensōji teahouses created and nurtured an erotic culture that gave birth to such legendary teahouse belles as Okita of the Naniwa teahouse and Oroku of the Minato teahouse. Their beauty dominated the curiosity and gossip of Edoites.

Okita was "so beautiful and lovely that nobody treated her lightly," and "there was no one who had not heard of her fame." It is even said that so many people once swarmed in front of the Naniwa teahouse just to catch a glimpse of her that the owner had to spray water to scatter them away. Okita even became a model for the ukiyo painter Kitagawa Utamaro (1753–1806; see Fig. 10). And Oroku was so renowned for her trussed hairstyle that everyone tried to copy it. It was as if Oroku "trussed Edo ladies" through her fashionable hairstyle.[66] Obviously, the "exhibitory" presence of teahouse waitresses was a major force behind the "tea-selling" business and Sensōji's asobi environment.

Clearly, it would be ludicrous to characterize Sensōji during the late Tokugawa period solely as a Buddhist center of prayer: it was also a Buddhist center of play and entertainment. For Edoites, as Komori Takayoshi aptly puts it, Sensōji was a place for *taberu* (eating), *kau* (buying), *miru* (watching), and, eventually, *asobu* (playing).[67] Visitors to Sensōji were fascinated by the abundant choices of pastimes, which ranged from street markets, noodle shops, restaurants, storytelling halls, theaters, circuses and other street arts, and archery halls to the attractions of toothpick shops and teahouses. There were also scenic buildings of unusual significance. Taking advantage of such opportunities, visitors were easily absorbed into this sphere of play and relaxation. The play culture of Sensōji was never in short supply (as long as it was not being hindered by the bakufu).

From an economic perspective, Sensōji's prosperity depended to a great extent on this popular play culture—even though it had nothing to do with the Buddha's original teachings. Throughout the late Tokugawa period, the rental income that this play culture provided to the coffers of

Fig. 10. Okita of the Naniwa teahouse. An ukiyo painting by Kitagawa Utamaro (1753–1806) (from Unno Hiroshi, *Edo no sakariba*).

Sensōji remained steady and significant, yielding hundreds of gold pieces every year. More significant, however, was the ripple effect of this culture. Play culture converted the whole area of Sensōji into a sort of amusement park (*sakariba*), and this magnet attracted crowds that benefited the entire Sensōji operation, both religious and nonreligious.

Late Tokugawa Sensōji culture was based on two core functions: prayer and play. People from all walks of life visited Sensōji to pray to the Asakusa Kannon, to enjoy the pastimes found on the spacious grounds of the temple, or (most often) both. In a society in which daily life was often vulnerable and insecure, people dealt with their anxieties through prayer (kitō). For those who sought a "miraculous" solution to a problem, Sensōji's Asakusa Kannon was essential. Sensōji was Edo's mecca for prayer worship. By the same token, in a society in which daily life was dictated by feudal order, Sensōji provided an ideal place for relaxation, through the various forms of asobi offered there. For Edoites who had to deal with the hectic tempo of urban life and the stresses caused by a rigid class system, Sensōji offered a breathing space that dispensed with social inequalities. Along with the Ryōgoku area, the precincts of Sensōji emerged as one of Edo's most popular amusement centers.

The rise of Sensōji as a center for both popular prayer culture and popular play culture, however, did not please the Tokugawa bakufu. From the standpoint of the bakufu, Sensōji deviated from normative funerary Buddhism into a form of Buddhism premised on the commercialization of prayer and play. The bakufu's unhappiness with the sprawling Sensōji culture was, in fact, expressed in a series of countermeasures that aimed to deprive Sensōji of the right to manage its hefty income as well as of the right to its lands. As noted in the Introduction, the magistrate of temples and shrines (*jisha bugyō*) expelled Sensōji's head monk, Chūun, from office in 1685, demolished the post of head monk in 1740, and then appointed a deputy administrator chosen from outside the Sensōji community. Furthermore, Kan'eiji assumed control of Sensōji's finances by appointing two or three treasurers from among its own officials. As a result, the sizable cash income of Sensōji fell into the hands of Kan'eiji officials. For Sensōji, which had vigorously promoted its sources of income, this was a smashing blow. Worse yet, in 1745 the bakufu put all 20,000 or so residents of the twenty-two units in the Sensōji front districts under the direct jurisdiction of the city magistrate (*machi bugyō*). This deprived Sensōji of its proprietary power over the monzen residents, the major suppliers of its culture.[68] Nonetheless, Sensōji culture never slowed: cultural trends are not easily reversed by administrative measures.

In many ways, Sensōji's prosperity reflected the rising power of commoner consumers, who strove to expand their cultural space in the commercialized and diversified society of Edo. In the late Tokugawa period, Edo society was less and less guided by the principles of a status-oriented feudal system. Firmly rooted in the crisscrossing currents of folk piety (prayer) and entertainment (play), the popular culture of Sensōji posed a potential threat to the Tokugawa system, which aimed to cement social order and harmony on the dictates of Confucian moral distinctions. In the eyes of Confucian critics, popular Buddhist culture was nothing but corruption and decay. Buyō Inshi, the pseudonymous author of *Seji kenbun roku* (An account of events seen and heard), written in 1816, lamented that Buddhist priests were preoccupied with prayer activities that generated income and had abandoned the way of Buddhist Law. He charged that in capitalizing on the fervor of popular worship, "Buddhism [had fallen] into the business of carnal desires."[69] And, he continued, temple lands had been turned into "a hell that violates the minds of people and robs them of their money" through the operation of so many restaurants selling meat and fish, crowded teahouses, and a variety of other forms of entertainment—all within the sacred Buddhist sanctuary.[70] All these commercial elements, which he viewed as antithetical to the teachings of the Buddha, led him to conclude that "Buddhism [had become] an enemy of the nation."[71]

Bakufu leaders appreciated neither the popular prayer culture nor the popular play culture at Sensōji. Yet they could not easily change this Buddhist culture through administrative measures that were blind to the cultural reality of Edo society. For the populace, the culture of folk piety and popular entertainment was part of their daily lives. Sensōji, blessed with the Asakusa Kannon as well as with a sakariba environment, became Edo's center of popular Buddhist culture. At Sensōji, the conjunction of prayer and play blossomed.

TWO
The Built-in Unity of Prayer and Play

One early morning in the eighth month of 1796, undercover bakufu police officers rounded up more than seventy Buddhist monks as they were sneaking out of the Yoshiwara red-light districts and other brothel areas in Edo. On the same day, the police publicly pilloried these monks at Nihonbashi and then banished them to remote islands. According to bakufu officials, these monks had violated the Third Precept of Buddhism, which prohibits sexual contact with women. The harsh punishment that summarily removed these unlucky monks from society served as a strong warning to the entire Buddhist community.[1]

Why did the bakufu suddenly crack down on so many monks under the pretext of enforcing the Third Precept of Buddhism? Was the Buddhist prohibition of sexual relations an urgent and serious concern to the public authorities at this particular time? Or did the bakufu hope to achieve other goals by chastising these monks?

We can situate these questions in the context of the bakufu's long-standing policy toward Buddhism, as seen in the edict of 1722—an edict applicable to monks of all sects (*shoshū sōryo hatto*). The bakufu clearly spelled out what was and what was not expected of "those who have renounced the world" (*shukkesha*). The essential functions of Buddhist monks were studying (*gakugyō*), performing rituals for promoting the Buddhist dharma (*hōji zazen*), preaching the sutras (*sekkyō*), and conducting funeral and memorial services (*ekō*). In carrying out these functions, the bakufu emphasized, entertainment (*kōgyō*) was not to be utilized as a means of attracting lay followers.[2]

Despite the regulations, bakufu leaders observed that Buddhist culture seemed to be persistently off-course. They repeated their warnings and made efforts to ensure that Buddhism did what they wanted it to do. An ordinance of 1788 deplored the state of observation of Buddhist precepts and dharma-like behavior in the Buddhist community; an edict of 1790 focused on unruly business activities in Buddhist precincts; and in 1829 bakufu leaders strongly condemned the widespread debauchery and violations of Buddhist precepts among monks.[3] In the view of bakufu leaders, the rampant "transgressions of precepts" (*hakai*), which they categorized under the rubrics of "sexual indulgence" (*nyobon*) and "meat-eating" (*nikujiki*), were worrisome. The 1796 purge of lecherous monks was a clear warning to other monks and, indeed, to the Buddhist establishment in general, that immorality would not be tolerated.

Echoing the bakufu's concern over the unsavory goings-on within Buddhist culture, Confucian scholars also voiced anti-Buddhist comments and criticized precept-breaking Buddhist monks and their institutions. In the eyes of Nakai Chikuzan (1730–1804), Buddhist monks were so far steeped in corruption that they casually drank, ate meat, and hung out at bars or brothels.[4] Yamanashi Inakawa (1771–1826) singled out the decline of the Law of the Buddha as the most lamentable phenomenon in Tokugawa society, saying it was even more worrisome than the problem of poverty.[5] For many Confucianists, Buddhist degeneration was evident from the fact that drinking, gambling, street theater, the singing of *kouta* (ditties), dancing, adultery, abortion, venal preaching, and the pursuit of luxury, and so on were all occurring within Buddhist precincts. Angry domain leaders, such as Tokugawa Nariaki (1800–1860), the lord of the Mito domain, confiscated temple lands, demolished temple buildings or converted them to other uses, and made the monks into farmers in an attempt to purge Buddhism of those religious who were violating Buddhist precepts and exploiting the people.[6] Matsudaira Sadanobu (1758–1829), the architect of the Kansei reforms, agreed that Buddhist monks were helpful neither to the people nor to society, but he was not sure that all Buddhist temples should be closed down. He believed that Buddhism was so deeply woven into the fabric of Tokugawa society that he feared a national upheaval should a forcible separation be attempted.[7]

In response to these condemnations, some Buddhist leaders attempted to defend Buddhism from Confucian criticism; others tried to improve the image of Buddhism by launching self-regeneration movements. In 1666 a Zen monk, Echū, remorsefully conceded in his book *Kaijō monogatari* (A tale of the sea) that all Buddhist sects had forgotten the Way of the Buddha and had ceased to be the treasure of the state. The essays of the Tendai monk Jitō (?–1819) and the Jōdo shinshū monks Erin (1715–89), Tokuryū (1772–1858), and Nankei (1790–1873) acknowledge that Buddhist corruption had indeed reached a serious level and called for grave reflection.[8] More positively, Jiun Sonja (1718–1804), leader of a Buddhist reform movement, urged not only Buddhist monks but also lay followers to daily practice a moral philosophy that featured the *jūzenkai* (ten good precepts), which prohibited killing, stealing, adultery, lying, frivolous language, slander, equivocation, greed, anger, and wrong views. Jiun soon expanded this movement, arguing that it was "an all-encompassing guide for humanity, beneficial in both the secular and the sacred realms of life."[9] Jiun's preachings were typical of those of Buddhist leaders involved in self-regeneration movements in the Tokugawa period.

In any case, most critics tended to measure the health of Tokugawa Buddhism by the yardstick of Buddhist precepts. For them, Buddhism was normatively defined in terms of a precept-abiding monastic life and the conducting of appropriate funerary and prayer services. As far as Buddhism's social role was concerned, it was crucial that funerary and prayer rituals, the two core religious functions of Buddhism, be pursued in an environment far removed from mundane interests, entertainment, luxury, and loose morality.

Was the ideal of Tokugawa Buddhism relevant in any way to Buddhism as it was practiced at Sensōji in the late Tokugawa period? Obviously, there was an unbridgeable gap between the two. Given the bakufu's prescription of Buddhism emphasizing prayer and its opposition to play, critics of Sensōji Buddhism could simply label its play aspects an example of Buddhist degeneration. As far as they were concerned, Sensōji Buddhism's laissez-faire mixture of prayer and play had no social rationale.

Could prayer have been forcibly separated from play within Sensōji Buddhism, as Buddhist critics hoped? The answer, as explained in Chapter 1, is no. Prayer and play were so intertwined that it was unrealistic to expect visitors to Sensōji in the late Tokugawa period to distinguish worship from play according to the lines laid down in such dichotomies as Buddhist versus anti-Buddhist or sacred versus profane. Unlike the Tokugawa ideologues and Confucian critics who refuted (albeit to no avail) the intermingling of prayer and play, the general populace embraced Sensōji Buddhist culture without reluctance.

What these Tokugawa critics failed to understand in their abortive endeavor to redress "Buddhist degeneration" was that the inherent fabric of Japanese religious culture resisted the forcible separation of prayer and play. To the common folk, the combination of prayer and play was not odd. Indeed, throughout Japanese religious history, this combination was never perceived to be self-contradictory. As we shall soon see, in their private lives (when free from ideological constraint) even high-ranking Tokugawa officials and eminent Buddhist monks seemed to believe that prayer and play merged naturally. For the general populace, Sensōji culture was unimaginable without both elements. In order to understand the inherent strength of this culture, we need to examine the context that nourished the merging of prayer and play.

The Cultural Unity of Prayer and Play

Despite the clout of the precept-obsessed public discourse, Sensōji culture prospered in the late Tokugawa period precisely because of its precept-defying mix of prayer and play. Sensōji's persistent prosperity seemed to discredit the anti-Buddhist critique of hard-line Tokugawa ideologues, but were prayer and play really inseparable in Sensōji Buddhist culture? All the evidence seems to suggest that the blending of prayer and play was a natural development within late Tokugawa urban Buddhism. Perplexingly, the bakufu seems not to have pressured Sensōji to curb the mixture of prayer and play and to have limited its coercion to a few institutional sanctions at the administrative and financial levels. What message was the 1796 purge of precept-violating monks meant to deliver to the Buddhist community? Was it just a passing episode? Or was the bakufu unable to overcome the fundamental structure of Japanese Buddhist culture, which was not responsive to its high-handed pro-precept policy? As far as Sensōji Buddhism is concerned, the public authorities, restricted by their own ideology, were out of step with the general public when it came to dealing with Tokugawa Buddhist culture. As I argue in this chapter, Sensōji Buddhism thrived within a cultural context that necessitated the intermingling of prayer and play. This intermingling was so deeply rooted that the bakufu could not easily eradicate it.

Interestingly, the mixing of prayer and play in Sensōji Buddhism was sometimes appreciated by the highest authority of the nation, the shōgun—at least within his private sphere. The Sensōji diaries contain numerous records of dealings with shōguns or shōgunal heirs. As the diaries show, the usual agenda of a two- to three-hour shōgunal visit (*shōgun onari*) to Sensōji featured a brief service dedicated to the Asakusa Kannon, a meal, and a lengthy inspection of entertainment performances. Sensōji also served as a place to stop for a meal and a rest during shōgunal hunting excursions in the Sumida River area. Whatever the reason for the visit, shōguns or shōguns-to-be rarely bypassed the pleasures of popular culture that Sensōji offered. In light of the tradition of shōgunal onari, the shōgunal interest in Sensōji Buddhism appears to be an aberration. When freed from the ideological canopy that cast a shadow over his public functions, the nation's top authority took advantage of both aspects of Sensōji Buddhism.

Up to the time of Shōgun Hidetada (r. 1605–23), a shōgunal visit was a strictly political event solemnly conducted according to the precedent allegedly set by Minamoto no Yoritomo's visit to the residence of Adachi Morinaga (1135–1200), the warlord during the early Kamakura period, on the third day of the first month of 1182. Following this example, the Ashikaga shōguns further refined the shōgunal onari, turning it into a major New Year's ceremony during which, for the purpose of consolidating shōgunal overlordship, they visited, in yearly rotation, a *gokenin* house (a direct vassal of the shōgunate).[10] The first two Tokugawa shōguns, Ieyasu and Hidetada, inherited this traditional "warrior house" (*buke*) onari ceremony and used it as an occasion to demonstrate their control over the daimyō by conducting a sword exchange ceremony that symbolized the daimyō's oath of loyalty (and his subordination) to the shōgun. The ceremony involved the presentation of a sword by the host daimyō to the shōgun, followed by the shōgun's bestowal of a sword upon the daimyō. Although after the ceremony a dinner was served in honor of the shōgun and a noh play was performed to amuse him, the early Tokugawa shōgunal onari preserved a strong political flavor.[11] From the time of Shōgun Iemitsu (r. 1623–51), however, the political implications of shōgunal visits were significantly diluted. Iemitsu often dropped into daimyō residences or other places en route to falconry expeditions, swimming, or recreational tours, and he tended to bypass ceremonial procedures in favor of informal entertainments. After Iemitsu, a shōgunal onari became simply an occasion for "private" excursions, and it began to include diverse destinations—one of which was Sensōji.

How did Sensōji handle a shōgunal visit, and what did the shōgun expect from Sensōji? According to descriptions in the Sensōji diaries, upon receiving notice of an upcoming shōgunal visit, Sensōji administrators carefully prepared a welcome. Preparations, made under the supervision of bakufu inspectors, involved procuring food and drink and setting up a temporary dining facility, with a seat for the shōgun, carpets, tents, tatami mats, a rattan blind, and a set of hand-washing vessels.[12] Sensōji officials paid special attention to the visitor's entertainment. Although, on his arrival, the shōgun customarily stopped by the Main Hall and paid homage to the Asakusa Kannon, this religious gesture was a mere prelude to the next part of his schedule—recreation. Sensōji officials, who knew better than anyone else the real intent of the shōgunal onari, made every effort to provide the best possible entertainment—which was presented on a specially installed stage. From a seat specially prepared for him, the visitor enjoyed an array of exotic performances, such as noh plays, puppet shows, acrobatics, juggling and tumbling exhibitions, equestrian feats, and dancing. The shōgunal visitors sometimes even ventured to take in the street markets and the misemono attractions of Okuyama (*SN*, 3: 445; 5: 331, 538; 7: 474–76, 622–23; 13: 160). On one occasion, Sensōji administrators were surprised when a storyteller dared to stop and amuse Shōgun Yoshimune (r. 1716–45), who loved to listen to street stories. In the 1770s, the youthful future shōgun Ienari (r. 1793–97) often played archery or a blowgun game, enjoyed watching Matsui Gensui's acrobatics, and liked to stroll around the streets of the precinct (*SN*, 3: 446; 5: 331).

The image of Sensōji as a place where piety and play were fused overwhelmed even top-ranking Buddhist priests. The Rinnōji monzeki, the overlord of Tendai Buddhism in the Kantō (of which Sensōji was a part), was the highest-ranking prelate to visit Sensōji. When an imperial prince from Kyoto assumed the position of Rinnōji monzeki and moved into the Kan'eiji residence in Ueno, he usually made an inaugural visit to Sensōji, which was, after all, one of the best-known temples in the Eastern Tendai system. The initial visit to Sensōji of the eleventh Rinnōji monzeki, Buddhist Prince Kuchō, on the eighteenth day of the third month of 1792, started with a ceremonial parade. Accompanied by his retinue of officials from Kan'eiji, Kuchō proceeded through the Kaminari Gate to the Main Hall. Along the route, the new monzeki inspected front district representatives, Sensōji's administrative deputies and ritual priests, and confraternity officials. After briefly paying homage to the Asakusa Kannon, the new monzeki presided over a gift-exchange ceremony that officially confirmed his overlordship of the Sensōji institution. During the ceremony, the representatives of Sensōji's various communities first presented their tribute, usually money or Asakusa staples, to their lord, and then the new monzeki bestowed gifts on them (*SN*, 6: 653–55).

As soon as he had completed the ceremonial aspects of his visit, however, Prince Kuchō wasted no time before proceeding to the next part of his schedule, which had nothing to do with his inauguration ceremony, namely, the private enjoyment of what Sensōji could offer—entertainment. Sensōji officials proudly presented a course of entertainment, including a demonstration of Matsui Gensui's acrobatics and a drinking table, and their new superior was greatly satisfied (*SN*, 6: 655–56; for other examples, see *SN*, 4: 475–76; 9: 725–29; 11: 203–7, 747–51; 13: 385–88). To a high-bred Kyoto Buddhist priest such as Kuchō, who had never been to Edo, Sensōji was well known as a place of piety. Yet, from the time of his first visit, it was even more a place of entertainment. After his initial encounter with the fascinations of Sensōji, Kuchō began to frequent it for fun and recreation. Throughout the late Tokugawa period, many Rinnōji monzeki enjoyed idle pastimes on their visits (*miyasama onari*) to Sensōji. Sensōji officials were attentive to the personal tastes of each monzeki and greeted their overlords with a customized entertainment program. For example, when the Rinnōji monzeki visited Sensōji in the second month of 1813, his host delighted him with a specially arranged sumō show. Even though this visit did not occur during the regular sumō season, Sensōji officials were able to organize 200 sumō wrestlers into forty teams and to produce a grand tournament of spectacular variety. The *miyasama* of Rinnōji was so amused that he even shared a meal of "red-bean rice" (*sekihan*) with the wrestlers after their performance (*SN*, 12: 461). On other miyasama onari, Sensōji officials offered noh theater, dancing performances, acrobatics, storytelling, and other forms of entertainment from the rich repertoire available (*SN*, 14: 115–17, 192–95; 15: 181–83).

Not only high-level visitors but also Sensōji administrators themselves pursued the amalgamation of prayer and play. To these administrators, prayer and play were complementary and indeed inseparable. A typical example of this attitude of Sensōji officials may be found in the practice of kaichō (the opening of a curtain), the exhibition of a secret deity, which was held in expectation of financial benefits. During the Tokugawa period, the usual schedule for holding a kaichō was once every thirty-three years for a period of sixty days (extendible by another ten to thirty days),[13] but exceptions to this schedule were not uncommon. In any case, the Sensōji administration took advantage of the popularity of its secret main deity as well as its attractive location in Edo and held thirty-one kaichō of the Asakusa Kannon after the first in 1654. Most of these occurred in the late eighteenth and early nineteenth centuries. In addition, it hosted twenty-seven *de-gaichō* (the opening of a curtain away from home) of visiting deities from other religious institutions.[14]

In theory, kaichō was a purely religious event designed to provide an opportunity for lay Buddhists to appeal directly to the compassion of a secret deity through a face-to-face encounter. But this opportunity was not available for free. Viewers of the secret deity were expected to express their gratitude by making a generous monetary donation to the host temple, in addition to paying a minimum entrance fee. Kaichō proved to be an effective means of raising funds for special projects or extra income. Rather than being an event of religious importance, the practice was, by and large, a fund-raising device. And to ensure that this practice was successful, Sensōji officials counted on the union of prayer and play, which would ignite both folk piety and the desire to be entertained.

The 1814 kaichō illustrates how the exhibition of the secret Asakusa Kannon deity capitalized on this combination of prayer and play. As soon as a date for the exhibition of the Asakusa Kannon (actually, the wooden substitute statue known as Maetate Kannon) was set, the Sensōji administration proceeded with its preparations. First, it advertised the event as widely as possible by erecting bulletin boards at the main entrance gate (Kaminarimon) on the south side of the precincts and at the eastern entrance gate (Zuijinmon) and at each of Edo's major urban hubs (Itabashi, Yotsuya, Shibaguchi, Ryōgoku, Senju, Kuromonmae, and Nihonbashi). It also distributed leaflets all over the city (*SN*, 12: 534). Four months before the event, an intensive campaign to publicize the miraculous stories and chronicles of the Asakusa Kannon was launched (*SN*, 7: 383). Helped by confraternity members and monzen residents, Sensōji officials were able to complete sundry other preparations, including building temporary kaichō offices, setting up additional offertory boxes, making a list of prospective donors, and organizing volunteer helpers.[15] With a grand opening ceremony, the Sensōji kaichō of 1814 was started on the eighteenth day of the third month, as planned.

For the Sensōji administration, which had impeccably orchestrated the preparations, the goal was to raise as much money as possible. The Asakusa Kannon was so well known that it was not difficult for Sensōji officials to rouse excitement about its upcoming advent. The bulletin boards, leaflets, and printed chronicles all advertised the imminent manifestation of the Asakusa Kannon. But Sensōji officials knew that folk piety alone would not be enough to ensure the success of the exhibition. And so to attract more viewers, they tapped into Sensōji's other attraction—play. In a well-coordinated scheme, Sensōji administrators arranged special performances of kabuki theater, puppet drama, noh plays, and Shintō dancing on an eye-catching stage erected in front of the Main Hall.[16] At the same time, they encouraged misemono merchants in the Sensōji area to deploy their best skills, exhibitions, and entertainment services. As a result, during the kaichō the whole area of Sensōji experienced a business boom, transforming it into a super-sakariba for three months.

The kaichō of 1827 again proved the importance of play. The Sensōji administration was delighted to accommodate misemono merchants who wanted to set up more archery booths during the event (*SN*, 17: 96). As Utagawa Hiroshige (1797–1858) succinctly captured in an ukiyo print, the 1827 kaichō was dominated by popular entertainers and kabuki actors, who extended their roles to selling medicine, cookies, bonsai, candies, and toys in the street markets.[17] Indeed, a kaichō was almost unimaginable without a high dose of play and entertainment.

During the kaichō period, in order to encourage larger donations, the Sensōji administration posted donors' names and the amount of their offerings on a bulletin board in front of the Main Hall. More aggressively, Sensōji fundraisers sometimes advertised the "blessed" names of big donors, presenting them to the public as exemplary beneficiaries of the Asakusa Kannon's miraculous compassion.[18] Sensōji officials also insisted upon "special" donations from confraternity members and merchant guilds. Despite these tactical schemes, saisen (offertory coins), which ordinary viewers offered in lieu of a formal donation, were still the most significant source of Sensōji's income. Offertory boxes were gold mines that netted the equivalent of at least 500 and sometimes as many as 1,000 gold pieces within a single kaichō (*SN*, 12: 668–69). Naturally, the Sensōji administration paid the utmost attention to these treasure boxes. At the opening ceremony, Sensōji officials staged a special ritual to ensure the abundant saisen. This ritual consisted of special divine dance (*kagura*) performed by a group of *shugenja* (Shugen priests) atop the offertory boxes in order to imbue them with luck (*SN*, 12: 642; 17: 277–78).

No matter what tactics were used, the outcome of a kaichō was measured by the number of visitors that it attracted. Sensōji officials clearly understood that the best way to ensure success was to capture the people's interest in play (asobi) and to fuse it with their folk piety. The amalgamation of religion (prayer) and entertainment (play) was most spectacular at Sensōji during the late Tokugawa period, but this was not a special cultural mutation or a deviation from the traditional religious culture. On the contrary, the association of prayer and play is deeply rooted in Japanese notions of asobi, which has a distinctly religious undertone.

In ancient times asobi was a way of communicating with the world of deities. When Amaterasu sequestered herself in the cave of heaven because of Susanō's rowdy behavior, thus plunging the universe into darkness, half-naked Amenouzume and shamans aroused much laughter among the gods with their bawdy dancing performance, in which they engaged in order to entice the Sun Goddess out of hiding. Other stories in the *Kojiki* and *Nihon shoki* chronicles tell us that the vengeful spirit of Amewakahiko was appeased by singing, dancing, and other musical entertainments. All these activities, referred to as *kami asobi* (divine plays) were, as Orikuchi Shinobu suggests, prototypical examples of how ancient Japanese were able to communicate with deities, pacify disgruntled spirits, revive the dead, and energize their spiritual power.[19] The ancient Japanese believed that they could achieve intimacy with a deity if they were able to "play with" it and that they could even affiliate themselves with it if they were able to amuse it. For that reason, the religious specialists at the Yamato imperial court who dealt with supernatural spirits were called *asobi-be* (play functionaries). Within that cultural tradition, play was not differentiated from religious worship, as is evidenced in the playfulness of Shintō festivals.[20] Also, medieval plays such as *dengaku* (field music), *sarugaku* (monkey music), and other theatrical forms of entertainment, which were often staged for *kanjin* (promoting [religious] merit) fund-raising campaigns at Buddhist temples or Shintō shrines, had their origins in kami asobi.[21] Watching kanjin shows was not simply a matter of being entertained: it also symbolized the making of an offering to deities and communing with them through play. In other words, play was a religious act.

In a discussion of the four paths to salvation (*rokudō-bakku* [escape from suffering in the six courses]) in medieval Buddhism, William R. LaFleur suggests that asobi was the fourth path and that it offered a way of transcending the suffering of the six courses. He defines this type of salvational path as "the ludization of transmigration along the taxonomy of value, to indicate that the entire rokudō system is conceived of as an arena of play." Medieval Japanese, he notes, "displayed a remarkable capacity for enjoyment—one that over the centuries produced much humor, festival, spoof, the pleasures of a 'floating world,' the lyrics of an Ikkyū or a Ryōkan, and the comedy of kyōgen. In short, the medieval Japanese displayed a capacity for ludus in its many forms."[22] Thus Japanese religious tradition had in it an element of play, as may be seen in the fourth salvational path. So it should not be surprising that the element of play forms a strong undercurrent within Sensōji culture.

During the late Tokugawa period, the Buddhist space of Sensōji was literally an amusement quarter inundated with all kinds of "play" activities that catered to Edoites in search of recreation, pleasure, and entertainment. Street markets, misemono exhibitions, circuses, sumō shows, archery booths, toothpick shops, and teahouses were certainly not what the critics of Tokugawa Buddhism thought proper. Nevertheless, at Sensōji the worlds of entertainment and religion were in perfect harmony with one another. For visitors to Sensōji, the composite culture of religion and entertainment was a great source of cultural enjoyment; and for Sensōji officials, it was a lucrative source of "Buddhist" business. Clearly, the cultural union of play and prayer was the foundation that nurtured Sensōji Buddhist culture.

In fact, play at Sensōji, from archery to misemono to commercial trade, had a religious undertone. Street markets were not purely places for trade. As the terms for market, *machi* (the etymon of *matsuri*) and *ichi* (shamaness), indicate, the ancient Japanese believed that deities were involved in markets.[23] Some scholars even suggest that the first form of trade had a religious component: prospective traders first ritually offered their commodities to deities and then proceeded to deal with customers.[24] In ancient times, markets, usually protected by *ichigami* (deities of the market) and demarcated by sakaki trees or rocks, also functioned as stages for performing worship or prayer rituals, hosting community meetings, as well as dancing and singing parties (*utagaki*), and executing criminals.[25]

The religious elements of Japan's ancient markets could still be found, albeit in vestigial form, in Sensōji's street markets. As noted in Chapter 1, the special fairs held on the twelfth and thirteenth days of the seventh month (Bon'ichi) and on the seventeenth and eighteenth days of the twelfth month (toshi-no-ichi) were, above all, occasions to procure religious items for the observance of the two most important ancestral memorial services: the Bon matsuri and the New Year. The religious overtones of toshi-no-ichi were particularly evident, since it occurred at the point of sending off an old year and greeting a new one. On the thirteenth day of the twelfth month, a few days before toshi-no-ichi, a grand purification rite, dubbed *susu harai* or *susu haki* (to sweep soot off), was usually performed in temples and shrines. Sensōji's year-end grand purification rite featured replacing the old lining in the Asakusa Kannon receptacle with a new one and cleaning the inside of the Maetate Kannon container with a bamboo duster. With this rite, the old year was officially concluded, and an altar for greeting the new year was installed. Toshi-no-ichi, held after the installation of the new altar, was the ritual period during which the sacrificial offerings that were to fill that new altar were prepared.[26]

Permanent street markets, centering around the nakamise (inner stores), also preserved some ancient religious elements. As Matsudaira Kanzan noted in his *Sensōji shi*, the *miyage* (staple products) available in these markets did not consist of ordinary goods such as rice, cloth, or fish, which one would find in abundant quantities in the downtown commercial areas. Rather, the stores featured such items as edible seaweed (Asakusa nori), Asakusa liquor, rice cakes, and dumplings.[27] These items, which were acclaimed as *hare* ("clean" or "divine") foods, were most often used for religious purposes. Thus Asakusa staples were sold for their miraculous effects rather than their practical value. Seaweed collected from the nearby Sumida River, for example, was supposed to facilitate the salvational power of the Asakusa Kannon.[28]

Misemono of manufactures were not simply commercial exhibitions, either. Misemono shows at temples or shrines were not unusual in the late Tokugawa period.[29] As Asakura Kamezō reminds us in *Misemono kenkyū* (A study of misemono), an exhibition of products at a religious site was not as absurd as we might think. According to him, such items originated in the *saiku* (delicate handiworks). Originally, saiku were items often used as sacrificial offerings in the traditional Shintō matsuri, especially in the ceremony designed to promote unity and collaboration among the members of a village community.[30] Over time, the traditional function of saiku changed in medieval cities, where shrine parish members paid more attention to the spectacular procession of the matsuri than to the communal worship service. As matsuri processions became more flamboyant, parish members began to use saiku sacrificial offerings as mere accessories to their portable shrines and spear-floats. Saiku decorations were sometimes carried by dancers, singers, and horseback riders in the matsuri procession, all in the name of creating *furyū* (showy spectacles). The Gion festival of the Yasaka Shrine in Kyoto pioneered this trend in urban matsuri.[31] The medieval fashion of furyū, which transformed the nature of saiku, filtered down into religious ceremonies in the early modern period. Religious institutions found that the exhibition of fancy handiworks could attract visitors. The exhibition of saiku eventually emerged as a sort of side attraction. In this process, artisans and merchants gradually took over saiku exhibitions at temples and shrines, establishing them as their specialty.[32] Misemono at Sensōji in the late Tokugawa period were far removed from the original religious overtones of saiku, but to the extent that they were exhibited and sold at religious sites, they remained within the traditional religious structure of saiku.

Likewise, the misemono performers of street arts also insisted on using religious spaces—the front streets, or precincts, of temples and shrines—for their business. Although the term "misemono" was coined during the Tokugawa period, such performances had been part of Japanese religious culture as far back as the divine dances of the traditional Shintō matsuri and were closely related to the fund-raising shows (*kanjin kōgyō*) put on by many religious institutions most often during the Sengoku period. Buddhist temples that had no steady source of income because of the rampant warfare of the period hired professional entertainers and staged misemono shows in their precincts in order to raise money through admission fees.[33] For ordinary spectators, such an occasion was an exciting opportunity to enjoy, for a few coins, a leisure culture that was not generally available in those days. With the passage of time, however, groups of professional entertainers sought to transform such shows into independent commercial enterprises. As part of this process, in early modern times misemono merchants and street performers came to dominate popular entertainment.[34] Although no longer used to raise funds for temples, popular entertainment retained its associations with religious institutions. Sensōji's misemono culture was a testament to the historical legacy of the kanjin show.

The religious roots of play indeed persist across the whole spectrum of Sensōji culture. Take, for example, sumō wrestling. A popular pastime during the Tokugawa period, sumō evolved from the religious asobi of dancing (called *sumai*, the etymon of *sumō*) performed at a demarcated stage (altar) in order to pacify resentful spirits, to pray for good harvests, or to foretell the fate of the year's crops.[35] Even today, the archaic form of sumō is still observable in some regions (e.g., in the "one-man sumō" in which a dancing priest mimics a wrestling match with a deity for the deity's pleasure).[36] Notwithstanding sumō's original religious purpose, during the late Tokugawa period Sensōji's misemono merchants staged a variety of playful quasi-sumō shows to attract people to their business. In one extreme case, in 1769 spectators were treated to a lewd sumō exhibition in which a half-naked woman wrestled eight lascivious blind masseurs. It was a great success. Not surprisingly, sumō matches between women and men continued to be staged until the Meiji government banned them in 1872.[37] No matter how much their shows diverged from the religious origins of sumō, sumō entrepreneurs at Sensōji never missed an opportunity to capitalize on that legacy: the wrestlers were decked out in Shintō style, the sumō stage (*dohyō*) resembled a ritual altar, a purification ritual (the sprinkling of salt) was performed before the match, and the umpires wore priestly vestments.[38]

Archery also had religious undertones at Sensōji. Archery on horseback, known as *yabusame*, was originally a form of divination performed during a Shintō festival. Tokugawa entertainment merchants saw the potential attraction of this ritual and quickly transformed it into a popular pastime. The young female attendants (*yatori onna*, or *yaba onna*), who beat a drum when an arrow struck the bull's-eye and collected the arrows, were an added attraction for the largely male clientele. As Terakado Seiken observed, "A girl runs an archery hall; charmingly made up and beautifully dressed, she flirts and lures customers."[39] For many male customers, the real joy of archery lay in being served by these young women.

Salesgirls were an integral part of Sensōji culture not only at archery booths but also at toothpick shops and teahouses. Hundreds of young women worked in these businesses, adding to Sensōji's play culture as both sales promoters and service providers. The owners of the incredibly crowded toothpick shops may sometimes have advertised that their wares were made from branches of Buddhist "teeth-cleaning trees" and would not only prevent cavities but also bring prosperity to one's descendants. However, the most effective way of surviving the fierce competition was to employ attractive young salesgirls.[40] As Edoites often satirized in *senryū* (short verses), these young salesgirls seemed to promote business through their physical attractions rather than through the quality of merchandise.

Some senryū even offer quite intriguing witticisms—a female attendant at an archery booth is "dispatched" somewhere for "private" business, and the Yamato teahouse "is temporarily closed" during the daytime.[41] Erotic play was not unknown at Sensōji (see Fig. 11). Reflecting this reality, the plots of some popular novels focused on teahouse love affairs (often conducted in the backrooms). Ryūtei Tanehiko (1783–1842), for example, describes in detail a love affair between Ohatsu (a teahouse girl) and Tokubee (the owner of a dry-goods store in Tamachi), which was carried out in the darkly curtained backroom of one of Sensōji's Nijikken teahouses.[42] And indeed, some salesgirls did provide "private" services, even in the Buddhist precincts of Sensōji.

The fusion of prostitution and religious space was not exceptional in the world of popular religious culture in Tokugawa Japan. Other religious sites for pilgrimages and popular worship were also hotbeds of prostitution. Zenkōji in Shinano, the Ise Shrine, Narita Shinshōji, Konpira in Sanuki, and the Usa Hachiman Shrine, to cite a few, all fell into this category.[43] Although it reached an unprecedented pitch in the late Tokugawa period, prostitution had long been associated with religious institutions in Japan. In ancient times, prostitutes often represented incarnated deities, and relations with them amounted to a kind of divine asobi whose purpose was communion with deities. In this context, prostitutes were called *asobime* (play girls), and in the colloquial language, sexual contact with a play girl was dubbed *omatsuri*, or Shintō worship.[44] During the medieval period such semi-religious figures as itinerant female shamans, Kumano nuns, puppeteer-prayer nuns (*kugutsu*), blind street diviners, and fishmongers (*katsurame*) were all known occasionally to practice prostitution while offering their religious specialties.[45] From the sixteenth century on, itinerant entertainers were forced to settle in sections of castle towns, transportation nodes, or commercial routes, as "brothels were institutionalized and taxed."[46] Professional prostitutes no longer performed religious functions, but their appellations still echoed

Fig. 11. A scene at a teahouse featuring teahouse girls and male clients. An ukiyo painting by Suzuki Harunobu (1725–70) (from Unno Hiroshi, *Edo no sakariba*).

the time when they had. Ordinary prostitutes were often called *gozen* (those who serve deities), and high-status prostitutes were given the title of a Shinto priest—*tayū*. Clearly the Sensōji prostitutes belonged to the Japanese religious tradition associated with play.

A Sensōji legend known as the *Asakusa hitotsuya* (A house in Asakusa) sums up the unity of prayer and play in Japanese religious culture.

A daughter lived in a house (*hitotsuya*) in Asakusa with her parents, and the parents had their daughter sleep with travelers. The parents killed the travelers while they slept on stone pillows (*ishimakura*), by knocking their heads against the stone pillows, and they then stole their possessions in order to make a living. One day, the daughter deeply repented her sins and disguised herself in male attire before sleeping with a traveler. The next morning the parents awoke to find they had killed their own daughter and, in remorse, begged Asakusa Kannon's mercy.[47]

Edo people were quite familiar with this story, a folktale that had many different versions across the country. Myōon-in, a subtemple of Sensōji, even claimed that it preserved the actual ishimakura as a religious treasure. By publicizing the hitotsuya stone, Myōon-in was able to attract many visitors to its exhibition hall in the late Tokugawa period (*SN*, 2: 76).

The hitotsuya story thematized the relationship between a prostitute and her stone pillow. According to Yanagita Kunio, a prostitute was originally a female shaman, and the stone pillow was her religious medium. When shamans tried to communicate with their deities, they often relied on the mysterious powers of a stone pillow or, in some cases, of a key stone (*kanameishi*).[48] Within the structure of the hitotsuya story, the prayer of a shaman may be replaced with the play of a prostitute. In this sense, the story alludes to the cultural unity of prayer and play.

But in relating the deeds of the prostitute to the destinies of her clients, the geographical setting of "a house" (hitotsuya) played an integral role. A house's location, whether between villages or on a desolate mountain ridge, was, in fact, a key feature of most such folktales. Symbolically, the location of Sensōji, as a hitotsuya, at the northern entrance to the shōgunal castle town of Edo was more than a geographical fortuity: it was the demarcation of a liminal space between this world and another world—the one that separated death from life. During the Tokugawa period, the area beyond the Asakusa Bridge over the Sumida River was simply called "an unknown world," and Sensōji, as a hitotsuya, was the entrance to that world.[49] The location of Sensōji in Edo had a symbolic spatial dimension.

The Social Geography of Prayer and Play

During the Tokugawa period, the Sensōji administration claimed that its space was a "no-killing" zone. This assertion was based on a bylaw, issued by the Edo city magistrate in the ninth month of 1692, that confirmed the special status of Sensōji space: "With regard to the matter of killing that might occur in the Asakusa River and in the areas between Suwa-chō in the south and Shōden-chō in the north, laws have been issued, and bulletin boards [proclaiming them] erected. From now on, killing is to be strictly prohibited in these areas. Those who violate [this] will be, without fail, punished."[50] Sensōji officials reiterated this prohibition by posting bulletin boards bearing the statement at the major entrances to temple land (*SN*, 1: 509; 3: 342).

The most noticeable landmark demarcating the entrance to Sensōji space was Komakata Hall, which was located on the southern boundary and housed a "horse-head" Kannon (Hayagrīva or Batō Kannon) statue. The Horse-head Kannon, which people believed to be a tutelary deity of the Sensōji lands, was a counterpart of the real "divine horses" (*jinme*) that belonged to the Main Hall of the Asakusa Kannon. On the first day of each month, Sensōji officials led these divine horses in a procession from north to south to mark the borders of Sensōji land. Komakata Hall was the southern limit of the procession, and here the divine horses were led around the hall and then proceeded toward the northern limit (Shōden-chō), as though separating Sensōji from the rest of Edo.[51] The symbolic spatial significance of Komakata Hall was clear to any visitor who confronted the words carved into the landmark at the southern tip of the Komakata Hall precincts: "a stone monument admonishing against killing." The message on the bulletin board beside this monument was unequivocal: "[The public authorities] strictly prohibit the killing of living beings in the districts between Suwa-chō in the south and Shōden-chō in the north."[52] In fact, during the Tokugawa period, fishing was not allowed in the waters of the Sumida River along Sensōji lands.

The Sensōji administration used the prohibition against killing as a pretext to assert its own proprietary rights over the area. The no-killing rhetoric, being both doctrinally expedient and multipurpose, was useful in preventing external intervention at Sensōji. Because of its appeal to the populace as a reflection of the First Precept of Buddhism ("I will not willingly take the life of a sentient being"), the no-killing zone was even used to challenge the authority of the bakufu. When Edo was hit by a massive flood in the seventh month of 1786, bakufu officials tried to enter Sensōji to collect birds as food for the shōgun's hunting falcons. At that time, the Sensōji precincts were filled with ducks and other wild birds that had come to this well-protected haven to escape the heavy rains and the muddy water of the Sumida River. To the bakufu gamekeepers, who were having trouble finding feed for the falcons, the ducks and birds shivering in the Buddhist enclave of Sensōji were easy targets. They brought documents from the shōgunate authorizing them to catch birds at Sensōji. Sensōji officials blocked their entrance, however, on the grounds that killers were not to be admitted to the no-killing sanctuary, and they reminded them that Sensōji had been the first Buddhist prayer hall for Tokugawa Ieyasu. At the same time, Sensōji officials ordered the merchants under their control not to sell or purchase meat or any fish, birds, or other living beings. It was a strong argument, for bakufu officials feared the curse of the Asakusa Kannon should they breach Buddhist law. To the jubilation of Sensōji officials, the bakufu hunters quietly retreated. Soon after its successful challenge to shōgunal authority, the Sensōji administration held a grand ceremony to release fish (*hōjōe*) into the Sumida River in celebration of the Asakusa Kannon's mercy toward the Sensōji community and all sentient beings (*SN*, 5: 343–49).

Marked off from the secular world, Sensōji was securely established as a prominent religious sanctuary in Edo, with its own logic and principles of divine protection. And Sensōji did indeed constitute a distinctive and divine world. All kinds of divine beings, both Buddhist and Shintō, filled the Sensōji sanctuary and ensured that it was unrivaled as a religious institution in Edo. In addition to the Main Hall (where the Asakusa Kannon, the Maetate Kannon, six other Kannon images, and a group of celestial deities were enshrined), in the inner precincts alone, there were, among others, several Fudō halls (Acalanātha), a Kōjin Shrine ("a violent deity"), a Kōshin Hall (a Taoist deity), four Jizō halls (Ksitigarbha), a Bishamon Hall (Vaiśravaṇa), a Monju Hall (Mañjuśrī), a couple of Benten (or Benzaiten) halls (Sarasvatī), a Daikoku Hall (Mahākāla), a five-story pagoda, the Arasawa Fudō Hall (Acalanātha), the Sanja Daigongen Shrine (the founders of Sensōji), the Kumagai Inari Shrine (Inari), a Hōsō Shrine (a smallpox deity), an Akiba Daigongen Shrine (a fire deity), a Shaka Hall (Śākyamuni), the Jūsha Daigongen Shrine (ten mowers), a Nenbutsu Hall (Amitābha), an Enma Hall (Yama-rāja), a Kumano Shrine, a Hashimoto Yakushi Hall (Bhaiṣajyarāja), a Daijingū (a branch of the Grand Ise Shrine), an Awashima Shrine (Awashima deity), a Kishibo Shrine (Hārītī), a Rokkaku Hall (Kṣitigarbha), multiple Inari shrines, a Sannō Gongen Shrine (a Hieizan deity), and the Nishinomiya Ebisu Shrine (Ebisu deity). Furthermore, each of thirty-four semi-independent subtemples had its own Buddhist halls and Shintō shrines.

The inner precincts of Sensōji, ensconced at the center of the temple's lands, were a paramount sanctum numinous with salvational power. For this reason, many people, during the most difficult moments of their lives, put their last hope in the mercy of Sensōji deities. In particular, for those who were crossing the threshold of death, Sensōji was often the final destination. The Sensōji diaries contain numerous records of "people dying on the street" (*yukidaore*) as they made a final journey to Sensōji in quest of the compassion of the Asakusa Kannon.

Many terminally ill people, beggars, and homeless people found their way to Sensōji as death approached so that the Asakusa Kannon might lead them to the other world and a better life. Each year the Sensōji administration had to deal with numerous dead bodies in the precincts. When a corpse was found, Sensōji officials immediately reported the matter to the Magistrate's Office of Temples and Shrines, and as soon as bakufu officials had completed their inspection, they cremated the body during a simple ceremony involving a funeral prayer. Sensōji officials handled yukidaore bodies quite matter-of-factly, but for these unfortunate souls who died in the streets the idea of commending themselves at the final moment to the care of the Asakusa Kannon must have been an incalculable consolation.[53] Suicides also favored Sensōji as their last stop in this world, and they received the same treatment as street deaths. Bakufu officials inspected the dead body and issued a public notice so that the deceased's relatives could claim the corpse; if no one showed up, the body was sent to Kotsukappara for cremation.

Sensōji's fame as a threshold to the other world made it a favorite place to abandon babies (*sutego*). Some parents who decided (or had) to forsake their children chose Sensōji, commending their infants to the mercy of the Asakusa Kannon. Sensōji officials handled the matter of foundlings with care. When an abandoned child was found, Sensōji officials first reported the matter to the Magistrate's Office of Temples and Shrines and then made a search for the parents; if the search failed, then, through front district officials, they arranged for the child's adoption. Sensōji officials usually gave the foster family two or three gold pieces on the condition that the child be well raised and not abandoned and, in the case of a girl, that she not be sold to the pleasure quarters (*SN*, 1: 491–93, 495–97; 3: 432, 436; 16: 396–400, 600, 636).

It was also common to find sick mendicants or pilgrims who had collapsed on the streets of Sensōji. In order to take care of these people, the

Sensōji administration even kept a medical doctor (from the Aoyanagi family of Hanakawado-chō) on the payroll. This doctor was under contract at the annual salary of 500 copper coins and, not surprisingly, was particularly busy during special events (*SN*, 2: 424). Sensōji, with its aura of divine care and compassion, offered a caring refuge not to be found elsewhere in the often forlorn metropolis of Edo.

No wonder that, during the late Tokugawa period, there were always many white-robed pilgrims streaming into the Sensōji sanctuary. Sensōji was the focal point of the nation's most popular pilgrimage circuits. Among those renowned tours of "numinous places" (*reijō*) were the three circuits of thirty-three Kannon sanctuaries, regionally grouped in Kansai, Kantō, and Chichibu; the Kumano pilgrimage courses; Zenkōji; and the eighty-eight sanctuaries of Kūkai in Shikoku.[54] Sensōji was the thirteenth stop on the Kantō Kannon circuit of thirty-three shrines as well as the final stop on the circuit of 100 Kannon shrines that combined the Kansai (Saigoku Kannon reijō), Kantō (Bandō Kannon reijō), and Chichibu (Chichibu Kannon reijō) circuits, along with one more site in Chichibu, which was added in 1536.[55]

As the Sensōji chronicles boast, pilgrims to Sensōji found themselves totally overwhelmed by the numinous aura of the Asakusa Kannon once they entered the sanctuary. The primary concern of these pilgrims was to form a personal connection with the Asakusa Kannon by placing before it evidence of their pilgrimage, such as a wooden board or paper (*junrei fuda*) on which were written their name, place of birth, and the reason for their visit. The popular belief that all sins committed in one's lifetime could be annihilated by the merits accumulated through pilgrimages propelled people's religious zeal. Pilgrimage, which was relatively affordable, attracted ordinary worshippers who could not afford such costly merit-making offerings as stone lanterns, stupas, or financial contributions to new temple buildings.[56] Moreover, pilgrimages were, Buddhists preached, as efficacious as other religious endeavors in gaining merit. Pilgrimage was based on the belief that the more pilgrimages one made, the more merit one accumulated toward the annihilation of one's sins.[57] As a result, pilgrims never stopped coming to Sensōji during the late Tokugawa period. Once they entered the sanctuary of the Asakusa Kannon, these pilgrims found themselves standing in a world free of the bondage of social status and feudal hierarchy. Their white robes, in the style of robes of the dead, were a claim to equality and freedom.[58]

In the 1730s a new pilgrimage circuit of thirty-three Kannon sanctuaries was created in Edo (Edo Kannon *fudasho*), and in the 1830s another was created in Asakusa (Asakusa Kannon *fudasho*): both of these had Sensōji as the first stop.[59] These "localized amulet-issuing circuits" (*chihō fudasho*), all conveniently arranged within the boundaries of Edo (or even within the districts of Asakusa), eased to a great extent the burden of traditional pilgrimage, which required at least a month or two and expenses for accommodations and meals. As the center of these new "mini" Kannon circuits, Sensōji hosted more and more pilgrims. Over time, however, the convenient shortcut for the completion of a full circuit of visits to the thirty-three Kannon sites facilitated the merger of prayer and play.

Pilgrimage now provided a good excuse for Edoites to take refuge from the tedium of their daily life and monotonous routines.[60] People could easily complete a pilgrimage in the space of a few days without adhering to the formality of the traditional tour and while idly enjoying the pleasure of travel, scenery, street markets, and misemono attractions. The distinctions between visiting a temple or shrine (*jisha mōde*) and "looking at things and playing around" (*monomi yusan*) were greatly diminished. For the casual "pilgrim," Sensōji offered a perfect combination of religious fulfillment and recreational pleasure. For Edoites who had to endure the increasing pressures of urban life, Sensōji was indeed more than a pilgrimage temple: it was an urban oasis within the sprawling metropolis of Edo.

Edo, which had been a small town with a population of several thousand at the beginning of the 1600s, was, during the late Tokugawa period, one of the largest cities in the world. As the political center of the Tokugawa shōgunate, Edo had gone through four major urban planning projects by 1657, when it was hit by the Meireki Fire. The Meireki disaster was a classic example of the danger and stress to which the inhabitants of this rapidly growing metropolis were exposed. History has it that a fire started in Hongō shortly after New Year's Day and swept through the city for three days, devouring "most daimyō mansions (some 500 of them) along with 779 hatamoto residences, 350 temples and shrines, and

400 blocks of densely packed commoner neighborhoods. It destroyed most of the castle's buildings, including its great central keep, and killed over a hundred thousand people, perhaps one in five city residents."[61] This disaster was so devastating that the shōgunate shifted its notions of urban planning radically: the city was no longer constructed with an eye to the defense of Edo Castle; rather, the emphasis shifted to the building of fireproof districts. Temples, shrines, and pleasure quarters were transferred to the outskirts, spacious fire lanes (*hiyoke-chi*) were created at the major intersections of the inner city, and several new business districts were established outside the original city zone.[62] By the year 1700, Edo had 800,000 residents; a quarter century later it had over one million.

Nevertheless, the samurai class, who made up less than half of Edo's population, continued to command nearly 70 percent of Edo's lands. Samurai holdings included daimyō establishments in the propitious locations of the Musashino uplands, hatamoto residences in the areas surrounding Edo Castle (as well as in Yotsuya and Ichigaya), and group residences for low-ranking warriors in the western and northern areas and in the southern Aoyama and Azabu areas. In contrast, the more than 500,000 townspeople (chōnin) had to live squeezed within a space that occupied less than a quarter of that occupied by samurai lands. After the Meireki Fire, commoner quarters expanded, in accordance with an increase in population, further into Honjo, Fukagawa, and Asakusa; into the valleys of Koishikawa, Ujigome, Ichigaya, Yotsuya, Akasaka, and Azabu; and into the original chōnin districts in the Nihonbashi, Kyōbashi, Kanda, and waterfront areas.[63] But all these areas, including the newly expanded districts, were not spacious enough to accommodate half a million commoners. The lives of commoners in late Tokugawa Edo were literally stifling, and the tensions caused by overcrowding ran extremely high.

Compared with the amount of space occupied by the typical commoner dwelling, the *jisha-chi* (lands of temples and shrines), which included the precincts of temples and shrines as well as the front districts (monzen machi), were exceptionally spacious, given the size of their population. In the late Tokugawa period, there were approximately 1,000 temples and shrines in Edo, with a few tens of thousands of priests and their families. The monzen machi population numbered a bit more than 60,000 in 1733 and 74,000 in 1844—less than 15 percent of the ordinary commoner population.[64] Including Buddhist monks and Shintō priests and their families, the number of inhabitants on the religious lands never exceeded 100,000—one-fifth of the population of the chōnin class. Nonetheless, this population occupied almost the same land area as the remaining population of ordinary townspeople—approximately 15 percent of the space in Edo.

Moreover, many Edo temples and shrines were private prayer halls associated with daimyō and hatamoto families. These private prayer halls for upper-class samurai families, most of which were small structures, were not open to the public.[65] Consequently, the temples and shrines that were open to the public were relatively fewer in number and quite large in size, and they were usually located on the outskirts of the city. Accordingly, their front districts naturally sprawled away from the bustling hubs of the inner city. To list a few typical examples, one can easily identify districts that developed adjacent to such temples as Sensōji (Asakusa), Ankanji (Koishikawa), Kan'eiji (Shitaya), Eitaiji (Fukagawa), Kan'ōji (Yanaka), Shōchiin (Kobinata), Zenkōji (Aoyama), Zenpukuji (Azabu), Denzūin (Koishikawa), Nezu Gongen (Shitaya), Yakuōji (Ichigaya), Zōjōji (Shiba), Gokokuji (Koishikawa), and Reiganji (Fukagawa).

Many of these temples had been transferred from the inner city after the Meireki Fire. Along with the already existing temples and shrines on the city's outskirts, these newly transferred temples composed a sort of belt along the boundaries of Edo, surrounding its inner districts. As townspeople spread into suburban areas in the late Tokugawa period, the somewhat segregated residential areas in the front districts of these temples and shrines naturally absorbed them. Religious lands were not immune to Edo's increasing urbanization during the late Tokugawa period. Despite the unstoppable urban sprawl, however, the spacious yet sparsely inhabited inner precincts of religious institutions somehow remained protected from the intrusion of the urban population and insulated from the hectic mundane world. It is no wonder that these religious enclaves offered a breathing space for Edo residents, particularly for commoners.

Among these religious enclaves, the Sensōji precinct and its neighboring areas were the most conspicuous and most captivating in Edo. As a center of folk piety and popular entertainment, the Sensōji space welcomed the public, and the environs of Sensōji, which included the Sumida River resort and waterfront areas, offered an additional attraction. The whole area was a vast amusement quarter unrivaled in Edo. The Sensōji administration even managed to extend its extraterritorial protection over the Sumida River.[66] Cherry blossoms along the banks of the river enchanted people in the spring, a boating excursion aroused excitement in the summer, and the beauty of the river never diminished, even in the winter season. Seasonal changes and scenic views along the Sumida River combined to produce natural beauties known as *Asakusa hakkei* (the eight scenes of Asakusa), all within walking distance of Sensōji.[67] Thus Edo residents had access to a year-round resort.

In particular, the Yoshiwara pleasure quarters in the northern neighborhood of Sensōji, which contained several thousand prostitutes, were an integral part of the world of popular culture in the Sensōji area. As the only government-authorized brothel quarters in Edo, Yoshiwara was a place not only for the sex trade but also for a different kind of social life. Attracted by the freer social norms and etiquette customary in Yoshiwara, an increasing number of commoner men sought moments of equality and liberation there.[68] Yoshiwara and the Sensōji space formed a sort of liberated zone. In the witty short verses (senryū) of Edoites, the pleasure quarters and religious precincts were, indeed, undifferentiated.

> Entering Kaminari [Gate], [one] passes through [to Yoshiwara] like *kaminari* (lightning)
> Dangling to [Asakusa] Kannon, [Yoshiwara] stands out conspicuous.
> What fun to fool around [Asakusa] Kannon on the way [to Yoshiwara].
> [Asakusa] Kannon is a Buddha who is of long-lasting use [for Yoshiwara].
> Inside the venerable [Sensōji] temple, [one] cuts a crossroads [to Yoshiwara].[69]

Yoshiwara and Sensōji were as close together culturally as they were geographically. Together, they produced one of the most popular sakariba in Edo.

Sakariba ("crowded plazas" or "amusement quarters") were part of Edo's cultural whirlpool. Besides the Sensōji sakariba, Edo had three other prominent amusement quarters: Ryōgoku, Ueno Hirokōji, and

Edobashi Hirokōji. Despite characteristic local features, all these amusement quarters shared common socio-geographical elements that seem to attest to the inherent association of prayer and play.

From the Kyōhō era (1716–35), the Ryōgoku area developed as a prosperous sakariba, with the emergence of numerous misemono shops, street artists, and circus performers on the sidestreets of fire lanes (*hiyokechi*). By the Hōreki era (1751–63), the Ryōgoku plaza was a central urban rendezvous, offering all kinds of pastimes and excitement. The Sumida River, which flowed under the Ryōgoku Bridge, was full of excursion boats, roofed restaurants, and floating bars in the summer. Teahouses, theaters, street circuses, gift shops, food vendors, and fireworks combined to create a kaleidoscope of popular culture. In the 1760s, Hiraga Gennai expressed, in his *Nenashi gusa* (Grasses with no roots), his impression of the crowds at the Ryōgoku sakariba: "One would marvel at these crowds, and wonder if they had emptied the houses of all the provinces."[70] Likewise, the Ueno sakariba, developed on the wide fire lanes down the southern hills of Ueno Mountain, produced a similar scene (albeit on a lesser scale). Edobashi was somewhat unique because it was the city's central produce and fish market. Over time, the flourishing commercial trade proved to be a catalyst for transforming the Edobashi area into a hub of popular culture. According to a 1791 bakufu record, the fire lanes of Edobashi were home to seventy-one vendors selling notions and gifts, fifteen diviners, eleven food hawkers, and seven used book stores. In addition, relatively permanent business establishments on both sides of the fire lanes included teahouses, archery booths, storytelling halls, barbershops, and wonder drug shops.[71]

Despite their individual characteristics, the Ryōgoku, Ueno, and Edobashi sakariba shared a common feature with the Sensōji sakariba: entertainment culture was closely associated with religious culture. Just as the Sensōji sakariba was centered around the Main Hall of the Asakusa Kannon, so the focal point of the Ryōgoku amusement center was the Ekō-in Buddhist temple. The Ekō-in was erected in 1657 as a prayer hall for the spirits of unidentified victims (*muen botoke*) of the great Meireki Fire. The government reportedly collected more than 108,000 corpses after the fire and buried them with a grand funeral ceremony at the site just across the Sumida River. After the funeral ceremony, Ekō-in was erected at the funeral site, and its priests were thereafter obliged to conduct, once a year with the support of the bakufu, a memorial service devoted to appeasing the homeless spirits of those fire victims who met violent deaths, lest they wander the city and menace people.[72] To the inhabitants of Edo, Ekō-in, located just across the Ryōgoku Bridge, symbolized an entrance to the other world. At the same time, with Ryōgoku's development as one of the most thriving sakariba, Ekō-in evolved as the most favored host temple for de-gaichō—the exhibition of other institutions' secret deities. Altogether 166 de-gaichō were held at Ekō-in between the first exhibition in 1676 and the end of the Tokugawa period. Thus the Ryōgoku sakariba owed its prosperity to the close association of prayer and play. By the same token, the Edobashi sakariba was centered around a Shintō shrine dedicated to the Inari fox god. The First Horse Day (*Hatsuuma*) festival of the Edobashi district, held at this Shintō shrine early in the second month of the year, was the most important annual event in Edobashi, for it was believed to open the entire Edobashi community to the spirits of spring. Finally, the Ueno sakariba had a charming shrine for Benzaiten, a tutelary deity. Along with the nearby Kan'eiji Temple and Momijiyama Tōshōgū Shrine in the Ueno hills, this shrine imbued the bustling amusement center with religious serenity.

The association of prayer and play at these sakariba was more than a mere spatial coincidence. First of all, all these sakariba spaces were located near water. Both the Sensōji sakariba and the Ryōgoku sakariba were situated near the Sumida River. Edobashi was a quintessential waterfront market. Even the Ueno sakariba, situated a short way inland, had as its backdrop a large artificial body of water—the Shinobazu Pond. As Jinnai Hidenobu suggests, such settings were conducive to the rapport between prayer and play.

> The presence of water was an important factor in the growth of an entertainment center. It is well known that a large number of "rendezvous teahouses" [*deai chaya*]—the equivalent to today's "love hotels"—were built in the romantic neighborhood of Shinobazu Pond. The area around the central island, which houses a shrine to Benzaiten and was built in imitation of Chikufujima at Lake Biwa (one of Japan's five famous Benten shrines), was particularly favored with such establishments.[73]

Water was indeed a common geographic element in the locations of popular temples or shrines associated with amusement centers. Aside from the Sensōji sakariba and others discussed above, other popular religious sites, such as Nezu Gongen Shrine in the Nezu district and Tomioka Hachiman Shrine in the Fukagawa district, were also located near water. As historians of Japanese religions often point out, water was an important ritual medium that was traditionally used in purifying social defilement or appeasing vengeful spirits. Moreover, Japanese believed that water would create a new life when a person's spirit returned to the other world. In Japanese religion, water, because of its life-giving power, was closely associated with new spirits, or the "source of life."[74]

In addition, sakariba temples and shrines were all geographically peripheral. Like Sensōji, most of the major temples and shrines in the commoner districts were situated "on sites that jutted toward the water's edge" and that "in every instance, were set apart from the profane space of the city streets."[75] Religious spaces in the lowlands naturally formed at the waterfront, just as temples and shrines in the uplands naturally formed at the edges of hills—another peripheral space. The moving of many temples and shrines to the outskirts of the city after the catastrophic Meireki Fire further removed Edo's religious spaces to the periphery. Sensōji, Zōjōji, Kanda Myōjin, Yushima Tenjin, Ichigaya Hachiman, Hie Sannō, Shiba Shrine, and Kan'eiji, to name just a few, were all situated in the border areas that separated the inner city of Edo from its outlying areas. These liminal spaces provided Edo people with an environment in which they could enjoy entertainment without having to worry about the class structure that predominated in the center of the city. The peripheral grounds of temples and shrines were all spaces of popular entertainment.

As Amino Yoshihiko convincingly suggests, during the medieval period in-between places such as riverbanks, bridges, temple and shrine entrances, markets, and transportation nodes served as a carefree public arena (*kugai*) unrestricted by the social norms of worldly relations. Itinerant artisans, vagabond artists, peddlers, and social outcasts gathered at such places to find relief from social discrimination and oppression. For them, the peripheral world was a "liberation zone" (*kaihōku*) imbued with an aura of sacredness—a place of "freedom" (*jiyū*) and "peace" (*heiwa*) built on the principle of "social non-attachment" or "untied-to-anything" (*muen*).[76] Inheriting this "public arena" atmosphere, religious spaces situated at the fringes of Edo's urban society offered a safe haven for cultural self-expression, where wandering performers gathered and created a world of freewheeling entertainment. For Edo's inhabitants, these spaces formed an ideal cultural asylum from the social bonds and regulations constraining their daily lives. From the standpoint of the government, these spaces served as useful outlets for people's sometimes volatile energy, which might otherwise have spilled over into social unrest. Shōgun Yoshimune, for example, sought to create a liberation zone for Edo commoners in the early eighteenth century. He directed bakufu officials "to build temples and shrines and to plant pine and cherry trees in places away from the built-up areas, hoping to draw the cultural energies of the populace to exhaustion." The Sumida embankment, along with Asukayama and Gotenyama, were made into public parks, where teahouses, restaurants, and other vendors gathered and catered to Edoites.[77] Thus the peripheral spaces occupied by religious institutions proved to be natural places for popular entertainment.

Among the many religious-cum-entertainment sites in Edo, Sensōji's northeastern quarter stood out because of the presence there of the Main Hall of the Asakusa Kannon and, behind it, Okuyama. Situated deep in the interior (*oku*) of the temple precincts, the Main Hall was the symbol of Buddhist spiritual protection, and Okuyama ("an interior mountain"), a spacious area studded with cherry trees to the rear of the building, was the stage for popular entertainments. The Asakusa Hall and Okuyama combined to form a perfect meeting point for prayer and play. As Maki Fumihiko suggests, such a geographical setting symbolized interiority and must have offered people a nostalgic return to the origin, where they could slip away from social attachments and experience salvation.[78]

The physically peripheral, yet spiritually central, space of Sensōji fit into the larger cosmological design of Edo. Located at the southern terminus of the Ōshū highway, Sensōji formed, along with Zōjōji in Shiba at the southwestern fringe of the city and Kan'eiji in Ueno at the northeastern boundary, a triangular spiritual blockade for the protection of Edo Castle. Sensōji and Kan'eiji were expected to guard the northeastern approaches to Edo, and Zōjōji was expected to guard the southwestern.

Between these vanguard temples were innumerable smaller temples, which together seemed to form a protective wall around the inner city. Removed from the crowded city streets and situated along watercourses, or surrounded by thick greenery on the radial boundaries of the city, these religious spaces came to harbor amusement quarters under the shield of divine protection. Sensōji, as an urban center for prayer and play, was in harmony with Edo's overall symbolic layout.

The geo-cultural dimension of Sensōji space was further strengthened by the unique cultural functions assigned to adjacent neighborhoods. Located north of Sensōji were the red-light district of Yoshiwara, residential quarters for Edo's outcasts (who worked as peddlers or vagabond entertainers or handled corpses and dead animals), the execution grounds, the Kotsukappara cremation center, Senju Station on the Sumida River, and dozens of lesser temples and shrines. In terms of Edo's layout, the Sensōji area was analogous to the Shinagawa area in the southwest, which contained the shōgunal funerary temple Zōjōji, the red-light district around Shinagawa Station, residential quarters for Edo's outcasts, a shōgunal execution ground at Suzugamori, and the Tama River. Along with Zōjōji and its neighborhoods, which were situated at the starting point of the Tōkaidō highway, Sensōji and its neighborhoods composed a "magical" (*ju teki*) cosmology for Edo. These symmetrical locations at the city's principal gateways constituted a liminal world within the shōgunal capital, where religion and entertainment were fused and the social evils and defilement emanating from the inner city were dissolved. Religious quests were fulfilled at Sensōji, sexual energies were absorbed at Yoshiwara, death pollution was handled by outcasts at Kotsukappara, and social evils and criminals were terminated at the execution sites.[79]

When all these elements are taken into account, the sociocultural geography of Sensōji points to the inherent association of prayer and play. As the Asakusa hitotsuya story reminds us, Sensōji was a place where entertainers, spiritual mediums, and travelers mingled in search of pleasure. It was also a space where both killing and repentance were encompassed by the mercy of the Asakusa Kannon.

Nevertheless, in reading of the Asakusa hitotsuya story, we must not overlook the role of the prostitute's parents. The parents, despite the apparently foreseeable consequences, arranged for their daughter to make a living by sleeping with travelers. It was, after all, the parents, not the daughter, who killed the travelers, and they killed for financial gain. In this sense, the parents may be seen as symbolizing the institution of the hitotsuya, in which religion and entertainment merged into a business enterprise. Here we can see the institutional unity of prayer and play.

The Institutional Unity of Prayer and Play

Some episodes in the history of late Tokugawa Yoshiwara reveal the extent to which Sensōji was institutionally oriented toward the unity of prayer and play. For example, a fire destroyed the brothel quarters of Yoshiwara in the eleventh month of 1812, as well as large parts of the Asakusa district, including seven of Sensōji's subtemples. Sensōji officials immediately undertook relief measures to help out the devastated subtemples. Their compassion had limits, however. Sensōji's deputy head monk ordered his subordinates to watch closely for prostitutes from Yoshiwara who might try to sneak into its precincts and districts to ply their trade until the Yoshiwara houses were rebuilt (*SN*, 12: 367–68). No sooner was the order issued than the heads of four front districts (Yamanojuku-chō, Shōden-chō, Ta-machi, and Kawara-machi) petitioned the Sensōji administration to take pity on the Yoshiwara prostitutes and allow them to conduct their business in their front districts. They expressed humanitarian concern for the now-homeless prostitutes and cited numerous precedents of similar temporary permissions (*SN*, 12: 382). The Sensōji administration eventually yielded to their urgent entreaties and allowed Yoshiwara prostitutes to conduct their business on its lands.

This special dispensation, granted in 1812, was the eighth time such permission was given in the late Tokugawa period. Whenever Yoshiwara was ruined by a fire, prostitutes employed in the walled pleasure quarters petitioned the Sensōji administration through the ward heads of neighboring districts to be allowed to set up business temporarily on its lands in *karitaku* (rent-houses). Sensōji officials usually responded sympathetically. In such cases, the Sensōji administration usually designated five districts near Yoshiwara (Yamanojuku-chō, Hanakawado-chō, Shōden-chō, Shōdenyoko-chō, and Kinryūsan Shitakawara-machi), out of its twenty-two front districts, as areas where prostitutes could temporarily carry on their business. The durations of such permission ranged from 100 days to two years, depending upon the time needed to rebuild the Yoshiwara district.

Despite the unilateral stipulations of the Sensōji administration, licensed prostitutes, unshackled from the fetters of Yoshiwara, did not remain within the confines of their new business territory. These venturesome entrepreneurs often spilled beyond the designated zones, and Sensōji officials were quite tolerant of this, even when the territories in question were their own backyard.[80] Furthermore, at such times "private" street prostitutes from other parts of the city often sneaked into the Sensōji area and took advantage of the business opportunities. During periods of sanctioned "rent-house" business, the Sensōji precincts, particularly Okuyama, were spectacles indeed. The teahouses lining the precincts were soon rented out to the "outside" intruders, and street pimps endeavored to attract customers to their "special business" parlors by decorating them with red lanterns and colorful curtains. Some business owners even distributed free jackets, with the logos of their rent-house businesses printed on the backs, to young men in the Sensōji area.[81]

The rent-house business in the Sensōji precincts and front districts was very popular with Edo commoners. For Yoshiwara prostitutes, who were, like "birds in a cage," generally strictly confined to their walled quarters, the rent-house business was certainly more than a change of place—it was an occasion on which they could breathe the air of liberation. In fact, Yoshiwara prostitutes, who endured harsh lives in the slavish world of the sex trade, often deliberately set fire to their own residences in order to escape the stifling and dire conditions of Yoshiwara. All of the thirteen fires between 1804 and 1807 in Yoshiwara were intentionally set by Yoshiwara prostitutes themselves.[82] When released from their cells, Yoshiwara prostitutes sought their own pleasures: boating excursions along the Sumida River, picnics under the cherry blossoms, recreational outings in the Sensōji sakariba, and visits to temples and shrines.

Although supposedly only when granted special permission due to disaster could Yoshiwara prostitutes venture into Edo streets, the reality was quite different. With or without permission, it was not unusual to find "private" prostitutes, known as *kakushi baita* (hidden streetwalkers), in the Sensōji area in the late Tokugawa period. The presence of unauthorized prostitutes and private prostitution in the Sensōji area was not simply a matter of defiance or deception: it was a structural feature of Edo society. Yoshiwara was the only sanctioned red-light district in a city with a population of over one million. In light of the floating cultural fashions of Edo society in the late Tokugawa period, the glittering pleasure culture of Yoshiwara, located on Edo's northeastern periphery, was too lavish and too segregated for such a buoyant urban society. Consequently, various types of pleasure businesses prospered at restaurants and teahouses, on the streets, in the excursion boats floating on the Sumida River, and at public parks. In particular, the front districts of temples and shrines (and even their inner precincts), because of the tolerant and supportive attitudes of religious institutions toward entertainers, often turned out to be hotbeds of illicit pleasure.[83]

The Sensōji administration was quite tolerant of "hidden streetwalkers" who sneaked across its borders. It is understandable why front district residents were so supportive of the hidden streetwalkers. For some residents of Sensōji's front districts, unlicensed prostitution meant extra rent income and other fringe benefits (*SN*, 15: 275–76). But the Sensōji administration did not benefit directly from the rent-house business, because all temporary business quarters for private prostitution were sublets leased out by merchants. Nevertheless, Sensōji officials were quite sympathetic to the illegal operations of private prostitutes and, indeed, were indifferent to the fact that prostitution was taking place in the heart of their own sanctuary. One might argue that Sensōji's position on this issue was an example of Buddhist compassion toward pitiful street entertainers. Sensōji was, however, a Buddhist sangha and was supposed to be bound by a strict set of behavioral guidelines, one of which was the strict prohibition of any sexual contact. Even under the laxest interpretation of Buddhist precepts, permitting the practice of prostitution in the Buddhist sangha was absolutely unthinkable. Not, however, at Sensōji.

As a matter of fact, the Sensōji administration did not deal with prostitution from the stance of Buddhist precepts. It is true that the Sensōji sangha, as a Tendai Buddhist temple, did not keep the full set of Buddhist precepts (*gusokukai*); rather, it followed the much less strict "bodhisattva precepts," which the founder of Tendai Buddhism, Saichō (767–822), had introduced from the *Fan wang ching* (*Bonmōkyō*) and which were based on the early ninth-century theory that enlightenment is inherent within all sentient beings.[84] Furthermore, the idea of original enlightenment (*hongaku shisō*) in Tendai Buddhism was so inclusive that its advocates even maintained that the doers of the most evil deeds still had "the innate capacity to attain Buddhahood," and they used the argument as "a rationale for affirming all things in their present state."[85] Nonetheless, as far as life within the sangha in this tradition was concerned, at least ten major and forty-eight minor precepts were, in principle, imposed on all Buddhists. Sexual activity, adultery, and lewdness were considered serious violations of these precepts.[86]

Within the Sensōji community, however, not only laypeople but also lifetime practitioners of Buddhism seemed to pay no attention to the most basic strictures of their religion. In their minds, there was little ethical contradiction between Buddhist life in the sangha and prostitution in a Buddhist temple. What Sensōji officials heeded most was the government's occasional, yet inconsistent, reactions against prostitution on temple grounds, expressed in the form of ordinances or regulations. In dealing with external regulations occasionally imposed from above, Sensōji officials reacted in a purely administrative manner. This would seem to indicate that, at a deep level, Sensōji monks were basically inured to the Buddhist spirit of "artificial" norms and precepts. From the stance of the Sensōji institution, prayer and play were compatible.

Sensōji's institutional embrace of play in the form of prostitution did not stop at the level of passive approval. The Sensōji administration, with its keen interest in finances, made efforts to reach out to the wider public through various other play opportunities. For example, it sponsored a *tomitsuki* (lottery), in which patrons bought chances at a prize. By the late Tokugawa period, tomitsuki at temples and shrines, which had originated in the religious custom of drawing *shūshō* talismans at Ryūanji Temple in Settsu in the late Kamakura period, had been transformed into a commercial enterprise for raising funds.[87] With the permission of the shōgunate, a temple or shrine conducted public lotteries and collected the profits from the games.[88] In 1745, on the grounds that it desperately needed at least 100 gold pieces to repair the Main Hall of the Asakusa Kannon, the Sensōji administration succeeded in obtaining permission to hold a lottery from the Magistrate's Office of Temples and Shrines. Sensōji continued to enjoy the right to conduct a lottery game once a month for nearly a century, until the time of the Tenpō reforms in the early 1840s.[89]

As far as finances were concerned, Sensōji monks did not differ much from any secular loan broker or banker. Sensōji had plentiful cash reserves, and Sensōji priests stepped into the loan business and sometimes got involved in legal disputes because of the temple's activities in this area. In 1762, Myōon-in, a Sensōji subtemple, brought a dispute with the daimyō of Tsushima, Sō Yoshiari, to the bakufu's court. Myōon-in had lent a sum of ninety gold pieces to the Tsushima daimyō, who promised to pay it back within a month with an interest of twenty-two gold pieces. After one and a half years, the loan still had not been repaid, and angry Myōon-in officials petitioned the bakufu to resolve the case (*SN*, 3: 16–19). In the same year, Nichion-in, another Sensōji subtemple, accused the daimyō of the Kameda domain, Iwaki Takayoshi, of defaulting on a loan of 1,050 gold pieces plus interest. Nichion-in complained that the daimyō had so far paid back only twenty-nine gold pieces (*SN*, 3: 21–23). Although all these legal disputes were instigated by subtemples, the source of money was the *shidōkin* (money of a religious hall) of the central Sensōji administration, which it operated as part of its loan business. The Sensōji administration was very adroit at circulating its vast cash reserves through its subtemples for loans or capital investment, all in the name of raising funds for the maintenance of temple buildings. In 1817, for example, Sensōji's cash reserves reached 6,865.8 gold pieces (*SN*, 13: 667–68), and the temple authorities were constantly engaged in a search for prospective borrowers of their extra capital.

Given the institutional and financial worries of the Sensōji administration, a little sexual play in its backyard would not have been a major concern. More serious headaches for the administrators arose from problems among its own members—financial misconduct, sexual scandals, gambling, and alcoholism. In spite of tight regulations on money transactions, the unlawful pawning of temple property was frequent, as were the use of fake signatures and flights of indebted monks (*SN*, 4:

105–11; 5: 213–14; 8: 293; 11: 627). Sex scandals were particularly notorious. Some monks set up lovers in private housing outside their temples; others, alone or in groups, often ventured into Yoshiwara (*SN*, 10: 337–40). Gambling was so rampant that the head monks of some subtemples even rented out temple halls to gamblers (*SN*, 12: 85, 370). This misconduct led to such punishments as admonition, confinement to one's residence, dismissal from one's post, divestiture, and banishment to remote islands—all of these enriched the gossip of late Tokugawa Sensōji. But nothing changed.

Driven by the dictates of entrepreneurship, Sensōji officials remained sympathetic to the world of play, which they adeptly linked to the world of prayer. Sensōji managers endeavored to channel religious visitors to the Asakusa Kannon to their play business and vice versa. Play culture was thus both a beneficiary and a benefactor of prayer culture. The ways in which the temple took advantage of Edo's frequently devastating fires illuminate how artfully play and prayer were interlinked at Sensōji. As discussed above, when a fire damaged Yoshiwara, the Sensōji administration used it as an excuse to boost play culture. By the same token, the Sensōji administration could sometimes convert fire into a religious boon. The Hinoetora Fire of 1806, which ravaged large parts of Edo, is an example of this.

The damage caused by the Hinoetora Fire was enormous—eighty daimyō residences, twenty shrines, and sixty temples (including the five-story pagoda of Zōjōji) were destroyed. About 530 districts were ruined, and the death toll reached approximately 1,200. As this ferocious fire was about to spread to the Sensōji precincts after devouring nearby Higashi Honganji Temple, Sensōji officials evacuated the Asakusa Kannon statue to Enmyōji Temple (an affiliate of the Mimeguri Inari Shrine) in the Honjo district.[90] But a miracle, Sensōji monks claimed, occurred in the nick of time: thanks to the protection of the Asakusa Kannon, it suddenly started to pour rain. Sensōji was saved, and the Asakusa Kannon statue was safely returned. Soon after this event, Sensōji officials dedicated a grand service of thanks to the Asakusa Kannon and used this fire for propaganda for the omnipotent powers of the Asakusa Kannon.[91]

The Main Hall of the Asakusa Kannon was threatened by fire many times in the late Tokugawa period. None of these fires, however, reached the hall, and Sensōji monks never failed to attribute this to the protective power of the Asakusa Kannon. The Gyōninzaka Fire in 1772, one of the three greatest fires in Edo (along with the Meireki Fire and the Hinoe-tora Fire), was also stopped by a sudden rain right before it was about to leap into the Main Hall, after having killed many people and destroyed the administrative headquarters (Denbō-in) and nineteen subtemples (*SN*, 3: 696–99). In 1821 a fire started in Hanakawado-chō, one of Sensōji's front districts, spread into the inner precincts, and devoured, in a flash, the Niō Gate, the five-story pagoda, and even the Nijikken teahouses. Again, just before the Main Hall was about to catch fire, a sudden rain saved the shrine of the Asakusa Kannon from destruction.[92] Rebuilt in 1650, the Main Hall was to survive for almost 300 years, until it was turned into ashes by American bombs in 1945.

Sensōji officials readily attributed the unusual longevity of the Main Hall to the miraculous protection of the Asakusa Kannon. The fire episodes, however easily we might dismiss them as a matter of luck, certainly helped to enhance the aura of awe and wonder surrounding the Asakusa Kannon. Thus, Sensōji capitalized on fires for play as well as for prayer. Of course, it may be too much to say that fire was a key contributing factor in the prosperity of Sensōji's prayer and play culture. It is unlikely that destruction of the Main Hall through fire would have brought an end to Sensōji culture. The point is, rather, that Sensōji missed no opportunity to expand the base of its prayer and play culture. One such opportunity happened to be fire, and it worked well. Other such opportunities included exhibiting the secret Asakusa Kannon statue (Maetate Kannon) and holding ennichi (a day for connection [with the Asakusa Kannon]). By offering these opportunities to connect with the Asakusa Kannon, Sensōji was able to attract more visitors and channel them into the bustling plaza of its play culture and vice versa. The working of prayer and play was mutually beneficial.

The tactics that Sensōji officials used to promote the prayer culture paralleled those they used in the play culture. One of these was publicity. Just as the rent-house business was promoted through advertisement, so was the Asakusa Kannon. In order to spread the religious reputation of the Asakusa Kannon to a wider audience, the Sensōji administration exhaustively collected "miraculous" stories about this deity and circulated them in the form of published "chronicles" (engi). The story of the origins of the Asakusa Kannon statue was first published in 1719, and thereafter similar stories were frequently printed. Stories such as the hitotsuya legend and tales about miraculous events during fires and various divine happenings involving the Asakusa Kannon were widely circulated among the populace.[93] The publication of these stories gave great impetus to folk piety and the popular worship of the Asakusa Kannon.

More interestingly, just as the play culture had external supporters (the residents of front districts), so did the prayer culture (laypeople who organized religious "confraternities" [kō]).[94] These organized groups of lay supporters emerged from the need to circumvent the status barriers of Edo society, and their collective support proved indispensable to Sensōji's prayer culture. It was not practical for individual commoners to have access to the Sensōji bureaucracy in order to receive the privilege of priestly services. One solution was collective interaction. Once formed, on obtaining approval from the Sensōji administration, religious confraternities served as an institutional linchpin connecting lay members to the prestigious religious services dispensed by Sensōji priests.[95] These confraternities of laypeople were useful to Sensōji, for their members could provide extra labor during special events, fund-raising campaigns, and so on. In the late Tokugawa period, many religious confraternities supported the prayer culture of Sensōji from without.

Among the confraternities, the largest was the Confraternity of One Hundred Thousand People (Jūmannin-kō). It was founded in 1718, when the head monk Kunen tried unsuccessfully to obtain financial aid from the government in order to repair the Main Hall. To raise the necessary funds, Sensōji officials resorted to exhibiting the Kannon statue (kaichō) and to conducting a donation campaign. In 1719, a regular kaichō in the thirty-three-year cycle was held, and soon after its completion Sensōji officials kicked off an unprecedentedly massive donation campaign under the banner of *jūmannin-kō*. In order to garner 100,000 donors, Sensōji officials divided the Kantō area into ten regions and assigned an official to each. The three-year campaign turned out to be quite successful, and 2,500 gold pieces were collected—over half the total costs of the repair work. To thank the donors, which included 148 daimyō, the Sensōji administration erected a Buddhist stupa and held a memorial ceremony on the fifteenth day of the fifth month of 1723. The donor-members of the Confraternity of One Hundred Thousand were enlisted as loyal patrons of the Asakusa Kannon.[96]

In addition to the Confraternity of One Hundred Thousand, there were ten other religious confraternities at Sensōji, all devoted to prayer and the Asakusa Kannon. Unlike the Confraternity of One Hundred Thousand, these confraternities were organized by laypeople seeking more direct access to the Asakusa Kannon and to Sensōji monks. Members interacted with Sensōji officials as a group by providing the Kannon altar in the Main Hall with ritual items. In return, Sensōji officials offered them customized prayer services. The costs of maintaining a grandiose altar for the Asakusa Kannon throughout the year were largely met by contributions from these ten confraternities. Their names are indicative of the ritual items they provided (*SN*, 7: 612).

Gozen (meal) kō: daily meal offered to the Asakusa Kannon
Darani (mantra) kō: expenses for mantra chanting and for maintaining the altar canopy
Rōsoku (candles) kō: candles lit on the altar throughout the year
Okashi (sweets) kō: cookies for offerings and desserts at banquets
Tōba (stupas) kō: flat wooden five-story stupas
Zōka (artificial flowers) kō: flowers for decoration and offerings
Gomamoku (*goma* trees) kō: cedar sticks to be burned in the *goma* (*homa*) offering
Higashi Takamori (eastern heap) kō: special meal offering piled up on the Eastern altar
Nishi Takamori (western heap) kō: special meal offering piled up on the Western altar
Otatami (tatami mats) kō: tatami mats for the floor of the Main Hall

Each confraternity had 100–200 members, most of whom were commoners. (Unfortunately surviving records do not allow us to reconstruct the nature of the membership in terms of sex, age groups, occupational categories, or residence locations.) In order to ensure that the confraternity could fulfill its donation pledges for the Asakusa Kannon, the Sensōji administration usually recognized a group only after it had raised a foundation fund and deposited it at the temple treasury. These funds guaranteed, in most cases, steady interest income to cover the regular costs of the specified donation.[97] As devoted followers of the Asakusa Kannon, the members of lay confraternities were faithful proponents of Sensōji's prayer culture in the late Tokugawa period.

How did Sensōji officials reconcile the probable conflicts in purpose between groups who supported play (the residents of front districts) and groups who supported prayer (the religious confraternities)? Play culture, dramatized by the presence of private prostitutes, had strong support from the residents of front districts, misemono merchants, and entertainers. By comparison, prayer culture, focused on the Asakusa Kannon, assembled pious confraternity members. Despite the seemingly contradictory nature of the cultural pursuits of these two groups, the Sensōji sangha was somehow able to accommodate both groups of supporters and to promote the institutional unity of play and prayer.

The Sensōji institution was in fact not a monochromatic Buddhist sangha but a heterogeneous organization whose structure served to integrate prayer and play into one culture. The core component of the Sensōji institution was, of course, ordained Buddhist priests. These people dominated the central administration and the thirty-four subtemples. But this did not mean that the Sensōji institution was run only by Buddhist monks. Members of two other groups—semi-monks and secular officials—served in the administration at various levels and had their own powers and functions. This triangular structure proved effective in running the narrowly defined community of Buddhist priests and, at the same time, in administering the affairs of laypeople, the residents of front districts, and temple merchants.

The top tier of the organization consisted of a group of approximately eighty Buddhist monks—in hierarchical order, a deputy head monk (*bettōdai*), managing administrators (*yakusha*), head monks of subtemples, ritual monks (*kusō*), and novices (*deshi*). As mentioned in the Introduction, the head of the Kan'eiji institution, the Rinnōji monzeki, appointed an administrator chosen from outside the Sensōji sangha and installed him as de facto head of the Sensōji administration under the title of deputy head monk. This outsider was, by and large, a political figurehead rather than a chief executive officer (*SN*, 5: 207–8). The general administration was left to two managing administrators, who were elected by a vote among the head monks of subtemples. Among the responsibilities of the managing administrators, the most important ones were to review all the petitions from members of the Sensōji community and to append their opinions before seeking the endorsement from the Kan'eiji and the Magistrate's Office of Temples and Shrines. Ritual monks were in charge of religious events in the Main Hall as well as the maintenance of the temple infrastructure. The head of the ritual monks, with the rank of head of subtemple, ran a warehouse and kitchen and led daily prayer offerings to the Asakusa Kannon and other deities (*SN*, 10: 45). In addition, the seventeen prayer monks assigned to Tōshō Daigongen Shrine at Mount Momiji in Ueno were in charge of daily prayer offerings to the spirit of Tokugawa Ieyasu.

The second tier of the organization consisted of a group of semi-monks: three assistant managers (*shōji*) at the Main Hall, several Shugendō priests, and quasi-Shintō priests. All of them were ordained at the Buddhist platform and allowed to wear black robes and a tonsure, but their offices were hereditarily transmitted as a family occupation. The three shōji, who were commonly known as Sanfudai (three hereditary deputies), were supposedly descendants of the three fishermen who had discovered the Asakusa Kannon statue in the Sumida River: the Sendō-bō family, descendants of Haji no Nakatomo, which was responsible for the general maintenance of the Main Hall; the Saitō-bō of the Hinokuma Hamanari lineage, responsible for arranging offerings to the Asakusa Kannon and other deities; and the Jōon-in of the Hinokuma Takenari lineage, in charge of beating gongs and other ritual instruments when prayers were held. These families also had the right to sell talismans and amulets to worshippers in the Main Hall.[98] A group of shugenja affiliated with Sensōji carried out purificatory rites to ensure safety and good results when special events, such as kaichō and the year-end market fair, were held. These shugenja, numbering nine in 1827, belonged to the Shōgo-in Temple of the Shugen Honzan Sect in Kyoto. However, in practice, as hereditary semi-monk priests, they were part of the Sensōji institution (*SN*, 10: 369, 372–73; 15: 91; 17: 277–78).

The third tier of the Sensōji organization consisted of secular personnel. Secular officials had nothing to do with the Buddhist order, but their role in the administration of the Sensōji sangha was far-reaching, particularly in the area of finances. The major secular officers were the two or three treasurers (*onando*), the two deputy managers (*daikan*) of Sensōji land and their two assistants, and the two assistant managers (*dōban*) of the Main Hall. Sensōji treasurers were highly independent, for they were dispatched from Kan'eiji on a monthly basis. They controlled Sensōji's monetary revenues, handled all expenses, and supervised the other secular officials. The major responsibility of deputy managers was to collect land taxes from the residents of front districts and rents from Sensōji's merchants and to supervise district heads (*nanushi*). Throughout the Tokugawa period, the office of deputy manager was monopolized by members of two families, the Honma and the Kikuchi. The two assistant managers of the Main Hall, whose positions were also hereditary, were, in cooperation with ritual monks and the three Sanfudai, responsible for the general maintenance of the Main Hall and other buildings.[99]

All in all, Sensōji was more than a Buddhist sangha; it was a special kind of enterprise. Its three-tiered administrative structure ensured that power was shared and controlled through a web of checks and balances. For example, the secular managers of the Main Hall set up ritual paraphernalia and procured materials to be offered at the altar; ritual monks performed prayer rituals; and the semi-monk Sanfudai managers sold the products of these rituals to the public. The worship of the Asakusa Kannon was handled not just as a religious undertaking but also as a business enterprise.

As an organization capable of dealing with any matter, Sensōji in the late Tokugawa period carried out a wide range of secular affairs in addition to religious ones. To mention a few of these, the Sensōji administration was obliged to inform and educate residents of its front districts regarding shōgunal decrees, to collect special taxes imposed on the residents for shōgunal projects, and to assist with such shōgunal tasks as distributing seeds imported from Korea and China to neighboring farmers (*SN*, 6: 79, 346). It also dealt with social problems such as foundlings, people dying on the street, suicides, and homeless sick people. Financial transactions received a considerable amount of attention, and administrators often found themselves in the middle of legal disputes.[100] The maintenance of temple buildings, whether they were to be reconstructed or repaired, was a constant concern of administrators, for a building's appearance served as an indicator of the religious efficacy of the deity enshrined within.[101]

In sum, the Sensōji institution was flexible enough to accommodate both prayer and play. Popular culture and Buddhist culture meshed perfectly at Sensōji. In terms of the hitotsuya story, the Sensōji institution played the role of the parents who arranged for the daughter to reconcile prayer and play, shaman and prostitute.

Sensōji culture in the late Tokugawa period was based on the unity of prayer and play. To those who view this in terms of the sacred (prayer) and the profane (play), Sensōji culture is simply a typical example of Buddhist degeneration. No doubt, Sensōji Buddhism did mix religion and entertainment. For this reason, critics invariably supported the "back to precept-centered Buddhism" movement, emphasizing the austere education of Buddhist priests and the strict study of Buddhist scriptures.[102]

As far as the Sensōji sangha was concerned, the Buddhist precepts imposed on its members were minimal, and education and training programs for new monks were almost nonexistent. At Sensōji, the head monk of a subtemple was allowed to take a disciple as a monk-candidate, and this candidate could easily be installed as an ordained Buddhist priest without having received any formal education.[103] The Tendai sect's traditional ordination platform (established by Saichō) was simply forgotten at the Sensōji sangha. The ordination ceremony for "shaving the crown of the head," which elsewhere featured the recitation of a renunciation *gāthā* (*jishin-ge*) and the sprinkling of water over the head of the candidate, had become a mere accessory to the presentation of gratitude money and gifts to the master monk. After the ordination ceremony, the novice monk served his mentor for several years, doing sundry jobs and learning priestly skills by observing his mentor. The practice of disciplinary precepts and the understanding of Buddhist scriptures were not necessary to the success of a new Buddhist priest. What was necessary was the polishing of skills and techniques for performing rituals, the wearing of splendid robes, and being surrounded by imposing buildings and statues.[104] The business of Sensōji Buddhism required entrepreneurial spirit and skill, and the unity of prayer and play fit right into it.

The coupling of prayer and play at Sensōji during the late Tokugawa period, however, cannot be imputed solely to the "deviance" of monks. Sensōji monks were simply part of a Japanese religious tradition in which prayer and play were not considered to be separate entities. Play was a way of communicating with deities, and prayer was a way of entertaining them. The unity of prayer and play at Sensōji was an expression of this cultural tradition. Both socio-geographically and institutionally, Sensōji was set up to accommodate prayer and play. Under the banner of being a Buddhist sangha (which provided certain immunities from shōgunal power), monks, semi-monks, and secular personnel cooperated to promote the business of worship and entertainment.

THREE

The Social Economy of Prayer and Play

The later years of the period when Tanuma Okitsugu served as head of the State Council of Elders (1767–86) were plagued with natural disasters, including the eruption of Mount Asama, massive famines in the Kantō and Tōhoku regions, and extensive floods in the Kantō region. These disasters further compounded the already deepening hardships of Edo residents and eventually led to the outbreak of urban "smashings" (*uchikowashi*) in 1787. When the daimyō of the Shirakawa domain, Matsudaira Sadanobu (1758–1829), replaced Okitsugu as head of the State Council of Elders that same year, Edoites had high expectations of relief from suffering. Some commoners even hastened to portray Sadanobu as a saint or a deity who would clean up the economic and social mess.

Matsudaira Sadanobu soon implemented a wide range of remedial measures that came to be known as the Kansei Reforms. For Sadanobu, the most urgent task was to remove the causes of social unrest and economic hardship. He and like-minded bureaucrats moved swiftly to execute reform policies designed to renovate the bakuhan social system, restore social morale, and revive the sagging economy. In order to restore the feudal order in Edo that his grandfather, Shōgun Yoshimune, had envisioned half a century earlier, Sadanobu placed special emphasis on redirecting the behavior and attitudes of Edo residents. He banned Edoites from producing, trading, and consuming luxury goods; enforced sumptuary regulations; strictly supervised the Yoshiwara and other private brothel quarters; controlled street performers and entertainers; and arrested gamblers. The popular culture of Edo commoners, which had gone largely unsupervised during the Okitsugu years, was now the prime target of suppression.

Contrary to Sadanobu's expectations, however, he soon found himself the object of ridicule and satire. Edo commoners began to grumble about the Sadanobu government's Neo-Confucian approach to their world. For them, the "upright" social order that Sadanobu tried to establish in Edo seemed far removed from the reality of their lives. A lampoon appeared in the eighth month of 1789, soon after the shōgunate had launched its campaign to straighten out the social order: "It is not easy to live in the clean stream of the Shirakawa River [Sadanobu was daimyō of Shirakawa, which literally means 'white river'], and [we] miss the water of the muddy Tanuma Lake [Tanuma literally means 'paddy lake']."[1] When strict sumptuary regulations were issued later that year, government officials began to hear complaints. Satirical verses and "mad songs" (*kyōka*), which appeared frequently on the streets of Edo in 1791, revealed the hardship caused by Sadanobu's reform policies. One such verse parodied a conversation between Sadanobu and Edo townspeople:

> *Sadanobu*: As regards treating the maladies of the people of our time with moxa—since we are in the latter days of the world, it shouldn't matter if they cry out.
>
> *Song by the townspeople in reply*: Even though curing the maladies of the latter days of the world, today we cannot stand the pain of moxa.[2]

In response to the outpouring of popular protest, the reformist shōgunate imposed even more suppression. *Kibyōshi* (yellow cover) writers of political satire were forced to concentrate on moral teachings; well-to-do merchants, who had dominated the salon culture, were culturally paralyzed. The Sadanobu government clamped down on prose literature, commercial painting, kabuki theater, street arts, entertainment, and popular worship. At the same time, the bakufu tried to mobilize popular culture to help restore and strengthen the Tokugawa feudal order. Popular culture, however, was not easily subdued, and the social order envisioned by the reformers did not come into being.[3] The Kansei reform measures failed not only to utilize popular culture for the cause of moral restoration but also to domesticate the cultural spirit of Edo commoners.

In this cultural milieu at the turn of the eighteenth century, the Sensōji culture of prayer and play prospered as if defying the moral design of the Tokugawa feudal system. The Sadanobu government wanted to contain the erratic cultural pursuits of Edoites at Sensōji. Contrary to the bakufu's hope, however, the prayer and play culture of Sensōji continued to gain in popularity, particularly in the Bunka and Bunsei eras (1804–29). The overarching framework of the Tokugawa feudal order seemed to have lost much of its relevance to Edo society, and the bakufu could not reverse this tendency with a few stopgap measures. Edo society was undergoing fundamental structural changes, and it placed less emphasis on status distinctions. And Sensōji Buddhism fit right in with Edo's new social economy.

The Social Base of Prayer and Play Culture

The annual festival of the Sensō Shrine, known as the Sanja matsuri (the festival of three shrines), was held on the eighteenth day of the third month of 1753. As usual, the monk-priests (*shasō*) of the Sensō Shrine performed a Shintō worship service for the Sanja Daigongen deities—the discoverers of the Asakusa Kannon statue. The *ujiko* (children of the clan) members of the Sensō Shrine (i.e., the residents of the Sensōji monzen parish) followed the worship service with a *mikoshi* (portable shrine) procession. But the participation of the ujiko members of the Sanja Daigongen parish seemed quite lackluster in comparison with the enthusiasm displayed by the Sensōji priests and bakufu officials. When the retinue of three mikoshi carrying the Sanja Daigongen deities was about to pass Suwa-chō, a number of residents tried to block the procession. Fistfights and squabbles erupted. Two residents were seriously injured, and the three portable shrines were severely damaged. The magistrate of temples and shrines immediately investigated the incident and punished those involved (*SN*, 1: 614–15).

On the surface, this incident might appear to be a mishap in which some unruly ujiko members of the Sensō Shrine disgraced their tutelary deities. Unruliness at the Sanja festival was, however, chronic throughout the late Tokugawa period. In 1759, for example, the Sensōji administration had to cancel the festival procession because of sabotage on the part of ujiko members who were supposed to carry the portable shrines. Because of their refusal to cooperate, following a brief worship offering to the Sanja Daigongen deities, Sensōji officials had to limit the procession of the portable shrines to a walk to the Main Hall of the Asakusa Kannon, which was just a few meters away (*SN*, 2: 451, 460). In 1769, monzen residents petitioned the Sensōji administration to cancel the upcoming festival due to a dull economy—the consequence of a large fire in the previous year. The fisherfolk of Ōmori Village, who were in charge of transporting the mikoshi by boat on the Sumida River, also wanted the festival canceled, citing poor fishing.[4] The Magistrate's Office of Temples and Shrines eventually approved a two-year postponement of the matsuri, as requested by the head administrator of Sensōji on behalf of the residents (*SN*, 3: 366–67, 369–72).

For the residents of the front districts, matsuri were financial burdens. In particular, the maintenance of the Sanja Daigongen's three portable shrines, for which ujiko residents were responsible, was quite an onerous task. The cost of repairing or rebuilding the shrines easily exceeded 100 gold pieces—a sum that would greatly encumber all the monzen residents of Sensōji. For example, it took four years for the ujiko residents of Sanja Daigongen to accumulate the necessary funds to rebuild the three portable shrines in 1772, at a cost of 100 gold pieces (*SN*, 3: 398–99). Seventeen years later, in 1789, when the subject of replacing the already dilapidated portable shrines was broached, ujiko members again had to find ways to raise the necessary funds.

In short, to ujiko residents, the Sanja matsuri, with its procession of the Sanja Daigongen's three portable shrines along the major streets of front districts and the Sumida River, was an unwelcome event. The residents' main concern was the heavy cost of the festival. Among the suggestions for ways to meet the festival expenses were the sale of liquor, street solicitations of contributions, and forced donations to fundraising shows such as the exhibition of Shintō dancing on the stage of Sensō Shrine (*SN*, 3: 445; 5: 151; 6: 134–35). In an extreme case in 1823, some ujiko members even pawned three street girls to the brothel quarters of Yoshiwara in order to raise money.[5] But no matter what method the ujiko contrived to defray the costs, none of them was better than canceling the matsuri itself. Ironically, the ujiko members of the Sanja Daigongen made every effort to stymie the Sanja matsuri, which was, in theory, supposed to provide them with the direct blessing of their tutelary deities. Over time, the repeated petitions for cancellation of Sanja Daigongen festivals resulted in changing them from an annual to a biennial event. Even this reduced schedule was rarely kept during the late Tokugawa period. There was a full-scale Sanja matsuri in 1772 and another in 1781, but for the next forty-two years (until 1823), the ujiko residents of Sanja Daigongen did not witness a procession of their tutelary deities.[6]

The attitude of the monzen residents toward the Sanja matsuri in the late Tokugawa period is puzzling. It was not an exuberant religious event for the ujiko community. The traditional spirit and images of Shintō festivals, as represented by the Gion festival of Kyoto, cannot be found in the Sanja festival. The conventional understanding of traditional Shintō matsuri is that the ujiko members of a Shintō shrine parish managed the festival in a communal manner and that such management helped strengthen their spirit of solidarity and autonomy. Shintō matsuri traditionally provided a "divine" opportunity for local residents to consolidate their community ties and thereby prevent the intervention of the authorities in their internal affairs. For Kyoto residents, the Gion festival was an inviolable symbol of their autonomy and solidarity.[7] But this communal spirit barely existed among the ujiko residents of Sensō Shrine. The greatest enemy of the Sanja festival was, paradoxically, the "children" of Sanja Daigongen themselves.

In fact, following its revival in 1823 at the end of a forty-two year hiatus, the Sanja festival once again disappeared until the end of the Tokugawa period. The reasons for its cancellation were various. One was that the festival would exacerbate a "disharmonious air" among ujiko residents (*SN*, 16: 23). For Sensōji monzen residents, the Sanja festival had the potential to trigger factional discord. In this sense, the real reason for forgoing the Sanja festival was the deterioration in communal bonds among the ujiko members. The financial burden of the Sanja festival was more a pretext than a cause. The Gion festival of Kyoto, which cost much more than did the Sanja festival, was held annually throughout the Tokugawa period, but it had the full support of its ujiko members. The

Sanja festival of Edo Asakusa, which could not rally communal support, turned out to be a cause of further communal discord.

The lack of communal spirit to support the Sanja festival was a reflection of the declining communal solidarity in the basic ward unit (machi) of Edo society. Unlike Kyoto townspeople, who still maintained strong communal bonds in the late Tokugawa period, Edoites were dispersing.[8] Amid the deterioration of the machi community in Edo, Shintō festivals, a traditional rallying point for communal unity, lost the appeal they once had for the scattering "children" of the *kami*. This very social trend, however, proved to be a contributing factor in the prosperity of Sensōji's culture of prayer and play. As the machi community began to decline, Edo society produced an ever-increasing number of uprooted, lonely urban inhabitants who thirsted for divine help (prayer) and momentary relief (play). Sensōji culture capitalized on these solitary urban crowds.

Contributing to the formation of a favorable social environment for Sensōji culture in late Tokugawa Edo society were three factors that led to the decline of the machi-based community. First, the increasing number of rental houses, or *kakae yashiki* (embraced estates), and tenants lessened the sociopolitical importance of owners-occupants (*iemochi* [those who own houses]), who had previously dominated the machi community. Second, the growing dominance of monopolistic chartered trade associations (*kabu nakama*) among powerful merchants weakened the business of independent machi-based petty merchants and facilitated their conversion into urban lower classes. Third, the rise of guild-like interest groups (*kaisho*), which instilled private entrepreneurship, had a negative influence on the conventional administrative affairs of the machi community. All in all, with the gradual collapse of the machi-based community, Edo society deviated more and more from the bakuhan's ideal social order. The shōgunate (*baku*) wanted to maintain autonomous, self-supporting local units (*han*) individually responsible for securing communal order. But this social design was destabilized by the gradual dissolution of its very foundation—the machi community. This trend worried bakufu leaders even as it aided Sensōji culture.

Amid growing concern about this trend, Matsudaira Sadanobu launched the Kansei Reforms in order to rebuild the crumbling social structure of Edo, and one of his key goals was to restore bakuhan order to the declining machi community. To that end, his administration disbanded a number of kabu nakama and kaisho organizations, imposed feudalistic urban policies on machi residents, and tried to strengthen the unity of the machi community.[9] These reactionary efforts seemed to be successful in the short run, but in the long run they could not stem the irreversible trends in Edo society.[10] The changes Edo society was experiencing were a menace to the social-engineering policies of the shōgunate but not to the Sensōji culture of prayer and play. Here we need to examine more closely the way in which the declining machi community of Edo society offered a favorable environment for Sensōji culture.

The machi community of seventeenth-century Edo was not so different from the one found in Kyoto. Each machi formed a geographically demarcated administrative unit and served as the most basic local community. Residents were expected not only to achieve mutual trust and social order among themselves but also to protect their properties collectively. Most households in the machi community possessed their own land and house, and all these homeowners (iemochi) participated in machi affairs as equals. When iemochi formed a majority, peace and harmony prevailed in the machi community, the spirit of communal solidarity and self-government (*kyōdōtai ishiki*) was attentively protected, and individual residents were expected to attend to communal interests before private interests.[11] The shōgunate embraced these principles and incorporated them into its own bakuhan order.[12]

The ideal self-governing system of the machi community, administered by the machi head (*nanushi*) in collaboration with iemochi residents, however, largely evaporated in the late Tokugawa period. As Yoshida Nobuyuki notes, the structure of Edo machi communities in the nineteenth century virtually eliminated the domination of iemochi. According to him, the commoner population of Edo in 1853 was a bit more than half a million, and the number of households was approximately 140,000. Among these households were only 13,822 iemochi—less than 10 percent of all households. Even the figure of 10 percent cannot serve as an index of the actual number of owner-occupants, because it included many absentee landlords who owned more than one dwelling. For instance, the Mitsui Echigo-ya alone owned ninety-two housing units in the city. It is estimated that fewer than 3 percent of Edo commoners were actual owner-occupants.[13] Kōji-machi Jū'ni-chōme, a typical downtown Edo ward, exemplifies the extent of structural changes in Edo machi communities by the late Tokugawa period. Among its 145 households in 1865 were three iemochi households, seventy-six land-tenant (*chigari*) households, and sixty-six house-tenant (*tanagari*) households. The iemochi households amounted to a mere 2 percent of the total number of households.[14]

These statistics suggest that, by the late Tokugawa period, the vast majority of Edo commoners were not landlords or homeowners but tenants, a total reverse of the early seventeenth-century situation. The drastic drop in the number of iemochi residents was, in fact, the result of a steady social change set in motion in the late seventeenth century when large-scale capitalists and great merchants made their way into the world of Edo commerce. From the beginning, these wealthy outsiders were eager to purchase property, for real estate, particularly land, was considered to be the safest and most lucrative investment. Surplus capital flowed into the real estate market, and great merchant families aggressively bought up real estate to rent commercially (*kakae yashiki*). In order to manage these properties, landlords hired salaried house managers, or *yamori* (house-keepers), who collected rent from tenants and handled property-related matters. The growth in the number of absentee landlords and, as a result, the rise of tenancy in Edo seem to have manifested the expansion of the urban commercial economy.

But the shrinking number of iemochi was not simply a reflection of economic change. Ironically enough, the bakufu, who favored a machi community based on iemochi, facilitated its demise. In 1690 the city magistrate summoned Edo's money-changers and asked if they would be willing to help the bakufu treasury by arranging for transfers of funds that would circumvent the procedures for the remittance of tax revenues and governmental disbursements then in operation. At that time, the usual procedure for handling the bakufu's tax revenues, which were collected in rice, was quite cumbersome: the rice was sold for cash (silver currency) in Osaka, the cash was shipped on horseback to Edo, the silver cash was exchanged in Edo for gold specie through the banking service provided by money-changers, and it was then deposited in the bakufu treasury. Conversely, when the shōgunal government purchased goods in

Osaka or Kyoto, the money to pay for the goods had to be shipped back to Osaka or Kyoto. Transporting cash back and forth between Edo and the Kansai region, which were hundreds of miles apart, was costly, onerous, and risky. In contrast, money-changers had already developed a safe and economic means of transferring funds between Edo and Osaka or Kyoto. For example, upon receiving goods from an Osaka supplier, an Edo wholesaler who used such a service would pay an Edo money-changer (i.e., a bank) and receive in return an exchange note (*kawase tegata*); the Edo wholesaler would send this to the Osaka supplier by express messengers (*hikyaku*); the Osaka supplier would then present the note to the Osaka branch office of the money-changer and cash it.[15] Many daimyō, who had to sell rice taxes for cash in Osaka, were already taking advantage of this banking service.

Responding to the bakufu request, twelve money-changers expressed their intention to provide the shōgunal treasury with the "public" service (*goyō*) of money transfer. The next year, 1691, the shōgunate appointed all twelve as shōgunal bankers on three conditions: (1) that within sixty days of having received the silver money from the bakufu revenues in Osaka, they deliver an equivalent value in gold pieces to the bakufu treasury; (2) that they process the exchange of silver and gold in Osaka before transferring the funds to Edo; and (3) that they put up real estate (*yashiki*) to the bakufu as collateral. Bakufu officials emphasized that delays in the delivery of funds would result in the confiscation of the collateral as well as punishment of those in arrears. In return for allowing a delivery period of sixty days, which was soon extended to ninety days, the bakufu exempted itself from service fees. This period of time was considered quite generous, for money-changers usually needed only ten days or so to complete a transaction between Osaka and Edo. During the remaining time, they could lend the "public" monies under shōgunal sanction.[16] It was an enormously lucrative enterprise that guaranteed profits, for debtors would not dare to default on loans that were eventually to be returned to the shōgunal treasury. Most of the profits from this business were invested in the Edo real estate market. Initially, this was to meet the bakufu's third condition about using real estate as collateral. But once the money-changers found real estate to be a lucrative investment, they bought far more land than was necessary to meet the bakufu's original requirement.

Consider, for example, the Mitsui family, one of the most successful money-transfer establishments. The Mitsui family had accumulated hundreds of building lots and houses and even whole blocks by the early eighteenth century. By 1836 it had as many as 1,130 units of real estate holdings. Other money-changers and merchant families followed suit, shaking the social foundations of machi communities, which had depended on the strong presence of independent, single-unit iemochi residents. In order to extract profit from their accumulated lands and houses (yashiki), these absentee landlords converted residential houses into commercial buildings, built new stores on empty lots, and then rented them to now propertyless merchants and artisans. The management of their commercial real estate was delegated to hired professionals, who were given a residence and paid a salary. Most of these professional real estate managers were from outside the local community, and their presence, therefore, introduced a heterogeneous element to the conventional machi community.[17]

Over time, big stores and chains shoved aside the businesses of traditional iemochi merchants and artisans. In place of owner-occupants, tenant populations came to fill the machi community.[18] In administration as well, small-scale independent business owners, who had previously run local communities, were pushed aside as real estate managers from outside created a new social force in Edo society. One side-effect of the diminishing role of iemochi residents was that the resident community leaders who once provided free administrative services to their community were gradually replaced by salaried administrators. And outside real estate managers assumed greater responsibilities in machi affairs. In sum, the original machi residents (iemochi) lost not only their rights over land and houses but also their control of the local administrative apparatus.[19] And so it is not surprising that the communal spirit and habits of the early Tokugawa machi community, which had been based on equality of iemochi residents, had become attenuated in the late Tokugawa period.

Machi administration was, in a sense, more professionalized than before, but its public authority was enfeebled. Fluid tenants now formed the majority of residents, and under the administration of hired machi elders and officials, the once-dominant spirit of communal management gradually yielded to functional principles (*SN*, 17: 533–34, 576–79). On the whole, traditional Edo society was in dissolution, and, by extension, so was the bakuhan notion of social order. Ironically, the erosion of the iemochi-based machi community was most seriously felt in the central area of the city, the birthplace of machi communities.

The inner city was dominated by commercial estate owners, mostly great merchants and money-changers, who further proceeded to form chartered trade associations (kabu nakama) to gain a commercial monopoly. When the bakufu expanded the commercial tax base during the years of the Tanuma administration (1767–86), these chartered trade associations soon expanded to the entire city. The cash-strapped government approved the formation of monopolistic trade associations in return for contributions of hundreds of thousands of gold pieces from these associations (in the form of licensing fees [*myōgakin*] and annual taxes [*unjōkin*]). By the mid-1780s, nearly all the great merchants in Edo were organized into protective trade associations that enjoyed exclusive monopolies on the purchase and wholesale of goods and services.

There were, of course, bumpy years for these protective trade associations. Internal strife often led to disarray, constant government policy changes required continual alertness, and challenges from without posed a threat. For example, in the Bunka era (1804–17), the Ten Groups of Wholesalers (Tokumi toiya) in Edo had to deal with a challenging commercial environment.[20] In response to the increasing advance of local Kantō suppliers and merchants into the Edo markets, the Tokumi toiya association successfully persuaded the bakufu, in return for increased "donations" to the bakufu treasury, to prohibit nonmembers from purchasing and selling cotton and other commodities produced in the Kantō area. Each wholesale group acquired the rights to define the range of items within its transactional monopoly in terms of *kabu* (shares), to issue a certain number of shares, and to decide who was eligible to obtain shares and in what quantity.[21] In order to tighten the Tokumi toiya's grip on the distribution networks in the Edo markets, the representative of the association, Sugimoto Mojūrō, exercised his political strength. After having established a financial foundation in 1809, Sugimoto approached the shōgunate with the promise that he could stabilize the falling price of rice and the rising prices of other commodities. He demonstrated the goodwill of his foundation, now referred to as Sankyō kaisho (Three bridges association), by building three bridges (Eitai Bridge, Shi'nō Bridge, and Okawa Bridge) that the shōgunate could not afford to build itself. Through this sort of leverage, in 1813 Sugimoto was able to obtain shōgunal authorization to reorganize the Tokumi toiya association into a more comprehensive trade association known as Higaki kaisen zumi toiya nakama (Association of *higaki*-vessel wholesale shipping agents). In the same year, the sixty-five groups of wholesalers belonging to this newly organized association raised a donation of 10,200 gold pieces for the bakufu and, thus, secured their trade monopoly. Despite its dwindling operation after Sugimoto was expelled in 1819 for mismanagement, the Higaki kaisen association remained a dominant force, at least in the central markets of Edo, until its temporary dissolution in 1841.[22]

On the whole, trade associations and their commercial monopolies marginalized the economy of independent petty merchants and destroyed the original commercial foundation of inner-city machi communities. There were, of course, some economic trends that worked against the trade associations. The scope of inner-city markets, once so crucial to the Edo economy, was shrinking due to the city's outward expansion in the late Tokugawa period. Moreover, privileged wholesale merchants were losing market shares because of the more diversified trade activities of nonmember merchants as well as the increasing incorporation of the Kantō *jimawari* (neighboring places) economy into the Edo markets. Furthermore, these chartered wholesalers were often blamed for price gyrations, and they were even temporarily suspended by the shōgunate from 1841 until 1851.[23] Nevertheless, it is no exaggeration to say that, until the demise of the Tokugawa bakufu, these monopolistic merchants were one of the most critical factors in the transformation of the social foundation of the Edo machi communities. Exerting their influence over and beyond the conventional boundaries of machi communities, privileged trade cartels and their wholesale members destroyed the tight communal solidarity that independent petty merchants and artisans had preserved within their local community. These new economic forces drove iemochi commoners to the periphery of the city, demoted them to the status of tenants, and created a space of "absentee" power in the machi community. By the eighteenth century, iemochi residents of inner-city wards had been reduced to 10 to 20 percent of the population; a century later, they accounted for less than 5 percent.[24]

Compared with the previous population of owner-occupants, tenants, who frequently moved in and out, were not as attached to their "rented" ward. Understandably, the fluid movements of tenants caused problems in ward administration. As far as city administration was concerned, the bakufu envisioned a sort of self-government in which iemochi residents were expected to deal with affairs in their own machi (except for those related to the military and the police) in a communal manner. Under this system, an individual machi was responsible for maintaining social order within its precincts. But as the number of iemochi residents steadily decreased, various new forms of administration were created in an attempt to deal with the increasing number of tenants and unsettled lower classes.

Among these new forms of administration, associations known as kaisho (meeting places) offered makeshift solutions to the changed social structure of the machi community. For instance, professional firefighters, who formed their own kaisho organizations, began to take over the fire service during the Tanuma years. Before that, firefighting had been a communal responsibility that each machi assumed by imposing a voluntary corvée tax on each household. This system, however, faced difficulties once communal solidarity ebbed. Many households often sent children, old people, or hired laborers to perform the "communal" service of firefighting. Such fire corps were almost useless when a fire broke out. This soon prompted some entrepreneurial residents to petition the city magistrate to establish a "private" fire company made up of professional firefighters. Despite the objections of some machi officials that a commercial fire company might be untrustworthy, the government approved the establishment of fire companies in the expectation that they would lessen the enormous financial burden caused by Edo's chronic fire disasters. Professional firefighters, chosen from among a group of artisans known as "scaffolding men" (*tobi*), were organized into fire brigades, and these organized forces gradually took over firefighting in Edo.[25] In the Tenmei period (1781–88), there were eight firefighting organizations employing 200 scaffolding men in the Sensōji area alone.[26]

As the case of entrepreneurial firefighting indicates, communal management of machi affairs was increasingly being replaced with impersonalized, contract-based management. This was especially evident in regard to new tenants moving into the machi community. There was no guarantee that the new residents would pay their rent on time, share the burdens of the cost involved in dealing with machi affairs, or cause no trouble. Previously, all new tenants had to be guaranteed by relatives or friends living in the same community, and the tenant-landlord relationship was personal rather than contractual. This personal network could hardly be sustained in late Edo society, and private commercialized kaisho organizations took over the function of guaranteeing newcomers. By the late eighteenth century, dozens of newly established private insurance kaisho organizations provided new tenants, who could not find relatives or friends to sponsor them, with their service. These organizations charged fees to, and took financial responsibility for, their customers.[27] Following suit, various types of commercial kaisho organizations emerged and took hold in Edo society. Bridge kaisho took over the management of Edo bridges (which had hitherto been maintained by local wards or the shōgunate); loan kaisho started underwriting and pawning services for those who had difficulty getting loans; and sanitation kaisho took over garbage collection. All these organizations sought to capitalize on the decline of communal machi functions.

The idea of *yaku* (public duties) itself was in flux. Machi elders and officials used to provide their services for free, and machi affairs used to be dealt with through personal connections or communal collaboration. But as the principles of a money economy penetrated the community, public duty was transformed into a paid professional service, and machi elders were replaced by salaried professional administrators.[28] As with the functions of kaisho organizations and private associations, the administration of machi affairs became impersonal and was contracted out in accordance with the mechanisms of a commercial economy. Even the most basic security and safety of the machi community were delegated to professional "gatekeepers" who policed the streets as their private business. Each machi had a checkpoint (*tsujibansho*) blockaded by an entrance gate (*kido*). Kido guards were responsible for maintaining order in the community, posting shōgunal decrees or machi bylaws, taking care of people who collapsed on the street, traffic control, and watching out for thieves or intruders. All these services were once communal responsibilities. But again, with the decline of communal spirit, it became almost impossible to recruit volunteers from among residents. Machi officials had no option but to hire professional gatekeepers who worked on contract. For their part, these professional gatekeepers privatized their service into a "business right," sellable or purchasable among themselves, that was immune to the intervention of their employer—the machi community.[29] Naturally, there emerged a sort of "public service" market, within which the gatekeeping business was transacted in the form of kabu ("stocks" or "licenses"). The kabu holders of gatekeeping services did not have to be gatekeepers themselves; many of them were entrepreneurs or capitalists who managed public service businesses by hiring the actual gatekeepers or by subcontracting their rights to someone else.

In similar fashion, most of the administrative functions of the machi community were transformed into a form of private "property right." The position of yamori became transferable through commercial transactions, as did that of machi elders (nanushi). Once freed from the bondage of obligatory public service to the machi community, ward administrators, whether yamori or nanushi, formed guild-like associations of their own and promoted their "private" interests in "public" service. In short, Edo society in the late Tokugawa period commercialized Tokugawa Japan's cherished "public duties" (yaku). And in this trend, Sensōji was no exception: many of its administrative functions were delegated to private business. These functions included the maintenance of an incense-burning canopy in front of the Main Hall, a nearby water container with a fountain for washing hands, a water fountain by the Eastern Gate (the Zuijin Gate), guard boxes for the Zuijin Gate, the Niō Gate, the Kaminari Gate, a stable for "divine horses," and the Komakata Hall. The running of these auxiliary facilities was delegated to independent private contractors who received, in return, the right to collect donations from visitors. Once they obtained the right to run these facilities, the service providers could sell their contracts or bequeath them to their children (*SN*, 3: 432, 435, 555, 709–12; 14: 121, 719–22).

To be sure, the profit-seeking organizations that took over many of the administrative functions of the machi community contributed to the disintegration of status barriers in Edo society; however, at the same time they expedited the dismantling of the machi community itself.[30] All in all, such social changes posed a substantial challenge to the Tokugawa system. Social conflicts and disharmony stemming from the increasing role of kaisho and nakama organizations reached a high point in the 1770s and 1780s and finally exploded with the urban smashings of 1787. Matsudaira Sadanobu tried to reverse the trend in the 1790s by enforcing policies that would dissolve private administrative organizations and strengthen the communal bond of the community. His administration reorganized firefighting brigades, restricted chartered trade associations, and established a system for providing shelter and food to the urban poor in times of emergency.[31] Under the reform-minded shōgunate, Edo machi seemed to recover their previous solidarity.[32] This recovery, however, turned out to be short-lived and eventually succumbed to the irreversible decline of "community consciousness" (*kyōdōtai ishiki*). Edo society was fragmenting.

In addition to the transformations brought about by these socioeconomic changes, Edo society was physically in constant metamorphosis because of the frequent reconfiguration of districts themselves. The frequent fires forced machi residents who had lost their homes and/or business establishments to relocate. The impact of fires was most keenly felt in the core districts of the inner city. As Nakai Nobuhiko notes, "the central wards of Edo were destroyed by fire on the average of once every six years in the 178-year period between the middle of the seventeenth century and the 1830s."[33] Following a fire, the reorganization of a district often prevented former residents from settling in the same community. Even those able to maintain permanent residences were psychologically affected by having their neighbors constantly change. Their interactions with new neighbors were limited and, by and large, short-lived. Edo society was becoming structured in such a way that individual isolation was inevitable.

This social environment nurtured Sensōji's prayer and play culture during the late Tokugawa period. As was previously discussed, the prayer culture at Sensōji lacked strong communal elements. The major objects of worship were not the parochial deities of the Sensō Shrine—the Sanja Daigongen—who were supposed to protect the "children" of their parish. In fact, the nominal parishioners of the Sensō Shrine community tried to avoid festivals for their tutelary deities. Most of the patrons of prayer culture at Sensōji individually solicited the divine help of Buddhist and minor Shintō deities. Likewise, Sensōji's play culture was highly individualized and scattered. It was not at all like the communal play that could be found in agricultural villages or in traditional Shintō festivals. Visitors to Sensōji sought recreation and entertainment on an individual basis through the medium of commercial exchange. They formed a lonely crowd milling around in search of moments of relaxation and pleasure.

A closer examination reveals that the prayer culture of Sensōji was indeed well suited to individual religious quests. Of course, religious confraternities provided their members with opportunities for collective prayer, but their worship activities were rather sporadic. As Edo society became more fluid and diversified, people's religious attempts to deal with disease, epidemics, natural disasters, and other hardships became more individualized. A religious booklet, *Edo Shin-Butsu gankake chōhō ki* (A double precious record of wish-prayer to kami and Buddhas in Edo), published in 1814, clearly shows why prayer temples such as Sensōji were so appealing to Edoites in the early nineteenth century. The author surveyed the issues Edo people sought to solve through prayer and the deities most often entreated to help solve them. Among thirty-one cases, disease was the number-one concern (nineteen cases), followed by "general well-being" (*shogan*) (seven cases), and disasters and misfortunes (three cases). Two cases were unclassified. For help with these concerns, people turned most often to the Asakusa Kannon.

As the statistics in *Edo Shin-Butsu gankake chōhō ki* indicate, Edoites were hardly free from the peril of epidemics, which often spread after natural disasters such as floods and earthquakes.[34] In particular, smallpox epidemics, usually accompanied by measles, hit the residents of Edo hard (e.g., in 1782, 1796, 1799, 1806, 1819, and 1825–26). Epidemics and natural disasters posed a constant threat to the lives of Edoites throughout the Tokugawa period. In the early Tokugawa period, when the machi community was still solid enough, hardships in the aftermath of epidemics and disasters could be buffered by mutual assistance and relief measures. As the local community gradually disintegrated in the late Tokugawa period, however, Edoites had no option but to deal with misfortunes as isolated individuals. This situation was further aggravated by an increase in the number of urban poor, who drifted around the city. The machi community no longer provided help to lessen the pains consequent upon epidemics and disasters. Great merchant families sometimes offered relief donations to the urban poor or ran soup kitchens for the disadvantaged and street beggars. But their sympathy was usually limited to those who were somehow connected to their business or to those who belonged to the same neighborhood.[35] Government action, if any, was usually belated, and when it did occur, it often took the form of moral exhortation rather than practical action. Worse yet, the suffering urban poor were easily exploited. Kaisho organizations extended their business to the urban poor under the pretext of insuring them when they went broke, in expectation of collecting commissions once they found jobs.[36] Given this social environment, Edo residents found themselves turning to individualized prayer.

The play culture of Sensōji provided another kind of blessing for unattached Edoites. Edo was a predominantly male society with an unquenchable thirst for pleasure and entertainment. At the turn of the eighteenth century, the ratio of men to women in Edo remained at six to four in spite of a steady increase in the female population. There was clearly a structural disparity between the number of men and the number of women.[37] There are several reasons for this. First, according to one estimate made circa 1800, about 300,000 local samurai accompanied their lords back and forth between Edo and their domains, in accord with the alternating attendance system. This population of unattached males had an insatiable appetite for Edo's flourishing popular culture. Second, hundreds of large-volume stores hired great numbers of single male workers from local areas. These stores, such as Echigo-ya, Shiroki-ya, Matsusaka-ya, Takashima-ya, Kuroe-ya, Izu-kura, Echizen-ya, and Yamakata-ya, were open to males only. (Echigo-ya was the first department store in Japan to hire female employees, and this occurred only in 1904.)[38] Third, as population statistics for the mid-nineteenth century show, approximately 20 to 30 percent of Edo's commoners were migrants, and they included thousands of male laborers seeking seasonal jobs (*dekasegi*). In addition, Edo contained approximately 5,000 celibate Buddhist monks.[39]

Edo's male-dominated population was obsessed with entertainment. Its unappeasable, sometimes unruly, craving for pleasure spilled out in all directions and took in kabuki theater, prose literature, ukiyo paintings, travel, *aragoto* (rough-stuff) matsuri, and street arts. Sensōji's sakariba culture proved most attractive to these uprooted men. No class boundaries hindered one from enjoying a variety of play opportunities at Sensōji. As if enjoying single-theme ukiyo paintings piece by piece, isolated Edoites sauntered around the Sensōji sakariba in search of whatever would satisfy their craving for fun and relaxation. During the late Tokugawa period, Sensōji space offered an oasis of play in the desert of Edo.

Prayer, Play, and Edo Commoners

In the early Tokugawa period, when status dictated almost everything, hierarchical distinctions between the samurai and other classes were strictly maintained "not only in their functions, but also in the quality of their dress, food, and housing, in behavior and speech, and in intellectual and cultural activities."[40] But nothing is permanent. By the mid-eighteenth century, due to changing socioeconomic realities, Edo society had lost many of its class-bound cultural distinctions. This brought to the fore the cultural role of commoners.

To what extent did commoners play a dominant role in Sensōji culture? How did commoners come to take central stage in the realm of Edo culture in general? In understanding the socioeconomic matrix of Edo and Sensōji culture, the world of entertainment (which included brothels, theaters, teahouses, and restaurants) can serve as a guide, for it offers a clear reflection of socioeconomic change.

This was particularly evident in changes in the patronage of licensed brothel quarters. When bakufu officials allowed a ward elder, Shōji Jin'emon, to establish an enclosed brothel quarter in Yoshiwara in 1617, they assumed that its customers would be mostly samurai. The bakufu thought that the walled quarter would help control masterless samurai (*rōnin*), who often snuck into the mushrooming pleasure quarters of the city.[41] The Tokugawa campaign against the forces of Toyotomi Hideyori in 1614–15 produced tens of thousands of masterless samurai. Those who were not absorbed into the Tokugawa system posed a potential threat to its political and social stability, since they roamed around the shōgunal capital forming street gangs and bullying the local populace.[42] Initially, the Yoshiwara quarter proved to be effective in keeping unruly samurai under surveillance and in fostering "good" customs.

The Yoshiwara pleasure quarter was, however, soon transformed into a "public" place where wealthy merchants (mostly under contract to the bakufu and daimyō) were allowed to mingle with samurai officials and to entertain them with lavish parties. A few wealthy merchants even joined the pleasure culture of the samurai at Yoshiwara. Responding to the extravagant mingling of people of different status, Yoshiwara developed a sophisticated system of entertainment that was stratified by the ranks of its entertainers. In early Tokugawa Edo society, Yoshiwara led a status-conscious entertainment culture measured by money and symbolized by *tayū* (the highest rank of prostitutes). In this cultural world, tayū, who were available only to a privileged few, were viewed as the symbol of beauty, cultural cultivation, and achievement. In some cases, they were even "held up as models of womanhood for ordinary young girls because of their constancy, dignity, and generosity toward the less fortunate."[43] But this culture of Yoshiwara tayū and high-ranking entertainers gradually dwindled, after peaking in the late Kan'ei years (1624–44). This is indicated by the declining number of tayū: seventy-six in the 1640s, eighteen in the 1660s, ten in the 1730s, and two in the 1750s. After the 1750s, the culture of the tayū was a thing of the past, and its passing was the death knell of the intensely status-bound culture of early Tokugawa society. In place of tayū, the cultural enfranchisement of commoner customers brought about an upsurge of lower-class prostitutes (*tsubone*): 2,500 in the 1730s, 4,000 to 5,000 in the 1750s, 6,000 in the 1830s, and 7,200 in the 1850s.[44] The Yoshiwara entertainers of the late Tokugawa period catered to a wide range of customers and especially welcomed well-to-do commoners eager to compensate for their inferior status by spending money.

The world of Yoshiwara entertainment soon expanded beyond the confines of its walled quarters. As seen in the *karitaku* (rent-house) business at the time of disastrous fires, Yoshiwara entertainers, blind to social status and class distinction, sought a wider spectrum of commoner patronage. As I briefly discuss in Chapter 2, there were twenty official occasions, mostly during the late Tokugawa period, on which Yoshiwara entertainers conducted their business in rent-houses in the Sensōji precincts and districts.[45] Once they ventured onto Sensōji land, dozens of temporary "teahouses" (which were fronts for prostitution) were set up on the front grounds of religious halls and in empty spaces within the temple precincts (*SN*, 5: 550–53; 15: 417, 420; 16: 144). Moreover, the rent-house business in Sensōji, which, in theory, required permission from the Sensōji administration, was not limited to designated periods or places. It was not uncommon to find permanent Yoshiwara rent-houses on the Sensōji grounds at any time during the late Tokugawa period (*SN*, 6: 483; 13: 131).[46]

Combined with other illicit sex businesses conducted at teahouses, restaurants, archery booths, and toothpick shops, street prostitution contributed to a mobile pleasure culture that soon expanded into ever-wider segments of Edo society. Private brothel quarters, called *okabasho*, mushroomed all over the city between the Hōreki and the Kansei periods (1751–1800).[47] Sumō wrestling, which during the early Tokugawa period was an asobi held only at samurai residences, had, by the late Tokugawa period, become a sleazy spectacle involving half-naked women wrestling on temple grounds. Sumō misemono shows now casually catered to a popular appetite for entertainment: it was no longer a mark of cultural distinction reserved for samurai. Kanjin fund-raising shows, which used to be held for solemn purposes at shrines or temples, also became daily sideshows and could be found at any amusement center in the city. Most cultural activities that had once been symbols of privilege had trickled down to the world of commoners. All this points to the popularization of play culture in Edo society.

Clearly, in the late Tokugawa period there was an extensive popular market for cultural pastimes and commodities in Edo society. In defiance of the Confucian feudal order, commoners now emerged as major consumers in the cultural market. When seventeenth-century bakufu leaders envisioned culture, they flatly excluded commoners. In achieving the "equilibrium and harmony" of society, they assumed that the ruling (state officials) and the ruled (peasants, artisans, and merchants) should adhere strictly to their heaven-mandated places, according to hereditary privilege and duty. In this social scheme, commoners were not expected to enjoy the luxury of "idle" cultural pleasures.

To the consternation of bakufu leaders, however, during the late Tokugawa period commoners began to create and expand their own cultural spaces. According to bakufu leaders, the biggest threat to the Confucian social order, which was hierarchical and immutable, came from "profiteering merchants" who strove "to garner ill-gotten gains in mercantile activities," just like "ants racing to putrid meat."[48] Edo townspeople were indeed successful within a developing commercial economy, and the fruits of their economic labors were directed toward cultural activities. The ruling samurai class could do nothing about the economic rise of commoners. Basically, the government was unable to absorb the wealth of urban merchants through taxation, being "deterred not only by the physiocratic notions of economics but also by a lack of understanding of the new commercial processes."[49] As time progressed, the economy advanced so much as to diminish the significance of class and to level cultural distinctions between the ruling and the ruled. Some well-to-do merchants even dared adopt a lifestyle that had been the particular preserve of the upper samurai class, even as the bakufu struggled to deal with the increasing impoverishment of the samurai class in general. The trend toward the popularization of culture was not simply an ideological issue of cultural leveling; it was intimately connected with fundamental socioeconomic changes.

Nevertheless, bakufu leaders and Confucian intellectuals tended to view cultural popularization in late Tokugawa Edo as an ideological problem stemming from degradations in the status order, and they blamed that on the "ill-directed" townspeople. What they could not grasp was that socioeconomic changes were causing the impoverishment of the samurai class. The diminishing cultural influence of samurai lay with the samurai class itself, which failed to adjust itself to Edo's new commercial economy. The problem lay, above all, in the constant real income level of the samurai class amid the expanding economy. Samurai income was measured in terms of fixed amounts of rice, which by and large remained constant throughout the Tokugawa period. These fixed salaries, which had been set at an austerity level in the early Tokugawa years, could not match patterns of increasing consumption over the years and caused the decline in their cultural dominance. The cultural hegemony of the samurai was gradually replaced by the cultural hegemony of the commoners—a replacement that enlarged the economic base of Sensōji culture in the late Tokugawa period.

According to Kozo Yamamura, even many of the privileged 5,200 shōgunal hatamoto retainers did not remain untouched in their cultural pursuits by financial difficulties. The problem was that with their stagnant purchasing power they suffered in a growing commercial economy that continued to offer more and more goods and services. The situation of 17,000 shōgunal vassals (gokenin), who had much smaller salaries than did the hatamoto, was very bad; even worse off were the lesser liege vassals and foot soldiers, who totaled more than 200,000.[50] As a result, from the eighteenth century on, shōgunal samurai frequently resorted to various forms of loans in order to deal with their increasing expenditures, and this further aggravated their financial situations. Despite the bakufu's various attempts to lessen the vicious cycle of indebtedness, too many shōgunal samurai threw themselves on the mercy of commoner money-lenders. A short verse (senryū) pointedly conveyed the sentiment of an indebted shōgunal samurai: "Please share this misery with me, my dear keepers of pawnshops. You are the only ones who truly know of this pain."[51] By the Kansei years, the samurai, burdened with debts, were experiencing real poverty. This pain rippled through the entire samurai class, gradually diminishing their cultural hegemony.[52] In this context, understanding the cultural rise of commoners entails understanding the impoverishment and consequent cultural decline of the samurai class.

To begin with, the poverty of shōgunal samurai was structured by the static *kokudaka* system, which was outside the developing commercial economy. In an economy in which rice served as the basis for calculating taxes and land values, and samurai received fixed salaries in amounts of rice, rice seemed to be most responsible for samurai impoverishment. For this reason, fluctuations in the price of rice were of the utmost concern to the bakufu, for their own subsistence was closely linked to the economic power of salaried samurai. In fact, on the surface the problem in the late Tokugawa period was that the price of rice fluctuated unfavorably for the samurai class, who had to sell their rice stipends in order to purchase other daily necessities such as clothing, fuel, foods other than rice, and gifts, as well as to pay the wages of servants, to maintain their houses, and so on. While the prices of other commodities remained relatively high, the price of rice remained depressingly low, except during crop failures and famines in the early 1780s and the 1830s.[53] Understandably, bakufu leaders defined the problem as the low price of rice in comparison with the high prices of other commodities.

The indebtedness and increasing economic difficulties of shōgunal retainers and vassals, represented by an acute concern about the price of rice, posed a serious problem for the bakufu. After all, hatamoto and gokenin were the most trusted supporters of the Tokugawa regime, and their well-being was a barometer of the competence and virtue of shōgunal rule. On top of the chronic deficits in the shōgunal treasury (in the early seventeenth century, over half a million gold pieces annually), in the early nineteenth century the impoverishment of shōgunal retainers and vassals emerged as a political liability for the bakufu, which had to depend on their military capacity to protect itself. As their economic predicament persisted, the morale of the hatamoto and gokenin ebbed to such a low level that bakufu leaders were compelled to take steps to alleviate their economic difficulties. But the trouble did not stop with shōgunal retainers and vassals.

Japan's entire samurai class, including daimyō and their local retainers and vassals, faced similar financial pinches. The economic foundation on which they laid claim to status and privilege was beginning to crumble. The samurai class was finding it increasingly difficult to milk the resources of its agricultural domains, which were developing a strong tendency toward peasant uprisings. Many daimyō were deeply indebted, and their local administrations struggled to find revenues to reduce their budget shortfalls. In this financial situation, it was impossible to save their retainers and vassals. There are some telling examples of the seriousness of the problem. The Satsuma domain, one of the most powerful, had accumulated a debt of five million gold pieces by 1831—an amount so large that the domain had given up trying to eliminate it. Satsuma leaders took radical measures, including the unilateral repudiation of all debts owed to local merchants (300,000 kan of silver) and a rescheduling of payments to merchants in Osaka and Edo over a period of 250 years. The

Chōshū domain's debts were equal to twenty years' worth of domain income. "In the case of Saga, the domain authorities magnanimously offered to settle with one of their Edo creditors, provided he was willing to accept just 20 percent of the principal."[54] Some domains defaulted on their debts, and others offered the samurai status to merchant financiers in return for professional assistance. All kinds of unconventional methods were devised to extract more tax revenues, and these invited protests, noncooperation, and violent confrontation. No matter what the daimyō did, most local governments were headed for financial disaster. Amid the insolvency stemming from huge debts, low-level samurai were often threatened with salary cuts and changes in sumptuary regulations. Under such circumstances, it was ludicrous to expect the samurai class to maintain high morale and dignity, not to mention its exclusive claim to status-specific cultural pursuits.

Moreover, the economic hardship that deprived the samurai class of its cultural distinction called into question the bakuhan system itself. In the late 1830s, as local governments began to devote their full attention to solving their fiscal problems, many domains were pitted against each other, and sometimes against the bakufu, in a race to gain a monopoly over the rights to produce and sell local products. This trend outlived reform efforts and, by the mid-1860s, had shattered the governing structure of the bakuhan system.[55] The growing fiscal liability of the samurai class that accompanied these socioeconomic changes had far-reaching ramifications for almost every aspect of Tokugawa Japan.

Bakufu leaders scrambled to find ways to rescue the troubled samurai class. Because of the deficits experienced by the bakufu itself, bailing out insolvent samurai retainers and vassals was not an option; instead, in the belief that a strong shōgunal treasury would provide room for easing the financial difficulties of the samurai class, the bakufu sought to fill its own coffers by expanding its revenue base and tightening its budgetary expenditures. The bakufu implemented measures designed to maximize the existing resource base. These included the reuse of construction lumber, the use of night soil as fertilizer, new agricultural techniques, measures to improve labor efficiency, the further development of natural resources, and even territorial expansion into Hokkaidō.[56] None of these measures was, however, effective. In earlier years, the Tanuma administration had tapped the merchant community and collected licensing fees and special taxes from chartered trade associations and issued new coinage and paper money in order to pocket the difference in value resulting from currency debasement. These commercial fiscal policies proved to be both short-lived and destructive. The bakufu also made a strenuous effort to decrease expenditures on an ongoing basis, including cutting or withholding vassals' salaries and economizing on government operations.[57] These austerities further exacerbated the declining morale of the samurai.

Through trial and error in their efforts to address the financial problems of the samurai class, bakufu leaders learned to pay close attention to price changes at the micro-economic level. In their understanding, fluctuations in the price of goods and services were causing the deterioration of samurai purchasing power. To preserve a sociopolitical structure that would ensure the privileges of the samurai and their cultural distinction, it was essential to have an economic system insulated from change. The ideal economic system should guarantee the purchasing power of samurai by providing a bottom limit on the price of rice.[58] Whenever economic problems became pressing, Tokugawa leaders and Confucian intellectuals persistently resorted to rice-based economic measures designed to boost the well-being of the samurai class. Such economic measures were, however, unsuccessful in late Tokugawa Japan. The samurai class continued to be mired in financial difficulties and, as a result, continued to lose its cultural clout. The failure of a rice economy meant the failure of the samurai class and the diminishing of their cultural hegemony. Put another way, fluctuations in the price of rice led to the proliferation of popular culture in Edo society.

What happened to the rice-based economy in Edo society? Did the failure of the ideal Tokugawa economic system help the popular culture of prayer and play at Sensōji? To understand the dynamics of Sensōji culture in the larger socioeconomic context, we need to examine the structural limitations of the rice-based economy in some detail.

In *Keizai roku* (An account of political economy), Dazai Shundai (1680–1747), a Confucian political economist, spelled out the ideal economic system for the samurai class. He observed that the trend toward a monetarized economy, with gold and silver as the basis for all economic transactions, was irreversible. Moreover, Edo had already become the commercial center of the nation, where everyone, including the daimyō, lived like sojourners. Within this fluid environment, the only way to preserve the economic privileges of the samurai class, Shundai argued, was to maintain the price of rice at a high level. His logic was rather simple: because the samurai have to sell their rice stipends to buy goods and services, their purchasing power would increase as the price of rice went up, to the eventual benefit of merchants and artisans; if the price of rice went down, the samurai would suffer from a decline in their purchasing power, and this would in turn harm the merchant and artisan classes, who would have fewer customers. Dazai Shundai argued that the price of rice should be set at a high level in expectation of this trickle-down effect. As an example to support his argument, he cited the economic prosperity between the Genroku (1688–1703) and early Kyōhō (1716–35) years, when the price of rice had been maintained at a high level and the economic activities of the four classes had expanded.[59] Dazai Shundai was enthusiastic about his samurai-centered economic theory: if the samurai were better off, then money would circulate better, and as a result, commerce would be stimulated, benefiting merchants, artisans, and farmers. This trickle-down view of economics was the standard view of bakufu leaders and Confucian intellectuals.[60]

Whenever the price of rice fell and the samurai suffered in the late Tokugawa period, bakufu leaders put into practice the rice-centered economic theory of Dazai Shundai. They were, of course, aware that many factors drove down the price of rice: good harvests, increases in rice production due to land reclamation, the forced selling-off of rice by daimyō and shōgunal vassals to pay back their debts, and so on. No matter what factors were responsible, however, the bakufu leaders usually tried to influence the price of rice either through monetary measures or by manipulating the rice supply. In most cases, however much sense the bakufu analysis made on paper, it did not work in practice. Price fluctuations, including those in rice prices, were much more complex than bakufu officials tended to think, particularly when the price of rice fell relative to the prices of other commodities.

In the Kansei years (1789–1800), for instance, the price of rice dropped, but other prices did not. This caused tremendous stress for the bakufu, which had just launched the Kansei Reforms in order to restore the financial strength of the samurai class. As an emergency measure to rescue shōgunal retainers and vassals from rampant bankruptcy, in 1789 the bakufu issued an edict unilaterally canceling debts. The terms of this cancellation were draconian: all debts and accumulated interest six years old or older were canceled; debts that had been assumed within the past five years were to be paid back along with interest calculated at the rate of 6 percent per year; and the interest rates for new loans was at 12 percent per year. Shōgunal hatamoto and gokenin cheered in unison for the measures put forward by Matsudaira Sadanobu. But their jubilation did not last long, for Edo rice dealers (*fudasashi*), who lost 1,187,000 gold pieces overnight, began to find ways to retaliate. They refused to provide new loans to those who took full advantage of the cancellation order. Some heavily indebted shōgunal samurai went bankrupt and even resorted to robbery or theft.[61] In 1790 the bakufu directed merchants to lower the prices of goods other than rice so as to offset the slump in rice prices, and they gathered statistics on these price changes in order to figure out what caused them. Thereafter, the bakufu carefully scrutinized price movements on a yearly basis. The next year the price of rice improved a bit, but this did not last long.

Despite repeated threats by the authorities, who ignored the mechanisms of the commercial market, wholesalers and retailers usually outmaneuvered bakufu officials. In 1791, chartered trade associations enticed bakufu officials with the suggestion that they would lower the prices of goods by 7 percent and, thereafter, by another 20 percent if the bakufu would allow them to exercise monopoly rights over the supply and sale of certain major commodities.[62] The bakufu accepted their suggestion, but the outcome was not satisfactory. In the ongoing price wars during the 1790s, merchants usually outsmarted bakufu officials.[63]

The economy of the first decade of the nineteenth century was again haunted by the steady decline in rice prices relative to the prices of other goods and services. The average price of rice in the Kansei years was 60 monme or more per koku, but it plunged to 55 monme in 1803 and to 50 monme in 1804. On the other hand, the stock of rice in Osaka grew steadily, from 2.36 million *hyō* in 1803 to 2.60 million hyō in 1806 to 3.42 million hyō in 1812, which put additional downward pressure on the price of rice. The policy of currency debasement that the bakufu implemented in the late 1810s in order to halt deteriorations in the fiscal situation helped to push up the price of rice and netted the bakufu treasury an income of 5.57 million gold pieces by 1835. But the benefits of the debasement policy did not come free: the excessive supply of currency pushed the prices of other goods and services even further above the price of rice.[64] The bakufu could neither understand nor overcome inflation. When irritated by the puzzle of unfathomable price fluctuations, the bakufu wielded its heirloom sword—the issuance of edicts and exhortations—which proved to be too obsolete and too irrelevant for an advanced market economy. Frustrated Confucian political economists sometimes echoed the unrealistic recommendations of Ogyū Sorai, who believed that samurai should be transferred from cities back to the land so that they could exercise direct control over rice crops.[65] Despite the bakufu's manipulative efforts, the price of rice was never stabilized in favor of the samurai, and price fluctuations persisted throughout the late Tokugawa period. On the surface, it seemed that "the complexity of the money system, mutual incompatibility among Edo's monetary goals, and political barriers that obstructed movement of goods undercut policy effectiveness."[66] But the real obstacle was more fundamental and structural: the late Tokugawa economy was progressing in a direction that was no longer compatible with the assumptions of feudalistic trickle-down theory.

Simply put, the Edo economy was no longer a surrogate samurai economy. The advanced commercial economy of late Tokugawa Japan far exceeded the size at which it could be arbitrarily manipulated for the benefit of a tiny segment of society (the samurai class constituted approximately 6 percent of the nation's population). It is true that the ruling minority expropriated half the land's agricultural bounty, but the nation's market economy was interested in more than that. As far as trade was concerned, value-added products, whether processed, handcrafted, or manufactured, were gaining in volume as well as in value. With the development of nationwide trade networks centering around Edo and the Kantō region, Edo commoners were being incorporated into the growing processing, manufacturing, shipping, unloading, transporting, advertising, and selling sectors. Combined with the burgeoning of street markets and entertainment enterprises, these new market forces helped transform Edo commoners into major consumers. Thus, it is no wonder that trickle-down policy measures focused on the well-being of the samurai class could not produce the desired effects.

Too many samurai in the late Tokugawa period lost not only their financial vigor but also their moral and cultural strength. As Buyō Inshi lamented in his *Seji kenbun roku*, many samurai "are making a living by borrowing [money] from townspeople throughout the year; on the surface, they have high [status] name, but in practice they have lost it; if they cut themselves off from the favor of townspeople, they perhaps will not be able to manage even a single day." Buyō Inshi concluded, "In a real sense, eight or nine out of ten samurai are not samurai. . . . The way of martial arts has diminished as much as seventy to eighty percent, and now only twenty to thirty percent of it remains."[67] Edo commoners filled in the economic vacuum left by the impoverished samurai and further expanded their market power. The fiscal power of well-to-do merchants, for example, represented by the Asakusa Kuramae rice dealers known as the eighteen *daitsū* (great masters), was great enough to dwarf the status of samurai rulers.

As time progressed, the class lines between samurai and commoners blurred so much that there emerged a sort of middle stratum, within which the lower samurai and upper commoners merged and exhibited one cultural orientation.[68] As a bakufu official observed in 1802, samurai and commoners came to share the same space in the realm of popular culture.

> The samisen became extremely popular during the 1740s-60s. Eldest sons of good samurai families and even other sons all took lessons; from morn till night samisen sounds were always to be heard. Eventually they began to perform other Kabuki music and full dramas etc., and followed this depravity to the extent of performing amateur Kabuki plays in residences. High hatamoto officials mimicking riverbed beggars (actors), aping female impersonators and stage heroes![69]

In late Tokugawa Edo society, hereditary status distinctions gradually lost their past rigidity. The cultural space of commoners was enlarged, and that of samurai was diminished. Edo commoners emerged as the major force behind Edo culture.

The prayer and play culture of Sensōji succinctly illustrates the central role of commoners in late Tokugawa culture. Sensōji had been a privileged prayer hall and had depended on the support of shōgunal and other prominent samurai families. By the late seventeenth century, the financial support of these elite samurai families had faded away and was replaced by that of commoners (who offered casual alms and donations). The reconstruction of the Kaminari Gate (see Fig. 12) demonstrates the shifting socioeconomic base of Sensōji culture. During the Tokugawa period, the Kaminari Gate was demolished by fire three times—in 1642, 1767, and 1865. When it was burned down in 1642, the Sensōji administration threw itself on the mercy of the shōgunal family. Responding to Sensōji's request, in 1650 Shōgun Iemitsu paid for the rebuilding of the main entrance gate—a total of 457 gold pieces.[70] At this time, the Sensōji administration did not have to turn to commoners for help.

More than a century later, in 1767, when the gate was destroyed for the second time, the situation was quite different. The shōgunal family was already dissociated from Sensōji, and other samurai patrons were not in a position to make the hefty donations needed for its reconstruction. The Sensōji administration appealed to the bakufu for financial help three times over a space of more than two decades, but to no avail. In 1783, nine commoner followers of the Asakusa Kannon—including a landlord; a builder; and owners of such businesses as pawnshops, lumber stores, a dry goods store, and a pharmacy—approached Sensōji officials and said that they would raise 2,000 gold pieces to rebuild the gate (*SN*, 4: 761–72). Although their overly ambitious suggestion did not materialize, thereafter many other lay followers pledged special donations out of their veneration for the Asakusa Kannon. As the devastating Tenmei famines, which had started in 1781, lingered on into 1788, Edo people began to heed the folk notion that the famines were caused by the anger of a pair of Sensōji guardian deities (thunder and wind deities) who had been housed in the Kaminari Gate.[71] The Sensōji administration aggressively sought ways to reconstruct the gate and finally came up with a plan. The bakufu eventually responded with a special grant of 50 silver pieces, and a commoner donated 100 gold pieces in 1793 (*SN*, 7: 17, 153). The next year the Sensōji administration took a loan of 500 gold pieces from a moneylender (*SN*, 7: 226) and solicited bids for the reconstruction. Although some troubles occurred during the bidding competition as well as at the start of construction, the Kaminari Gate project somehow began on schedule. The biggest problem was raising funds to pay for the skyrocketing construction costs of more than 2,000 gold pieces. This was an enormous amount of money, but the enthusiastic financial and moral support of commoner patrons was unprecedented. Confraternity members installed special donation boxes at key points throughout Sensōji and appealed to patrons and visitors (*SN*, 7: 292–93). A group of monzen merchants donated to Sensōji a business location worth 450 gold pieces, which would generate significant rent income (*SN*, 7: 410–11). The Sensōji administration held a special kaichō, during which laypeople and confraternity members demonstrated devout support and cooperation, in order to raise additional funds. Donations of small amounts of money and offerings such as lanterns and stupas flooded in, and all of it contributed to the project's successful completion in 1795. This remarkable achievement was made possible by the commoner faithful, not by the samurai.

Commoners were indeed a dominant force in the prayer culture of Sensōji during the late Tokugawa period. From humble crowds of worshippers to prominent merchants and moneylenders, financial contributions stretched from saisen offerings to designated donations, mostly made in the name of the Asakusa Kannon. For example, the head of the Three Bridges Association, Sugimoto Mojūrō, made a *kagura* (Shintō dance) offering to the Sanja Daigongen in 1810 in order to pray for the prosperity of his business organization, and in the following year he again offered a special prayer that combined kagura and *goma* (an esoteric prayer that features the burning of pieces of sumac trees) offerings (*SN*, 12: 6–7, 343). A group of commoner patrons approached the Sensōji administration in 1816 with an offer to pave the pathway between the Kaminari Gate and the Main Hall with stones (this path turned into a muddy lane on rainy days). A year later, this project was successfully completed with a collective donation of 300 gold pieces and the full collaboration of the Sensōji administration (*SN*, 13: 168, 190, 201, 543). Three years later, in 1820, a group of monzen residents and merchants made an additional donation to repave the stone path between the Niō Gate and the Main Hall (*SN*, 14: 483, 486, 561). In 1826, three commoners even

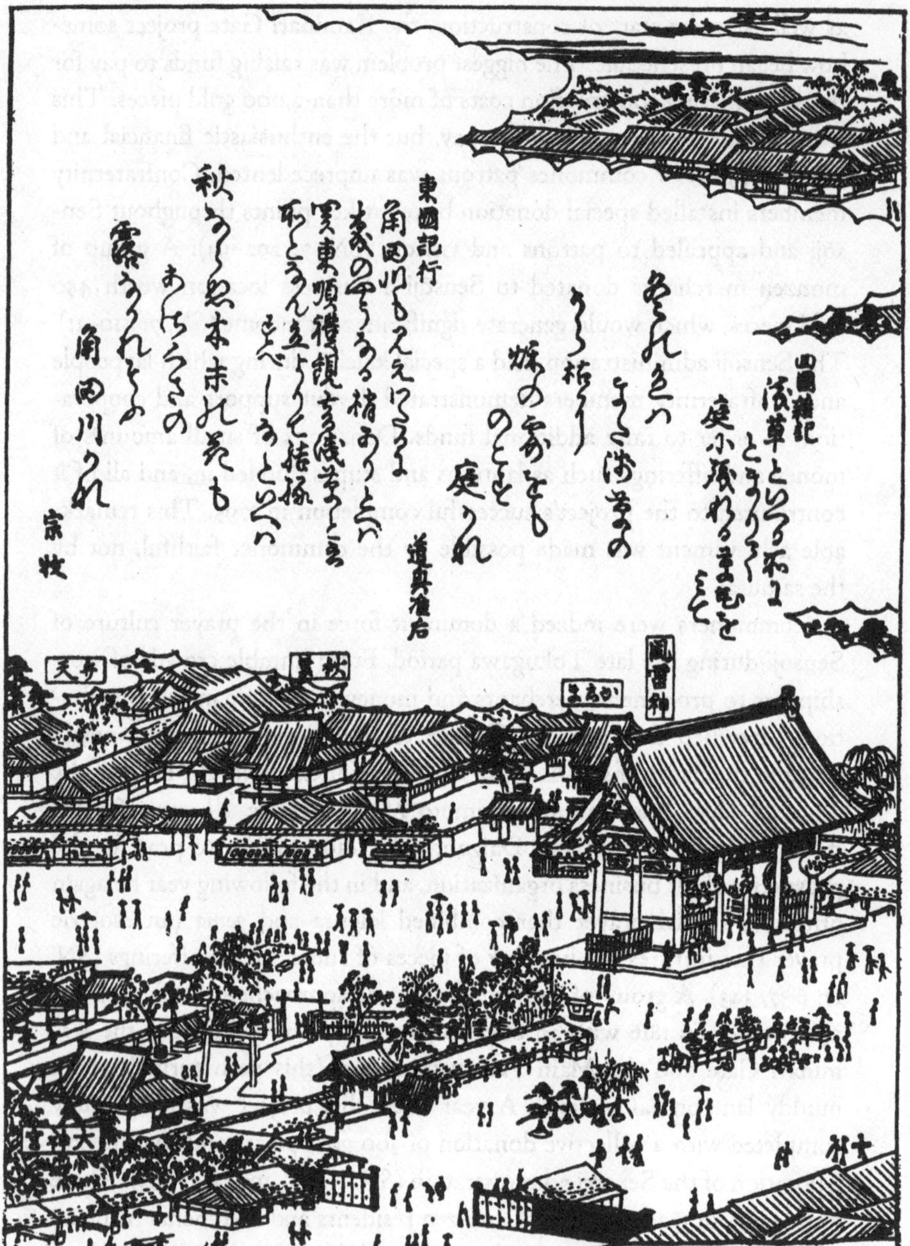

Fig. 12. A scene at Sensōji featuring the Kaminari Gate (from Saitō Gesshin, *Edo meisho zue*).

金龍山浅草寺全圖
共五枚
隅田川
花川戸

donated a sacred horse along with 300 copper coins. This was considered quite exceptional during a period in which offerings of *ema* (horse paintings), not real horses, were the norm (*SN*, 16: 462–63). Large sums of cash donations from commoners were not unusual. Wealthy confraternity members often made, collectively or individually, cash donations of tens or even hundreds of gold pieces—donations that were usually completed in multiple installments over a period of one to five years.

Even commoners of the lowest social classes patronized Sensōji. A good example of this is the devoted support of Yoshiwara prostitutes and pimps. A Yoshiwara brothel manager named Iyo donated a Kannon statue in 1797 (*SN*, 8: 46). She wished to offer a bronze lantern in 1804, but the bakufu blocked the donation on the grounds of sumptuary regulations (*SN*, 10: 382, 398, 402–3, 423). Many Yoshiwara prostitutes were faithful followers of the Asakusa Kannon, and their votive offerings ranged from stone lanterns and stupas to ema. Confraternity members, monzen merchants, and residents also offered generous donations, such as endowments for lantern oil, funds for repairing or constructing buildings and religious structures, lanterns, stupas, and sundry other items. Edo residents in general were not sparing in their generosity to Sensōji. Two merchant brothers donated a set of implements for the tea ceremony along with ten gold pieces in 1813, and the Echigo-ya store presented a decorative canopy for the central altar of the Main Hall in 1814 (*SN*, 12: 526, 640). Innumerable cases in the Sensōji diaries tell of the unwavering support and involvement of commoners in the religious culture of Sensōji. This, of course, does not mean that samurai simply vanished from the scene of Sensōji prayer culture. There were still some devoted samurai patrons, but as far as Sensōji was concerned, their support no longer compared with that of the commoners.

By the same token, the play culture of Sensōji in the late Tokugawa period also belonged to the commoners. They were both the producers and the consumers of play culture. The dominance of Edo commoners in the play culture of Sensōji reflects the late Tokugawa spirit of play, which manifested itself in the fashion for learning, reading, recreation, and entertainment among townspeople. Shikitei Sanba (1776–1822), in his *Ukiyo buro* (The bathhouse of the floating world), depicts the popular cultural fashion by looking at the daily lives of young commoner girls.[72]

A conversation between two ten- or eleven-year-old girls, Omaru and Okado, is revealing. Okado complains:

> Listen, [Omaru]. As soon as I get up in the morning, I should go to the terakoya and arrange the seats [for the day], and then I should go to the samisen teacher and practice playing samisen. Upon returning home and having breakfast, I should go from a dancing lesson to the terakoya, and then return around two o'clock in the afternoon. And then I take a bath at the public bathhouse, and without a break, go to the koto ("a Japanese harp") teacher. Upon returning home, I should practice playing samisen or dancing. I can play a little [until the sunset]. When it gets dark, I will again practice playing the koto.[73]

Edo mothers may have pushed their daughters too much with regard to taking private art lessons and reading and writing classes. Young girls who had been exposed to the arts and "polite accomplishments" would certainly have a better chance of marrying men of samurai stock or of rich merchant families, or of entering the service of an upper-class family. Enhanced social mobility aside, however, this fanatic fashion for cultural education speaks to the level of cultural activity in Edo at this time. The enjoyment of arts, music, and other pastimes was no longer the monopoly of the samurai class.

Cultural activities indeed became an integral part of the daily lives of commoners in the late Tokugawa period. In the publishing world, for example, from 1775 to 1806 more than 2,000 kibyōshi titles were published, and each usually sold as many as 10,000, or sometimes 15,000 to 17,000, copies. In addition to kibyōshi, there were *gōkan* (bound-together volumes), *sharebon* (witty books), *kokkeibon* (humorous books), and *ninjōbon* (books about human feelings). All these fictional works enjoyed a tremendous popularity, and the market for popular novels in Edo was huge. Those who could not afford to purchase original copies could borrow them, for a period of fifteen days to a month, from book-lending stores, which prospered all over the city. By 1808 there were 656 such stores, and their number had increased to approximately 800 by the 1830s. Since each store served around 50 households on average, approximately 40,000 households regularly patronized these stores.[74] Among many publications, a guidebook to the Yoshiwara pleasure quarters, *Yoshiwara saiken* (A close look at Yoshiwara), was probably the most popular. This guidebook, which first appeared during the Hōreki years (1751–63), was a sort of perennial underground bestseller among male commoners, now the major patrons of the Yoshiwara.[75] The vibrant mass market for cultural commodities, which included kabuki theater, ukiyo prints, *haikai*, tourism, street arts, and mass entertainment, testified to the ascent of commoners in the cultural world of Edo.

In this cultural milieu, Sensōji offered abundant opportunities for play to Edo townspeople. As one of the most popular amusement centers in Edo, Sensōji was a cultural melting pot for mass entertainment. Its street markets attracted urban crowds of old, young, men, women, merchants, laborers, itinerants, peddlers, and others. Other major amusement centers in the city also took advantage of the social ascension of commoners. The original inner-city regions of Edo had, with the decline of the samurai, lost much of their previous cultural vitality. Now, areas along the city boundaries, which before had scarcely been populated, were becoming vibrant and energetic as the inner-city economy steadily expanded outward during the late Tokugawa period.

In retrospect, when procurement merchants or quartermasters functioned as official suppliers for the bakufu and daimyō, the central area of Edo was an area of economic prosperity. Responding to the high demands of privileged samurai families and government offices, merchant-financiers and specialized wholesalers concentrated in this area, collectively known as the Hon-chō neighborhood (Hon-chō 1 and 2 chōme, Ōdenma-chō, Minamidenma-chō, and Kodenma-chō). But with the steady downturn in samurai consumer markets, the Mitsui store, for example, moved its major branch from Hon-chō to Suruga-chō, on the eastern boundary of the inner city. After the move, in 1683 the Mitsui store introduced new methods of doing business—cash sales at cheap prices for the emerging mass market.[76] By the Kyōhō era, the business of cloth stores in the Hon-chō area had drastically dropped off, and by the 1820s it had almost disappeared.[77] *Edo kaimono hitori annai* (A guide to shopping in Edo), published in 1824, introduces fifty-eight cloth stores in Edo. In their early stages, all these stores had been located in Hon-chō 1 and 2 chōme, but by the time this guidebook came out, none of them was there.[78] Business centers were dispersed from the inner city to the outer city in the search for commoner consumers. The Sensōji area was one of the places to which they came.

Although commoners emerged as the major socioeconomic foundation of Sensōji culture in the late Tokugawa period, this does not mean that they formed a homogeneous class. The Confucian class category of urban commoners, which encompassed artisans (*kō*) and merchants (*shō*), is too vague to capture the diverse roles played by commoners in Sensōji culture. In order to better understand the dynamics of Sensōji culture, we need to examine how and in what manner Edo commoners were involved in it.

The Culture of Prayer and Play and the Edo Economy

The power of Sugimoto Mojūrō, a flamboyant patron of Sensōji, collapsed in 1819. For some years he had been instrumental in suppressing inflationary fluctuations in commodity prices. But the bakufu abruptly abandoned him when he failed to mobilize the members of his Three Bridges Association to maintain the high price of rice.[79] Although a powerful tycoon, Sugimoto was not immune to the bakufu's whimsical politics. Powerful rice dealers as well at Asakusa Kuramae had to keep a low profile in the early nineteenth century, even after they recovered from the debt cancellation edict of 1789. No doubt, privileged merchants played a vital role in promoting the popular culture of late Tokugawa Edo, but they also fell easy prey to bakufu scapegoating. Given this fact, the power of the upper levels of townspeople over the world of Edo culture remained sporadic throughout the late Tokugawa period. Those who steadily nurtured Edo culture were the lower layers of society.

As part of the Edo milieu, the prayer and play culture of Sensōji could not prosper without the wider socioeconomic involvement of commoners. The lower stratum of commoners living in the Sensōji area was especially indispensable to its culture. Unlike visitors to Sensōji who occasionally gave alms and played the passive role of consumers, these people in the low social stratum were more directly involved in Sensōji's world.

In fact, for the lower classes of Edo, the ever-proliferating popular culture was more than a mere object of enjoyment—it was a source of livelihood, as can be seen in the close association between the two in the bakufu's policy on popular culture. For example, as a part of the Kansei Reforms, in 1787 the bakufu imposed strict sumptuary regulations on the populace for three years in an attempt to encourage frugality in private life and austerity in public expenditures. Understandably, the primary targets of this sumptuary policy were the inhabitants of Edo, who were, in the view of bakufu leaders, tainted by a corrupt urban lifestyle full of excessive material desires and disorderly cultural pursuits.[80] In 1788 the bakufu police rounded up street gangs and clamped down on irregular and unlicensed prostitution. In 1794, when the sumptuary law was extended for ten more years, the bakufu issued a torrent of moral injunctions and frugality measures (including a ban on sumptuous Shintō festivals and Buddhist rituals). In response to the bakufu's sumptuary edicts, the Sensōji administration repeatedly admonished its monks and monzen residents to refrain from lavish gift-exchanges and spending. When, in 1811, the bakufu insisted that all expenditures be minimized, the Sensōji's head administrator indicated what should be done at Sensōji and its monzen districts. Among other things, he forbade building repairs or reconstruction; enjoined against accepting donations during sumptuary years; restricted the purchase of ritual implements, whether Shintō or Buddhist; and prohibited the purchase of new ritual robes (*SN*, 12: 278–79).[81] Along with edicts banning prostitution, pornography, gambling, alcohol, and entertainments, the bakufu reintroduced its sumptuary regulations whenever social order or moral health was called into question—in 1818, 1820, 1823, 1828, and so on, with terms of three, five, seven, or ten years. The Tenpō Reforms of 1841 were nothing but a rehash of the bakufu's lingering concern with the moral health of the Tokugawa social order. In the 1840s, the bakufu even forbade "decorations at the Tanabata festival, elaborate hats and kites, costly children's toys, certain brands of fireworks, sumptuous clothing, gourmet specialties, and expensive houses and garden furnishings (including lanterns, basins, and trees)."[82]

But no matter how seriously the bakufu considered the matter of social order or moral health, it had to implement sumptuary measures with discretion lest it invoke urban riots. As Tōyama Kagemoto (1793–1855), a celebrated city magistrate during the years 1840–43 and 1845–52, correctly pointed out, sumptuary measures always backfired (in the form of economic recession) when they too rigidly limited popular culture. Citing past experiences, he opposed the hard-line position of Mizuno Tadakuni

(1794–1851), who wanted to implement stern sumptuary moves as part of the Tenpō Reforms.[83] In 1733, when an uchikowashi riot broke out in Edo, the city magistrate was considerate enough to issue an edict stating that construction projects (*fushin*) and excursions (*yusan*) should not be discouraged while the price of rice was too high for the townspeople. The same cautionary approach was repeated in Osaka in 1746, when the bakufu announced a similar sumptuary law in that city. The bakufu's directive to city officials mentioned that it would be counterproductive to discourage people from conducting excursions and "musical performances" (*narimono*). In the Tenmei years, amid a series of injunctions on austerity, the bakufu indicated that the measures should be implemented prudently and only if the extravagance of the townspeople became too visible. Bakufu officials and ward elders clearly understood that the harsh repression of construction projects and popular cultural activities such as excursions, pilgrimages, street theater, religious rituals, spectacles, and street arts might jeopardize the livelihood of many commoners.[84]

For the bakufu, the view that construction and popular culture were important sources of income for the urban lower classes and that, therefore, sumptuary measures should be implemented with discretion did not arise from feelings of sympathy toward the urban poor. It was, rather, based on a painfully learned historical lesson. Because of a relatively high level of material consumption and public spending, the bakufu was tempted to make construction projects, whether public or private, a prime target of its sumptuary fiscal policies. But a ban or restriction on construction had to be implemented cautiously, for unduly harsh belt-tightening measures that dried up jobs in the construction sector invited a much more serious problem: fire. When construction workers, day laborers, and lumber merchants were pressed too hard, Edo often suffered massive destruction and social turmoil because workers who had lost their jobs intentionally set fires in order to create new jobs for themselves.[85] Fire was a final resort for unemployed laborers and the urban poor. After a disastrous fire, the bakufu usually had to subsidize reconstruction, which translated into new construction jobs. It is no wonder that soon after Shōgun Yoshimune launched the Kyōhō Reforms and enforced sumptuary measures on construction in the 1720s, Edo was hard hit by a spate of suspicious fires.[86] As Matsudaira Sadanobu took pains to acknowledge while wrestling with chronic fiscal deficits, fires had to be prevented in the first place, due to their consequences for public finances and social stability. With the drastic increase in the numbers of urban poor in the late eighteenth and early nineteenth centuries, bakufu officials found it increasingly difficult to enforce sumptuary laws.

As a source of livelihood for the urban poor, the economy of popular culture, such as that found at Sensōji, was basically no different from the economy of construction. Andrew L. Markus hints at the job-creating potential of popular culture in his description of Edo's street culture near a theater at the Ryōgoku Bridge in the mid-1800s:

> The entire square to the other side of these teahouses was occupied by the Muraemon-za Theater, the "Three Sisters" female kabuki, peep shows . . . raconteurs, archery booths, barbershops, massage healers, and around them peddlers of toys, loquat leaf broth . . . as well as wandering masseurs and Shinnai balladeers, peddlers of all sorts, blowgun booths, *dokkoi-dokkoi-dokkoi* [snatches of a refrain], fortune-sellers with lanterns dangling from their collars, vendors of "streetwalker" noodles.[87]

For the unemployed, a world of flourishing popular culture such as this offered abundant job opportunities as acrobats, street musicians, dancers, raconteurs, entertainers, peddlers, food vendors, healers, diviners, itinerant shamans, restaurant workers, teahouse girls, barbers, souvenir shop helpers, and sundry goods storekeepers. The Sensōji precincts were as thriving as the Ryōgoku area in this respect.

The high demand for pastimes among Edoites helped popular culture flourish and generated new job opportunities, but the job-seekers' strenuous, sometimes desperate, efforts to find a livelihood within popular culture contributed to its further proliferation. Popular culture was too fertile a source of income for the lower classes of Edo to pass up. With the increase in the population of the urban poor and the unemployed in the late Tokugawa period, socioeconomic pressure to liberate popular culture grew. The urban lower classes tried to exploit all forms of popular culture as a potential source of livelihood. For the bakufu, such pressure was, however, a menace with the potential to create cultural disorder and moral decay. The government made various efforts to curb popular culture and to discourage the frivolous cultural spirit of commoners. The tensions between the two could not easily be overcome.

Edo, which had grown to be the nation's economic and cultural center by the late eighteenth century, was a sprawling metropolis. More than half of its populace belonged to the commoner class, and transient menial laborers, male and female entertainers, and assorted poor accounted for a large segment of this class.[88] By the early nineteenth century, Edo had accumulated an even thicker layer of urban poor, which posed an additional challenge to the already crumbling machi communities. In particular, the most pressing problem was the increasing population of occupants of tanagari (tenements), who could not settle in one place and who had chronic difficulties finding a steady means of livelihood. According to one estimate, in the 1820s Edo's tanagari residents made up more than 70 percent of the entire commoner population. This was an extremely high number of people for the bakufu to deal with adequately, especially while suffering from severe fiscal deficits and from the demoralization of the samurai class.[89]

The social stability of the shōgunal castle town became an object of acute concern for bakufu leaders, for nobody could forecast when the worst would come. When the rebellion led by Ōshio Heihachirō (1798–1837) broke out in Osaka in 1837, the reverberations were felt throughout the entire nation. Even though the rebellion itself (which occurred in Japan's second largest city—a city under the direct control of the shōgun) was contained within twelve hours, it revealed the fragility of the Tokugawa system. Ōshio Heihachirō demonstrated what happened when the urban poor were heedlessly neglected. In fact, the situation in Edo, which had expanded far beyond the optimal size for feudal management, had been extremely volatile since the late eighteenth century. Worse yet, frequent fires had drained the shōgunal treasury, and anomic urban communities had lost their mechanisms of social stability.

Complicating the problem in Edo was that it did not stop with Edo alone. The failure of Kantō villages in the hinterlands of Edo compounded the problem through the migration of poor farmers into the city's social margins. The quick conversion of these migrants into members of Edo's urban lower classes was not so much a reflection of a sluggish economy as a by-product of the impoverishment of Kantō villages under the direct rule of the shōgun. One-fourth of the shōgunal lands (*tenryō*) lay in the Kantō area—a bit more than one million koku out of the bakufu's 4.5 million koku holdings. Despite the bakufu's utmost attention to the Kantō area, where shōgunal lands were extensively scattered, many villages in the region began to face gradual privation from the late eighteenth century due to an increase in abandoned fields and a decrease in the number of farmers. For example, between 1721 and the time of the Tenmei famines in 1786, the population of Shimotsuke decreased from 560,000 to 435,000 (22.3 percent) and that of Hitachi from 710,000 to 515,000 (27.7 percent). By the first year of the Bunka era (1804–17) these domains had experienced further decreases. The situation in the Mito domain was not so different. It lost approximately 30 percent of its population over a period of four or five decades beginning in the mid-eighteenth century.[90] To be sure, the Tenmei famines of 1783 to 1786 caused large-scale starvation and death. But the magnitude of the loss of population far exceeded what was due to the famines. Moreover, this demographic trend in the Kantō area continued into the early nineteenth century, even though food was relatively abundant. In fact, contrary to the national trend of modest demographic growth during the Kasei years (1804–29), the Kantō area outside Edo kept losing its farmers. These farm families were migrating to Edo.[91]

It is not hard to imagine who migrated to Edo. Rural samurai and wealthy farmers (*gōnō*), who formed the local elite, had no compelling reason to abandon their hereditary landholdings and well-established status. More than anyone else, these privileged few enjoyed what the local society and economy could offer, and their connections with the public authorities enabled them to dominate village affairs. The local elite had ample reason to relish the economic affluence and social influence that they held. The problem was poor farming families, who were experiencing increasingly hard times in the late Tokugawa period. Many such families fell into poverty and despair. Ironically, the destitution of Kantō farming villages was growing even as local gentry were benefiting from advances in the economy. Agriculture was becoming more commercialized, and local industries were booming. The Kantō economy was closely interwoven with the vast consumer markets of Edo. The so-called Kantō jimawari (neighboring villages) economy that connected Edo and its immediate hinterlands prospered to such an extent that it dwarfed that of Osaka (hitherto known as the "kitchen of Japan") and ushered in a new period of "Edo-centrism." Despite the development of a robust commercial economy in the Kantō area, however, many farming families were ruined and were forced to abandon their fields and head for Edo in search of a new livelihood.[92]

The incorporation of the Kantō jimawari economy into Edo markets barely touched poor Kantō farmers. The commercialization of agriculture and the growth of local industries benefited only a small number of wealthy farmers who were closely connected with Edo wholesalers and local merchants. These wealthy farmers operated agricultural processing industries, ran banking businesses, and even controlled the rapidly expanding distribution networks for local staples in close collaboration with Edo merchants. By the early nineteenth century, the distribution networks of the Kantō economy had surpassed those of Osaka merchants in terms of the quantity of goods shipped to Edo markets. During the 1720s, Edo consumer markets still depended heavily on the supply of *kudarimono* (goods that come down) from Osaka. For example, Osaka supplied 100 percent of the ginned cotton sold in Edo, 34 percent of the cotton, and 76 percent of the soy sauce and oil. By the 1850s, these respective numbers for these commodities were 34, 18, 6, and 60 percent. Among the five commodities that were most actively traded in the Edo markets, sake was the only one whose shipments from Osaka actually increased over this period: from 22 to 86 percent. The increase in sake shipments reflected the abundant production of rice in the Kinai region and Osaka's tradition of sake-brewing skills.[93]

In any event, during the late Tokugawa period Kantō farming villages experienced a tremendous transformation, with the increasing cultivation of commercial crops and the development of processing industries. Nevertheless, the benefits of commercial agriculture and processing industries were limited to a small number of wealthy farmers. Moreover, the overall agricultural productivity of Kantō farming families, particularly those who grew grain, lagged far behind that of Kinai farming families. This was at the root of what polarized the rich and the poor. As Matsudaira Sadanobu correctly and painfully observed, poor farming families who could not milk the flourishing jimawari economy "were driven to abandon their fields and move to Edo."[94] Echoing the same concern, in 1816 the author of *Seji kenbun roku* lamented: "Among Kantō villages, Hitachi and Shimotsuke are left with more than half of their fields and houses deserted . . . a thing that has never been seen before. . . . Farmers in other areas as well have moved to Edo for *dekasegi* [earning one's bread away from home], and population has decreased to a great extent."[95] The depression in Kantō farming villages continued until the 1840s, when they slowly began to recover with the arduous efforts of the bakufu and local governments as well as through self-help movements led by reform agriculturalists such as Ninomiya Sontoku (1787–1856) and Ōhara Yūgaku (1797–1858).

By the mid-nineteenth century, with the constant influx of migrants from Kantō villages, the population of Edo had snowballed. Most of these migrants were easily absorbed into the already thickened lower rung of Edo society (in spite of the bakufu's anti-vagabond decrees).[96] Job opportunities for these urban lower classes were relatively abundant in Edo compared with the employment situation in the poverty-stricken villages of Kantō. But most of these jobs were low paying and temporary. A class of urban poor known as the residents of *uradana* (rear tenements) made a living as peddlers of used clothing and recycled goods, street hawkers (*botefuri* or *furiuri* merchants), sellers of sundry dry goods and food, palanquin bearers, cargo handlers, street entertainers, construction workers, and other day laborers. For example, in mid-nineteenth century Edo, there were about 6,000 peddlers trading used clothes, 4,500 dealing in used tools and implements, and 2,000 collecting scrap metal. Since for commoners clothes and tools were major property items (after real estate), commercial transactions in these recycled goods (whether stolen from or pawned or discarded by samurai and upper-level townspeople) were brisk.[97] The networks developed by wandering peddlers were very extensive, encompassing Edo, Kantō villages, and even Ōshū. On the other hand, street hawkers and palanquin bearers in late Tokugawa Edo were more or less under the control of the bakufu, which used its licensing power to create a stable income from these sources for poor self-supporting commoners.[98] There were tens of thousands of street merchants, both licensed and unlicensed, catering to Edo inhabitants. Other lower-class members of Edo's economy included day laborers, workers employed at samurai or upper-level chōnin residences, shop helpers, gatekeepers, gardeners, carpenters, plasterers, itinerant healers and diviners, popular entertainers, and so on.

No matter what their occupation, however, most of those living in the tenement houses along back alleys faced a daily struggle for survival. They were vulnerable to the slightest change in conditions. Along with small retailers selling produce and sundry goods in the quarters facing the front street, these uradana dwellers formed the world of Edo commoners. On the surface, their lives seemed to be peaceful, as Jinnai Hidenobu describes in a nostalgic scene depicting the sleepy alleyways that are still observable today in Tokyo:

> The inhabitants of cramped tenement houses had no yard space of their own and therefore had to turn to the backstreet for all their open space. It was not only a front yard for potted plants and a place for children to play, but an indispensable makeshift kitchen for housewives to make fires for cooking. A common toilet and well were also found there. In the furthest recesses of the alley the Inari fox god was enshrined, providing a spiritual bond for the denizens of the alleyway.[99]

Under favorable conditions, the world of the uradana constituted part of the Pax Tokugawa. But in hard times it was easily transformed into a tinderbox of social discontent.

A prime example of just such a social explosion is the uchikowashi of 1787. When rice suddenly became scarce and the price jumped to unprecedented heights, the rumor spread that the jump was caused by rice dealers' hoarding of rice stocks. Some five thousand enraged commoners rioted and, within the space of five days, destroyed 980 rice stores and smashed a significant number of other stores selling cotton, paper, and cloth. To uradana residents who were barely scratching by, suddenly raising the price of rice was like throwing a stick of dynamite into a fire. These people "did not have extra pennies for getting over even one night." When they saw their lives being jeopardized by the "unjust" greed of wealthy rice merchants, these uradana dwellers did not remain submissive. Uradana dwellers demanded that rice merchants lower prices, petitioned (through ward officials) the city magistrate to intervene and ease their suffering, and attempted to negotiate with the rice merchants for a peaceful solution (while warning of possible violent confrontation). When negotiation proved fruitless, they began to smash things in order to force the merchants to sell the rice at cheaper prices (*yasuuri*). Although uchikowashi was a violent protest, rioters tried to maintain their own rules, such as a strict prohibition on theft, attention to the sources of fire, a ban on provoking trouble in their own neighborhoods, and advance warnings to targeted stores. To the urban poor, uchikowashi was a deserved punishment visited upon "greedy rice merchants."[100]

Probably for that reason, the bakufu arrested only forty-two men during the 1787 uchikowashi.[101] Instead of meting out heavy punishments, the Matsudaira Sadanobu government launched constructive programs designed to stabilize the lives of Edo commoners, particularly low-income residents, and also attempted to restore Kantō farming villages. Urban policies were closely linked with farming village policies so as to contain a "fluid population." Right after the uchikowashi the bakufu ordered the Kantō intendant Ina Tadataka to relieve the hunger of the starving populace and reduced sake brewing by one-third. In 1789, in order to establish an emergency reserve of rice for the famished, the bakufu issued a *kienrei* (order of abandonment) that forced the daimyō and hatamoto to "donate" 50 koku of rice per each 10,000 koku of landholdings for five years. A more comprehensive scheme to deal with the urban poor came in 1791, with the plan to establish an Edo-wide relief fund based on *shichibu tsumikin* (installment savings of seven out of ten). According to the instructions of Matsudaira Sadanobu, each Edo machi was to trim its expenditures and to contribute 70 percent of the savings annually to the relief fund, which would then be used to purchase enough reserve rice to feed a half-million commoners for thirty days. All 1,511 machi in Edo participated in this citywide program, to which the bakufu itself contributed 10,000 gold pieces. This program served as a great buffer in times of famine and epidemic at the end of the Tokugawa period. On the other hand, in order to contain the increasing numbers of street beggars and homeless people, the bakufu established a housing camp (*ninsoku yoseba*) at Ishikawajima. Homeless people who flowed in from poverty-stricken Kantō villages often became involved in theft and crime, and the bakufu wanted to segregate them from the rest of Edo society (*SN*, 16: 412–13).

These relief plans, however, were not a permanent solution to the structural problem of Edo's growing lower classes. In an effort to reverse the influx of poor migrants to Edo, the bakufu repeatedly issued edicts that encouraged or ordered them to return to their home villages, and sometimes provided them with travel expenses. But the effects of those edicts were limited due to the bleak economic prospects that faced those who returned. Kantō villages were trapped by the widening disparities between the wealthy and the exploited. The wealthy lived like urban aristocrats, wearing swords and taking surnames. The exploited despaired in their barren farming fields and were sorely tempted by a more commercialized economy. Many Kantō villages suffered from an increase in vagrants, robbers, and gamblers. From 1805 on, the bakufu took steps to restore law in the Kantō area by dispatching eight inspectors charged with patrolling their circuit and implementing laws to "correct" evil customs.[102] Despite the strenuous efforts of the bakufu, the lawlessness in the Kantō region was not easily subdued and, even worse, spilled over into the streets of Edo. Edo's problem with its urban poor was not something that could be solved by shock therapy ordered from above; it required structural solutions in line with the economic trends of the late Tokugawa period.

One such structural solution was to create new job opportunities for the unsettled urban poor. Even though this seemed logical, job creation was not in line with the ideology of Tokugawa society and feudal rule. Bakufu leaders and their conservative Confucian advisors were concerned mostly with preserving the hereditary privileges of samurai, and their policy proposals focused primarily on the well-being of the samurai class (the assumption being that the richer the samurai class, the better off the rest of the populace). Tokugawa leaders often paid lip service to the Confucian norm of "benevolent rule" (*jinsei*) in their public discourse, but when it came to policy, jinsei usually turned out to be nothing more than hollow rhetoric. When irritated by the social disorder caused by the economic hardships experienced by commoners, the bakufu tended either to hand out emergency help or to implement hasty stabilization measures. To redress the cultural excesses that were thought to lead to loose public morality, the bakufu was inclined to implement sumptuary measures (due to their quick and palpable impact). But these measures were usually shortsighted, and, worse yet, the strict enforcement of sumptuary measures was disruptive of the lives of the poor.

By the late eighteenth century, the Edo economy had become too diversified and diffused to be easily manipulated by a public authority that favored narrow unilateral policy measures. The fluid population of Edo commoners ignored the bakufu's top-down prescriptions and took advantage of Edo's expanding economy. There were jobs available in commerce, trade, transportation, construction, processing, small enterprise, and entertainment. Among these, popular culture had a potential for job seekers. Whether welcomed or suppressed, popular culture was more than something to enjoy: it was a source of livelihood for a large number of Edo's poorest commoners, including many uprooted rural migrants from Kantō villages.

Throughout the year, the Sensōji culture of prayer and play indeed offered numerous job opportunities for the tenant residents of the monzen districts, entertainers, and merchants. Moreover, the religious setting of Sensōji, with its extraterritoriality, provided entertainers and merchants with a protected venue for their business activities. The freedom found within this environment was an invaluable asset that benefited the entire Sensōji business community.[103] Sensōji and its monzen merchants and entertainers were interdependent and together created a robust economic zone at the northeastern edge of Edo.

Many merchants and entertainers belonging to the lower strata of Edo society were involved in the production of Sensōji's popular culture. Among them, those most closely associated with the inner precincts of Sensōji were petty entrepreneurs, called *yashi* or *gōmune*, who ran vending stalls, teahouses, and toothpick shops or sold "performing arts on the streets" (*daidōgei*). Although in legal terms most of these entrepreneurs had the status of townspeople, they were, in practice, under the control of Kuruma Zenshichi, the head house of the "non-person" (*hinin*) class segregated in the northeastern corner of Edo. The subordination to Kuruma Zenshichi stemmed from the reality that the yashi or gōmune made their living by soliciting alms from patrons, as the "non-people" did by begging generosity from the "people." In order to attract spectators to their commodities, these petty entrepreneurs developed and refined a wide range of such street arts as cat's cradle (*ayatori*), monkey shows (*saruwaka*), acrobatic feats at crossroads (*tsuji hōge*), ballad dramas, mimicries (*monomane*), "reading things" (*monoyomi*), puppet shows, storytelling, and street dances. All these street entertainments were the valuable source of subsistence for hundreds of families, whether they lived in the Sensōji districts or not.

Surrounding the inner precinct was the outer precinct (*sannai*), where three inner monzen wards, thirty-four subtemples, and the residences of three hereditary semi-monks were located. In the mid-1820s, there were 195 households in these three inner wards (Minami Umamichi-chō, Minami Umamichi Shin-machi, and Kita Umamichi-chō), and most of them depended on Sensōji for their survival. Among these households only twenty-nine enjoyed relatively stable business establishments; the rest of them consisted of poor tenant residents who struggled to make ends meet.[104] Businesses in the inner monzen districts were, however, not confined to these three wards. For financial reasons, many subtemples in the sannai precinct developed their own mini-monzen districts inside their allocated temple lands. For example, the Iō-in subtemple had parcels of land amounting to 3,256 *tsubo* (1 tsubo = ca. 36 sq. ft.); of this 2,505 tsubo were leased out or used as roads, and tenement houses were built on 310 tsubo. Another subtemple, Kongō-in, out of a total of 778 tsubo, allocated 347 for lease and 80 as a mini-monzen district.[105] Subtemples were very eager to develop monzen districts, particularly during times of financial difficulty, for the income from land leases and house rents was too significant to be ignored.[106] As a result, by 1825 there were 598 households living on lands owned by Sensōji subtemples, a number that far exceeded the entire number of households in the three major inner monzen wards. Including residents living in tens of monzen tenement houses run by two of the three hereditary Sanfudai families, the population of commoners in the sannai precinct was around 5,000 in the late Tokugawa period (*SN*, 10: 126–29). Undeniably, most of these residents relied, to one degree or another, upon the cultural economy of Sensōji for their subsistence. But as Sensōji officials pointed out in a report to their head monk in 1814, the number of residents seeking emergency allocations of rice or involved in financial disputes was on the rise, and the situation of sannai monzen residents was generally quite tough (*SN*, 12: 712–14).

Table 3
Number of Households in Each Monzen Ward, mid-1820s

Ward	Number of Households
Suwa-chō	287
Sangen-chō	562
Komakata-chō	195
Tawara-machi 1 chōme	267
Tawara-machi 2 chōme	342
Tawara-machi 3 chōme	280
Nishinaka-chō	339
Higashinaka-chō	451
Namiki-chō	149
Chaya-machi	48
Zaimoku-chō	168
Hanakawado-chō	520
Yamanojuku-chō	285
Kinryūsan Shitakawara-machi	131
Ta-machi 1 chōme	268
Ta-machi 2 chōme	292
Shōden-chō } Shōdenyoko-chō }	618
Saya Asakusa-machi	276
TOTAL	5,478

SOURCES: *Kyū Bakufu hikitsugi sho: Edo machikata kakiage—Asakusa* (1825), 2 vols., annot. and ed. Hayashi Rokurō, Hasegawa Masatsugu, and Asakura Haruhiko (Tokyo: Shin jinbutsu ōraisha, 1987), 1: 248–54, 287–302, 306–55, 357–424; 2: 49–63, 75–109.

The support base that Sensōji culture generated for merchants, entertainers, and temple residents sprawled beyond the keidai and sannai precincts to a monzen area known as *ryōnai* (proprietary land). During the mid-1820s, there were 19 monzen wards in this category; the number of households in each ward is shown in Table 3. With more than 5,000 households and probably more than 20,000 residents, the Sensōji monzen was the largest of its kind in Edo. These people depended heavily on the cultural economy of Sensōji for their livelihood and were very sensitive about anything that might affect their business in the Sensōji precincts.

The economic dependence of monzen residents upon the Sensōji culture of prayer and play was most acutely felt during mourning periods for prominent people, since construction and musical performances were either banned or restricted at such times. Whenever a shōgunal or imperial family member, an imperial court official, or a high-ranking Buddhist monk died, the bakufu ordered religious institutions to ban musical performances lest they dishonor the quiet observance of mourning and prayer for the posthumous well-being of the deceased. In the case of Sensōji, this order came through its head temple, Kan'eiji. The period of mourning varied from one to seven days, depending on the deceased's rank and his or her association with the Tendai Buddhist Sect or Kan'eiji. Sometimes such prohibitions were applied according to the administrative divisions of Sensōji lands. When Shōgun Ienari's young daughter died in 1800, Kan'eiji ordered Sensōji to ban musical performances for three days but did not ban construction (*SN*, 9: 115). When an imperial prince died at Fushimi Castle in Kyoto in 1802, the head monk of Eastern Tendai Buddhism (the head of Kan'eiji, the Rinnōji monzeki) rushed to Kyoto, and a strict order of abstinence was imposed on Sensōji. Construction was suspended for five days in the Buddhist halls and for one day in the precincts; musical performances were suspended for seven days in the Buddhist halls, for five days in the precincts, and for three days in the front districts (*SN*, 9: 614–16). During such suspension periods, Sensōji precincts and front districts virtually ceased to function. For many monzen residents, entertainers, and merchants, who depended on the boisterous crowds of Sensōji for their daily sustenance, such disruptions were life-threatening. Whenever possible, monzen residents petitioned the Sensōji administration to lift the suspensions or, at least, to shorten their duration. Sometimes they even asked for rent reductions or exemptions during these periods.

All this attests to the fact that the prayer and play culture of Sensōji was indispensable to the livelihood of many Edo commoners. As the most prosperous center of prayer and play in Edo, Sensōji was a magnet for business enterprises, which, in turn, generated thousands of jobs.

Most of these economic opportunities were, however, both transient and volatile. Sensōji merchants and entertainers had to conduct their businesses within the ephemeral environment of Sensōji's cultural economy. In order to open a business, prospective merchants had to petition Sensōji officials for permission to operate, and they had to negotiate a lease. For example, an entertainer approached Sensōji officials in 1780 to gain permission to promote the sale of medications along with children's sideshows at a space behind the Nijikken teahouses (*SN*, 4: 530). A resident of Minami Umamichi Shin-machi who set up an archery booth and a lunch box corner in 1813 negotiated a contract with the Sensōji administration that specified the payment of a monthly rent of 700 copper coins for most of the year but 350 coins during the three months of the winter season (*SN*, 12: 497). In the tenth month of 1826, and again in the first month of 1827, a monzen resident of Hanakawado-chō submitted a petition to the Sensōji administration, asking for the fifty-day lease of a block of land measuring eight by thirteen *ken* in Okuyama, where he planned to set up a misemono shop for displaying special bamboo artifacts. His petition was cosigned by four other monzen residents, who served as guarantors, and was confirmed by the ward head and a five-man group (*SN*, 16: 458–60; 17: 7–9). A commoner from a farming village in Musashi asked, through his village elder and mediators, if the Sensōji administration would rent him 300 tsubo in the precincts, where he wanted to set up four or five teahouses with a shared garden in their rear. He offered to donate twenty-five gold pieces if he could be exempted from paying rent for the next five years (*SN*, 17: 255–56). These are just a few examples of how business enterprises were set up in Sensōji. In most cases, the Sensōji administration was friendly and cooperative with its resident merchants and entertainers, who were in competition with each other.

With their talents, skills, or side services, Sensōji merchants and entertainers usually added play to their offerings of material commodities such as tea, homemade medications, toys, souvenirs, and staple products. In the highly fluid world of entertainment, one needed to be a jack-of-all-trades. Many artisans and laborers working by day as carpenters, roof tilers, plasterers, goldsmiths, metal workers, comb makers, tool makers, shop helpers, toothpaste sellers, street vendors, and fishmongers often converted themselves into entertainers at night in order to make extra money. Night shows, seasoned with a dose of the erotic, were tremendously popular. For instance, Kawashima Kayū, originally a comb maker, was enormously successful with his performance of *hachinin-gei* (eight-person arts), in which one person plays eight different roles. His pantomimes attracted some 300 patrons per day in the early nineteenth century.[107] Such success stories were rare—most performers enjoyed far more temporary successes. Nonetheless, the cultural economy of Sensōji remained integral to the lives of Edo's lower classes throughout the late Tokugawa period.

During the Kansei years, Matsudaira Sadanobu attempted to redress the social ills and moral decay of Edo society through a series of reforms. Although the aim of these reforms was, in theory, well defined, Edo society during the late Tokugawa period was not amenable to them. The disarray in Edo's administrative organizations, which used to uphold the communal management of machi units, was irreversible, and, by the mid-eighteenth century, more contractual forms of social relations had taken root. Status distinctions between samurai and commoners had lost their ideological vigor as well as their practical relevance as the increasing financial difficulties of the samurai led to their demoralization. In contrast, a growing number of commoners found more and more socioeconomic niches thanks to the commercialization of the economy. The status society was dying out, as the increasing numbers of urban poor further eroded the Tokugawa economic ideal. The expansion of the lower classes could not be contained within a samurai-centered trickle-down economy. These social changes troubled the shōgunal capital city and brought the Tokugawa system into serious question.

Edo's socioeconomic "problems," however, proved to be most beneficial to the prayer and play culture of Sensōji. Sensōji's popular Buddhist culture offered religious well-being as well as leisure pastimes. Edoites who had disengaged from the traditional communal bond of the machi and had become social drifters could easily find comfort at Sensōji. The Asakusa Kannon and other well-known deities were readily accessible, without the impediments of formal procedures or onerous financial burdens. Visitors could, at any time, readily satisfy their religious desires with a few copper coins unhampered by their status or their name. By the same token, the play culture of Sensōji enabled Edoites to enjoy casual moments and a variety of exotic experiences in the street markets and misemono shows.

It was townspeople, not samurai, who were most supportive of the Sensōji culture of prayer and play. As samurai gradually lost their economic strength in the late Tokugawa period, their previous level of cultural patronage could no longer be sustained. They were replaced by masses of commoners, who were better able to milk the expanding commercial economy. Sensōji had long since ceased to be a shōgunal prayer hall or an isolated religious institution on the quiet periphery of Edo. Sensōji had always been quite status blind when compared with Buddhist institutions such as Zōjōji and Kan'eiji. Nonetheless, it is remarkable that the unprecedented prospering of a prayer and play culture at Sensōji was attributable primarily to the collective contributions of the commoner class.

Indeed, Sensōji's culture of prayer and play was inconceivable apart from the world of Edo commoners—particularly the poor tenants on its own lands. While providing a major source of livelihood for many of the merchants, entertainers, and laborers living in its vicinity, Sensōji culture was, in return, further enriched and expanded by these people's economic activities. The interdependency of the proprietary temple and the people it controlled was so much a part of the cultural economy of prayer and play that it was impossible to separate the one from the other.

In short, Sensōji's culture of prayer and play and the world of Edo commoners were so firmly integrated that their association easily outlasted the reform measures of the late Tokugawa period. No matter how bakufu leaders viewed the social ills and moral decay of late Tokugawa Edoites, they could neither rectify the problems nor reorient cultural trends with coercive policy measures. Yet reform-minded bakufu leaders clung stubbornly to obviously ill-fated policies. They were persistent not only in pushing their policies but also in holding on to the conviction that the root of the problems lay in the minds of the populace. As time progressed, the bakufu paid greater attention to "correcting" the minds of the people, with the aim of "restoring" Confucian values and ethics to Edo society.

FOUR

The Cultural Politics of Prayer and Play

Matsudaira Sadanobu's Kansei Reforms, which aimed at returning "the polity to the simpler samurai standards of earlier days," made an enduring mark on nineteenth-century cultural life.[1] Compared with two other major reforms, the Kyōhō and Tenpō, Sadanobu's policies, with their sharp focus on a simpler social order, were particularly ideological in character. In order to reverse the escalating deterioration of the earlier Tokugawa social order, Sadanobu sought, first of all, to redress moral laxity with the proscription of heterodoxy (*igaku no kin*) and through the moral economy of exhortation. The Sadanobu government instructed the head of the Hayashi family, the rector of national education, to forbid the teaching of heterodoxy to students and to promote the upright public morality of earlier days. For that, the bakufu singled out the teachings of Chu Hsi as orthodox moral principles in the expectation that their propagation would restore the foundational order of the Tokugawa feudal system. In Sadanobu's view, too many "novel doctrines" were causing confusion and disarray in public morality.[2] The issue of moral order became so overwhelming a concern that his government diagnosed social problems and sought solutions for them according to Neo-Confucian doctrines.

As discussed in Chapter 3, however, by the late Tokugawa period Edo society had become more diversified and stratified and could not easily be amended by the moral teachings of Chu Hsi. Edo society demanded rather a flexible moral economy of eclecticism and pragmatism that could accommodate the changing realities of people's everyday lives. As many intellectuals suggested, eclectic thinking and a pragmatic approach certainly were better suited to dealing with the widening disjunction between social ideal and social reality. Doctrinal purity could no longer capture the imagination of the moralists of the Kaitokudō (a school for commoners in Osaka) and Shingaku ("heart learning," based on the teachings of Ishida Baigan, 1685–1744), the followers of Ogyū Sorai, and the scholars of Dutch or National Learning. These moralists and scholars concerned themselves with devising realistic and adaptable moral teachings applicable to a wider audience, including commoners.[3] Their ideas, which departed from the narrowly defined public ethics of the Tokugawa shōgunate, reflected people's diminishing trust in the established order.

Despite these diverse and critical comments on Tokugawa problems, ranging from fiscal matters, the causes of social disorder, village administration, agriculture, criminal law, popular culture to public projects, conservative Confucian thought did not fade away. The backlash against the ban on heterodoxy led to increased support among Chu Hsi scholars of the original Tokugawa system. Centering around the Hayashi school at Shōheizaka, the now-empowered orthodox scholars began to consolidate their control over samurai education and to monitor lines of liberal inquiry. The confrontational climate of polemics contributed to the gradual bifurcation of the intellectual, ideological, and cultural matrix of late Tokugawa Japan: on the one hand, there were those who desired to preserve the system, and on the other hand, those who desired to withdraw from established authority. The divergence between the guiding principles of bakufu leaders and orthodox Confucians on the one hand and the nonconformist discourses of disillusioned critics on the other became part of the larger context of cultural politics in late Tokugawa Japan.

Cultural politics in late Tokugawa Japan were especially salient in Edo society, where the traditional class lines between samurai and commoners were changing. Originally, samurai society (consisting of Edo Castle and the residential areas of shōgunal retainers and vassals and daimyō in the inner city) had been distinguished from commoner society (commoner residences, commercial areas, and religious spaces surrounding the inner city). Culturally, samurai society represented, in Kurimoto Shin'ichirō's words, a "sunshine city" (*hikari no toshi*), where hierarchy, subordination, status, privilege, and orthodox ideology were valued. As far as cultural politics was concerned, the "sunshine city" was supposed to subjugate commoner society. Over time, however, commoner society gradually evolved into a "shadow city" (*yami no toshi*) with its own autonomy, where liberation, anti-order, cultural expression, individuality, and practical learning were passionately sought.[4]

In the view of the samurai ruling class, commoners were problematic because of their tendency to succumb to loose moral standards. And the situation seemed to get worse as time went on with the steady influx of rural immigrants and the growth of the lower classes at the social margins. For their part, Edo commoners found Neo-Confucian moral teachings and exhortations increasingly irrelevant to, and even incompatible with, their world. Instead of passively subjecting themselves to the top-down imposition of public ideology, Edo townspeople tried to create a cultural niche of their own in the "shadow city."

Amid the rising conflict between rulers and ruled, the Sensōji culture of prayer and play in the late Tokugawa period represented just such a cultural niche. Not only could Edoites evade the established order at the Sensōji sanctuary, but they could also create their own counterculture. More specifically, the cultural vitality of play at Sensōji instilled in commoners a spirit of self-assertion, thereby helping them circumvent the established social boundaries. By the same token, Sensōji's popular deities, to whom people resorted in search of relief from suffering, offered an appealing alternative to the public protection that seemed increasingly obsolete. The cultural milieu of late Tokugawa Edo, as seen in Sensōji culture, was deviating from the prescriptions of orthodox cultural politics. Nevertheless, in an attempt to contain popular culture, the bakufu monitored, censored, suppressed, and punished those who it thought did harm to the foundations of the Tokugawa moral order.

Public Ideology and Private Ethics

Soon after Matsudaira Sadanobu assumed the office of state elder in 1787, his administration strengthened its control over publications by stipulating that all picture books and woodblock prints receive government approval before being distributed to the public. Special attention was paid to publications that might disturb public morals with depictions of salacious matters or discussions of current affairs.[5] The first victim of the Kansei censors was Santō Kyōden (1761–1816), who had just published a trilogy depicting the world of courtesans. This work contained elements that satirized the government's reforms. In 1791, the reform government sentenced Kyōden to fifty days in handcuffs and confiscated half of his publisher's (Tsutaya Jūzaburō [1750–97]) property. Other authors and ukiyo artists who did not escape the tight grip of government censorship and punishment were, to name a few, Hayashi Shihei (1738–93) in 1792, Shikitei Sanba (1776–1822) in 1799, Utagawa Toyokuni (1769–1825) in 1801, and Tamenaga Shunsui (1790–1844), Terakado Seiken (1796–1868), and Ryūtei Tanehiko (1783–1842) in 1842 (during the Tenpō Reforms).[6]

In line with the heightened censorship of erotic publications, the bakufu even extended the official ideology to Edo's public bathhouses, which numbered approximately 600 by the early nineteenth century. Bakufu officials were concerned primarily with "mixed bathing" (*konyoku*), and they banned it in 1791 and again in 1801. The bathhouses known as *furoya* had flourished as quasi brothels, where "bath girls" (*yuna*) had served customers until tightly regulated by shōgunal order in 1657.[7] One could no longer find furoya-style bathhouses in late Tokugawa Edo, but what did emerge and prosper were bathhouses catering to both sexes. In 1808, when the bakufu forced bathhouse owners to organize "associations" (*kumiai*) for the self-regulation of mixed bathing, there were still 371 bathhouses for both sexes, 141 for men, and 11 for women. It was totally unacceptable, lamented bakufu leaders, for the wives of commoners and their grown-up daughters to go to "mixed" bathhouses, where they could hear information on matters occurring in their district or city, slake their curiosity and relieve their boredom with rumors and gossip, and, above all, mingle with males in the nude. As Nishizawa Ippō (1801–52), a kabuki playwright from Osaka, observed in the 1840s, however, mixed bathing still existed in Edo. In the 1840s Edo seemed to have more bathhouses than ever, at least two in each ward, and many of them still seemed to offer mixed bathing in tight spaces.[8] A bath was an almost indispensable daily routine in windy and dusty Edo. Since commoner residents could not afford to build a bathtub in their cramped residences due to the danger of fires, the cost of firewood, and a shortage of water, the ideal solution was the public bathhouse, which not only was affordable (the fee was four to eight copper coins), but also offered a space for socializing. Mixed bathing attracted both females and males, who could exchange, if only temporarily, the tedium of a status society for the equality of naked bodies.[9] Understandably, bakufu leaders saw in mixed bathing a threat to Confucian ethics.

Confucian ethics were quite strict in differentiating men from women in terms of social roles and public etiquette. Confucian manuals that offered advice on educating daughters placed special emphasis on "feminine" virtues and upright moral attitude: mixed bathing was unimaginable. Young girls were even discouraged from reading "licentious and amorous stories such as the *Ise* and *Genji monogatari*," which, in the view of these manuals, would destroy core Confucian virtues such as female chastity and devotion to the family.[10] In the 1790s, the bakufu began to implement policies designed to remove ordinary women from male public spaces, which were deemed part of the pleasure culture, and to keep female entertainers under strict control. For instance, the bakufu banned secret prostitutes and unlicensed street entertainers in 1793, instructed women not to wear colorful and luxurious hair decorations in 1802, cracked down on geisha and teahouse girls, and intensified control over restaurants and teahouses with female servants in 1824. Needless to say, all these decrees were applied to the Sensōji precincts and districts.

Interestingly, however, in executing these anti-entertainment measures, the bakufu seemed to view the issue of "moral problems" mainly through the female body. For bakufu leaders, the "deterioration of good morals and customs" was plainly attributable to a pleasure culture that was linked to female bodies. Accordingly, the female body was castigated as a major source of ethical corruption. No matter in what form it appeared, whether on paper or on the street, the prime target of suppression and punishment was the female body itself throughout the late Tokugawa period. In 1793, the bakufu began censoring "indecent" woodblock prints and ordered painters and publishers not to include the name of the female model on the print. Two years later, in 1795, the bakufu banned the publication of "lecherous" or "expensive" woodblock prints depicting female bodies. Here and elsewhere the bakufu paid a great deal of attention to "commercialized" representations of prostitutes, teahouse girls, and kabuki actors playing the roles of females.[11] The commercialized bodies of females were even subject to frequent expulsion from the public scene, as seen in the occasional arrest of female entertainers on streets in the Sensōji area. When the Tenpō Reforms forbade the employment of teahouse girls, most of those at Sensōji shaved off their eyebrows, dyed their teeth black, and disguised themselves as married women pursuing legitimate businesses.[12] Overall, the bakufu's moral policies suggested that the root of moral and ethical problems was the public display of the female body. Against this backdrop, reform-minded bakufu leaders extended their surveillance to fictional stories that included female bodies or love affairs, and they cast a watchful eye on the some 800 book-lending shops (*kashihonya*).

Despite the bakufu's efforts, the world of popular culture, as seen in mixed bathing and Sensōji teahouses, did not yield easily to the Tokugawa notion of ideal social order. In prose literature, for example, the stories that fascinated Edoites reflected their self-expressive experiences and desires. Although there were fads in the types of novels that were popular, the stories were, by and large, not what the bakufu considered morally uplifting. Marius B. Jansen aptly summarizes the reversal of the normative platitudes of public duty and morality in the world of prose literature.

> [Santō] Kyōden, [Shikitei] Sanba, [Jippensha] Ikku, and others described a world of play filled with raucous laughter, physical indulgence, and crudity. Sanba's bathhouse patrons are a scruffy lot, remarkable for sores, flatulence, casual insult, and gross indecency. They live in a world in which people spend their lives in narrow quarters of the permissible and achievable. It is a society in which concern with the physical usually takes precedence over concern with the intellectual or spiritual.[13]

A world of play filled with the physical dominated prose literature. The literary world that mirrored late Tokugawa Edo society was full of tales of ghosts, demons, witches, romances, miraculous happenings, and vendettas; depictions of the licensed quarters; vignettes of mundane and familiar activities; travel accounts filled with fun and ephemeral pleasures; and sketches of human feelings. Under the close surveillance of the government, writers often labored to create plots highlighting the eventual triumph of "upright virtues" such as filial piety, feminine chastity, sacrifice, heroism, and dedication to righteousness—all in aid of the morality of reward and punishment.[14] Bakufu leaders enjoined writers to offer moral instruction to the public, but such enforced teaching could not be effective. In contrast to the spontaneous reflection of the sociocultural reality that "freewheeling" literature could convey, "moralistic" literature, which could not garner popularity, was an unmistakable indicator of the decline of Tokugawa ideology.

Understanding the limitations of passive surveillance and censorship in their endeavor to "moralize" the habits and minds of Edo inhabitants, reform-minded bakufu leaders also aggressively sought out cases of exemplary moral behavior as models for public education. From the third month of 1789 on, the bakufu and local governments literally ransacked the nation looking for exemplars of filial piety, loyalty, chastity, familial harmony, good customs, honesty, sacrifice, and diligence in farming. These people were honored with cash prizes and other gifts, and their names and deeds were published in the interest of public education. On the instruction of Matsudaira Sadanobu, Shōheikō Confucianists published a collection of stories about 8,614 exemplary lay Confucians under the title *Kōgi roku* (Records of righteousness and filial piety) by the end of 1789. The same project was launched again in the Bunka era (1804–18) and was completed by 1848. Throughout the late Tokugawa period, the shōgunate repeated its "righteousness and filial piety" project through local administrations, which it instructed to discover and reward model "Confucian" individuals.

Sen'yō eikyū roku (Permanent records of selected essence), a collection of records on Edo's machi administration from the Keichō era (1596–1615) to 1864, contains three stories about Asakusa women that exemplify filial piety. The first story concerns a woman called Tsuge, a resident of Asakusa Saruya-chō. When her father, a barber, became old and sick, Tsuge married his apprentice, Mannosuke, who was to inherit the barbershop business. But Mannosuke turned out to be a total decadent. Tsuge soon divorced him and decided to support her bedridden father on her own. She worked as a maid in the daytime and, after returning home in the evening, devoted herself to caring for her father. Whenever possible, she tried to make extra money through sewing so that she could get better food and medicine for her father. Despite her utmost care, however, her father got worse and eventually became a cripple. Nevertheless, Tsuge did not lose hope, and every day she prayed to the Asakusa Kannon for her father's quick recovery. The city magistrate noticed her devotion to her father and rewarded her filial piety with the prize of fifteen *kanmon* (1 kanmon = 1,000 copper coins) in 1844.

The second story is about a teahouse girl named Chiyo of Asakusa Higashinaka-chō, who supported her elderly mother. Soon after Chiyo had become a teahouse girl at the age of twelve, her mother completely lost her sight and became totally dependent on the medical as well as financial care of Chiyo. For her part, every evening Chiyo threw herself upon the generous compassion of the Asakusa Kannon. Pressured by time and money, Chiyo eventually became a geisha (a better-paying job) in order to make ends meet. Although Chiyo's hard work allowed her mother to enjoy a hot bath every day, Chiyo could not even afford to purchase the clothing a geisha needed, and she was soon forced to move to a cheaper place. Despite her increasing hardships, her faith in Buddhism remained strong. The city magistrate rewarded her filial piety with ten kanmon in 1853.

The third story deals with a Yoshiwara prostitute named Kane, who had an exceptionally warm heart. When she was two years old, Kane lost her parents; and when she was eight years old, she was sold to a Yoshiwara brothel as a maid. Life as a prostitute soon followed under the new name of Mayuzumi, but she never lost her spirit of generosity toward those less fortunate than herself. While temporarily working as a street prostitute at Yamanojuku-chō after a great earthquake had destroyed Yoshiwara in 1855, Mayuzumi saw many cases of suffering. Out of her compassion, she sold her hairpins, combs, and other decorative items, bought 1,160 bowls, and donated them to soup kitchens in the Asakusa area. The city magistrate honored her philanthropy with two silver pieces.[15]

The Sensōji administration often followed the bakufu's lead in preaching the ethic of Confucian filial piety. For example, in 1812, when the city magistrate awarded five silver pieces to a girl named Ken for her remarkable filial piety toward her ailing stepfather, the Sensōji administration offered her five kanmon. In recognition of the devoted care by Ken's mother, Seki, of her husband, the bakufu granted her a living allowance of ten gold pieces, to which the Sensōji administration added 1,500 copper coins. The story of Ken's filial piety was widely publicized because of the pitiful turns in her life. Ken was abandoned at the age of twelve by her stepfather, a rice merchant, who had adopted her at the age of seven and then sold her to a samurai family as a maid. Some years later, her stepfather fell ill and had to recall his son, who had been an apprentice at another store, to inherit his business—but to no avail. While he despaired, Ken voluntarily returned to her stepfather and carried out his trade, even though it was physically hard on her. At the same time, she nursed her sickly stepfather. Persevering through all kinds of difficulties, every day Ken prayed to the Asakusa Kannon for her stepfather's quick recovery (*SN*, 12: 379–82).

The bakufu seemed content to ignore the non-Confucian values in these stories (e.g., dependence on the supernatural help of Buddhist deities was not a Confucian value) and highlighted those aspects that were in line with their cultural politics. In fact, this kind of selectivity was already common in the 1760s to 1780s, when Neo-Confucian values were beginning to lose their ethical relevance to Edo society. No matter what social challenges they encountered, throughout the late Tokugawa period bakufu leaders stubbornly held to the belief that social problems could be solved through Confucianism and relied on social engineering through mind cultivation to prop up a deteriorating social order.

As Ogyū Sorai observed in 1725 in *Seidan*, life in Edo was, however, replete with excessive consumption, disorder, and material freedom. He worried that the long-term effect of such a highly commercialized society would be the total destruction of a Confucian moral order based on strict status distinctions. As bakufu leaders admitted, the status order was steadily deteriorating. Contrary to the Confucian political economy of the heterodox Ogyū Sorai, who called for samurai to leave the cities and return to a past arcadia, conservative bakufu leaders obstinately adhered to the Confucianism of Chu Hsi and emphasized the "restoration of mind." This seemed to be their prescription for all social problems.

Even in dealing with street beggars and wanderers, Matsudaira Sadanobu and his deputies applied the principles of Neo-Confucianism. Previously, social stragglers had been seen as criminals deserving harassment and punishment. Amid the rising wave of hard-line Neo-Confucian perspectives in the 1790s, however, bakufu leaders found in stragglers an experimental mini-laboratory for putting their ideas into practice. Here was the perfect opportunity for showing that they could reform social failures through "the correction of their minds." In order to rehabilitate street beggars, the bakufu accommodated them in residential camps (first built in Ishikawajima in 1790) and taught them moral lessons. The number of homeless in the Ishikawajima camp grew to approximately 500 by the Tenpō era (1830–43), but this was only a tiny portion of the estimated 100,000 poverty-stricken members of Edo's underclass. Still, with regard to bakufu social policy, this project represented a shift from an emphasis on punishment to an emphasis on rehabilitation.[16] From the standpoint of Neo-Confucianism, social failure meant moral failure, and moral failure meant a defiled mind, which could be cleansed through moral teachings and discipline. By extension, bakufu leaders attributed Edo's social problems to the failure to instill Neo-Confucian values and ethics, and they sought to remedy this through disciplinary exhortation.

Nevertheless, Edoites were not responsive to the Confucian cultural politics of the bakufu. The magnitude and spirit of Edo's commercial economy were far beyond the easy grasp of top-down ideological guidance. The economy was moving forward according to its own logic, and it resisted external intervention. Likewise, Edo townspeople were attuned to a socioeconomic life that was in line with their own values rather than with the feudalistic Confucian principles dear to the bakufu. This was the new spirit of Edo economism, which had been presaged by culture of the Genroku era (1688–73) in the Kamikata (Kyoto-Osaka) area at the turn of the seventeenth century. Clearly, the economic principles and values of the late Tokugawa period were increasingly incompatible with the feudal principles of the Tokugawa system.

As Ihara Saikaku (1642–93) and Chikamatsu Monzaemon (1653–1724) pointed out, the spiritual values of a commercial economy are basically twofold: (1) status is gauged by the medium of money; and (2) the logic of feudalistic discrimination based on a "given" status and privilege is no longer valid.[17] For them, an individual's wealth was a good that deserved to be protected and respected insofar as it was the result of hard work and creativity. The Genroku culture of Kamikata merchants valued commercial activities, the virtues of labor, and empirical rationalism. This was in stark contrast to conventional Confucian fatalism, which defined wealth as a "given" predetermined by the will of Heaven. The spirit of Genroku culture was eventually channeled into the Zeitgeist of late Tokugawa Edoites, who viewed wealth as the reward for hard work and entrepreneurial creativity. To Edo townspeople, wealth was achievable through individual initiative. By the late eighteenth century, as Yasumaru Yoshio suggests, in the consciousness of Edo commoners, "business and morality were reconciled, and economic salvation and moral salvation became interchangeable."[18] And, indeed, Edo townspeople began to justify their economic activities with their own "private" ethics and values, in defiance of bakufu "public" ideology.

Bakufu leaders and Confucian thinkers, however, remained unmoved by the new moral economy that was gaining currency among commoners. They insisted that the ideal order could be achieved only when each social class dutifully carried out its own designated function. This cardinal principle of Confucian order was expressed in such phrases as "equilibrium and harmony" and the "rectification of names," which were based on the notion of an immutable, class-based moral hierarchy. The assumption was that society was a zero-sum game—an increase in one place could come only as the result of a decrease in another place. Tokugawa rulers, interested in entrenching the hereditary hierarchical privileges of one social class, were naturally most concerned with the possible erosion of the benefits and privileges of the ruling class. This concern intensified from the mid-eighteenth century on, as the samurai class became increasingly impoverished. Who should be blamed for the crumbling of names? For Confucian thinkers such as Yamagata Daini (1725–67), the answer was obvious:

> The key to "rectifying names" was for the ruler to ensure that each person, or socioeconomic class, adhered strictly to the heaven-mandated line of work expressed in its status name. But this task had proved impossible because Japanese commoners were "wholly undiscriminating and incapable of reason." They would "seek profit and shrink from loss by nature."[19]

Yamagata Daini singled out mercantile activities as the prime danger to the Tokugawa system. His view reflected that of the ruling class in general. Confucian thinkers as well as bakufu leaders accused merchants of "selfish instincts" that were destructive of the "normative" Tokugawa order, and they tried to find ways to scapegoat "greedy" merchants so as to arrest the burgeoning forces of commercialism. Matsudaira Sadanobu's debt cancellation order of 1791 was one such attempt to curb the unquenchable power of money. Samurai indebtedness to the rice dealers (*fudasashi*) of Asakusa Kuramae, which totaled more than one million gold pieces, was abrogated with one edict.

The bakufu, however, could not deter the growth of the progressive socioeconomic spirit of Edo merchants. In the late Tokugawa period, the self-generated private ethic of Edo townspeople, with its emphasis on industry, thrift, harmony, and creativity, led them to clarify their new vision of selfhood and to seek a spiritual path premised upon "self-realization."[20] This contrasted sharply with the hegemonic Confucian ethic that the authorities were trying to impose through guidance, instruction, and exhortation.[21] The root of the conflict between the two was that, no matter how they were packaged, Confucian ethical values did not take into account individual subjectivity. In this Confucian moral economy, each social class was assigned a fixed morality that carried a hierarchical human value. Commoners were considered ethically and morally inferior to samurai. The intrinsic limitation of Confucian ideology was clear to commoners, whose selfhood was defined as a given rather than as something that could be created through their own subjective activities.[22] By comparison, the "private ethic" of commercialism, at least theoretically, offered Edo commoners the possibility of overcoming a mandated ethical passivity and of liberating themselves from the moral bondage of Tokugawa Confucianism.

Whether it was a matter of overcoming ethical passivity or moral bondage, Edo commoners endeavored to achieve self-realization through, above all, play (asobi). Ihara Saikaku commented in the late seventeenth century that two things seemed to occupy the minds of Kamikata townspeople: one was the making of money (*kasegi*); the other was the pursuit of pleasure (*yūraku*). As far as Saikaku was concerned, Kamikata townspeople seemed to believe that kasegi could be achieved through their own efforts—industry, steadiness, resourcefulness, discretion, endurance, honesty, thrift, concession, justice, mutual help, and harmony with the environment.[23] At the same time, Saikaku observed that, for Kamikata townspeople, wealth, achieved through the practice of their own ethic, was a means for realizing the pleasure of asobi. As a mantra popular in the Genroku era—"to work for playing" (*kaseide asobu*)—indicates, yūraku did seem to be the ultimate goal of townspeople.[24] Since they were shut out of political privileges, urban commoners paid attention to making money so that they could enjoy cultural activities.

The coupling of wealth and pleasure-seeking, which had begun in the Genroku period, took firm root among Edo merchants and artisans in the late Tokugawa period. Rai Kiichi has shown how seriously Edoites linked work (kasegi) to asobi through his examination of kibyōshi prose. For the Edo townspeople depicted in kibyōshi fictions the acquisition of wealth was still not totally free of the supernatural intervention of such deities as Daikokuten (Mahākāla) and Benzaiten (Sarasvatī). Moreover, bakufu economic policies tended to impede commercial activities, even though some privileged merchants in close association with the bakufu had access to preferential treatment. Nevertheless, Edo townspeople found these roadblocks bearable, for they did have hope in the growing commercial economy and its rationalism.[25] What they could not tolerate was the bakufu's attempts to prevent them from channeling their wealth into pleasure-seeking activities. In their consciousness, work and play were inseparable. When, for whatever reason, work was forcibly separated from play, Edo townspeople found themselves irritated and, consequently, critical of the bakufu.[26] For them, the Matsudaira Sadanobu government's censorship of popular literature was clearly a form of political suppression.

The Tokugawa government continued to attempt to suppress popular culture in the name of Neo-Confucian standards. Popular writers and ukiyo painters had to be cautious, and street performers and entertainers could not lessen their vigilance concerning the government's cultural policing. The tension between public ideology and popular culture grew particularly intense when bakufu leaders attempted to eradicate certain entertainment businesses during reform periods. In most cases, the bakufu, having unhampered power, was able to enforce its suppressive policy measures. But those who were targeted and, as a result, were in danger of losing their source of livelihood became more secretive about their endeavors. Many entertainers looked to set up in religious spaces, where they would be better protected (and sometimes even immune) from the authorities. And Edoites in general turned to religious spaces in order to elude the authorities' attempt to discourage the union of work and play.

The usefulness of religious spaces to play culture was well demonstrated when the government of Mizuno Tadakuni launched the Tenpō Reforms. In 1842, the government decided to ban the *yose* (storytelling) business, which was regarded as a major source of ethical contamination. In principle, licensed storytellers were supposed to tell "moralistic" stories; in reality, yose halls in late Tokugawa Edo turned out to be temporary playhouses where petty impresarios hired chanters, young boys and girls, samisen accompanists, and dancers and often staged such erotic shows as "parlor ballad drama" (*zashiki jōruri*), "women's ballad drama" (*onna jōruri*), and kabuki (somewhat sleazy plays peppered with lustful stories). Many yose managers were firefighters (*tobi*), plasterers, lumber carriers, and construction workers from the lower classes of Edo society who "simply converted permanent structures that were used for other purposes during the daytime into nighttime yose."[27] Who patronized these nighttime shows? Nishiyama Matsunosuke is unequivocal about this: "The audiences who packed these show houses included warriors and commoners from Edo or the suburbs. Unmarried men and women from the Edo working class especially enjoyed visiting the yose where they could hear comic monologues, riddle improvising, 'eight-role art,' and much else."[28] Boosted by contagious popular patronage, Edo contained roughly 400 to 500 yose halls by the early 1840s.[29] To the annoyance of the bakufu leaders and Confucian moralists, examples of "didactic justice" were never heard in these storytelling halls.

The city magistrate Tōyama Kagemoto finally ordered a reduction in the number of yose halls (from around five hundred to fifteen), banned female performers, and restricted storytelling topics to four subjects—commentaries on Shintō, commentaries on *shingaku* (heart/mind study), military stories, and old tales (*mukashi banashi*). Initially, the city magistrate decided not to impose the order on yose halls located in religious precincts, on the grounds that they were under the jurisdiction of the magistrate of temples and shrines. In addition, yose halls in the temples and shrines were not only far less numerous than were those in other districts, but they helped generate income for those religious institutions that the authorities could no longer afford to subsidize. Debates on the issue followed, and Tōyama Kagemoto eventually agreed to the equal application of *kōgi* (public authority), deciding that all but nine yose halls were to be removed from the compounds of temples and shrines.

Amid such hostility toward the yose business, Sensōji was fortunate to retain *three* yose halls (six other religious institutions were allowed only one hall each). Nonetheless, the number of yose halls at Sensōji was reduced from twenty-six to three. However, all active raconteurs were somehow accommodated in these three spots (apparently by rotating them).[30] Thus all Sensōji storytellers were saved because they had set up their business within religious spaces that were relatively free from the grip of bakufu cultural politics.

As far as cultural politics was concerned, the bakufu had a more difficult time in taming the cultural taste of consumers who melted away into the anonymity of the crowds. Throughout the late Tokugawa period, the bakufu had to rely mostly on moral exhortations in a fruitless attempt to redirect the cultural energies of the populace toward public ideology. Commoners easily found ways to defy the bakufu's cultural restrictions and, more important, came to justify their "play" by linking it to their own moral economy. Once people could afford to pay for their pastimes themselves, any play activity that they chose to enjoy was often seen as the ultimate goal of their own personal economic achievements. This was the built-in cultural economy of what Yasumaru Yoshio refers to as *tsū-*

zoku dōtoku, or "the people's morality."[31] The Neo-Confucian ideology of the Tokugawa period proved to be ineffectual in the cultural world of ordinary people armed with their own private ethics. And this ideology was especially ineffectual when it was imposed on the evasive and motley worlds of asobi.

Play, Disorder, and Cultural Vitality

Saitō Gesshin (1804–78), the ward elder of Kanda Kiji-chō, is representative of the spirit of play among Edo commoners in the late Tokugawa period. According to his diary, Gesshin allocated a great deal of time and money to his frequent attendance (at least several times a month) of kabuki performances, storytelling sessions, puppet shows, street plays and performances, misemono spectacles, circuses, and other activities. His outings, during which he was often accompanied by family members and friends, usually included dining out at various restaurants.[32]

Although Saitō Gesshin was relatively better off and had more leisure time than most commoners, his passion for pastimes was not unusual in late Tokugawa Edo. It was, rather, part of the fashion of the time in which he lived, easily observable among Edoites of every social class: everyone seemed to be preoccupied with pleasure-seeking. Asobi, which in most cases had once been pursued in the form of seasonal activities under the rubric of religious observance, was so secularized in the late Tokugawa period that Edoites could easily incorporate it into their daily routines. There was no longer any meaningful distinction between asobi and work (*shigoto*).

Traditionally, asobi was set aside for "pure" (*hare*) blocks of time and space, which were not to be adulterated with "impure," or ordinary, time and space. But for Edoites in the late Tokugawa period, time and space could be compartmentalized according to the dictates of their urban life, which was basically indifferent to cyclical change. In this environment, it was only natural for Edoites to pursue asobi activities in their daily lives.[33] For instance, polite accomplishments (*geinō*), formerly used to mark religious or ceremonial occasions, became a casual and general object of education and enjoyment. The *iemoto* (headmaster) system of geinō education, which historians regard as a distinctive characteristic of

Japanese culture, took root because of the widespread popularity of geinō activities.[34]

Routinized asobi proliferated in, among other spheres of endeavor, the performing arts, waka poetry, painting, reading, recreational activities, eating, drinking, watching, and travel. Travel, which took the form of pleasure tours of religious sites, summarily illustrated the secularized nature of asobi. Temples and shrines had been a favorite destination for religious visits among imperial family members, court nobles, and upper warriors in ancient and medieval times. When this custom spread down to commoners during the Tokugawa period, it was modified in the direction of pleasure seeking. In principle, the bakufu and local governments allowed commoners to travel outside their villages and towns only when they sought permission for a pilgrimage to a prominent temple/shrine or for a medical trip to a hot spring.[35] Despite these regulations, commoners could easily convert their "religious" or "medical" trips into pleasure tours.

When booming tourism industries promoted the package tour to a wider stratum of the populace, travel became further pleasure-oriented. In 1804, a comprehensive hostelry chain called the Naniwa-kō (Association of Naniwa [Osaka hostelers]) began to provide such travel services as transportation, accommodation, money exchange, and porters in the regions between Edo and Osaka. Responding to market demands, new hostelry chains such as Higashi-kō (Association of the Eastern [hostelers]) and Santo-kō (Association of Tri-City [hostelers]) soon entered the travel business and paved the way for a tourism boom. Along with these industries, easily available travel guidebooks also boosted the pleasure tour. Not surprisingly, a guidebook entitled *Miyako meisho zue* (A pictorial book of Kyoto's famous places) sold as many as 4,000 copies within a year of its publication in 1780, and Jippensha Ikku, thanks to reader enthusiasm, extended his travelogue depicting two Tōkaidō travelers, the *Tōkaidōchū hizakurige* (Shank's mare on the Tōkaidō Highway), into a series of eight volumes by 1809. Any information on pleasure tours attracted people's attention, as tourist routes were expanded from already famous places (such as Ise, Kumano, and Kyoto) to Konpira, Miyajima, Zenkōji, Haguro, Kyūshū, and other hot spring resorts.[36] Travel became almost an obsession during the late Tokugawa period, as we can sense from a number of common sayings: "One should visit Ise at least once in one's lifetime" and, particularly for Kyoto people, "Seven visits to Ise, three to Kumano, and a monthly visit to Atago in one's lifetime."[37] Although all the destinations in these sayings were religious sites, as though suggesting that *inori* (prayer) was still the *tatemae* (principle), it was an open secret that, for most travelers, asobi was the *honne* (real intention). Travel meant a temporary move into a liminal, transitional space in which one could create a social niche of one's own without the interference of daily rules.

Travel in the late Tokugawa period took various forms, ranging from a months-long pilgrimage to a remote place to a casual, day outing to a destination within walking distance. Urban dwellers in Edo did not have to spend considerable time and money on a long trip because there were many local opportunities for fun and recreation. Not a single day passed in the city without activities to break up the quotidian life of its inhabitants. Festivals, Buddhas and deities, special religious events (such as ennichi and kaichō), kabuki, circuses, spectacle shows, street markets, teahouses, restaurants, pleasure quarters, and seasonal scenery were all beloved by fun-seeking Edoites. Casual outings became a sort of cultural fad among Edoites. Not only commoners but also the samurai who filled daimyō residences and offices were bewitched by "making a tour of noted places" (*meisho meguri*). Caught up in the sweep of "seeing things and playing outdoors" (*monomi yusan*), even "virtuous" housewives rarely stayed home (which, of course, some critics lamented as a sign of the collapse of the good customs of Japanese women).[38] The constant moving, sightseeing, shopping, drinking, and eating created a cultural fashion of play that Nishiyama Matsunosuke has termed "action culture" (*kōdō bunka*).[39]

Within the action culture of Edoites, the Sensōji sakariba was a breeding ground for a wide range of play-oriented commodities. As discussed in the previous chapters, Sensōji's plentiful supply of play never suffered from a shortage of demand, but the relative popularity of the various modes of play was in constant motion according to the ephemeral appetites and desires of patrons. In their faddish pursuit of play opportunities at the Sensōji sakariba, Edoites seemed to be particularly fascinated with the delectations of the liberated body. As H. D. Harootunian points out, "Late Tokugawa cultural practice seemed to converge upon the body, making public what hitherto had remained private, whether in eating, drinking, speaking, bedding down with either a man or a woman, or relieving oneself, and often led to gargantuan indulgences coming from the joys of the flesh."[40] In this cultural milieu, the body naturally produced major themes for prose literature and ukiyo paintings. More significantly, as described in these artistic genres, the body "called into question the superiority of mental over manual skills" and claimed its autonomy as "the maker and consumer of things."[41] Physical skills and energies were appreciated more than ever before. Of course, when their craze for play could not be sated with epicurean joys alone, Edoites eagerly expanded the scope of their action culture to *haikai* composition, music, flower arrangement, the tea ceremony, calligraphy, reading, group study, religious devotion, and so on. Through a variety of these play opportunities, Edoites tried to disengage themselves from the cultural bondage of Japanese feudal society and constructed their selfhood in their own manner.

Despite the wide range of play activities available for cultural cultivation, Edoites molded the fashion of action culture in a rather passive manner through consumption. Moreover, as far as the pursuit of asobi was concerned, Edoites, who lived in a densely populated urban environment, were, ironically, isolated individuals. Edoite action culture did not feature strong collective or creative elements.[42] Its individualized and passive character was couched in mass cultural markets in which scattered Edoites "individually laundered their quotidian lives" through consumption. This was the operational dimension of popular play culture in the late Tokugawa period: individualized cultural indulgence but no serious cultural creativity.[43]

Despite their relative lack of cultural creativity, however, Edoites were serious in their efforts to elevate and refine their consumption of play commodities. The enjoyment of polite accomplishments (*yūgei*), for example, was sought in the name of achieving the "way" (*michi*) of arts (*gei*) or one's avocation (*dōraku*). Like the Way of Shintō, yūgei activities were objects of serious pursuit and required strict education and discipline.[44] Many other aspects of action culture followed the example of well-organized yūgei learning and teaching. For serious pursuers of asobi activities, they were more than a simple pastime involving little in the way of spiritual value. When commoners pursued asobi as the "way" of self-fulfillment, feudal cultural distinctions seemed to be greatly mitigated.

Beyond cultural avocation, commoners sometimes engaged in critiquing the feudal system when they played with the deliberate satire of "mad poetry" (*kyōka*) or short verse (senryū), or when they lent disproportionate importance to the different and exotic, thus relativizing the importance of hierarchy of Tokugawa society. Through play, autonomous individuals could distance themselves from the culturally imposed social status. This, of course, worried bakufu leaders and Confucian intellectuals, who were particularly concerned about the degree of popular disengagement from the collectivity. As Harootunian notes, "The activities of daily life that concentrated on bodily performance [or asobi activities] lost their link to common labor and a common social whole."[45] In their play, commoners were finding ways to express their own alternatives to the collectivity and public ideology.

Understandably, however, the disengagement from public ideology engendered by the consumption of asobi commodities never resulted in a direct collective challenge to the Tokugawa system. The asobi activities that constituted the action culture were fragmented and existed in isolation from one another. It is, therefore, not surprising to find that people's obsession with self-indulgence and self-satisfaction while engaging in their isolated cultural pursuits was often tinged with gloom and pessimism, for they could not affect the larger social system. It is too much to expect that Edoites could somehow have channeled their disengagement from the public domain into the creation of a new sociopolitical environment. Asobi existed for itself. As long as asobi remained asobi, it was an object of enjoyment detached from the real world. In the end, asobi activities were an escape from, not a solution for, the discontents feudal society engendered in commoners. For the discontented, those asobi spaces that accommodated their despair were often breeding grounds for gloomy, ominous creatures such as ghosts, apparitions, devils, goblins, shades, wraiths, and vengeful spirits. For disgruntled Edoites, these creatures, as depicted in theater, prose literature, or folk religion, gave form to their anger, unhappiness, and frustration. Edoites were fascinated with these underground creatures who served as their cultural proxies, sometimes projecting their ordained fates onto them.[46] And so Edo's action culture came to embrace a grotesque underground world. The diabolical world of devils and demons, which coexisted along with the celestial world of Buddhas and deities, functioned to absorb the unfulfilled desires and energies of Edoites.

Edoites found a repository for their unanswered questions about the nature of the world and society in the shadowy realm of devils, demons, and evil spirits. They were especially drawn to religious places that housed evil spirits or condemned creatures. In fact, many temples and shrines in Edo had underground creatures in their backyards that counterbalanced the divine beings in their frontyards (*omote*). Sensōji, one of them, renowned for its "front" Asakusa Kannon, was also well-known for its "rear" (*ura*) world of "evil" deities.

According to several legends originating in the early seventeenth century, Sensōji had at one time been haunted by ghosts and apparitions. One of these legends tells of eerie ghosts encountered by a courageous falconer at the Main Hall during the Genna era (1615–23). One night the falconer happened to stay over at the Main Hall; at midnight, two strange men holding golden cudgels in their hands suddenly appeared and warned him that the hall was not a place for a vulgar person like him. When the falconer stared at them without moving an inch, the two disappeared. Soon fifty to sixty monks emerged, threatened the man, and disappeared again. A boy monk then appeared, quickly grew so big as to fill the hall, and then disappeared. The next morning, a servant came to greet him and gave him a horse. When the mounted falconer began to tell the servant what had happened during the night at the Main Hall, the servant revealed that he was the boy monk. The falconer tried to kill the servant, but fell from the horse in a faint. Another legend tells of a love story that ended tragically. In the Kan'ei era (1624–43) a young merchant came to Edo and opened a shop. Soon he fell in love with a girl living nearby, and since her parents opposed their marriage, they decided to run away together. At night they happened to stay at the Main Hall at Sensōji. When the young merchant woke up, he could not find his lover.

An old man suddenly appeared and pointed to a big tree standing outside the hall. The merchant was shocked to find the girl's body, torn into two parts, hanging from the tree.[47]

As a relatively obscure temple in pre-Tokugawa days, Asakusa Sensōji had been haunted by shadowy ghosts, spirits, and underworld demons. Behind the shiny images of Buddhist and Shintō deities, visitors to Sensōji in the late Tokugawa period still found things with which to sate their fascination with the diabolic (e.g., King Yama [Enma], an old guardian demon called the Sanzu-no-Kawa Hag in the Enma Hall, a murderer-turned-Shintō-deity known as Kume, a smallpox deity, and so on). All these spirits and deities responded to the nihilistic and pessimistic aspects of people's psyches. Edo townspeople in the late Tokugawa period were still tightly bound to the traditional household, feudal social status, five-man associations (*go'nin-gumi*), and the governing administration—all of which limited the scope of their cultural pursuits. Social restrictions and economic difficulties sometimes placed the underprivileged in an almost helpless position within the markets of the play culture. All this indicates that even the desire for passive play often remains unsatisfied. These unfulfilled desires and unrelieved grudges found expression in the angry, vengeful faces of shadowy beings. The world of inauspicious creatures was the other side of late Tokugawa play culture.

In fact, late Tokugawa Edo was a cultural arena within which clashed the interests and concerns of people of differing social backgrounds. Edo society itself was highly volatile: jobs were abundant, yet insecure and unstable, and the social order was crumbling. In such a society, Edoites welcomed ghosts and evil spirits who embodied the unpredictability of their life and the uncertainty of their survival. They were fascinated with the topsy-turvy world of underground creatures emanating volatile and violent energies. For these Edoites, the world of fierce-looking deities and evil creatures was a fertile source of disorder, hallucination, gloom, and indecency that slaked their thirst for an upside-down society. Among various cultural genres that enriched the "shadow city" of Edoites, Tsuruya Nanboku's *Tōkaidō Yotsuya kaidan* (Tōkaidō Yotsuya ghost stories) and Takizawa Bakin's *Nansō Satomi Hakken den* (A tale of Hakken [the Samurai Hakken with eight Confucian Virtues] of the Satomi House in Nansō [Kazusa]) are representative of what was found in prose literature, and Utagawa Kuniyoshi's creative pictures of ghosts illustrate what was offered in ukiyo painting. The explosive popularity of these artistic genres in the early nineteenth century was a reflection of the insatiable energies and desires of Edoites.[48]

In particular, Edoites found an outlet for their suppressed psychology at such prominent Shintō festivals as Sannō-sai and Kanda matsuri (known as *tenka matsuri*, or "mundane festivals") as well as at a kabuki genre known as *aragoto* ("ruffian's business," or "wild acting"). Compared to Kyoto's highly communal and harmonious festivals, the tenka matsuri of Edo were carnivals of explosive energy that were often characterized by such terms as "razzle-dazzle" (*bakasawagi*) and "pushing each other's sword-guard" (*tsubazeriai*). Incendiary Shintō festivals offered a legitimate opportunity for Edoites to vent their wild energies and unfulfilled desires.[49] It is no wonder that the Sanja matsuri at Sensōji, which shared the cultural spirit of tenka matsuri, was far from an occasion for celebrating communal harmony.[50]

Similarly, in Ichikawa Danjūrō's aragoto, which defied the norms of samurai society, Edoites found their hidden angst expressed through the abusive, revengeful, or retributive actions of tragic heroes, petty criminals, gangsters, and bandits.[51] Danjūrō superbly acted out Edoites' feelings of resistance, discontent, sorrow, resentment, and anger in a "bombastic and rebellious" manner. For Edo commoners who still found the social restrictions of feudal order stifling and unbearable, the tragedy, wrath, and eventual revenge of their "imaginary" heroes offered a thrilling catharsis.[52] Gunji Masakatsu has succinctly characterized the "new patterns of taste" in the early nineteenth century: "On the Edo stage, one might almost designate this period as the age of abusive language (*akutai*), so popular was cynical or abusive language and behavior. . . . During this latter phase of kabuki, plays depicting the activities of petty criminals and rogues who made their living by fraud and extortion increasingly won favor."[53] Danjūrō always staged *Shibaraku* (Wait a moment) at the end of the year and *Tale of the Soga Brothers* (*Soga monogatari*) at the beginning of the year.[54] The spirits of the Soga brothers, who schemed to take vengeance for their father's wrongful death, captured the psychology of Edoites. Since the Kyōhō era, it had been an annual custom for three major theaters (Nakamura-za, Ichimura-za, and Morita-za) to stage the Soga story in the first month as part of their "early spring season" and so to open another promising year. This strategy always proved popular with Edoites.[55]

The theater of ghost stories and outlaw-like heroes offered an alternative worldview to that of feudal society by twisting or reversing its seemingly immutable realities. The many different versions of the Soga brothers story, ghost stories, and "raw life" (*kizewa*) plays—all forms of a theatrical genre known as *akutai shibai* (billingsgate theater)—were filled with back-street fighting, intimidation, terrorism, killing, vengeance, betrayal, and turmoil.[56] For the bakufu, billingsgate theater was the total inversion of the normative society it desired. By reversing good and evil, however, Edoites somehow found an abreaction for their frustrations arising from class, status, gender, and wealth.[57] To many Edoites, Danjūrō was almost a deity—someone who provided them with a sacred space of relief and salvation. In that sense, Danjūrō's aragoto performances were "not just theatrics, but prayers."[58] Alarmed by the kabuki fad, in *Seji kenbun roku* Buyō Inshi deplored the tendency of popular *shibai* (theater) to drag Edoites into a world of fantasy and delusion bedeviled by morally ruinous suggestions. To his annoyance, he found that "shibai is not something that just mimics the real world; to the contrary, the shibai becomes the real world, and the real world becomes the shibai."[59]

Thus Edoites were entangled with multiple social realities in late Tokugawa Edo society—a society in which social disorder and disunity were keenly felt amid the influx of poor immigrants into the social margins. Native-born residents, who referred to themselves as Edokko (children of Edo), tended to blame the intrusion of "non-Edo people" for the city's deteriorating social order. The propensity for conflict between poor immigrants and longtime residents was quite visible in the early nineteenth century, and the Edokko often measured their well-being against that of the "outsiders." The more the "within" (*miuchi*) consciousness of Edokko intensified, the more it became expressed in a negative fashion.[60] Early in the nineteenth century, new immigrants became a prime target for the pomposity and resentment of Edokko. By scapegoating outsiders, Edokko tried to find ways to divert the anger stemming from Tokugawa society. But as the continual influx of immigrants became just one more aspect of life in Edo, the Edokko found a more appealing means of dealing with their discontents and frustrations in the anti-structure of billingsgate theater and the underground world of ominous creatures. Edokko transformed this gloomy world into a source of comfort, self-justification, and inspiration. Over time, not only Edokko but Edo inhabitants in general also found themselves morally uplifted in the upside-down world of social norms. Edoites' fascination with "evil" creatures and alternative forces was more than just a way of escaping from seemingly unalterable social realities: it was also a way of finding pride and cultural redemption.

For Edoites, the pleasure quarters, theatrical districts, and "shadow" streets offered the possibility of overcoming the strictures of a moralistic Confucian society. The places at which Edoites were able to foster their pride, resistance, and cultural accomplishments were, however, the very places that the bakufu categorized as "evil spaces" (*akubasho*). Tokugawa leaders condemned akubasho as hotbeds of crime and immorality and, for fear of contamination, separated them from the rest of society.[61] For example, the bakufu regarded kabuki actors as "a social group lower than merchants, and only a little above the pariah class. This attitude remained throughout the Tokugawa period. Restricted in where they could live, and legally administered as beggars, they were considered male prostitutes and accordingly the theater district was put near the Yoshiwara pleasure quarter [by the Tenpō reforms], far from the center of Edo."[62] Paradoxically, these segregated pockets of the city served as "unordinary spaces" (*hare no ba*), where Edoites could pursue their own individual desires and values and nurture their spirit of resistance and freedom through asobi activities.

So far from succumbing to the hackneyed negative images of asobi perpetuated by the public authorities, Edoites saw it as a way of liberating themselves from the bondage of a feudal order.[63] As Nishiyama Matsunosuke notes, "contemporary society was severely constricted by the boundaries of feudal rank and status. In order to surmount such barriers, people devoted themselves to the world of play."[64] Play was Edoites' gateway to a new horizon of hope. This is reminiscent of the traditional understanding of asobi: asobi was a ritual dedicated to the deities, and pursuing asobi to its ultimate limit was not unlike pursuing the sacred realm of the deities—a pursuit in which the pursuer and the pursued eventually became one.

The ultimate goal of such cultural pursuits and enjoyment was conceptualized in the aesthetic value of *tsū* (connoisseurship). Tsū, the final stage of *sui* (quintessence), generally referred to a state of ultimate cultural mastery, wherein one had acquired the ability to appreciate the quintessential quality of an asobi. The aesthetics of tsū could be applied to any asobi activities, whether the tea ceremony, haikai poetry, calligraphy, painting, dancing, singing, noh drama, or whatever. Among these, the activity that Edoites most often used to illustrate the different stages of cultural mastery was the "way of color" (*shikidō*; here "color" refers to "sex"). The fifth volume of Fujimoto Kizan's (1626–1704) magnum opus, *Shikidō ōkagami* (Great mirror of ways of color), which was in print in 1678, was widely cited with reference to the ascending stages of cultural achievement.[65] Following the twenty-eight-chapter structure of the *Lotus Sūtra,* Kizan divided the way of color into twenty-eight stages grouped into six grades: pre-uncouth, uncouth (*yabo*), half-quintessential, quintessential (sui), upper quintessential, and ultimate quintessential. Here, Kizan likened the final stage to the state of *sokushin jō-Butsu* ("attaining enlightenment," or "becoming a Buddha in this existence"), where one no longer needed sex. This was the ultimate state of tsū, and upon achieving it, one could return to one's quotidian life with an enlightened mind, thus resolving any possible duality of the real and the unreal.[66]

It was the ideal of tsū at which the Edo spirit of asobi aimed. Tsū referred not to techniques of cultural enjoyment but to a style of cultural pursuit. Cecilia Segawa Seigle puts it this way:

> The *tsū*'s ideal characteristics were generosity, courtesy, consideration, intelligence, wit, candor, refinement, and urbanity. The consummate *tsū* was an elegant man-about-town who dabbled in music, painting, poetry, popular song, haiku, tea ceremony, flower arrangement, and calligraphy. A sign of the *tsū*'s worldly sophistication was for him to be seen at the theater and the Yoshiwara, and to be knowledgeable about the pleasure quarter.[67]

Tsū was a refined aesthetic pursuit undertaken in a spirit of self-redemption; compromise with vulgar entertainment was not allowed. In theoretical terms, as Nishiyama Matsunosuke suggests, the spirit of *hari* (strength of character) and *iki* (refinement) define tsū as an aesthetic consciousness, and tsū, as a principle of action, completes the spirit of hari and iki. In other words, when one pursues the aestheticism of hari and iki to its end, one performs a spontaneous act of non-purpose that leads one to absolute self-liberation.[68] This is the state of tsū. Commoners who had to endure the barriers to social mobility in feudal society found a fantasy of self-realization in the triangular aesthetic of hari-iki-tsū.

In practice, tsū aestheticism, however sublime in theory, was not something Edoites could easily attain. In the Hōreki-Tenmei eras (1751–88) some rich merchants, intellectuals, and samurai attempted to dedicate themselves, as *bunjin* (lettered men), to the pursuit of tsū. They dissociated themselves from the public domain and devoted their time and energy to artistic cultivation. Among many cultural genres available (e.g., singing, calligraphy, haikai composition, prose literature, kabuki, and philosophical studies), these rather nonchalant connoisseurs singled out *nanga* (southern painting) in imitation of the Chinese "bamboo" hermits.[69] But the artistic cultivation of the bunjin ideal was limited to a small number of lettered men who promoted a form of "salon" culture. Even for them, the aesthetic of tsū was merely a cultural experiment, not something that was ultimately realizable.

Although the aesthetic spirit of this salon culture trickled down to a wider audience over time, for most Edoites the ideal of tsū was an empty quest that seemed to be open only to the few with the economic resources to embark on it. Even so, the spectacularly lavish asobi parties frequently held at Yoshiwara in the Tanuma years (1772–86) and staged by the wealthiest rice dealers (known as eighteen Great Masters) seemed to be nothing but hollow attempts to reach the ultimate way of tsū.[70] Tsū aestheticism remained, in the final analysis, a cultural ideal precisely because it was attainable only in theory.

Over time, culminating in the Bunka and Bunsei eras (1804–29), popular forms of tsū aestheticism gradually diffused among the general populace. Right after the Tenmei famines, the social base of asobi culture was markedly widened by the fashion of action culture, but this came at the expense of the further erosion of tsū idealism. The aesthetic ideal of tsū, which, during the Hōreki-Tenmei years, was likened to the seats in the proscenium box (*sajiki*) of kabuki theater, quickly dissipated, as is seen in such terms as *yabo* (uncouth) and *kiriotoshi* (cheap seats), which were used to describe the cultural spirit of the Bunka-Bunsei years.[71] As time progressed, asobi culture in the late Tokugawa period came to accommodate mass consumption.

As the national center of cultural consumption, Edo showed no sign of cultural decline, even during the difficult years of the 1830s, when the nation was suffering from famines, frequent peasant uprisings and urban smashings, and the military rebellions led by Ōshio Heihachirō (1798–1837) and Ikuta Yorozu (1801–37). In 1838, the bakufu ordered the deputies (*daikan*) of shōgunal lands to assess the mental health of peasants and report to the government. What bakufu leaders found to be common in those reports, and most worrisome, was the strong yearning of peasants for Edo culture. One of the goals of the Tenpō Reforms of the early 1840s was to terminate this "vain" yearning of peasants—a yearning that could only erode their upright "agricultural morality."[72] Despite the derisive label "uncouth," however, the popular culture of late Tokugawa Edo could not be "corrected" by forced measures from the top.

The strength of Edo culture in the late Tokugawa period stemmed from the cultural vitalism of asobi. As Delmer M. Brown suggests, such vitalism seemed to be endemic, something that evolved from the traditional traits of Japanese culture. According to Brown, Japanese vitalism is rooted in the traditional belief in the life-giving, mysterious power of kami. In this cultural tradition, all human activities, particularly (kami) asobi, are related to "the [vitalistic] power of a *kami* to create or enrich any form of life, here and now."[73] The Japanese belief in kami as sources of life-giving or life-restoring energy was behind the vitalism of popular Edo culture. The pursuit of (kami) asobi connoted a path toward the life-affirming power of kami.

Endemic vitalism aside, what is so unique about the asobi culture of late Tokugawa Edo is that it flourished within its own moral economy. This was more than a lingering reflection of traditional cultural traits: popular asobi culture contained a moral element—the value of "life strength" (*ikioi*) that energized the daily lives of Edoites. Even though the idea of "life strength" was rooted in the vitalistic power of kami,[74] asobi culture generated far more than a ramification of kami power. As the saying "to work for playing" (*kaseide asobu*) indicates, the value of life strength was increased in the dialectic between the pursuit of asobi and people's private ethic. The idea of life strength was elevated to a "spiritual virtue" (*toku*) that had its own self-justification in asobi culture. For late Tokugawa Edoites, asobi could lead them to the realization of a spiritual virtue essential to sustaining their social being. For this reason, Edoites strove not only to make money but also to direct that money toward asobi activities, which harbored the virtue of life strength.

Despite its inherent virtue of life strength, however, asobi culture in late Tokugawa Edo still could not create a life space free from the status distinctions and the feudal order of the Tokugawa system. The desires and concerns of Edoites that could not be accommodated within that system rarely mattered to the ruling elite. The Tokugawa shōgunate simply tried to suppress what was incompatible with its Confucian moral economy. In this environment, Edoites turned to the medium of prayer in their search for an alternative authority.

Prayer, New Divinities, and Alternative Sources of Authority

Edokko, who were said "not to have extra pennies for getting over even one night" but were known "not to worry about the next day," represented the optimistic and carefree spirit of Edo townspeople. Whenever they had time and extra pennies, Edoites indulged in play activities, without worrying about the future. The concerns of tomorrow were superseded by the pleasures of today.

This seemingly optimistic spirit was, however, counterbalanced by the realities of everyday life. Edoites were quite helpless in the face of frequent encounters with misfortunes and sufferings, for which the public authorities proved to be of little use. Two problems in particular were chronic sources of trouble for Edoites: disease and natural disasters. For the majority of Edo's poor, urban life meant "living in the long-tenement building" (*nagaya kurashi*). As Susan B. Hanley describes it: "The families of daily laborers in Edo were often crammed into one-room apartments approximately nine feet square with a small entry for storing tools and footgear and for cooking. They shared toilets and access to water with other tenants in the block."[75] High density and its inevitable side effects (e.g., poor sanitation and psychological stress) made living in Edo a daily struggle.[76] In addition, in the late Tokugawa period Edoites frequently suffered from disasters such as fires, floods, storms, and earthquakes. And these most keenly affected the lower classes.

Disease was the most feared enemy of Edo inhabitants. For commoners, disease was by and large beyond their control: medical knowledge and effective medicine were still limited, and, when available, medical services were often far beyond their economic reach. Once an epidemic occurred, it tended to quickly spread through the entire ward, then through the entire district, and finally through the entire city. Outbreaks of smallpox, often in combination with measles and other diseases, were quite extensive and devastating in the late eighteenth and early nineteenth centuries.[77] Young children in particular were vulnerable to smallpox, the prime cause of an infant mortality rate that reached the incredible level of 70 to 75 percent in the Tokugawa period.[78] Edo inhabitants in general (whose diet depended heavily on rice, soy products, and salt) suffered from such maladies as eye disease and beriberi due to the lack of vitamins and other vital nutrients supplied by vegetables and other foods. Other diseases (such as internal diseases with sharp pain [called *senki* and *shaku*], food poisoning, toothache, influenza, syphilis, and hemorrhoids) were also constant causes of suffering.

In theory, the authorities, who justified their existence on the basis of the Confucian ideal of "benevolent rule," were supposed to succor those in distress. But the bakufu, which was mired in its own fiscal problems and the crumbling Tokugawa system, proved to be quite indifferent to the personal agonies of Edo commoners. Edo, which by 1800 was a sprawling metropolis overburdened with a large transient population, simply slipped out of the bakufu's control. It was a mega-city, spawning urban problems and hardships for its inhabitants. Impromptu, ad-hoc policy measures were of no help to those in trouble. The bakufu, for example, implemented a policy designed to eliminate the transient population by returning immigrants to their native places, but the policy could do nothing for those with nowhere to go. To new residents of Edo (and probably to all Edoites), Edo was a forlorn city in which they had no direct access to the production of clothing, food, and shelter. In a society that was still overwhelmingly agricultural, this would have made them feel even more helpless.[79]

In the helplessness, Edoites took refuge in prayer and threw themselves on the mercy of deities. No doubt the world of kami and Buddhas was the most familiar source of hope and comfort. However, the prayer culture of Edoites in the late Tokugawa period was, in two respects, quite distinct from the prayer culture of earlier periods. First, there was a great concern for "this-worldly benefits" (*genze riyaku*), which included even this-worldly solutions to other-worldly wishes. Edoites wrestled with their daily predicaments in the context of the here and now, not in the context of the next life. Compensation in the other world was less meaningful than it had been. Furthermore, their concern was not to be met by simply overcoming their current predicament. Edoites sought almost boundless this-worldly benefits. Bakufu leaders and Confucian intellectuals were highly critical of this tendency, and they accused Buddhism of creating values premised on "vanity" and desires premised on "fantasy." Armed with Confucian ethics, government officials castigated the genze riyaku form of Edo Buddhism as a stumbling block to rationalistic efforts to improve conditions in this world.[80] Despite their scorn, genze riyaku prayer continued unabated.

Second, Edoites of the late Tokugawa period were suspicious of the religious efficacy of traditional deities. As Buyō Inshi insightfully noted with regard to early nineteenth-century dissatisfaction with the insipidity of conventional religions, Edoites seriously questioned the efficacy of age-old deities and their representatives: "In today's society, the representatives of Shintō and Buddhism resemble national traitors. All the kami have ascended to heaven; the Buddhas have left for the Western Paradise; and all present and other worlds have fallen into disuse. Providence and retribution have been exhausted. All the Buddhist priests have fallen into hell and have ended [their mission] by becoming sinners."[81] As far as Buyō Inshi was concerned, older, more established divinities had often ceased to be functional. People were beginning to search for new divinities.

Changes in a guidebook to Edo entitled *Edo sǫ kanoko meisho daizen* (A complete collection of Edo's famous places) illustrate what was happening in the religious world of Edo. Compared with the first edition published in 1690, the second edition published in 1751 introduced far more

Buddhist and Shintō deities who were the objects of popular worship. For example, the number of images of Benzaiten went from 13 in 1690 to 134 in 1751, of Kannon from 15 to 52, of Yakushi from 10 to 34, of Fudō from 7 to 19, of Amida from 20 to 35, of Jizō from 0 to 47, and of Inari from 24 to 124.[82] New divinities were constantly being created in response to new religious needs. With the increase in the population of popular deities, pilgrimage courses were created inside Edo that connected religious sites housing newly emerged "miraculous" divinities belonging to the same genealogy. There were no Kannon pilgrimage sites in Edo in the seventeenth century, but by the mid-eighteenth century there were more than ten. Not only Buddhas and kami, but also obscure deities rumored to be efficacious in the treatment of certain diseases or the alleviation of misfortunes sometimes captured popular attention.

These new deities were not immune to the fate of many older deities, however. In fact, most of them did not remain popular long. Edoites were quick to take up the worship of new deities and just as quick to discard them. A new deity's fame was subject to situational factors, and its divinity was never permanent. The prayer culture of Edoites in the late Tokugawa period has been characterized as *hayarigami shinkō* (belief in fashionable deities).[83] According to fashion, people moved from one deity to another. But no matter what deities people invoked, their prayers were framed within the context of this-worldly benefits. Fashionable deities were most successful in satisfying such concerns as the alleviation of misfortune and suffering and the acquisition of good luck, health, and prosperity.

In catering to Edoites' this-worldly cravings, Sensōji was the most renowned warehouse of fashionable deities. Besides the Asakusa Kannon, Sensōji boasted tens of other highly popular deities. As far as Edoites were concerned, traditional Buddhas seemed to be increasingly insensitive to the this-worldly aspects of life, and Shintō deities were somewhat indifferent to individual and personal matters.[84] The following are some of the most notable hayarigami at Sensōji in the late Tokugawa period.

1. The Niō (the king who holds a *vajra* or diamond cane) statue at the Niō Gate. Originally a Buddhist guardian deity called Kongō rikishi (Diamond superman), it suddenly became popular during the Kan'ei era (1624–43), when it salivated. From the Kyōhō era (1716–35), it began to

attract large crowds of worshippers, particularly on the sixteenth day of the first and seventh months during the weeks of the equinoxes, who would pray for prosperity.[85]

2. The Old Woman Sarasvatī (Rōjo Benzaiten) statue enshrined in the Benten Hall on Dai-Butsu Hill. The term *rōjo*, or "old woman," referred to the fact that the statue was covered with white hair. Previously a water deity residing in an old pond at Sensōji, it gained a reputation as a popular deity in the late Tokugawa period. Thanks to a legend that a large quantity of coins had erupted from that pond and to the Benzaiten's reputation as a god of wealth, Rōjo Benzaiten was popularly believed to bring economic fortune to her worshippers.[86]

3. The Sanzu no Kawa Hag statue housed in the Enma Hall. The Hag is an old female guardian demon in the second court of hell, who strips off the clothes of the deceased before they cross the river flowing between this world and the next. This ominous underworld gatekeeper was transformed into a benevolent deity believed to respond sympathetically to wishes. Because the statue lacked two of its front teeth, people believed that it would promptly lessen toothache. Edoites suffering from this malady usually offered toothpicks to this deity when they worshipped it. It was also renowned for its ability to protect children's health. Dolls, coins, or rice were usually offered for that purpose.[87]

4. The Fudō (Acalanātha) statue enshrined in the Arazawa Fudō Hall. This statue was said to have flown into Sensōji from an unknown place during the Enbō era (1673–80). Sensōji monks soon enshrined this statue as a guardian deity. In the late Tokugawa period, Edoites came to worship this deity in the belief that it would protect them from fires and epidemic diseases.[88]

5. The Yakushi (Bhaiṣajyarāja) statue of the In-Yakushi Hall. This popular deity was believed to cure all kinds of eye disease. Monks attached to this hall concocted eye lotions called *musō no megusuri* (eye lotions found only in dreams) and sold them to worshippers at the price of sixteen copper coins per container. At the same time, they never forgot to caution customers to have faith in the miraculous power of this particular Bhaisajyarāja image, for the efficacy of the medicine was contingent on the "one element" (*ichimi*) of faith that the deity would add to it. This statue was later transferred to the Myōtoku-in subtemple.[89]

6. The standing Jizō (Kṣitigarbha) statue in Shōchi-in. As the fifth of Edo's well-known set of six Kṣitigarbha, this statue was particularly famous for helping to open the eye of wisdom and for bringing wealth and luck.[90]

7. The stone statue of Kume enshrined in the Kume Heinaibee Shrine. According to legend, Kume Heinaibee was an invincible warrior who wandered around and tormented many innocent folk with his infernal deeds. After he died, his son made a stone statue in the shape of a meditating monk, in accord with Kume's promise that if his son erected a stone statue of him on a busy street, he would atone for his crimes by suffering exposure to harsh weather. For reasons unknown, the statue came to be housed at Sensōji and later became a popular deity of power, marriage, and ague (see Fig. 13). Worshippers who sought its divine help wrote a letter (*ofumi*) to express their wishes, offered it, and then took a letter previously offered by someone else on the assumption that it was an answer from the Kume deity.[91]

8. Kumagai Inari. This deity was commonly called Anzaemon Inari, after its first worshipper, Kumagai Anzaemon, who lived in the late seventeenth century. According to one version of the chronicles, Anzaemon played a crucial role in saving the lives of a family of foxes while serving as a retainer of a lord of Echizen. When the daimyō planned a hunting excursion in a nearby brush, a fox appeared to Anzaemon and begged him to save his family. Upon hearing of this, the daimyō forbore from touching the fox family. A few years later Anzaemon became a masterless samurai and moved to Edo. While living a poverty-stricken life in Edo, Anzaemon relied on a bottle of sake and a parcel of food wrapped in bamboo leaves that someone would leave on his doorstep three or four times a month. One day an old man appeared to Anzaemon and informed him that an "auspicious event" (*kichiji*) would occur within the next year. As foretold, Anzaemon was hired by a daimyō family as a retainer at a salary of 200 koku of rice. Anzaemon later discovered that the old man was the head of the fox family he had helped to save. In order to honor the fox family, Anzaemon enshrined the old fox as his family's tutelary deity. This fox deity (Inari) eventually came to be housed at Sensōji, where it gained popularity in the late Tokugawa period.[92]

Fig. 13. The stone statue of Kume Heinaibee (from Saitō Gesshin, *Edo meisho zue*).

9. The smallpox deity of the Hōsō (smallpox) Shrine. Edoites believed that children suffering from smallpox could avoid harm if they would put under their pillow leaves of the *nandin* trees that grew around the Sensō Shrine.[93]

10. The Koyasu no Ishi (Stone of easy delivery) of Konzō-in. A couple from the Shinano domain received a revelation from an unknown deity while dreaming. The deity said, "It has been a long time since I came to lurk in your backyard. I now want to become a follower of the Three Treasures (Buddha, dharma, and sangha) as you are and devote myself to the Great Vehicle. I will then protect you, help your posterity prosper, and lessen the pain of difficult delivery for those who would make a connection."[94] The couple immediately dug out their backyard, found this special stone, and worshipped it wholeheartedly. Thereafter, they were blessed with five sons, four daughters, forty-six grandchildren, and 141 great-grandchildren. In the early eighteenth century, this stone was moved to Sensōji and soon became a popular deity believed to provide easy delivery and prosperity to offspring.

Besides these notable deities, Nishiyama Ebisu, an Avalokiteśvara statue with eleven faces, and a group of 100 Avalokiteśvara statues in Senzō-in were also popular objects of veneration. All these hayarigami deities attracted the worship of Edo people in the late Tokugawa period. Compared with the Asakusa Kannon, however, their popularity fluctuated and tended to be rather short-lived. The Sensōji administration tried to market these deities through such measures as *engi* (religious chronicles), ennichi, kaichō, and the refurbishing of the buildings housing them.[95] Nevertheless, the fate of these "fashionable deities" depended on the whimsical religiosity of their worshippers, who would turn off their veneration whenever they found better deities elsewhere.

According to Miyata Noboru, the Japanese people readily and arbitrarily create a new divinity through either *matsuri age* (to worship and then send up) or *matsuri sute* (to worship and then send off). Deification involves two stages: (1) granting divinity to any possessor of uncommon power by paying homage (*matsutte*) to it and (2) sending it up (*ageru*) if it is benevolent or sending it off (*suteru*) (i.e., outside the community) if it is malevolent.[96] The process of deification is so malleable that, in theory, any object can be installed as a deity if it is believed to possess extraordinary power. Once divinity is granted, the deity thus created is treated with the utmost devotion lest it harm its own creators.[97]

For Edoites, once an object was erected as a deity, it no longer mattered whether it had originally been an evil person or the cause of disease. Kume Heinaibee, who senselessly murdered innocent people, was a typical example of a villain-turned-deity in the form of *ikigami* (a living deity), that is, something transformed from an actual person. By the same token, the *hōsōgami* represented a smallpox-turned-deity in the form of *akujin* (an evil deity).[98] Beings with vicious natures could be elevated to the status of deities when people worshipped them and thus purified them of their evil elements. Edo people transformed the terrifying Niō, the Hag of Sanzu-no-Kawa, King Yama, and Acalanātha into benevolent deities through worship and prayer.[99] Even a stone (Koyasu no Ishi) could acquire divinity if Edoites showed a religious interest in it. Underlying this seemingly capricious creation of divinities was a deep-rooted belief that negative elements could be nullified by purificatory rituals and prayer. In this sense, divinity was a human construct.

Moreover, Edoites seemed to believe that these deities were neither permanent nor possessed of monopolistic powers. Justifying their actions through chronicles, miraculous stories (*reigenki*), scriptural narratives, customary beliefs, and even physical appearance, Sensōji worshippers assigned functions to their deities according to their own needs. The specialties of Arazawa Fudō, Rōjo Benzaiten, In Yakushi, Hōsōgami, and Koyasu no Ishi at Sensōji more or less corresponded with those of deities in Japan's traditional religious culture. But the decision to make Kume a marriage maker and curer of ague, to make the Hag of Sanzu no Kawa a protector of children's health, and to make the six Jizō statues givers of wisdom was quite arbitrary.[100] Furthermore, a deity's specialty could be quite fluid, depending on the needs of its worshippers. The Kume deity and the Hag of Sanzu no Kawa were typical: the former used to be a deity of power but was transformed into a deity of marriage making and ague curing, and the latter was transformed from a deity who protected children's health into a deity who cured toothache.

All these features attest that the nature of hayarigami deities was contingent on the life world of Edoites. When their living conditions and daily concerns changed, so did the world of their popular deities. Such constant change led to Buyō Inshi's lament that "traditional" deities, whether Buddhist or Shintō, had all died out. To him, divine authority should officially be defined within the framework of the Tokugawa system. But in late Tokugawa Edo people had lost their respect for government-sponsored religious authority. By implication, they had also lost their respect for the bakufu, which had proved all but useless to them. Those who hoped to improve their situations were left to create their own "miraculous" authorities. Thus distrust in conventional authority, whether religious or political, was translated into the proliferation of faddish prayer activities.

Given the trends of the time, the lasting popularity of the Asakusa Kannon was quite exceptional. The people of Edo believed that the Asakusa Kannon could respond to all prayers concerning *sainan* (disasters), *saiyaku* (misfortunes), or *shogan* (all wishes). There was no functional limitation to the power of the Asakusa Kannon, and worshippers never doubted its boundless compassion. The infinite supernatural faculties of the Asakusa Kannon were a source of great comfort to Edo people, who yearned for the omnipotent care of an overarching divine authority. The Asakusa Kannon's comprehensive salvational capacity was rarely questioned, thanks to the twenty-fifth chapter of the *Lotus Sūtra*, which was widely circulated in Japan as an independent sutra under the name of *Kannon kyō*, or *Fumon bon*.[101] This chapter explicitly sets forth the scope of Avalokiteśvara Bodhisattva's compassion, which reaches everyone and everywhere. The Avalokiteśvara Bodhisattva will save one from the "seven difficulties" (*shichinan*) and the "three poisons" (*sandoku*), and it will grant the "two desires" (*nikyū*).[102] The numbers seven, three, and two have been interpreted as representing, respectively, "external" obstacles, "internal" sufferings, and the "ideal" of a happy life; thus, they are symbolic of the Bodhisattva's omnidirectional compassion.[103]

Following the description of the universal compassion of Avalokiteśvara Bodhisattva, the *Lotus Sūtra* states that its salvational power is attainable by easy paths (*igyō*): by single-mindedly calling on its name, by being constantly mindful and humbly respectful of it, and by making offerings to it. In responding to each request, the scripture continues, Avalokiteśvara will appear in one of thirty-three forms (depending on which is most suitable), ranging from the body of a Buddha to the body of Vajrapāṇi, and deliver its salvational power. The number thirty-three is a Buddhist metaphor for infinity and signifies the ubiquity of Avalokiteśvara's compassion.[104] Both Avalokiteśvara's omnipresence and the idea that there were easy paths for attaining its divine help attracted worshippers.

Still, such doctrinal hermeneutics fall short of explaining the spectacular popularity of the Asakusa Kannon or, to be more precise, the popularity of the Asakusa Kannon statue enshrined in the Main Hall of Sensōji. Most Buddhist temples in the Tokugawa period housed more than one Kannon statue, but all Kannon images were not equally venerated. Only a few of them attracted popular worship, and the case of Sensōji was a rare exception even among those few. In the Sensōji precincts alone, there were five other Kannon halls of various sizes, and flanking the Asakusa Kannon statue in the Main Hall were six more Kannon images positioned shoulder to shoulder.[105] But none of them was considered comparable in power to the tiny Asakusa Kannon statue. Buddhist doctrine makes no mention of a deity's efficacy being dependent on the size of a statue of it. In fact, it makes no mention of a deity's needing to be represented by a statue at all.

The extraordinary religious power of the Asakusa Kannon was, in a word, a cultural construct. A wide range of factors that may have been involved in the popularity of the Asakusa Kannon have been mentioned in previous chapters: the wide circulation of chronicles dealing with it; the role of the prominent monk Ennin, who made the statue a secret Buddha; Sensōji's affiliation with the Tokugawa leadership; and Sensōji's geographical location, which served as a cultural, social, and institutional linchpin between Edo and the outside world. Undeniably, all these factors contributed to one degree or another to building the religious reputation of the Asakusa Kannon.

Nevertheless, the construction of the religious power of this small image cannot be fully understood without considering the Japanese conception of a deity's manifestation at a lodging place. A deity was believed to manifest itself and its power in a more appealing manner when it was worshipped at a designated lodging place and at a designated time. Based on this traditional idea of divine epiphany, Sensōji monks highlighted the special presence of the Asakusa Kannon at its golden statue through such special occasions as ennichi and kaichō.

In traditional Buddhism, any day that one pays worship to a Buddhist deity is one's connection-day (ennichi), and the religious merit gained by worshipping should not vary by the date. However, the Sensōji Buddhists promoted the idea that by worshipping the Asakusa Kannon on its designated connection-day, the anniversary of the day on which the statue was discovered (the eighteenth day of the third month), one would acquire far greater religious merit than would be the case on an ordinary day.[106] This idea was in tune with the traditional idea of a worship day (referred to as *sainichi* in Shintō)—the day when a deity was invited to its temporary lodging place, worshipped, and then sent back to its permanent residence.

No matter the theoretical grounds, the idea of a connection-day for the Asakusa Kannon was further developed in two directions: (1) the multiplying of connection-days from a yearly to a monthly event on the eighteenth day of each month (Sensōji advertised that those who worshipped the Asakusa Kannon on these particular days would attain hundreds [or even thousands] more merits than those who worshipped on other days) and (2) the creation of new quasi-connection-days in the name of *kudoku nichi* (merit-making dates), which were added to or overlapped the regular monthly dates. The annual schedule of merit-making dates and the amount of their obtainable merits are shown in Table 4. In the late Tokugawa period, the Sensōji administration distributed fliers advertising the annual schedule of merit-making dates widely, a tactic that proved to be very effective. The tenth day of the seventh month, known as *Shiman rokusen nichi* (46,000 days), attracted the largest crowds of worshippers, particularly in the nineteenth century.

Kaichō were also extraordinarily effective in raising the religious fame of the Asakusa Kannon. This ceremony featured the limited public exhibition of the secret statue of the Asakusa Kannon. Despite its Buddhist rhetoric, kaichō was unique to Japanese Buddhism and probably evolved from the tradition of keeping the *shintai* (the body of a Shintō deity) out of people's sight.[107] When the Asakusa Kannon supposedly manifested itself in its own lodging statue at a kaichō, Edo people almost held their

Table 4
Merit-Making Days for Worshipping the Asakusa Kannon

Month/day	Merits obtainable
1/1	100
2/30	90
3/4	100
4/18	100
5/18	100
6/18	400
7/10	46,000
8/24	4,000
9/20	300
10/19	400
11/7	6,000
12/19	4,000

SOURCE: Amino Aritoshi, *Sensōji shidan shō*, p. 460.

breath in anticipation of making direct contact with the deity. It is no wonder that Sensōji enjoyed so many visitors and an enormous income whenever a kaichō was held.

In the final analysis, Sensōji worshippers played a determining role in constructing the divine authority of the Asakusa Kannon. On the surface, Sensōji officials seemed to take the lead in this process but, in practice, it could never have taken place without the high demand for the numinous authority of the Asakusa Kannon. The Asakusa Kannon had remained a perennial, secret hayarigami until the Meiji government implemented a policy of separating kami from Buddhas. On the pretext that the secrecy of the Asakusa Kannon was a hoax to cover up its nonexistence, the Meiji government inspected the actual Asakusa Kannon in 1869. It was proved to exist, yet the government's action damaged its "absolute" secrecy. The public authorities thereafter continued to harass the prayer culture of Sensōji.[108] As for the other popular deities at Sensōji, their credibility was fragile even before the Meiji age.

Whether their popularity was perennial or short-lived, Sensōji hayarigami in the late Tokugawa period were a major source of alternative divine authority for Edoites. No matter how bad their living conditions, late Tokugawa Edoites were disinclined to take their troubles lying down. Since the bakufu and communal organizations failed to provide them with protection, Edoites became increasingly estranged from the public authorities and, instead, sought solace in their own actions or in their own religious quests.[109] An individual's handling of daily predicaments was now in his or her own hands. Although, with their decreasing respect for the bakufu, Edoites sometimes turned to violence and disorder, it was more usual for them to turn, through individual prayer, to the world of "fashionable deities." The popular world of Sensōji deities provided Edoites with a spiritual buffer zone that served to lessen their socioeconomic hardships and their psychological anguish.

Matsudaira Sadanobu's orthodox ideology was geared to arresting the "strayed" morality of Edo townspeople (as evidenced in their indulgence in the popular culture of prayer and play). However, despite strenuous efforts, he could not easily subdue the cultural trends of the time. To his disappointment, the popular play culture of Edo society not only caused the class boundaries of Edo inhabitants to be further blurred but also encouraged Edoites to develop their own modes of self-expression. Similarly, the prayer culture provided Edoites with a fertile source of new divine authority, and this served to relativize the stature of Tokugawa public authority. As we have seen in the popular Buddhist culture of Sensōji, fashionable popular deities seemed to enchant Edoites and to take the place of an inadequate bakufu. But despite the apparently deteriorating plausibility of the Confucian rule of "benevolence," bakufu leaders stubbornly insisted on trying to restore the vertical hierarchy of Confucian moral values and social class.

As a result, the moral fissure between the ruling and the ruled continued to widen in the late Tokugawa period. The flourishing popular culture of prayer and play, which was nurtured by the gradual dissipation of Tokugawa ideology, naturally came to exert more and more impact on public ethics, values, morals, and authority. More specifically, the rise of fashionable popular deities, which offset the decline of conventional deities, encouraged Edoites to seek their own spiritual authority as a way of overcoming the ironclad Tokugawa order. The ruled readily transformed themselves into lay priests, and they tailored prayer rituals so as to address their specific problems. Meanwhile, play, which had become routinized for all walks of people, provided a cultural venue for developing strength and a different system of values. For Edoites, the culture of prayer and play was a gateway to a new form of social perception and moral imagination. It is no wonder that Edoites, struggling within a feudal society, tried to convert prayer and play into an arena within which they could pursue their own cultural politics, meaning, and lives.

In their daily lives, Edo commoners were, however, still subject to the Tokugawa feudal system, and they were never really free from socioeconomic exploitation. Understandably, there was much gloom and despair. Despite this, Edo commoners strove to nourish, through their cultural pursuits, a sense of autonomy and legitimacy in the shadow world of Edo society. The upper classes' monopoly over prayer and play was greatly diminished by the common people's attempt to establish their own cultural space. Outside the dictates of established authority, Edoites vindicated their own notions of ethics and virtue. The prayer and play culture of Sensōji was one such cultural attempt at moral justification.

Nevertheless, the prayer and play culture did not result in a cultural revolution or a social revolt. In fact, direct challenges to the Tokugawa system were never tolerated. Edoites carefully avoided any hint of sedition, whether in the form of ideas or actions, since this was sure to end disastrously. In this sense, the Edoite prayer and play culture in the late Tokugawa period was a culture for helpless petty bourgeois (*shōshimin*). Edoites pursued liberation, but it was an internal liberation and was, by definition, invisible and premised on self-satisfaction. There was no cultural shake-up that would have affected the feudalistic Tokugawa system. Edo commoners justified their own moral values, expanded their self-understanding, and established new modalities of relating things, but they did all this within the boundary of private self-satisfaction. Accordingly, Edoites fell far short of establishing a new cultural framework that would entail political change. For this, they had to await a new polity. When it finally came, they were no longer Edoites, but Tokyoites. A new age was opened by political initiative from the top, not from the bottom.

CONCLUSION

The Cradle of Prayer and Play

In the early nineteenth century, the inhabitants of Edo used the word "kaichō" (to open a curtain) as slang for a crowd lost in the heat of gambling or a person lost in the pleasures of sex—within a religious space.[1] In theory, kaichō, the exhibition of a secret deity at a Buddhist temple, was the highest point of religious sanctity—the point at which a worshipper has direct personal contact with a mysterious deity. But in daily conversation, the word referred to a frolicsome activity occurring in an unusual place.

This usage of "kaichō" was something more than a derogatory reference to Buddhist institutions: play was indeed part of Buddhist culture in the late Tokugawa period. No matter what religious site they visited, Edoites expected opportunities for play as well as opportunities for prayer. There was no dichotomy between the sacred and the profane in Edoite consciousness, and neither gambling nor sexual pleasure was a stranger to the world of religious culture. Whether dealing with entertainment or piety, Edoites used the same vocabulary. Thus "kaichō" as a signifier for both prayer and play captures the essence of late Tokugawa Buddhist culture.

Because of the phenomenal popularity of its secret Asakusa Kannon statue, the Sensōji administration endeavored to hold kaichō as often as possible. For laypeople, the public revelation of the Asakusa Kannon was the high point of Sensōji Buddhism; for Sensōji as an institution, it was a prime opportunity to collect income. Spurred by worshippers' fervid response to the exhibition of the Asakusa Kannon and its own expectations of a sizable income, the Sensōji administration made every effort to circumvent the normal once-every-thirty-three-year schedule for kaichō. In the late Tokugawa period, Sensōji held at least seventeen special kaichō, in addition to four regular ones, in the space of about a century (see Table 5).

Sensōji offered various reasons to the bakufu in the attempt to obtain permission for special kaichō. On the occasions of visits by a shōgun or a shōgunal heir, Sensōji officials usually argued that the boundless compassion of the Asakusa Kannon should be shared with the general public. In 1773, when an epidemic ran rampant in Edo, killing thousands of people (allegedly as many as 119,000), Sensōji held a special kaichō to pray for relief. Fund-raisings for repairing or rebuilding the Main Hall and subtemples were also a good reason for a special kaichō, as were the centennial or fifty-year anniversaries to celebrate the discovery of the Asakusa Kannon statue. Furthermore, Sensōji hosted a number of de-gaichō events to display celebrated secret deities from other renowned religious institutions (e.g., the set of three secret Amitābha statues of Zenkōji).[2]

In all cases, the kaichō of the Asakusa Kannon at Sensōji, which were presented alongside the kaichō of play, attracted large crowds who sought both the firsthand blessing of the Asakusa Kannon and an array of uncommon opportunities for recreation and entertainment. Kaichō benefited all parties. For Sensōji, they brought a bonanza of saisen income that sometimes exceeded a thousand gold pieces. For kaichō viewers, misemono merchants, and entertainers, kaichō meant an exorbitant windfall, whether religious or economic, that they could otherwise hardly expect. It is, therefore, no wonder that resourceful religious institutions such as Sensōji made every effort to hold a kaichō whenever possible. As a result, displays that lasted sixty to eighty days were not uncommon in late Tokugawa Edo, and there were often five to ten simultaneous "exhibitions" in any given time.[3]

In the eighteenth century, the bakufu intervened in this situation through the mechanism of permission-granting in order to regulate the competition in this lucrative business. The bakufu decided to control the frequency and duration of kaichō by granting only five permits per season

Table 5
Kaichō at Sensōji, 1751–1860

Year	Duration (days)	Reason
1751	80	Regular
1769	30	Shōgunal visit
1773	1	To eradicate epidemics
1774	30	Shōgunal heir's visit
1777	50	1,150th anniversary of the discovery of the Asakusa Kannon
1781	15	Shōgunal visit
1783	80	Regular
1783	7	Shōgunal visit
1791	50	Fund-raising
1795	60	To rebuild the Kaminari Gate
1801	15	Shōgunal visit
1807	70	Fund-raising
1814	80	Regular
1817	15	Shōgunal visit
1827	80	1,200th anniversary
1830	15	Shōgunal visit
1832	60	Shōgunal visit
1841	60	To celebrate the restoration of the Main Hall
1848	60	Regular
1856	80	Fund-raising
1860	50	Fund-raising

SOURCE: Armino Aritoshi, p. 576.

and limiting exhibitions to sixty days per permit. In an attempt to prevent a temple or shrine from depending on kaichō for its finances, the bakufu further stipulated that an institution could hold one only at intervals of thirty-three years.[4] As we have seen, however, the bakufu was quite lenient about granting special permission to hold kaichō more often.

The bakufu's leniency toward special kaichō was not incompatible with its own policy intentions. As Hiruma Hisashi points out, the hidden agenda of the bakufu's policy was to cope with its own deteriorating finances. With the increase in budget deficits, in 1758 the bakufu was forced to abandon its long-standing policy of direct grants-in-aid to temples and shrines; in place of these grants, it allowed them to raise funds through kaichō or direct solicitation (known as *kange* [exhortation of Buddha's teachings]).[5] Since the bakufu's policy was intended to transfer the burden of preserving what was often referred to as the spiritual pillars of the nation to the people, the bakufu tried to establish regulations that would enable religious institutions to be self-supporting. Apparently, the bakufu began to perceive kaichō less as a matter of religious devotion and more as a means of financial gain. When it found itself unable to fulfill the traditional role of supporting "public" religious institutions, the bakufu opted to disguise its own financial problems by passing the responsibility for providing financial aid to those who patronized the temples and shrines themselves. In this ambivalent situation between the regulations and policy intentions of the bakufu, the Sensōji administration was quite successful in persuading the authorities and frequently obtained permission to hold kaichō, especially special ones.

With the self-contradictory sanction of the government, kaichō at the sakariba enclave of Sensōji blossomed into the culture of prayer and play. When the Sensōji sakariba was transformed into a space for religious quest and relaxation on the occasion of a kaichō, Edoites rushed to withdraw from the hustle and bustle of urban life in search of a moment of liberation from the constraints of feudal society. The Asakusa Kannon was status-blind and free from the formality of priestly service, and misemono entertainment was available to all classes.

Sensōji kaichō, which negated the principles of feudal bondage, added fluidity to Edo society. In this sense, the prayer and play culture of the Sensōji sakariba represented what Asai Ryōi (1612?–91) called the culture of the ukiyo (floating world). Just as Ryōi had already sensed in the mid-seventeenth century the growing laissez-faire spirit of urban culture, visitors to Sensōji in the late Tokugawa period pursued the comforts of faddish deities and the pleasures of the misemono, "caring not a whit for the pauperism staring [them] in the face and refusing to be disheartened, like a gourd floating along with the river current."[6]

Whether driven by a desire to pray for genze riyaku (this-worldly benefits) or by a desire to enjoy the pleasures of the moment, Edoites devoted their time and energy to floating on the cultural tides of the Sensōji sakariba. As casual lay Buddhists, they rarely relied on the services of Buddhist priests. Sensōji priests were unconcerned that lay Buddhists had to establish direct contact with the deities through their own devices. As anonymous, isolated monads practicing their own form of Buddhism, Edoites developed an individualized credo of this-worldly benefits. And, as casual cultural connoisseurs, they also searched for play opportunities. Deprived of political power and social prestige within feudal society, Edo commoners turned their full attention to expanding the inner space of individual freedom and enjoyment at the Sensōji sakariba. They were anonymous yet enthusiastic consumers looking for a release from the Tokugawa world.

Nevertheless, Edoites' seemingly carefree pursuit of Sensōji culture was more than a matter of indulging in momentary relief or relaxation. It had a sociopolitical dimension that was the antithesis of Tokugawa feudal society. When Edo society was relatively stable and had well-established communal organizations and associations, ward communities served as a scaffolding for social harmony and integration. From the mid-eighteenth century on, however, with the intrusion of monopoly capitalism, the influx of rural immigrants, and the massive emergence of the poor, Edo society began to undergo structural changes. Frequent fires destroyed neighborhoods, and residents were constantly being relocated to unfamiliar districts. The rapid increase in the number of impoverished samurai made Edo even more unstable. Edo society in the late Tokugawa period may have been dynamic, but it was also precarious and sometimes disruptive. Yet the bakufu's policy remained unchanged, and, even worse, the bakufu obstinately enforced that policy in an attempt to undo irreversible social changes.

Frustrated by the irrelevance of the Tokugawa feudal system, Edoites retreated into their own world of self-redemption. They were helpless before the high wall of feudal power and hereditary social status. The outside world was frozen and fixed, and their social standings were predetermined. The only escape was the religious world and a private ethic of pleasure seeking. The more Edo commoners desired something better, the more they turned to supernatural beings. Genze riyaku prayer was a convenient outlet for them.

In fact, as far as Edo commoners were concerned, improving their lives in this world certainly seemed more contingent on the help of deities or self-serving ethical values than it did on the workings of the Tokugawa political economy. Religion could be a substitute for a public authority that had failed to solve the problems of Edoites.[7] In this context, genze riyaku emerged as a suitable and promising mode of problem solving for Edo commoners. It is ironic that the social well-being of feudal Edoites was relegated to a prayer culture that was generated by none other than the feudal society they were attempting to escape. The well-being of the feudal body was itself ensured by feudal religiosity.

Similarly, the world of play culture at the Sensōji sakariba offered an outlet for those feelings and desires that ran counter to the ideology of Tokugawa moral order. Edo commoners did not dare to challenge the mandated link between the feudal body and the Confucian mind; rather, they directed their energies toward seeking the pleasures of the moment through any number of activities, all of which were conducted within an environment that was relatively free of bakufu harassment. The public authorities were lenient toward sakariba misemono, street arts, acting, and ukiyo paintings when they were performed in a setting that was segregated from normative society. And Edo townspeople did not miss the opportunity to enjoy what this setting had to offer.

However, pastime activities at the Sensōji sakariba could never be more than a fictional world of "acting" staged in an extraordinary setting. Once Edoites returned to their ordinary lives, they had once again to subject themselves to the social norms of Tokugawa society. It is in this context that the obsession of Edo commoners with the world of kabuki theater becomes understandable. Gender was erased by heavy makeup, and the kabuki body (as an agent of an inverted Tokugawa society) freed people from feudal norms. The kabuki audience could, through the medium of the theater, find itself momentarily liberated from a world governed by feudal principles.

Ukiyo paintings also fascinated Edoites. By separating the feudal body from its normative world and elevating it to an object of artistic appreciation, ukiyo artists introduced Edoites to an imaginary world of beauty. Beauty, as presented in a painting, was beyond the powers of the bakufu to mold. In retrospect, the vogue for *shunga* (spring paintings) in the Kan'ei era (1624–43), if short-lived, suggested the equality of all human beings through naked bodies and sexual images that dissolved social status and rank.[8] For Edo townspeople, shunga were a cultural manifesto that asserted the possibility of equality and liberation; for the ruling class, they were an ominous menace that threatened to undermine the Tokugawa social order. The bakufu soon banned "perverted" shunga paintings and suppressed other ukiyo paintings. It also regulated the world of kabuki.[9] Despite repeated bakufu attempts at control and suppression, however, popular play culture did not easily subside. Indeed, it mushroomed in the late Tokugawa period as if challenging the Tokugawa design of the Confucian feudal mind.

It is therefore arguable that the Sensōji sakariba culture of prayer and play had anti-feudal connotations. Visitors to Sensōji sought the assistance of its popular deities for what they could not otherwise deal with or expect the authorities to deal with. These deities were available, without the mediation of Sensōji priests, to anyone with a few coins. What the government could not provide could now be sought through prayer. Similarly, play opportunities in the Sensōji sakariba offered Edoites not only momentary relief from the endemic inequalities of Tokugawa society but also the possibility of imaginatively transforming them. Play culture, which eschewed political suppression, prospered in the highly commercialized environment of the Sensōji sakariba.

Nonetheless, although the Sensōji culture of prayer and play was imbued with anti-feudal potential, its soteriological praxis was both unrealistic and self-contradictory. For instance, genze riyaku prayer in the pursuit of material well-being was, in theory, incompatible with Buddhist teachings on compassion toward sentient beings. The legendary story of the fishermen at Sensōji, which inspired Buddhist worshippers to seek material blessings through the divine help of the Asakusa Kannon, illustrates the unbridgeable dichotomy between Edoites' faddish quest for this-worldly benefits and the cardinal teachings of Buddhism. According to the *Kannon myōō shū* (A collection of Kannon's miraculous responses), with which Edoites were familiar, after discovering the Asakusa Kannon statue, the three fishermen prayed to it when they cast their net into the Sumida River and then found it full of fish. "From that time on, whenever they went out to catch fish, they first prayed to the sacred Kannon image, and then threw their nets, which would then be full of all kinds of fish. They earned a lot of money, all thanks to the miraculous help of the Kannon."[10] Sensōji monks loved to tell this story to show that the Asakusa Kannon could bless worshippers with worldly benefits.

A closer examination, however, reveals that the message behind this story is a violation of the Buddha's compassionate teaching about the sanctity of life. "Do not willingly take the life of a sentient being" is the First Commandment of the Buddha. Yet these fishermen prayed for the Buddhist deity to bless the killing of sentient beings. Sensōji monks eagerly preached this story as an example of the boundless this-worldly benefits that could be obtained through the miraculous working of Buddhist merits: "To kill more, just invoke more compassion from the Kannon." But other Sensōji stories reveal that these three fishermen knew full well that they were violating the Buddha's commandment against killing. No doubt, they feared karmic retribution. The stories nonetheless remind us more strongly that merits could be accumulated by supporting monks and donating materials to temples and that such merits were great enough to excuse sins and evil deeds.

The story of the Asakusa fishermen illustrates the main characteristics of the genze riyaku soteriology of Tokugawa Buddhism. The concern with material benefits was so overwhelming that worshippers manipulated the salvational modus operandi of Buddhist compassion for their own convenience. Buddhist soteriology was easily subjected to situational genze riyaku concerns. More important, encouraged by such malleability, Edoites could readily pull their this-worldly concerns out of the contemporary realm (*genze*) of the Tokugawa political economy and find a refuge for them in the spiritual power of divinities that they themselves created. Consequently, Edoites opted out of the Tokugawa body politic instead of confronting it. True, there were a number of rebellions in the form of "urban smashings" and other collective protests. These actions were, however, infrequent and incidental. In general, escaping from social reality by seeking refuge in a salvational fantasy was the motivation behind Tokugawa Buddhist soteriology. And it is this that fashioned the genze riyaku prayer culture of Sensōji in the late Tokugawa period.

The limitations of the anti-feudal connotations of play culture were no different from those of prayer culture. Edoites pursued popular play opportunities as a way of liberating themselves from Tokugawa feudal society, but they also failed to relate their momentary pleasures to the larger context of the Tokugawa political economy. The problem was that the liberated feudal body achieved through play was no more than a product of ephemeral acting (as seen in kabuki theaters or in ukiyo paintings) and, therefore, remained detached from the hard reality of Tokugawa politics. Edoites did not politicize their feudal bodies as independent agents of an anti-feudal struggle. The independence of the feudal body from the feudal mind was simply an illusion confined to the world of play.

The Edoite fascination with the kabuki play *Tōkaidō Yotsuya kaidan* unequivocally illustrates the ephemerality of fictive emancipation from Tokugawa society. The story, which Tsuruya Nanboku wrote for the Nakamuraza theater in 1825, is horrifying: The protagonist Iuemon murders a man, takes the victim's daughter, Oiwa, as his wife, and then plots to have her killed. Soon after his wife has been murdered, he inherits her sizable property. At that moment, his murdered wife becomes a fiery ghost who tries to take revenge on him, but to no avail.[11] Edoites were thrilled by the inverted social norms and ethics promulgated by the protagonist of this play. The world of kabuki acting offered them a cathartic moment within which the concerns of the real world were drowned. Edoites eagerly entered into plots that featured the reversal or negation of the norms of Tokugawa feudal society, an act that must certainly have been easier than confronting that society directly.

For Edoites, the Sensōji sakariba was truly a fictional utopia, where even the lowest classes could freely search for self-liberation in the commercialized play markets. The commodities available at these markets provided Edo townspeople with nothing less than a cultural ghetto of spiritual communitas.

As has been stated, however, the culture of prayer and play fell far short of enabling Edoites to challenge the Tokugawa system. Whether pursued through prayer or through play, moments of salvation, autonomy, self-liberation, and enjoyment were merely temporary alternatives to the feudal social order. Arguably, what the prayer and play culture of Sensōji offered, in the final analysis, was the illusion of self-satisfaction and the absence of power. By retreating into a hermitic space of anti-feudal praxis, Edoites depoliticized their position in the real world. Relief, autonomy, and pleasure were vigorously sought, but they were detached from the governing principles of Tokugawa society.[12] In other words, the dominance of illusory pleasure over political engagement was an absolute precondition of the prayer and play culture.[13]

Despite the political passivity of the sakariba culture, bakufu leaders in the late Tokugawa period did not condone the separation of the politics of the Tokugawa system from the cultural orientations of the ruled. For the stability of Tokugawa feudal society, bakufu leaders could not let culture (the spiritual) deviate from politics (the physical). In a system within which the life of commoners was expected to be simple and harsh and to take place within the boundaries of social class, the holistic integration of the physical and the spiritual was a social mandate. Under the dictates of this mind-body holism, the ruled were not supposed to talk freely about "passion and feeling as essential to human nature."[14] Instead of following a class-bound prudent life, lamented bakufu leaders, townspeople were pursuing undisciplined consumption, play, and debauchery, not to mention following an indiscriminate prayer fad that seemed to instill distrust in the authorities. As H. D. Harootunian reminds us, all these passions and desires, which affected samurai and peasants alike, in fact drove the populace into a "dangerous libidinal economy."[15] In order to preserve the Tokugawa order, bakufu leaders insisted that such cultural perversity be redressed through belt-tightening measures and moral exhortation.

That was the ultimate direction of the Kansei Reforms of the 1790s, which aimed to reinstate public morality by suppressing undesirable bodily expressions as well as unorthodox ideas. The Tenpō Reforms four decades later again tried to restore the moral health of urban life, which, according to the bakufu, had been severely tainted by religious superstition and the passion for play activities.[16] Bakufu leaders, who were accustomed to attributing all destructive moral problems to the mind, condemned the fun-seeking activities and religious quests of Edoites as deviations from Confucian morality. Given this ideological stance, the popular culture of prayer and play was readily targeted as the object of mind-centered reform measures throughout the late Tokugawa period. But once the initial push for reform ended, the sakariba culture of prayer and play always reasserted itself.

When the zeal for the Tenpō Reforms drew to a halt in 1844, for example, Edoite cultural energy again burst into full bloom. The sakariba culture of prayer and play was especially spectacular during the eras of Kōka (1844–47) and Kaei (1848–53). In response to exploding demand, the production of cultural commodities such as ukiyo paintings, *kusazōshi* (illustrated storybooks), and popular street plays returned to the levels of the Bunka and Bunsei eras. Storytelling halls, which had been hammered by the Tenpō Reforms, mushroomed all over the city with amazing speed, and soon numbered more than a thousand. Misemono businesses also quickly recaptured the resurgent appetites of Edoites and upgraded their displays and performances.[17] By the same token, religious commodities rode the fad of genze riyaku prayer. Edoites, who combined their religious cravings with their asobi cravings, crowded into religious places and downtown sakariba. There also appeared several popular mini-circuits for pilgrimages, featuring Kannon, Jizō, and Amitābha. Given this cultural mood, it is only natural that Sensōji's regular kaichō in 1848, along with two special fund-raising kaichō in 1856 and 1860, were great successes. The power of orchestrated commercialism demonstrated itself once again.

After successfully holding thirty-one kaichō during the Tokugawa period, in the modern period Sensōji still continued the legacy of urban Buddhist prayer and play culture. This is most evident in de-gaichō. Sensōji ventured to hold the first de-gaichō for the Asakusa Kannon at the Matsusakaya Department Store in Nagoya in 1929. It was a tremendous success. Since then, more than twenty de-gaichō for the Asakusa Kannon have been held at various commercial locations, from Kyūshū to Hokkaidō. On each occasion, Sensōji conducted an aggressive advertising campaign to promote the exhibit of its "hidden treasures" (*hihō*) and the secret Asakusa Kannon. These Sensōji de-gaichō were designed to "open the curtain" of commercial Buddhism within the ambiance of prayer and play. Commercial de-gaichō in the modern period are the true legacies of Sensōji's Buddhist culture in late Tokugawa Japan and its seamless synthesis of prayer and play.

Reference Matter

Notes

For complete author names, publication titles, and publication data, see the Works Cited, pp. 265–80.

Introduction

1. Matsudaira, 1: 482.

2. *Shintei zōho kokushi taikei: Tokugawa jikki*, 38: 221; and Amino Aritoshi, pp. 218–19.

3. Matsudaira, 2: 483.

4. Naitō Akira and Hozumi Kazuo, 1: 11; and Tokoro, "Edo no machi," p. 100.

5. Matsudaira, 1: 495–97; Amino Aritoshi, p. 215.

6 Matsudaira, 1: 482; and Amino Aritoshi, pp. 182–210.

7. *Shintei zōho kokushi taikei: Tokugawa jikki*, 39: 353.

8. Naitō Masatoshi, pp. 82–83.

9. The gargoyle had a monkey-like face and two horns. Because of its monkey (*saru*) face, people believed that it would be able to remove (*saru*) any kind of misfortune. See Amino Aritoshi, pp. 374–75.

10. Matsudaira, 1: 495–97; Amino Aritoshi, p. 215; and Tokoro, "Go-shuinjō," pp. 84–85.

11. Sueki, pp. 37–38.

12. Itō Yuishin, pp. 175–226.

13. Dozens of versions of the Sensōji chronicles survive today. The earliest one is presumed to be a product of the late medieval period, and the rest were written in the Tokugawa and Meiji periods, usually on the occasion of a kaichō of the secret Asakusa Kannon image. See Amino Aritoshi, pp. 1–22; and Asakura Haruhiko.

The year 628 is doubtful, but archaeological finds in the Sensōji area strongly suggest that a temple existed on the present site at least in the early Nara period (710–84). The earliest document containing the name "Sensōji" is a section of the *Azuma kagami* written in the fifth year of the Jishō era (1181).

14. Amino Aritoshi, pp. 70–71.

15. Due to its connection with Ennin, Sensōji switched its affiliation from the Hossō sect to the Tendai sect; in 1950, it changed affiliations again and became head temple of the newly established Shō Kannon sect.

16. The statue that Ennin carved was twenty-five inches (two *shaku* [60.5 cm] and two *sun* [4.9 cm]) high. This does not mean, however, that the original Asakusa Kannon statue was the same height; its dimensions have never been recorded, and no one has ever seen it. A widespread folk tradition has it that the original statue is exactly 1 *sun* and 8 *bun* high (approximately 5 cm); these dimensions correspond precisely to the day on which it was discovered: the "eighteenth" day of the third month. See Amino Aritoshi, pp. 78–79, 86–87.

17. Matsudaira, 1: 478–79, 483.

18. Takano, *Kinsei Nihon*, pp. 132–36.

19. Tokoro, "Go-shuinjō," pp. 81–82.

20. More specifically, for example, in the 1640s the total yield from the landholdings consisted of 467 koku from paddy fields and 33 koku from dry fields. See Kitahara Susumu, "Jiryō to nengu." The Sensōji administration imposed a fixed tax rate (*jōmen*) of 35 percent of rice yields throughout the Tokugawa period, but was flexible about collecting this tax, particularly in years of drought or flood. See *SN*, 3: 258, 264, 267–71; 4: 755–68; 5: 366.

21. Terakado, 1: 63.

22. Ibid., pp. 69–77.

23. *Shintei zōho kokushi taikei: Tokugawa jikki*, 39: 353. There was a larger political scheme behind this reshuffling, which was to transplant the model of the triangular cosmology of the imperial court, Kyoto, and Enryakuji on Mount Hiei (the head temple of the Tendai sect) to Eastern Japan. This scheme was promoted by Tenkai, who envisioned connecting Edo Castle, Edo, and a new hegemonic Buddhist center. For the site of the temple, Shinobugaoka (in Ueno) was chosen and named Mount Tōei (Eastern Hiei), and Kan'eiji, which would replace Sensōji as a major Buddhist prayer hall for the Tokugawa family, was built there in 1625.

24. According to a survey by the Meiji government early in the 1870s, Sensōji's original farmlands were preserved almost intact at the end of the Tokugawa period. The rice yields (in koku) from the Sensōji farmlands were Senzoku Village, 346.149 koku; Yamanojuku-chō, 17.996 koku; Namiki-chō and

Chaya-machi, 5.222 koku; Komakata-chō, 5.500 koku; Suwa-chō, 9.712 koku; Sangen-chō, 14.845 koku; Nishinaka-chō, 7.576 koku; Higashinaka-chō, 10.579 koku; Tawara-machi, 21.639 koku; Shōden-chō and Kawara-machi, 21.540 koku; Ta-machi, 9.040 koku; Zaimoku-chō, 9.677 koku; Hanakawado-chō, 33.104 koku; and Saya Asakusa-machi, 3.570 koku. Total production was 516.149 koku (Kimura, pp. 53–54).

25. All income statistics are estimated from records in *SN*, 9: 173–285.

26. Hirai, 6: 177.

27. Yanagita, "Nihon no matsuri," 10: 261–84; and Miyata, *Onna no reiryoku*, p. 176.

28. It was not only in years of slumps or natural disasters but also in years of economic boom that merchants petitioned for reductions, or at least for no increases, in taxes and rent. See *SN*, 5: 190–92. In particular, during the winter season, or during periods of musical performances (*narimono*) on the occasions of the funerals of Tokugawa family members or monzeki abbots, merchants in the precinct usually appealed for rent exemption on the basis of slow business. See *SN*, 1: 493–94.

29. Gill, 11: 489–94.

30. Turner, pp. 30–34.

31. Sutton-Smith, pp. 3–5.

32. For a discussion on the role of the concept of public duty (*yaku*) in Tokugawa Japan, see Bitō, pp. 27–52.

33. Ooms, *Tokugawa Ideology*, pp. 50–62; and Chiba, p. 48.

34. Umeda, pp. 359–61.

35. Ibid., pp. 351–53.

36. Ibid., p. 98.

37. The *Tokugawa jikki* records: "On the sixth day [of the eighth month], the chief priest of Asakusa Kannon Chiraku-in, Chūun, brought a legal proceeding against the Nikkō abbot [of Kan'eiji] and also slew a dog of a gatekeeper. Because his actions were against the law for followers of the Buddha, he was divested of the post of chief priest of the Kannon as well as the duty of Mount Momiji [Tōshōgū]." This account tells of two charges: Chūun's challenge to the authority of his head temple, the Rinnōji monzeki of Kan'eiji; and his violation of Shōgun Tsunayoshi's Edicts on Compassion for Living Beings (*shōrui awaremi no rei*), which prohibited cruelty to animals. See *Shintei zōho kokushi taikei: Tokugawa jikki*, 42: 553.

38. Tokoro, "Jōkyō ni nen Sensōji bettō tsuihō jiken."

39. This refers to the destruction of Hieizan Enryakuji in 1571, Nichiren

Buddhism in 1579, Ishiyama Honganji in 1580, Kōyasan in 1581, and Negoroji in 1585.

40. For more details, see Tsuji Zennosuke, p. 9.

Chapter 1

1. For more details, see Reader, pp. 55–106.

2. A well-known but forged temple document, *gojōmoku shūmon danna ukeai no okite* (Regulations on articles for confirming religious sects and danna houses), shows how the danna house system was abused. Most temples in the Tokugawa period preserved a copy of this document, which contained fifteen articles prescribing the conditions under which a danna temple could refuse to include a family in its non-Christian registry—known as *shūmon ninbetsu chō* (registry of religious sects and people's identification). Danna households could not ignore these regulations, since their temple could retaliate by declining to issue non-Christian identification certificates. According to the regulations, a temple could refuse to issue a certificate when a household failed to pay its annual or special fees, when it did not cooperate in the events of its danna temple, or when it intentionally neglected to ask its danna temple priests to preside over mortuary or memorial rituals. Each year the head monk of a temple would reiterate these articles to his danna households before renewing their registration certificates. This temple document was also widely used as a textbook to give children in the *terakoya* educational system reading and writing practice. For how this forged document was circulated, see Tamamuro, "Bakuhan taiseika no Bukkyō," pp. 31–38.

3. Matsudaira, 2: 212–88.

4. Nomura, pp. 183–84.

5. See Takizawa.

6. Matsudaira, 1: 370–438.

7. The shūshō ritual was originally performed on the first through seventh days of the first month, but in 1689 it was moved a day forward (in accordance with its performance at Kan'eiji). See Amino Aritoshi, pp. 392–93.

8. Shioiri, pp. 328–29.

9. The shūshō ritual derived from an indigenous New Year's ceremony that featured a prayer rite for ensuring good harvests and national peace. Shūshō rituals at Buddhist temples usually contained procedures designed to invoke the protective power of Buddhist deities as well as procedures to ensure purification. For more details about the shūshō ritual in general, see Gorai, "Shūshōe Shūnie to minzoku"; and Nakazawa, pp. 46–50.

10. For purification, most temples counted on the *kichijō* (Śri-mahādevī) re-

pentance ritual, which is based on the seventeenth chapter of text no. 665 in the *Taishō shinshū daizōkyō*, 16.402a–456c. See Hayami, pp. 105–8.

11. For a lay observation of the tsuina ceremony in the late Tokugawa period, see Saitō Gesshin, *Tōto saijiki*, 1: 19–20.

12. Among the various mantras, the Senju darani was singled out as the most efficacious spell after it had been introduced by the head monk, Kuzen, from the Kinzanji in Okayama in 1712. The text of the Senju darani is the *Ch'ien-shou ch'ien-yen Kuan-shih-yin p'u-sa ta-pei-hsin t'o-lo-ni ching* (*Taishō shinshū daizōkyō*, no. 1064, 20.115b-119c). For the actual practice of the mantra at Sensōji, see Matsudaira, 2: 377; and Saitō Gesshin, *Tōto saijiki*, 1: 79–80.

13. Shioiri, pp. 337–40.

14. For detailed statistics concerning Sensōji's prayer patrons and confraternities, see Matsudaira, 2: 212–88. Subtemples sometimes organized a temporary confraternity in order to raise funds for special purposes—usually for small-scale projects such as erecting a stupa or lantern stall. After the completion of the projects, the confraternity soon disbanded. See *SN*, 4: 768–69.

15. This prayer schedule format, referred to as *sanki* (three periods), was derived from the daimyō's ceremony for the shōgun. On the fifth day of the fifth month (Dango), the ninth day of the ninth month (Chōyō), and the twenty-first day of the twelfth month (Seibo), all daimyō in residence at the capital had an audience with the shōgun, at which time they presented him with gifts for the occasion—respectively, two sets of *katabira* (a hemp garment), *noshime* (a ceremonial robe worn by a samurai under the *kamishimo*), and *somekosode* (a wadded silk garment). See Kitahara Akio, 10: 262.

16. Among many examples, see *SN*, 1: 517; and 13: 483. In particular, Sensōji administrators conducted, without fail, a special prayer ritual in the year corresponding to the unlucky ages (25, 42, and 60 years old) of the shōgun as well as the Rinnōji monzeki, and presented them with special talismans for their safety and peace. See *SN*, 8: 627; 9: 5; 10: 3; and 12: 402, 555. For studies of the traditional religious measures used to deal with unlucky ages, see Watanabe.

17. For example, see *SN*, 2: 213 (residency in the home domain); 2: 402–3 and 429 (bad crops); 3: 730 (earthquake and bad crops); and 4: 341 (sumptuary laws).

18. Other important nation-protecting sutras were the *Suvarṇaprabhāsottama Sūtra* (*Konkōmyōkyō*) and the *Ninnō Hannyakyō*, a Chinese apocryphon.

19. The six stages of an esoteric prayer ritual are: (1) purifying the body, words, and mind of the priest; (2) establishing a sanctum for the performance; (3) establishing an altar for the main deity; (4) sending a jeweled chariot to invite the main deity; (5) purifying the inside and outside of the altar once more; and (6) making an offering to the main deity. See Yoritomo, "Mikkyō to shuhō," pp. 78–81.

For comparison with other Kannon rituals, see Kakuzen (1143–?), ed., "Shō Kannon-hō" and "Jūhachinichi Kannon-ku," in *Dai Nihon Bukkyō zensho: Kakuzen shō* (Tokyo: Kōdansha, 1972), 54: 97–116; Shōchō (1205–82), ed., "Shō Kannon," in *Dai Nihon Bukkyō zensho: Asaba shō*, 58: 226–30; and Jōkei (1155–1213), "Kannon kōshiki," in *Taishō shinshū daizōkyō*, no. 2728, 84.886a–887c.

20. For a discussion of the role of mantras in esoteric prayer ritual, see Yoritomo, *Mikkyō to mandara*, pp. 96–150.

21. Amino Aritoshi, 386–89.

22. According to Gorai Shigeru's ("Minzoku shinkō") interpretation, the well-known message of the *Dai-Hannya Sūtra*, the wisdom of "emptiness" (*śūnyatā*), was powerful enough to transmit an allegorical understanding of purification. The idea of "emptiness" was interpreted as a magical power that could "purify," or "empty," one's life of malicious elements.

23. For example, a messenger from the Izumi daimyō, the Tōdō family, rushed into Sensōji around eleven o'clock at night on the twenty-seventh day of the sixth month of 1770 and asked for a special prayer ritual. The messenger said that his lord had been suddenly struck by extreme pain from a serious disease, and in the hope of alleviating his pain, he immediately wanted to receive a Sensōji talisman and votive offerings. Sensōji priests promptly conducted a Dai-Hannya ritual and sent a talisman along with a votive offering (an item that they had planned to offer to the Asakusa Kannon the next morning). See *SN*, 3: 469–70. For the development of talismans or religious fetishes embodying the religious power of deities in general, see Yabe, pp. 3–23.

24. The Buddhist custom of producing the kumotsu fetish has a parallel in the Shintō worship service. For details, see Yanagita, "Nihon no matsuri," 10: 261–84; and Tani, pp. 205–35.

25. "Enyū nikki" and "Enyū nikki betsuroku," in Yanagisawa, vol. 13.

26. Ibid., p. 571.

27. Matsudaira, 1: 1–2.

28. For some examples of the religious concerns of *ōoku* women, see *SN*, 3: 664–69 (well-being of the shōgunal family), 4: 8 (recovery of an ill shōgunal heir), 5: 425 (recovery of the shōgun), 6: 764 (healthy growth of a shōgunal infant), 12: 426 (safety and health during pregnancy), and 13: 147–49 (safe delivery).

29. Matsudaira, 2: 632–34, 670.

30. See Nishiyama, *Edo Culture*, pp. 80–90.

31. Hayashi, "Kannon sama to Sutejirō."

32. See "Jijiroku," in *Mikan zuihitsu hyakushū*, ed. Mitamura Engyō (Kyoto: Rinkawa shoten, 1927), 6: 49–51.

33. Saitō Gesshin, *Bukō nenpyō*, 2: 35.

34. See Saitō Gesshin, *Saitō Gesshin nikki shō.*

35. For more details, see Nishiyama, "Edo no machi nanushi Saitō Gesshin," 4: 463–502.

36. Komori, *Edo Asakusa machina no kenkyū,* p. 256.

37. Takeuchi, "Shomin bunka no naka no Edo," p. 39.

38. Nishiyama, "Dai-Ei Hakubutsukan no Asakusa eken."

39. Since subtemples did not have the power to levy taxes on their front streets, an effort to develop front-street markets involved petition and approval. See *SN,* 3: 274–75, 5: 566, 6: 785–86, 7: 84–85, and 10: 147–51. For a detailed report on the front streets of some subtemples in the early 1820s, see "Sensōji jichū Kongō-in monzen yokka in monzen shirabe kakiage" and "Kakiage Asakusa Iō-in monzen," in *Kyū bakufu hikitsugi sho: Edo michikata kakiage,* 2 vols., annot. and ed. Hayashi Rokurō, Hasegawa Masatsugu, and Asakura Haruhiko (Tokyo: Shin jinbutsu ōraisha, 1987), 2: 63–68.

40. Matsudaira, 2: 289–91.

41. Ibid., 2: 444–68.

42. Ibid., 2: 439–54; Mizue, "Meibutsu no ryūkōsei" and "Yone manjū to so no hayari"; and Kitahara Susumu, "Kaminari monzen no meishu."

43. Amino Aritoshi, pp. 467–72.

44. Saitō Gesshin, *Tōto saijiki,* 3: 94.

45. Matsudaira, 2: 420.

46. Yanagisawa, p. 731.

47. Matsudaira, 2: 574–92.

48. Saitō Gesshin's *Bukō nenpyō* records in some detail the display of "living figures" in 1855:

> "Living figures" from Osaka were put on display at Asakusa Okuyama. These figures were manufactured by Matsumoto Kisaburō from Bingo in Kumamoto; they are said to be made, not of wood or clay, but rather of papier-mâché. Many figures were exhibited: inhabitants of the island of long arms, the island of long legs, the land of perforated chests, the land of no stomachs, and figures from other exotic lands. Figures of courtesans from the Maruyama area [of Nagasaki] were also displayed. All of these figures, both men and women, are completely lifelike. (trans. from Nishiyama, *Edo Culture,* p. 235)

49. All examples are extracted from Matsudaira and Asakura Kamezō. Asakura offers the most comprehensive collection of misemono shows of the Tokugawa and early Meiji periods. Since its publication, this book has been a standard reference for secondary studies of misemono. See Moriya, "Misemono kenkyū kaidai."

50. Asakura Kamezō, pp. 139–218; Furukawa, pp. 123–78.

51. For more detailed examples of the exhibition of human deformities in the late Tokugawa period, see Markus, "The Carnival of Edo," pp. 528–31; Asakura Kamezō, pp. 139–75; Furukawa, pp. 289–94; and Ono Takeo, pp. 88–90, 95–102, 105–10.

Exhibitions of natural history eventually suffered the same fate as did exhibitions of humans. Exotic fauna and flora, for example, ceased to be displayed at Sensōji when the Meiji government established the Ueno zoo in 1882 and, later, the botanical gardens. However, until then, the Sensōji misemono never failed to attract the Edo populace.

52. Asakura Kamezō, pp. 246–50, 278–80, 290–92; Furukawa, pp. 203–8, 270–80; and Ono Takeo, pp. 154–204.

53. Imada, pp. 126–27; Morioka and Sasaki, p. 133; for more details, see Okabe.

54. Imada, pp. 128–30. For other examples of storytelling that critiqued the established order, see Morioka and Sasaki, pp. 139–45.

55. These examples are from Matsudaira; Asakura Kamezō, pp. 1–137; and Furukawa, pp. 21–121.

56. Markus, "The Carnival of Edo," pp. 531–36; and for a comprehensive list of types of popular performing arts, see Nishiyama, *Edo Culture*, pp. 228–31.

57. For a list of performances specially arranged for the shōgun and other dignitaries, see Matsudaira, 2: 625–30.

58. Ibid., 1: 218; and Furukawa, p. 94. For the Matsui family, see Nishiyama, *Iemotosei no tenkai*, pp. 101–10.

59. Asakura Kamezō, pp. 33–57; and Furukawa, pp. 47–60.

60. For example, the acrobatic shows of Hayatake Torakichi and Sakurazuna Komaju in the early 1860s were so popular that the entrance fee was once set at 1,600 copper coins per gallery (*sajiki*) and 372 coins per head. The usual fee was a few copper coins. See Asakura Kamezō, p. 56.

61. In the seventeenth century, sumō was a leisure sport available only to the privileged few, and the shōgunate designated it as a symbol of samurai culture. Under the strict supervision of the Office of the Magistrate of Temples and Shrines, which oversaw applications, approval, and so on, a sumō game could only be held at a samurai's residence and was for invited guests only. Around the Genroku era (1688–1703) the shōgunate allowed sumō matches as a means of raising funds (*kanjin kōgyō*) for the upkeep of temples and shrines. Later, in the Hōei era (1704–10), the shōgunate partially deregulated sumō. See Takano, *Kinsei Nihon*, pp. 2–25. For the establishment of sumō *iemoto* by the Yoshida house,

which based its claim on the role of Yoshida Oikaze in the late seventeenth century, see Bolitho, "Sumō and Popular Culture," pp. 26–28.

62. Ishioka, 14: 329.

63. Komori, *Edo Asakusa machina no kenkyū*, pp. 252, 256–57.

64. Matsudaira, 1: 446–48.

65. Satō Yōjin, "Chaya," pp. 268–69.

66. Komori, *Edo Asakusa machina no kenkyū*, p. 258.

67. Ibid., p. 251.

68. Tokoro, "Monzen machi no shihai." For the implementation of the decree of 1745 at Sensōji, see *SN*, 3: 341–42.

69. Buyō Inshi, 1: 91–92.

70. Ibid., 1: 98.

71. Ibid., 1: 106.

Chapter 2

1. Tsuji Zennosuke, p. 477.

2. Umeda, pp. 100–102.

3. Ibid., pp. 110–17.

4. Tsuji Zennosuke, p. 164.

5. Ibid., pp. 195–96.

6. For more details, see Collcutt, pp. 147–50.

7. Tsuji Zennosuke, pp. 390–92.

8. Kashiwahara, "Gohō shisō to shomin bunka," pp. 547–48.

9. For a detailed treatment of the subject, see Watt, pp. 200–212.

10. For more details about the visits of the Ashikaga shōgun, see Satō Toyozō, "Shōgun-ke onari ni tsuite, 1" and "Shōgun-ke onari ni tsuite, 4."

11. Satō Toyozō, "Shōgun-ke onari ni tsuite, 6" and "Shōgun-ke onari ni tsuite, 7."

12. Although most of these items were supplied from the Kan'eiji, the Sensōji administration still had to spend sizable amounts in return for the privilege of having shōgunal visits. In order to lessen the frequent financial burden on Sensōji, in 1807 the shōgunate set up a special fund of twenty gold pieces at Kan'eiji, which was to use the interest on this fund to reimburse Sensōji for the expenses it incurred. See *SN*, 11: 302.

13. The idea of a thirty-three-year interval was derived from the thirty-three manifestations of Avalokiteśvara Bodhisattva, as expounded in the twenty-fifth chapter of the *Lotus Sūtra*.

14. For a complete list of Sensōji kaichō in the Tokugawa period, see Amino

Aritoshi, pp. 514–16; and for de-gaichō held in Sensōji, see Hiruma, *Edo no kaichō*, pp. 126–36.

15. For a detailed discussion of preparations for holding a kaichō in general, see Hiruma, *Edo no kaichō*, pp. 114–26, 183–87.

16. Hiruma, "Edo no kaichō," 2: 447–71.

17. Nishiyama, "Ichiritsusai Hiroshige ga."

18. The Sensōji administration appreciated the donation of material items such as lanterns, ema, tea bowls, rice, handiworks, and cloth, but preferred cash offerings to the point that it sometimes stipulated what percentage of a donation could be made in the form of material goods (i.e., 30 percent). See *SN*, 4: 720.

19. Orikuchi, "Nenjū gyōji," 15: 374–78.

20. For an excellent discussion of the Shintō festival and kami asobi, see Plutschow, pp. 41–74.

21. For a detailed study of kanjin campaigns in the ancient and medieval periods, see Goodwin.

22. LaFleur, *Karma of Words*, p. 54.

23. Miyata, "Toshi to minzoku bunka," p. 11. Even today people in the Tōhoku area call a place for trade a "machi." On the other hand, according to Yanagita Kunio, *ichi*, referring to a woman who serves deities, is derived from *itsukime* (a clean woman); see his "Yama no jinsei," 4: 125.

24. Kitami, pp. 27–28.

25. For detailed discussions of the function of markets during the ancient period, see Kobayashi; and Saigō. For a detailed discussion of *utagaki*, see Plutschow, pp. 118–28.

26. Miyata, *Edo no chiisana kamigami*, 251–52.

27. Matsudaira, 2: 441–60. For more on Asakusa liquor, see Kitahara Susumu, "Kaminari monzen no meishu."

28. According to a widely publicized story, one day in 945 the Asakusa Kannon appeared to the lord of Awa in a dream and informed him that if he would eat seaweed collected from the Sumida River, then, under the protection of the Buddha, he would be free from disease and the three poisons, and his family would be forever prosperous in this world and happy in the other world (Matsudaira, 2: 441–44). A handbill composed by Ryūtei Tanehiko (1783–1842) to advertise Asakusa seaweed for a store called Nakajimaya Heizaemon also boasts of the wonders of Asakusa seaweed: "With it, you make the flavors of whitebait come alive once more in the bowl; with it, plain tōfu becomes [tasty as] fishbones; the green of rice wrapped in isona wrack surpasses [in freshness] the voice of a Komatsu warbler; with it, 'bay-fried thin-spitted' eel passes for fragrant 'Edo kebab'" (Markus, *Willow in Autumn*, p. 117).

29. The vast majority of misemono shows were held in the precincts or front villages of temples and shrines. For example, the most prosperous places for misemono (their associated temples or shrines are given in parentheses) were the Ryōgoku area (Ekō-in), Asakusa (Sensōji), and Ueno Hirokōji (Shinobazu Benzaiten)—all in Edo; Naniwa Shinchi and Dōtonbori (Shitennōji) in Osaka; and Ōsu Kannon in Nagoya. The misemono show located on the Shijō riverbank in Kyoto is an exception to this tendency.

30. See Okamoto, pp. 168–82.

31. Yanagita Kunio argues that the most significant turning point in the history of matsuri was the emergence of "matsuri for showing," which the Gion festival of Kyoto pioneered. He distinguishes this new style of matsuri, which he labels *sairei,* from the traditional style. According to Yanagita, sairei are characterized by furyū, in contrast to matsuri, which feature *imi* (abstinence) and *komori* (seclusion). For more details, see Yanagita, "Nihon no matsuri," 10: 176–92.

32. Moriya, "Toshi sairei to furyū," pp. 423–58. Concerning the trickling-down of furyū, Moriya especially emphasizes the role of merchants, particularly of toy sellers who promoted the furyū of kite-flying (*tako-age*) in eighteenth-century Edo ("Kinsei no toshi seikatsu to furyū no tenkai," pp. 142–46).

33. Hayashiya, pp. 163–67.

34. Moriya, *Kinsei geinō kōgyōshi no kenkyū,* pp. 29–39.

35. On the relationship between *sumai* and *sumō,* see Miyata, *Yōkai no minzokugaku,* p. 134.

36. Misumi, pp. 91–92.

37. For more details, see Furukawa, pp. 68–72; and for sumō wrestling as a popular sport, see Bolitho, "Sumō and Popular Culture," pp. 23–25.

38. For a detailed discussion of the religious dimension of sumō, see Yamaguchi.

39. Terakado, 1: 64.

40. Unno, p. 178.

41. Komori, *Edo Asakusa machina no kenkyū,* p. 257; and Kasuya, p. 750.

42. Ryūtei, pp. 42–57.

43. Shinjō, pp. 723–36.

44. Nakayama, pp. 76–82; and Saeki, pp. 52–56.

45. For studies of the various functions of itinerant religious women involved in prostitution during the medieval period, see Amino Yoshihiko, "Chūsei no tabibito tachi," pp. 172–200; and Gorai, "Chūsei josei no shūkyōsei to seikatsu." On the other hand, Miyata Noboru (*Onna no reiryoku,* pp. 65–75) suggests that the special religious function of itinerant women was based on the composite religious power stemming from their movement across boundaries and their

femininity, which, when mediated by dancing or other artistic performances, has an innate potential for facilitating communication with deities. Barbara Ruch (pp. 521–28), however, cautions against such generalizations: "Because dancers, singers, and shamans shared a matrilineal professional line, mother to daughter or female-adept to adopted daughter-disciple; because the repertoires of singers of tales and songs included some sacred subject matter; because shaman ritual usually included dance; because all three types tended to be without husbands, independent, and unregulated and to travel in small groups, observers throughout history have tended to confuse them." That is why, she continues, "in the popular mind . . . shaman, entertainer, and prostitute were often not distinguished. Modern historians writing about this period, too, have so far treated them as degrees of one kind."

46. Ruch, p. 526; Seigle, pp. 8–9.

47. Various versions of the Asakusa hitotsuya legend, which are by and large identical, are found in *Kaikoku zakki* (late fifteenth century), *Edo meisho ki* (1662), *Edo suzume* (1677), and *Edo sunago* (1735). For these versions, see Matsudaira, 2: 67–74.

48. The theory that Japanese prostitutes originated from female shamans (*miko kigensetsu*) was suggested by Nakayama Tarō and Yanagita Kunio and was widely incorporated into the history of popular arts by Orikuchi Shinobu, Hori Ichirō, and others in that field. See Nakayama, pp. 82–88, 102–6; and Yanagita, "Itaka oyobi sanka." In comparison, Takigawa Masajirō (pp. 23–135) vehemently criticized miko kigensetsu, insisting that Japanese prostitutes were descendants of *paekchŏng* (a social outcaste class) from Paekche in Korea.

Based on a comprehensive reading of medieval documents, Amino Yoshihiko ("Chūsei no tabibito tachi," 180–87) criticizes Yanagita's miko kigensetsu as too narrow and Takigawa's theory as stemming from racial prejudice toward Koreans. Amino suggests that prostitutes originated from various sources: itinerant artists, female religious, women from seashore villages, and entertainers who had been dismissed by the government.

49. Miyata, *Shūmatsukan no minzokugaku*, pp. 97–114.

50. Kinsei shiryō kenkyūkai, 1: 285.

51. Matsudaira, 1: 343–45.

52. Ibid., 2: 294.

53. Miyata, "Sensōji ganbaru," p. 208.

54. For more details, see Kitagawa, pp. 127–36.

55. Saitō Akitoshi.

56. Tokugawa Japanese believed that pilgrimages could annihilate sins committed in this world. One reason for the popularity of pilgrimages was the wide

circulation of a story concerning Tokudō Shōnin, the founder of the Saigoku thirty-three Kannon circuit, who successfully conducted a pilgrimage known as "a tour of hells" (*jigoku meguri*). See Shimizutani, *Kannon junrei no susume*, pp. 71–91.

57. Chanting Japanese-style pilgrimage songs (*goeika*) at each pilgrimage site was also popular. Pilgrims believed that goeika could serve both as an alternative to making an offering of handwritten Buddhist sutras and as a form of spell (*shingon*).

58. Nishiyama, "Kannon junrei ni miru shomin shinkō," pp. 2–6; Shimizutani, *Junrei no kokoro*, pp. 74–86.

59. Saitō Gesshin, *Tōto saijiki*, 3: 107–13, 122–25; Shimizutani, "Sensōji to fudasho," pp. 6–9.

60. In the Tokugawa period, there was a saying about pilgrimages: "Seventy percent play and thirty percent piety still is not bad." For a detailed discussion of the pursuit of pleasure during pilgrimage, see Shinjō, pp. 723–36. A prime example of pleasure seeking under the pretext of pilgrimage is the Ise pilgrimage (Ise *okagemairi*); see Davis, pp. 45–80.

61. Totman, pp. 227–28.

62. Naitō Akira, "Edo no toshi kōzō," pp. 33–54; and *Edo to Edojō*, pp. 41–76.

63. See Gamō.

64. Tokoro, "Edo no machi," pp. 102–5.

65. Nishiyama, *Edogaku nyūmon*, pp. 223–25.

66. A dispute occurred in 1774 between the Sensōji administration and the city magistrate concerning proprietary rights over auxiliary facilities to which a wooden bridge over the Sumida River would be attached. The shōgunate argued that the river belonged to the public authority (kōgi) and that all facilities attached to the bridge should be controlled by the city magistrate; the Sensōji administration argued that it had paid special taxes for other riparian public projects and that at those times the shōgunate had treated Sensōji as the proprietor of the Sumida River. The Sensōji administration won the case. See Ikegami Akihiko, "Azuma bashi," pp. 125–27.

67. Nishiyama, "Asakusa hakkei," pp. 15–19.

68. Kurachi, pp. 358–59.

69. Shibundō henshūbu, p. 173.

70. Hiraga, pp. 77–84.

71. Yoshiwara, "Hirokōji," pp. 19–21.

72. For details of the Ekō-in *segaki* ritual, see Saitō Gesshin, *Edo meisho zue*, 2: 1852–58.

73. Jinnai, *Tokyo: A Spatial Anthropology*, p. 110.

74. For an excellent discussion of the association between water and the "source of life" in Japanese religious culture, see LaFleur, *Liquid Life*, pp. 14–29.

75. Ibid., pp. 83–85.

76. For a detailed study of the so-called public zone in medieval Japan, see Amino Yoshihiko, *Muen kugai raku*, pp. 41–152; and Jinnai, "Spatial Structure of Edo," pp. 132–33.

77. Jinnai, *Tokyo: A Spatial Anthropology*, p. 101.

78. Maki Fumihiko ("Oku no shisō") argues that the Japanese conception of "center" (*chūshin*), whether physical or spiritual, is the product of a culture that denies the notion of Absolute Being. Compared with Roman Catholic churches and towers in traditional Europe, which symbolize an axis mundi for the entire cosmos, every temple and shrine in Japan symbolizes an interiority (*oku*) that is at the center of its own cosmos. Cosmic centers in Japan, Maki argues, are dispersed and localized, corresponding to the multiple spiritual axes of their villagers and residents. According to Maki, approaches to a temple or shrine, through a path up a hillside or to precincts situated deep within thick greenery or near water, dramatize a nostalgic return to an interior origin. See also Jinnai, "Spatial Structure of Edo," p. 131.

79. Naitō Masatoshi, pp. 81–90.

80. In handling the rent-house business, Sensōji administrators were concerned primarily with two matters: the intensity of the government's regulation and criticism from other Buddhist sects. See *SN*, 3: 318–20. The Sensōji administration usually tried to avoid any awkward situation by offering slow and vague responses. When it had to tackle the matter resolutely, it did so by confiscating the rents that landlords collected from Yoshiwara people (*SN*, 13: 131), dismissing the officials responsible (*SN*, 13: 164), and confiscating and redistributing temple lands (*SN*, 13: 248–49).

81. Miyamoto, pp. 211–13.

82. For example, a Yoshiwara prostitute named Raisan attempted to set fire to her place of business in 1829 because of her employer's exploitive treatment. When Raisan failed to take a customer, her master tried to deny her food; one time she escaped but was soon captured; whenever she was idle, her employer blamed her lack of customers on her bad manners and lack of skills. The only way to escape, Raisan thought, would be to set fire to her place and to be transferred to other brothel quarters. She and two other disgruntled prostitutes planned to set the fire, but their conspiracy ended with failure. At first they were condemned to have their faces marked with fire after being displayed on the streets of Edo, but this sentence was commuted to banishment to a remote island. See ibid., pp. 210–11.

83. Komori, "Kakushibaita," pp. 564–65.

84. See Shirato.

85. Ōsumi, p. 561.

86. Saichō denied the *vinaya* precepts and, instead, adopted the *Fan wang ching* precepts as a minimum set of autonomous self-regulations for the Buddhist sangha. Since then, vinaya precepts, which refer to compulsory traditional precepts imposed on Buddhist monks, have been almost abandoned in Japanese Buddhism, regardless of sectarian divisions. For a detailed discussion of Saichō's view of the Buddhist precepts and his impact on Japanese Buddhism, see Groner, pp. 169–263.

87. Amino Aritoshi, p. 611.

88. In 1730 the shōgunate gave permission to Gokokuji Temple to hold the first tomitsuki in Edo, and this triggered a fashion for lottery gaming in the late Tokugawa period. Among religious institutions permitted to conduct the lottery business, Yanaka Kannōji, Meguro Ryūsenji, and Yushima Tenmangū were the most prosperous. For a collection of primary materials concerning the tomitsuki business in Edo, see Taitō-ku kyōiku iinkai.

89. Amino Aritoshi, pp. 612–14.

90. When a fire threatened Sensōji buildings, the Asakusa Kannon and its frontal statues were promptly evacuated to safe places. For example, at the time the great fire started at Gyōninzaka in 1772, the statues were transferred by boat along the Sumida River to Ekō-in in the Honjo district (*SN*, 3:693–708), and at the time of a less threatening fire in 1756, they were transferred to a boat standing by on the Sumida River (*SN*, 2: 202). In every case, the statues contained in the receptacles were placed intact into a palanquin, and their secrecy was strictly maintained.

91. Ikegami Akihiko, "Hinoetora no Edo taika," pp. 141–44.

92. Ibid., p. 145.

93. Asakura Haruhiko; Shimizutani, "Sōsō engi to reigen."

94. The term *kō* originated from a suffix designating the regular meetings of study groups that discussed Buddhist scriptures or of prayer groups that observed Buddhist rituals in the Nara period. With the popularization of *Hokke hakkō* (Eight lectures on the *Lotus Sūtra*) among Kyoto aristocrats during the Heian period, group meetings, particularly for prayer rituals, spread down to ordinary people. For details, see Tanabe.

As the synthesis of Buddhism and Shintō (*honji suijaku*) penetrated the religious world of medieval Japan, religious confraternities for Shintō as well as folkloric rituals began to gain wide popularity. In the Tokugawa period, such confraternal groups came to include any social association whose purpose was collective activity.

95. Yanagawa Keiichi (pp. 62–75), in his thesis on the "religion of the group" (*mure no shūkyō*), suggests that the primary orientation of traditional Japanese religions was not toward individuals but toward groups (e.g., a family, a clan group, an organization, a village, or a nation).

96. *SN*, 13: 450–51; Amino Aritoshi, pp. 269–82.

97. For example, the Sensōji administration withdrew recognition from a confraternity named the Benten (Benten deity) kō in 1783 because it repeatedly defaulted on its monthly donations (*SN*, 4: 746). In 1784 a group of merchants tried to organize a confraternity provisionally named Gofushin (construction) kō, with a pledge of 500 gold pieces. After the Gofushin kō several times failed to honor that pledge, it was also disbanded (*SN*, 5: 129–34, 146–48, 159–64, 194–98).

98. For more details, see *Kyū bakufu hikitsugi sho*, 2: 68–71; and Tokoro, "Sensōji Sanfudai ni tsuite," p. 228.

99. Matsudaira, 1: 96–100.

100. In order to minimize the causes of legal disputes, the Sensōji administration set up its own regulations for financial transactions. For example, loans, the most frequent source of trouble, could be transferable to new head monks only if they were first endorsed by managing administrators (*yakusha*) and members of the district association of subtemples. See *SN*, 2: 90.

101. In 1658 the shōgunate banned all construction of new temples; some local governments adopted even more draconian measures. For example, the Mito domain government demolished around 65 percent of Buddhist temples in the domain, and the Okayama domain government around 58 percent. The reason was that the excessive number of Buddhist monks was resulting in a paucity of taxable resources. For more details, see Tamamuro, *Nihon Bukkyō shi*, pp. 104–66. Moreover, in 1727, due to deteriorating finances, the shōgunate reduced governmental subsidies for building projects at temples and shrines. Eight years earlier, Sensōji administrators had been refused government financial aid to rebuild the Main Hall. From then on, Sensōji rarely received any subsidies from the Tokugawa government. See Amino Aritoshi, pp. 308–11.

102. In comparison, some Meiji Buddhist reformers even questioned the "veracity" of Mahāyāna Buddhism itself and called for a return to "fundamental Buddhism" (*konpon Bukkyō*), which referred to the primordial teachings of Śākyamuni. Inoue Enryō (1858–1919) believed that the "theory of Mahāyāna was not Buddha's teachings" (*daijō hi-Butsu setsu*), and, in line with Inoue, Anesaki Masaharu (1873–1949) advocated a return to "fundamental Buddhism." For

more details concerning the "cleansing movements" of Meiji Buddhism, see Kashiwahara, *Nihon Bukkyōshi*, pp. 83–92; and Ketelaar, pp. 207–12.

103. The records of the Sensōji diary between 1815 and 1817 provide detailed information about the recruitment of novice-monks, including data on the age when they "renounced the world," their home villages, their fathers' names and occupations, and their mentors and ordination temples. See *SN*, vol. 13.

104. In the Tokugawa period, the Tendai sect maintained a status system, and all Tendai monks were divided into fourteen ranks, distinguishable by different colors and styles of robe. Because of the status associated with these robes, Sensōji monks often attempted to wear robes of a higher rank than they actually occupied. In 1791, when the head monk of Genshō-in (a subtemple of Sensōji) was elected to the office of managing administrator (*yakusha*), he successfully petitioned Kan'eiji officials to allow him to wear the blue hat (*hanada*) given to those who attended the Lotus Conference at Enryakuji. Although he had never attended the conference, he maintained: "I am going to be despised by the members of the Sensōji community if I perform the office of *yakusha* without wearing a *hanada* hat." See *SN*, 6: 513.

Chapter 3

1. Rai, "Kusazōshi ni arawareta shomin no sekaizō," p. 255.

2. Ibid., p. 256; and Mizuno, *Yoshi no sōshi*, 1: 349.

3. For fuller accounts of the Kansei reforms, see Soranaka; and Ooms, *Charismatic Bureaucrat*, pp. 77–104, 122–50.

4. Legend has it that soon after the Asakusa Kannon statue was found in the Sumida River near Asakusa, the area was declared to be a sacred no-killing zone; fisherfolk in the area were relocated to Ōmori, a seashore village in Shinagawa. Once they settled there, auspicious-looking logs flowed down from the Sumida River, and tasty seaweed began to grow on those logs. Thereafter, the villagers of Ōmori made a good living by harvesting this high-quality seaweed. In order to repay the Asakusa Kannon, the villagers began to transport the three *mikoshi* containing the three deities who had discovered the Kannon statue along the Sumida River during the Sanja festival (see Kitahara Susumu, "Sanja matsuri," pp. 156–57).

5. *Edogaku jiten*, p. 826.

6. Kitahara Susumu, "Saikō sareta Sanja matsuri," p. 267.

7. Moriya, "Toshi sairei to furyū," pp. 423–25.

8. Tsukamoto, pp. 95–96. For a detailed discussion of the outbreak of fights during the Sanja festival, see Takeuchi, "Festivals and Fights," pp. 393–401.

9. Tsuji Tatsuya, p. 470.

10. Tsukamoto, pp. 69–70.

11. For example, the bylaws (*shikimoku* or *okite*) of Kyoto machi communities, which served as a prototype for those of Edo machi, clearly illustrate the idealistic communal spirit of the original machi community. Machi bylaws, without exception, mandated peace and harmony among machi residents, decision-making based on unanimous consensus, the exclusion and surveillance of strangers, and equality among fellow residents (see Yoshida, "Chōnin to machi," pp. 164–68).

12. Asao, "Sōson kara machi e," pp. 346–52.

13. Yoshida, "Omotedana to uradana," pp. 303–6.

14. Ibid., pp. 321–22.

15. Hayashi, *Nihon no kinsei*, pp. 115–18. In addition to the method of money transfer mentioned above, there was another method, called *gyaku kawase* (reverse exchange). In this case, an Osaka supplier would send goods to an Edo wholesaler and, at the same time, issue an exchange note. The supplier would then present the note to a designated Osaka money-changer and receive a certain percentage of the face value of the note. The Osaka money-changer would then send the note to an Edo branch office, which would collect the face value of the note from the Edo wholesaler.

16. Ibid., pp. 118–20.

17. Nishizaka, pp. 195–97.

18. Kurushima, p. 109.

19. Yoshida, "Chōnin to machi," pp. 164–69. For comparison, see Smith, "The Edo-Tokyo Transition," pp. 368–70.

20. The Tokumi toiya association was established in 1694 by Edo wholesalers who had encountered enormous financial burdens due to losses at sea when they began to purchase goods in Osaka and ship them to Edo. Up until then, Edo wholesale merchants had simply been sales agents for Osaka suppliers, who had been responsible for getting the goods to Edo. In order to avoid conflicts of interest with Osaka suppliers and to maximize commercial profits, Edo merchants unified the supply and sale of goods for the Edo markets and organized a protective trade association that functioned as an insurance institution designed to lessen the individual burdens related to loss of goods at sea. Nevertheless, frequent sea disasters eventually caused the association's strength to diminish. The number of cargo vessels belonging to the association steadily decreased from 160 in the Kyōhō years (1716–35), to 100 in the 1760s and 1770s, to 38 in 1808.

21. Kagawa, *Nihon no rekishi*, pp. 179–80.

22. Kagawa, "Toshi shōgyō no hatten," pp. 195–206. In 1813, the number of wholesaler-members in the association reached 1,187, and the number of licenses (*kabu*) 1,865. But twenty years later, in 1833, membership was reduced to 919 and

the number of licenses to 1,244, which means that many wholesalers had opted out of the association.

23. Ibid., pp. 207–9.

24. Tsukada, pp. 259–60.

25. Tsukamoto, pp. 79–80. For a fuller account, see Kelly, pp. 317–25.

26. Ikegami Akihiko, "Meiwa no kasai," pp. 23–24.

27. Tsukamoto, pp. 80–81. It is ironic that kaisho organizations contributed to the increase in the tenant population. By easing the process of renting houses, tenant kaisho facilitated the infusion of new tenants into the machi community but deterred the integration of these strangers into the communal life of the conventional machi community. For comparison with employment agencies that provided guarantorship for "the increasingly impersonal, if not mistrustful, relationship between masters and servants," see Leupp, pp. 69–72.

28. Tsukamoto, p. 71.

29. Iwata, "Toshi keizai no tenkan," pp. 283–90.

30. Tsukata, pp. 259–64.

31. The shōgunate established relief funds called *machi kaisho tsumikin* (reserve funds of ward offices) for the urban poor; previously such relief funds had come from private kaisho organizations, which had often established such funds in order to promote their own business interests. The city magistrate asked each resident of the machi community to contribute an amount determined by the value of his property, and the collected donations were used to establish relief funds to help the poor in the form of direct assistance or as low-interest loans (see Nakai, pp. 591–92).

32. Tsukamoto, pp. 102–4.

33. Nakai, p. 576. For statistics regarding wards destroyed by fire, see Nishiyama, *Edo Culture*, pp. 27–29.

34. Miyata, "Shomin shinkō no shoson," pp. 687–89.

35. Nishizaka, pp. 194–97.

36. Tsukamoto, p. 83.

37. According to Henry Smith ("The Floating World," p. 36), "For 1733–47, the ratio moved from 173 (males per 100 females) to 169; in 1798 it dropped to 135; and in the period 1832–67 it continued a steady decline, from 120 to virtual parity on the eve of the Meiji Restoration." See also Kitahara Susumu, "Rōkakko to Edokko," pp. 169–70.

38. Nishiyama, *Edokko*, pp. 122–23.

39. For more details, see Smith, "The Floating World," pp. 29–31.

40. Shively, "Popular Culture," p. 711.

41. Although the shōgunate was most concerned with taming masterless

samurai, other matters also required urgent fixing in Edo. For example, Shōji Jin'emon cited three reasons to build a centrally administered pleasure quarter: it would make it possible to apprehend those who had stolen money in order to afford prostitutes; it would prevent women from being kidnapped on the street and sold; and it would make it easier to control "evil bandits." For detailed discussions of the genesis of Yoshiwara, see Seigle, pp. 20–30; and Miyamoto, pp. 169–71.

42. For information on masterless samurai (*rōnin*), street bullies (*kabuki mono*), and the measures taken to suppress them, see Eiko Ikegami, pp. 204–9; and Totman, pp. 107–8.

43. Shively, "Popular Culture," pp. 745–46.

44. Kumakura Isao, "Yūjo to yūkaku," pp. 205–6; and Seigle, pp. 125–28.

45. Miyamoto, pp. 209–10.

46. In 1816 the shōgunate discovered that three of Sensōji's subtemples—Nichion-in, Myōtoku-in, and Myōon-in—were "embracing" secret prostitutes on their temple lands. This was not the first time that such a thing had happened, but the government struck immediately, punishing those subtemples by confiscating all rent collected from the prostitutes and shackling the hands of their head monks for two months (see *SN*, 13: 131, 164, 248–49, 255).

47. Satō Yōjin, "Okabasho," p. 560.

48. Wakabayashi, p. 70.

49. Shively, "Popular Culture," p. 710.

50. Kozo Yamamura, "Increasing Poverty of the Samurai," p. 393; and the section entitled "A Fixed Income and Increasing Wants," in *Samurai Income and Entrepreneurship*, pp. 41–48.

51. Yamamura, "Increasing Poverty of the Samurai," p. 396.

52. Conrad Totman notes that by the late eighteenth century some debt-stricken samurai abandoned the dignity of their status and engaged in commerce in order to make ends meet. The following comment that a contemporary made about the severity of samurai poverty is quite striking: "For years now, the samurai have suffered from poverty and their minds have been occupied by making a living. 'Buy this, sell that' and 'pawn this to pay for that' has become all of their lives. Even for those dedicated to their duties, it was inevitable to debase themselves and to engage in unsavory conduct" (cited in Totman, p. 328).

53. For statistical studies of the annual budgets of some typical samurai households that show how they were indebted, see Yamamura, "Increasing Poverty of the Samurai," pp. 396–98; and Totman, p. 292.

54. Bolitho, "The Tempō Crisis," p. 135.

55. Ibid., pp. 136–38.

56. Totman, pp. 260–79.

57. Ibid., pp. 328–33.

58. This opinion was in line with the highly respected view of Ogyū Sorai, who, in 1722, had already pinpointed three specific causes for the impoverishment of the samurai class in his *Seidan* (A discourse on government): rising prices, the scarcity of money, and the lack of credit. Among these, the biggest cause was, Sorai argued, the price of goods and services, particularly the price of rice, which the samurai could not control because they were not attached to farming fields. He assumed that if the samurai class returned to the soil, then they could set the price of rice and that this would affect all other prices. For a detailed discussion of Sorai's vision of Confucian political economy, see Lidin.

59. For more details, see "Shokka," in Dazai, pp. 487–543; and Najita, pp. 830–33.

60. Iwata, "Toshi keizai no tenkan," pp. 268–69.

61. For a fuller account of debt cancellation, see Ooms, *Charismatic Bureaucrat*, pp. 91–97; and Kitahara Susumu, "Rōkakko to Edokko," pp. 182–83.

62. Hayashi, *Nihon no kinsei*, pp. 248–53.

63. Concerning the eventual failure of the Kansei reform measures, which aimed at stabilizing the prices of other commodities in favor of the price of rice and, thereby, restoring financial strength to the samurai class, Isao Soranaka (pp. 156–63) emphasizes the self-interest of the *han* governments in addition to the intricate market mechanism of trade and the stratagems of merchants and trade associations.

64. Kagawa, *Nihon no rekishi*, pp. 172–76.

65. "Sorai wished to restore the physical vigor and fiscal well-being of samurai by ending their habits of urban indolence, extravagance, and dependence on merchants. So he recommended their transfer from cities back to the land" (Totman, p. 288).

66. Ibid., p. 334.

67. Buyō Inshi, pp. 11, 46.

68. Asao, "Jūhachi seiki no shakai hendō," p. 94. On the blurring of distinctions between samurai and commoners, see Smith, "The Floating World," p. 32; Smith discusses how these two groups forged a common language and a common culture, particularly in the world of leisure and entertainment.

69. Gerstle, p. 40.

70. Amino Aritoshi, p. 229.

71. Takeuchi, "Tenmei kikin," pp. 163–65.

72. For an introduction to *Ukiyoburo* and its sequel, *Ukiyotoko* (The barbershop of the floating world), see Leutner, pp. 92–111.

73. Shikitei Sanba, p. 185.

74. Takeuchi, "Shomin bunka no naka no Edo," pp. 17–18.

75. Nishiyama, *Edogaku nyūmon*, pp. 215–16.

76. Sakudō, p. 155.

77. By 1717, dry-goods stores occupied 88 percent of the total *maguchi* (front streets) of Hon-chō 1 and 2 chōme, with a total of 232.75 *ken*. But fourteen years later, in 1731, the rate of occupation decreased to a bit more than 71 percent, with a total of 187 ken—a drop of approximately 20 percent (see Iwata, "Toshi keizai no tenkan," pp. 292–93).

78. Nishizaka, pp. 185–86.

79. For more details, see Hayashi, *Nihon no kinsei*, pp. 236–48.

80. For a discussion of the Tokugawa bakufu's attempt at social engineering through adopting sumptuary and austerity measures in the early Tokugawa period, see Shively, "Sumptuary Regulation," pp. 123–63.

81. Similar measures were repeated in 1828 (see *SN*, 17: 631–32).

82. Bolitho, "The Tempō Crisis," p. 145.

83. Tsukamoto, p. 98. For more details, see Fujita.

84. Tsukamoto, pp. 97–98.

85. Right after fire broke out at Meguro Gyōninzaka in 1772, some construction workers offered generous donations to temples and shrines to express their gratitude for the destruction. This Gyōninzaka fire, which was recorded as one of the three most devastating fires in Edo, eventually devoured approximately 630 wards and killed thousands of people (see Yoshiwara, "Kaji," p. 572).

86. Ibid., p. 574.

87. Markus, "The Carnival of Edo," p. 509.

88. Totman, p. 477; and Rozman, pp. 106–8.

89. Kagawa, *Nihon no rekishi*, pp. 186–87.

90. Ibid., pp. 162–64; and Sekiyama, pp. 137–38.

91. For a fuller discussion, see White, pp. 25–33.

92. For example, a hatamoto family, the Utsu, had a parcel of land, rated at 5,000 koku, in Shimotsuke. At one point in the Genroku era (1688–1703), the land contained 433 farming households and 1,095 villagers. But by the year 1823 the number of households and the number of villagers decreased to 156 and 713, respectively. About 40 percent of the farming fields had become wasteland, and the remaining farmers continued to suffer from heavy taxes (see Kagawa, *Nihon no rekishi*, p. 256; see also Rozman, p. 104).

93. Taniyama, pp. 139–41; and Houser, pp. 38–40.

94. Houser, p. 150. Concerning "the ambivalence of the situation in the Kantō," which generated more and more impoverished farming villagers amid a growing commercial economy, David L. Howell (pp. 353–56) provides telling

evidence through the example of a Chōshi town that was well known for its soy sauce–brewing industry.

95. Buyō Inshi, pp. 63–64.

96. For example, Mizuno Tadakuni strictly "banned further in-migration to Edo and expelled those without families and permanent jobs from there and elsewhere and did have a temporarily depressive effect on at least the migrant populations of Edo and Osaka" (White, pp. 33–35).

97. Peddlers dealing with recycled goods were organized into eight guild associations (*kumiai*) by the order of the city magistrate in 1723. Through these self-regulatory associations, the bakufu hoped to control pawnshops and to halt rampant theft. However, given the rapid increase in the population of the lower classes, the bakufu never achieved control over merchants dealing in recycled goods. For more details, see Hayashi, *Nihon no kinsei*, pp. 155–68; Iwata, "Toshi keizai no tenkan," pp. 280–81; and Yoshida, "Omotedana to uradana," pp. 326–33.

98. In 1658–59 the bakufu issued "licenses for street-sale" (*furiuri fuda*) to the street hawkers who were already in the business as well as to old people, children, and the disabled—all of whom needed extra protection and assistance. Under this licensing system, which was designed to regulate the commercial transactions of fifty kinds of items, the bakufu specially designated fifteen items (including tobacco, salt, candies, wooden sandals, soy sauce) and banned able-bodied men between the ages of 16 and 49 from dealing in them. With the increase of street peddlers in the late Tokugawa period, however, this system could not be maintained (see Iwata, "Toshi keizai no tenkan," pp. 274–76).

99. Jinnai, *Tokyo: A Spatial Anthropology*, p. 62.

100. See Iwata, "Uchikowashi to minshū sekai," pp. 80–87; and Walthall, "Edo Riots," pp. 413–19.

101. For the list of those arrested or chased, see Takeuchi, "Uchikowashi," p. 585.

102. Jansen, pp. 74–75, 83–84.

103. Hiranuma, pp. 23–24.

104. Yoshida, "Kyodai jōkamachi: Edo," p. 164.

105. Hiranuma, p. 8.

106. The following chart shows the changing income structure of Sensōji's major subtemples in the eighteenth century. It clearly illustrates that income from land leases and house rents gained in importance for most subtemples. The data for 1745 are from "Bungen oaratame kakiage chō" in Matsudaira, 2: 515–47, and those for 1784–93 are from *SN*, vols. 4 and 5. All amounts have been converted into approximate values in gold currency (ryō).

Subtemple	Lease/Rent	Danna Fee	Others	Total
Iō-in				
1745	92	7	15	114
1784–93	105	3	6	114
Jissō-in				
1745	12	11	7	30
1784–93	9	3	21	33
Shuzen-in				
1745	7	18	14	39
1784–93	27	19	3	49
Chikō-in				
1745	36	1	9	46
1784–93	61	1	12	74
Konzō-in				
1745	12	24	4	40
1784–93	17	12	5	34
Nichion-in				
1745	50	68	10	128
1784–93	65	77	33	175
Zenryū-in				
1745	0	37	6	43
1784–93	12	7	5	24
Kongō-in				
1745	15	4	10	29
1784–93	41	20	26	87
Myōtoku-in				
1745	15	1	5	21
1784–93	52	1	24	77
Kakuzen-in				
1745	15	3	6	24
1784–93	20	10	5	35
Hōzen-in				
1745	30	10	18	58
1784–93	0	9	39	48
Chōju-in				
1745	7	26	7	40
1784–93	49	0	5	54

107. Nishiyama, *Edogaku nyūmon*, pp. 99–100.

Chapter 4

1. Jansen, pp. 52–53.

2. Ibid., pp. 55–56; and Ooms, *Charismatic Bureaucrat*, pp. 133–44.

3. For an apt discussion of diverse social discourses in late eighteenth-century Tokugawa Japan, see Totman, pp. 348–77.

4. Kurimoto, pp. 51–79.

5. Academic works dealing with current political or diplomatic affairs were also banned, lest they mislead an uninformed public and call into question the political monopoly of the Tokugawa shōgunate. One notable victim of censorship was Hayashi Shihei (1738–93), whose discussion of the Russian advance to the Japanese seas had an undertone that was critical of bakufu policy (see his *Kaikoku heidan* [A military discourse on the maritime country]). Another category of publication under strict government surveillance was Christian writings. For that, the Tokugawa shōgunate strictly censored Chinese books imported through Nagasaki from China (see Itō Tasaburō; and Jansen, pp. 58–59).

6. For a detailed discussion of Ryūtei Tanehiko and his works, see Markus, *Willow in Autumn*, pp. 183–212.

7. Hanley, p. 99; and Seigle, pp. 45–47.

8. For more details about the public bathhouse in Edo, see Jinbo.

9. In Shikitei Sanba's words: "There is, one realizes on careful reflection, no shortcut to moral learning like the public bath. It is, after all, the way of Nature, and of Heaven and Earth, that all are naked when they bathe—the wise and the foolish, the crooked and the straight, the poor and the rich, the high and the low" (trans. from Leutner, p. 137).

10. At the same time, traditional Confucian education for women also emphasized practical learning: the basic skills of making clothes and sewing bedding, cooking and cleaning, marriage preparations, taking care of children, household service, greeting etiquette, and cultural accomplishments such as flower arranging, tea, painting, calligraphy, singing and dancing, composition of poems, and playing a musical instrument (see Shively, "Popular Culture," pp. 722–23).

11. For a detailed chronology of the censorship of publications from the time of the Kansei Reforms on, see *Edogaku jiten* (1984), pp. 813–49. For an example of the censorship of ukiyo paintings, see Akai, p. 183.

12. Unno, p. 176.

13. Jansen, p. 69.

14. For an insightful, concise account of the world of popular novels during this period, see Totman, pp. 413–22.

15. Hayashi, "Asakusa no onna tachi," pp. 48–53.

16. Hirota, "Yonaoshi ni miru minshū no sekaijō," pp. 264–65.

17. Hirota, "Kinsei no seijuku to kindai," p. 321.

18. Yasumaru, p. 35.

19. Wakabayashi, pp. 69–70.

20. For example, Ishida Baigan opened up a new chapter in popularizing the thought of "subjective" *kokoro* (mind) in a systematic way. At an early age, Baigan wanted to teach people the five cardinal virtues and the five human relationships of Confucianism. But he was not sure of his own interpretation of them, and so he wandered around for a year or so in order to find an answer. This was of no avail until he came upon an old hermit monk named Kokuri Ryōun. The monk pointed out that Baigan understood the five cardinal virtues and the five human relationships as external norms that should be applied to human subjectivity. He pointedly reminded Baigan that one's own mind was the source of everything and that, therefore, morality must be realized through the mind. This meant, Ryōun continued, that "if you seek ethical norms outside yourself, and forget to cultivate mind in yourself, you [will] end up [by] alienating ethical norms from your own mind" (see Yasumaru, p. 30).

21. "Movements to work out one's salvation with one's own effort" (*jiryoku kōsei undō*) in the late Tokugawa period were most visible in the self-help movements that aimed at rehabilitating barren farming villages in the Kantō areas. In particular, Ninomiya Sontoku, who, starting in the Odawara domain right after the Tenmei famines, launched a movement known as "returning one's blessings" (*hōtoku*), served as a role model for other leaders, agriculturalists, late Mitogaku reformers, new religious leaders, Shinshū myōkōnin, *ikki* leaders, local National Learning scholars, and Shintō priests (see Yasumaru, pp. 10–11; and for Ninomiya Sontoku, see Howell, pp. 365–68).

22. Yasumaru, pp. 33–35.

23. Hirota, "Kinsei no seiritsu to minshū," pp. 27–29.

24. Rai, "Kusazōshi ni arawareta shomin no sekaizō," pp. 227–31.

25. Ibid., 231–39.

26. Ibid., 256–58.

27. Nishiyama, *Edo Culture*, p. 240; and for a discussion of workers in construction and other fields, see Leupp, pp. 134–37.

28. Rai, "Kusazōshi ni arawareta shomin no sekaizō," p. 241.

29. According to a conservative bakufu count, the number of yose halls in Edo was 211.

30. For details about the impact of anti-yose edicts on Sensōji and its subsequent adjustment, see Hiruma, "Keidai no yose."

31. For a detailed discussion of *tsūzoku dōtoku* in the late Tokugawa period in relation to the process of modernization in the following period, see Yasumaru, pp. 4–146.

32. Hiruma, "Samazama na kōdō bunka," pp. 324–28.

33. Kumakura, "Kinsei ni okeru geinō no tenkai," pp. 13–21.

34. The yūgei culture developed for three reasons: (1) a high demand for yūgei learning and an abundant supply of yūgei teachers, both of which existed within a system of private education; (2) the *iemoto* (the head of the ie) system, based on a custom of license granting that facilitated yūgei learning and teaching; and (3) the development of an asobi infrastructure (e.g., teahouses, restaurants, kabuki theater, and other play spaces). For a detailed discussion of the iemoto system, see Hsu.

35. Ishimori, pp. 101–2.

36. Ibid., pp. 102–3. Among these, Ise was the most popular destination for a pleasure tour. In addition to the main object of folk piety (the grain deity Toyouke at the Ise Grand Shrine, which was famous for bringing good crops and general well-being), Ise offered plenty of pleasure opportunities, particularly for male travelers. Upon arriving in Ise, male travelers usually conducted a sex rite known as *shōjin otoshi* (dropping a [religious] devotion) in the pleasure quarters of the city, which contained approximately a thousand prostitutes. For an excellent discussion of "travel as recreation" in late Tokugawa Japan, with a focus on "the development of a travel industry" and "the secularization of pilgrimage," see Vaporis, pp. 217–54; and for popular pilgrimage sites in the Edo period, see Nishiyama, *Edo Culture*, pp. 130–41.

37. Ishimori, p. 105.

38. Takeuchi, "Shomin bunka no naka no Edo," pp. 30–38.

39. For more details, see Nishiyama, *Edogaku nyūmon*, pp. 57–62.

40. Harootunian, "Late Tokugawa Culture and Thought," p. 173.

41. Ibid., pp. 173–74.

42. Rai, "Koyū bunka no seijuku," pp. 157–61.

43. Nishiyama, *Edokko*, pp. 188–89.

44. Kumakura, "Kinsei ni okeru geinō no tenkai," p. 42.

45. Harootunian, "Late Tokugawa Culture and Thought," p. 175.

46. Hirota, "Kinsei no seijuku to kindai," pp. 309–14.

47. Unno, pp. 168–70.

48. Tsuruya Nanboku's *Tōkaidō Yotsuya kaidan* was a tremendous hit as soon as it was first presented on the kabuki stage in 1825. Takizawa Bakin's *Nansō*

Satomi Hakken den, published between 1814 and 1842 (the longest novel to that date in Japanese), fascinated readers with its energetic movements and dramatic reversals involving ghosts and vengeful spirits. However, it had an undertone of moralistic retribution that was evoked by its depiction of vanished samurai glories. Utagawa Kuniyoshi (1797–1861) earned attention in 1843 with a work depicting the struggles of ghosts. This particular painting conveyed popular sentiment, which was against the Tenpō Reforms (see Hirota, "Yonaoshi ni miru minshū no sekaijō," pp. 270–71).

49. Nishiyama, *Edokko*, pp. 118–20.

50. For example, see *SN*, 7: 665–69, 683–86; and 16: 22–23.

51. For the origin of aragoto plays, see Kominz, "*Ya no Ne*."

52. C. Andrew Gerstle (pp. 35–36) quotes a comment by Danjūrō I on the essence of aragoto, which is recorded in the book *Kokon yakusha rongo sakigake* (Advanced actors' analects from the past and present): "When invited to a daimyō's residence, after sake was served, I was asked to show them *aragoto*. Therefore, to the chanting of the Nō play *Kegekiyo*, I stripped to my underclothes and violently smashed the *shōji* and *fusuma* (sliding doors) with my feet. Whereupon, the patrons asked what are you doing? When I replied that this is *aragoto*, the daimyō was delighted and rewarded me well. Even in front of daimyō you must never be afraid, or it won't be *aragoto*."

53. Gunji, pp. 207–8.

54. For a discussion of "Shibaraku" pieces performed by Danjūrō V in the 1770s and 1780s, a period known as kabuki's golden age, see Kominz, "Ichikawa Danjūrō V and Kabuki's Golden Age," pp. 63–65.

55. Hattori Yukio, "Soga mono," in *Kokushi dai jiten*, 8: 620–21. For a fuller treatment of the Soga story as New Year's theater in Edo, see Kominz, *Avatars of Vengeance*, pp. 182–94, 218–24; and Nishiyama, *Edo Culture*, pp. 214–21.

56. For a treatment of Tsuruya Nanboku's *Yotsuya kaidan*, under the heading of "the aesthetic of evil," see Nishiyama, *Edo Culture*, pp. 213–14.

57. Aoki, pp. 288–90. As Laurence R. Kominz (*Avatars of Vengeance*, p. 165) notes, Edoites went to a Danjūrō play because Danjūrō "converted fear and propitiation of Soga Gorō into awe, excitement, and celebration. The exorcisms by actors and offerings by audience members demonstrated that for many the awe inspired by the aragoto portrayals of Gorō and Fudō were more than mere amusement."

58. Gerstle, 36–37.

59. Buyō Inshi, pp. 242–43.

60. Based on the analysis of Nishiyama Matsunosuke, who relies on Santō Kyōden's characterization, we can say that an Edokko, who was most typically a

firefighter, a carpenter, or a fishmonger, distinguished himself from the non-native Edoite by having "a sense of pride in being born in the capital of the shōgun, looking up at the gold roof finials of the castle and taking his first bath in water supplied by the city aqueduct; an irresistible urge to part with his money as soon as it is earned, by spending a fortune to taste the first bonito of the season or selling a fine downtown house for a single fling in the Yoshiwara; having a classy upbringing, complete with a wet nurse under an umbrella and the best toys; having as his base the very center of the city, near Nihonbashi" (trans. from Smith, "The Floating World," p. 35; for more details, see Nishiyama, *Edokko*, pp. 93–95).

61. For example, according to the same policy measures previously applied to the Yoshiwara brothel quarters, in 1842 the bakufu relocated all kabuki theaters from the downtown Shibai-chō district to Saruwaka-chō (on the northeastern periphery of the city). This was partly designed to discourage the public by preventing casual access to vulgar entertainment as well as to put the kabuki business under stricter control.

62. Gerstle, p. 34.

63. In a similar vein, Anne Walthall, in her study of rural culture in late Tokugawa Japan, suggests: "Cultural pursuits [by peasants] became acts of resistance to the established order. . . . As local officials felt their control over these activities begin to weaken, their desire for a sense of communitas took second place to the fear of disruptive activities. . . . The inherent antagonism between popular and ruling-class culture became apparent, and the arts themselves became a form of resistance to the dictates of governmental authority." For a fuller discussion, see Walthall, "Peripheries," pp. 385–92.

64. Nishiyama, *Edo Culture*, p. 62.

65. The fifth volume, originally entitled "Twenty-Eight Chapters" ("Nijūhachi hon"), of *Shikidō ōkagami* (A great mirror of the way of color), an eighteen-volume encyclopedia of brothel quarters, was separated and published under the title of *Shikidō okagami* (A little mirror of the way of color) in 1699. For the text, see Noma, pp. 149–204. For a brief introduction to the *Great Mirror* and the author, see Rogers, pp. 32–38.

66. Kurachi, pp. 358–59.

67. Seigle, p. 131.

68. Drawing on Kuki Shūzō's *Iki no kōzō* (The structure of *iki*) and Asō Isoji's *Iki/tsū*, Nishiyama Matsunosuke (*Edo Culture*, pp. 53–54, 58) characterizes the aesthetic of Edo culture through the concept of *iki*: "The aesthetic consciousness crystallized in the word *iki* had come to center on three elements: a strength of character called *hari*; the allure referred to as *bitai*; and the urbanity

known as *akanuke*. *Hari* was a sharp, straightforward, coolly gallant manner that resisted all compromise, conciliation, and undue social adroitness or tact. . . . *Bitai* implied a kind of eroticism; but more important was the maintenance of a sense of charm. . . . The quality of *akanuke* demanded an unpretentious air, a thorough familiarity with all aspects of life, and an unconcerned, unassuming character." On the other hand, Nishiyama continues, "The aesthetic consciousness of *iki* is part of a refined culture of sensation; *tsū* is this aesthetic consciousness put into practice. In other words, *tsū* is the behavior brought forth by *iki*."

69. For more information on the rise of bunjin culture and bunjin consciousness, see Nakamura. For a fuller treatment of bunjin's cultural aesthetic, with a focus on Buson, see Morris, "Buson and Shiki," pp. 381–407; and Morris, "Group Portrait with Artist."

70. Among the eighteen great masters, Oguchiya Jiheigyo was the best known. According to H. D. Harootunian ("Cultural Politics in Tokugawa Japan," pp. 23–24): "When he cruised the Yoshiwara district he wore an edged, crested kimono of black silk, carried a sword in a sharkskin sheath and a pill box, and walked on clogs made of gold-threaded material. His presence constituted a spectacle by itself, inevitably commanding the attention of all. Once he entered through the great gate marking off the district from the rest of the city, women who worked in the teahouses gathered on both sides of the street and cheered, 'there goes Mr. Deity of Good Fortune.' . . . It was reported that after visiting the toilet he would pour generous amounts of salt on a large plate and wash his hands in it. His daily use of salt amounted to a yearly total equivalent to thirty-five pounds of rice!"

71. Aoki, pp. 285–87.

72. Ibid., p. 294.

73. Brown, p. 526.

74. Maruyama Masao ("Rekishi gishiki no kosō," pp. 14–19) has explored how the idea of "life strength" (*ikioi*) had been used to sanctify the genealogical origin and linear succession of the Yamato imperial line in ancient Japan. According to him, the Japanese emperorship was justified not by the Confucian concept of the "Mandate of Heaven," but by the blood lineage of the imperial house that successfully demonstrated "life strength." "Life strength" was a supreme virtue, on which political sovereignty could be asserted. See also Brown, pp. 526–35.

75. Hanley, pp. 126–74.

76. Hayashi, "Asakusa no onna tachi," pp. 47–48. Nevertheless, Edo tenants fared better, Susan B. Hanley (p. 127) notes, than did the inhabitants of European cities: "However densely these families were packed in, they were not on

top of each other in multistory buildings nor did people live in basements as Europeans did. The ever-present danger from earthquakes and the light construction precluded tall buildings, and the authorities forbade their construction by anyone who might be inclined to be so imprudent."

77. For more details, see Miyata, "Toshi to minzoku bunka," p. 127.

78. For demographic studies of the relationship between infant mortality and smallpox, see Jannetta, pp. 97–100; and Nakajima, pp. 10–11. For an archaeological study of the subject, see Tanigawa, pp. 93–94.

79. See Yanagita, "Toshi to nōson," p. 251, for a comparison of how the traditional Japanese psychology of security, which was attached to the production of clothing, food, and shelter, manifested itself in urban dwellers and rural producers.

80. For a discussion of critics of the genze riyaku fever of Edo Buddhism, see Kashiwahara, "Kinsei Shinshū to genze riyaku"; and Chikazu.

81. Quoted in Harootunian, "Late Tokugawa Culture and Thought," p. 215.

82. Hiruma, "Samazama na kōdō bunka," pp. 319–20; and for figures in the 1690 edition, see Edo sōsho kankōkai, pp. 62–68.

83. The term *hayarigami shinkō* was coined by Yanagita Kunio ("Ishi-gami mondō," pp. 29–30, 97, 144–46), who saw the volatile ups and downs of fashionable deities as a mysterious character of Japanese religion. For examples of faddish deities, Yanagita suggested Tokoyo no Kami (for wealth and longevity), Shidara no Kami (for dispelling epidemics), and Shutara-shin (for happiness) in the ancient times; and Kuwa-gami and Karakasa Jizō (for safe delivery) in the early modern times.

84. See Miyata, "Edo chōnin no shinkō," pp. 243–45. For example, the *Lotus Sūtra* is often cited as a source for the term *genze riyaku*, but the sūtra's real message is that genze riyaku is an extra reward to one who makes the effort to reach the dharma. See Chapter 5 of the *Miao-fa lien-hua ching*, which says, "These beings, having heard this Dharma, in the 'present age' are tranquil and are later born in a good place" (*Taishō shinshū daizōkyō*, no. 262, 9.19b, trans. from Hurvitz, p. 102).

85. Matsudaira, 1: 132–33.

86. Ibid., pp. 403–8; and Miyata, *Edo saiji ki*, p. 186.

87. Matsudaira, 1: 264; Miyata, *Nihonjin no kōdō to shisō*, p. 44; and Miyata, *Edo saiji ki*, pp. 188–90.

88. See "Kinryūsan Sensōji Arazawadō Fudōson ryaku engi," in Matsudaira, 1: 145–46.

89. "Kōnōsho: In-Yakushi go musō o-megusuri," in Matsudaira, 1: 342; and "Hashimoto Yakushi yuraisho," in ibid., pp. 88–91.

90. Matsudaira, 1: 609–11. For a set of six Jizō statues for pilgrimage in Edo, see Saitō Gesshin, *Tōto saiji ki* (1838), 3: 142–45.

91. For more details, including different versions of Kume's life story, see Matsudaira, 1: 411–30; and Miyata, *Edo saiji ki*, 186–87.

92. Matsudaira, 1: 161–76; and Miyata, "Kumagai Anzaemon Inari."

93. Matsudaira, 1: 182.

94. "Koyasu Hōshushin Engi," in Matsudaira, 1: 581–85.

95. Among these, the most effective way to enhance the reputation of a deity was to erect a magnificent shrine to it. The concern about maintaining religious halls is well reflected in the Sensōji diaries, which record in great detail every single building project.

96. The uncommon power of kami in Japanese traditional culture is independent of the binary opposition of good and evil. Kami might exert either benevolent or malevolent power, depending on the degree of treatment they receive from their worshippers. The most oft-cited reference regarding the indigenous conception of kami is Motoori Norinaga: "Kami include not only mysterious beings that are noble and good but also malignant spirits that are extraordinary and deserve veneration" (trans. from Matsumae, p. 318).

97. For more details, see Miyata, *Edo no chiisana kamigami*, pp. 80–93; *Toshi minzokuron no kadai*, pp. 177–89; and "Matsuri sute no ronri," pp. 65–72.

98. For the deification of human beings, see Miyata, *Ikigami shinkō*, pp. 14–39. For ritual appeasement and purification as a means of deifying evil spirits, see Miyata, *Toshi minzokuron no kadai*, pp. 181–89.

99. See Ōshima; and Kamiya.

100. For studies of the functional reformulation of Buddhist deities in Japan, see Takatori; and Itō Yuishin, pp. 175–213.

101. This refers to the twenty-fifth chapter (*Taishō shinshū daizōkyō*, no. 262, 9.56c–58b, "The Gateway to Everywhere of the Bodhisattva: He Who Observes the Sound of the World") of the *Miao-fa lien-hua ching*.

102. The seven difficulties are conflagration; drowning; attack by *raksasa*-ghosts; the threat of murder by knives and staves; attack by malignant ghosts; imprisonment in stocks, pillory, or chains; and attack by malicious bandits. The three poisons refer to lust, anger, and folly. The two desires are to have a son possessing happiness, excellence, and wisdom and a daughter possessing beauty and affection.

103. Gotō, pp. 36–50.

104. Ibid., pp. 167–89.

105. Matsudaira, 1: 53–63.

106. Amino Aritoshi, p. 447.

107. In Shintō, on the occasion of a matsuri a deity was believed to descend to its *shintai* (the body of a deity) (e.g., a mirror, a rock, a sword, a bell, or a comma-shaped bead), which was encased in the inner shrine (*honden*). For more details, see Yanagita, "Shinju hen"; Orikuchi, "Hige kago no hanashi"; and Ono Sokyō, pp. 209–10.

108. Amino Aritoshi, pp. 99–102.

109. Focusing on the religious activities of peasants in late Tokugawa peripheries, Anne Walthall ("Peripheries," pp. 376–77) suggests that "the appearance of *hayarigami* provided ordinary peasants an opportunity to seek salvation in a momentary escape from the restrictions of the status system and the unpleasant realities of their everyday existence."

Conclusion

1. Amino Aritoshi, pp. 571–72.

2. In addition to the Zenkōji Amitābha statues, other favorite guest de-gaichō deities included the thirty-three Kannon images of the Chichibu pilgrimage circuit. Edoites especially welcomed the Chichibu Kannon de-gaichō, which would not only multiply the salvational compassion of the Asakusa Kannon but would also enable them to complete a full cycle of pilgrimage to the renowned thirty-three Chichibu Kannon deities within the sanctuary of Sensōji. For an example of Chichibu Kannon de-gaichō at Sensōji, see *SN*, 4: 618–19.

3. For a comprehensive chronology of major kaichō, including de-gaichō, held in Edo during the Tokugawa period, see *Edogaku jiten* (Tokyo: Kōbundō, 1994), pp. 776–849.

4. Hiruma, "Edo no kaichō," pp. 330–34; and *Edo no kaichō*, pp. 31–36. The idea of the thirty-three-year interval was taken from the "thirty-three" manifestations of the Avalokiteśvara Bodhisattva in the twenty-fifth chapter of the *Lotus Sūtra*. For an analytical observation of a contemporary thirty-three-year Kannon kaichō, see Bodiford.

5. Hisashi, "Edo no kaichō," pp. 24–26. Kaichō were held mostly in Edo, Osaka, and Kyoto under the guidance of the magistrate of temples and shrines, and *kange* fund-raising campaigns were usually allowed, under the control of the Council of Elders (Rojū), in the local regions. For more details, see Kitamura, pp. 10–12; Yukawa, pp. 26–29; and Takano, *Kinsei Nihon*, pp. 117–24.

6. Totman, p. 206.

7. For a comprehensive anthropological discussion of the "technologies of power" behind culturally distinct constructions of the self, society, and the cosmos in the religious traditions of Christianity and Islam, see Asad.

8. Varley, pp. 176–80.

9. For more details, see Momokawa, pp. 20–24; and Shively, "The Social Environment of Tokugawa Kabuki."

10. Shimizutani, "Sōsō engi to reigen," pp. 29–32; and for a full version of the story, see "Kannon myōō shū," in Matsudaira, 2: 655–59.

11. Nishiyama, *Edo no seikatsu bunka*, p. 42.

12. Momokawa, pp. 16–18.

13. Not only in the popular culture, but also in the intellectual, moral, and new religious activities of the late Tokugawa period, fictive spiritualism (or moralism) was predominant. When the founders of new religions called for a world renewal (*yonaoshi*), their preaching was invariably based on kami possession, spiritual powers, and "divine" intervention. The privileging of spiritual faculty over manual labor was a core tenet of new religious movements in the late Tokugawa period.

14. Harootunian, "Cultural Politics in Tokugawa Japan," p. 14; and for a theoretical discussion of the issue of individual agency in relation to the deployment of cultural values, see Bell, pp. 82–83.

15. Harootunian, "Cultural Politics in Tokugawa Japan," p. 23.

16. Konta, pp. 269–84.

17. Nishiyama, *Edo no seikatsu bunka*, p. 45.

Works Cited

Akai, Tatsurō. "The Common People and Painting." In *Tokugawa Japan: The Social and Economic Antecedents of Modern Japan*, ed. Chie Nakane and Shinzaburō Ōishi, pp. 167–91. Tokyo: Tokyo University Press, 1990.

Amino Aritoshi. *Sensōji shidan shō*. Tokyo: Kinryūsan Sensōji, 1962.

Amino Yoshihiko. "Chūsei no tabibito tachi." In *Nihon minzoku bunka taikei, 6: Hyōhaku to teichaku—Teijū shakai e no michi*, ed. Amino Yoshihiko, pp. 153–266. Tokyo: Shōgakkan, 1984.

———. *Muen kugai raku: Nihon chūsei no jiyū to heiwa*. 2d ed. Tokyo: Heibonsha, 1987.

Aoki Michio. "Kasei bunka no ninaite wa dareka." In *Sōten Nihon no rekishi, 5, Kinsei hen*, ed. Aoki Michio and Hosokawa Satoru, pp. 285–94. Tokyo: Shin jinbutsu ōraisha, 1991.

Asad, Talal. *Genealogies of Religion: Discipline and Reasons of Power in Christianity and Islam*. Baltimore: Johns Hopkins University Press, 1993.

Asakura Haruhiko. "Sensōji kankei no engi rui." In *Kaminarimon Edo banashi*, ed. Sensōji hinamiki kenkyūkai, pp. 187–91. Tokyo: Tōkyō bijutsu, 1986.

Asakura Kamezō. *Misemono kenkyū*. Kyoto: Shimonkaku shuppan, 1977.

Asao Naohiro. "Jūhachi seiki no shakai hendō to mibun teki chūkansō." In *Nihon no kinsei, 10, Kindai e no taidō*, ed. Tsuji Tatsuya, pp. 45–94. Tokyo: Chūō kōronsha, 1993.

———. "Sōson kara machi e." In *Nihon no shakaishi, 6, Shakai teki sho shūdan*, ed. Amino Yoshihiko, pp. 323–62. Tokyo: Iwanami shoten, 1988.

Bell, Catherine. *Ritual Perspectives and Dimensions*. New York: Oxford University Press, 1997.

Bitō Masahide. *Edo jidai to wa nani ka.* Tokyo: Iwanami shoten, 1993.

Bodiford, William M. "Sōtō Zen in a Japanese Town: Field Notes on a Once-Every-Thirty-Three-Years Kannon Festival." *Japanese Journal of Religious Studies* 21, no. 1 (1994): 3–36.

Bolitho, Harold. "Sumō and Popular Culture: The Tokugawa Period." In *The Japanese Trajectory: Modernization and Beyond,* ed. Gavan McCormack and Yoshio Sugimoto, pp. 17–32. Cambridge. Eng.: Cambridge University Press, 1988.

———. "The Tempō Crisis." In *The Cambridge History of Japan,* vol. 5, *The Nineteenth Century,* ed. Marius B. Jansen, pp. 116–67. Cambridge, Eng.: Cambridge University Press, 1989.

Brown, Delmer M. "The Early Evolution of Historical Consciousness." In *The Cambridge History of Japan,* vol. 1, *Ancient Japan,* ed. Delmer M. Brown, pp. 504–48. Cambridge, Eng.: Cambridge University Press, 1993.

Buyō Inshi. *Seji kenbun roku.* 1816. Reprinted—Tokyo: Kaizōsha, 1926.

Chiba Noritaka. "Seiji to Bukkyō." In *Nihon Bukkyōshi,* 3, *Kinsei kindai hen,* ed. Tamamuro Taijō, pp. 19–72. Kyoto: Hōzōkan, 1967.

Chikazu Keishi. "Genze riyaku hitei no ronri." In *Nihon shūkyō no genze riyaku,* ed. Nihon Bukkyō kenkyūkai, pp. 324–41. Tokyo: Daizō shuppan, 1970.

Collcutt, Martin. "Buddhism: The Threat of Eradication." In *Japan in Transition: From Tokugawa to Meiji,* ed. Marius B. Jansen and Gilbert Rozman, pp. 143–67. Princeton: Princeton University Press, 1986.

Davis, Winston. *Japanese Religion and Society: Paradigms of Structure and Change.* Albany: State University of New York Press, 1992.

Dazai Shundai. "Keizai roku." In *Nihon keizai taiten,* 54 vols., ed. Takimoto Seiichi, 9: 379–671. Tokyo: Keimeisha, 1928–30.

Edogaku jiten. Tokyo: Kōbundo, 1984.

Edo sōsho kankōkai, ed. "Edo sō kanoko meisho taizen." In *Edo sōsho,* 3: 1–88. Tokyo: Meicho kankōkai, 1964.

Fujita Oboe. *Tōyama Kinjirō no jidai.* Tokyo: Kōshō shobō, 1992.

Furukawa Miki. *Zusetsu shomin geinō: Edo no misemono.* Tokyo: Yūzankaku, 1982.

Gamō Masao. "Edo no machi zukuri." In *Dai-Edo mangekyō,* ed. Nō-san-gyo-son bunka kyōkai, pp. 58–65. Tokyo: Kumimotosha, 1991.

Gerstle, C. Andrew. "Flowers of Edo: Kabuki and Its Patrons." In *18th Century Japan,* ed. C. Andrew Gerstle, pp. 33–50. Sydney: Allen & Unwin, 1989.

Gill, Sam M. "Prayer." In *The Encyclopedia of Religion,* 11: 489–94. New York: Macmillan, 1987.

Goodwin, Janet R. *Alms and Vagabonds: Buddhist Temples and Popular Patronage in Medieval Japan.* Honolulu: University of Hawaii Press, 1994.

Gorai Shigeru. "Chūsei josei no shūkyōsei to seikatsu." In *Nihon joseishi, 2, Chūsei*, ed. Joseishi sōgō kenykyūkai, pp. 103–36. Tokyo: Tōkyō daigaku shuppankai, 1982.

———. "Minzoku shinkō toshite no Dai-Hannya kyō." *Indogaku Bukkyōgaku kenkyū* 3, no. 1 (1954): 183–85.

———. "Shūshōe Shūnie to minzoku." In *Kōza Nihon no minzoku shūkyō, 2, Bukkyō minzokugaku*, ed. Gorai Shigeru et al., pp. 84–98. Tokyo: Kōbundō, 1980.

Gotō Daiyō. *Kanzeon Bosastsu no kenkyū*. Rev. ed. Tokyo: Sankibō Butsu shorin, 1989.

Groner, Paul. *Saichō: The Establishment of the Japanese Tendai School*. Berkeley: University of California Press, 1984.

Gunji Masakatsu. "Kabuki and Its Social Background." In *Tokugawa Japan: The Social and Economic Antecedents of Modern Japan*, ed. Chie Nakane and Shinzaburō Ōishi, pp. 192–212. Tokyo: Tokyo University Press, 1990.

Hanasaki Kazuo. *Edo no deai chaya*. Tokyo: Kinsei fūzoku kenkyūkai, 1972.

———. *Senryū zappai: Edo okabasho zue*. Tokyo: Kinsei fūzoku kenkyūkai, 1964.

Hanley, Susan B. *Everyday Things in Premodern Japan: The Hidden Legacy of Material Culture*. Berkeley: University of California Press, 1997.

Harootunian, H. D. "Cultural Politics in Tokugawa Japan." In *Undercurrents in the Floating World: Censorship and Japanese Prints*, ed. Sarah E. Thompson and H. D. Harootunian, pp. 9–28. New York: Asia Society Galleries, 1991.

———. "Late Tokugawa Culture and Thought." In *The Cambridge History of Japan*, vol. 5, *The Nineteenth Century*, ed. Marius B. Jansen, pp. 168–258. Cambridge, Eng.: Cambridge University Press, 1989.

Hayami Tasuku. *Nihon Bukkyōshi: Kodai*. Tokyo: Yoshikawa kōbunkan, 1986.

Hayashi Reiko. "Asakusa no onna tachi." In *Edo Asakusa o kataru*, ed. Sensōji hinamiki kenkyūkai, pp. 47–53. Tokyo: Tōkyō bijutsu, 1990.

———. "Kannon sama to Sutejirō: Edo-dana hōkōnin monogatari." In *Kaminarimon Edo banashi*, ed. Sensōji hinamiki kenkyūkai, pp. 29–33. Tokyo: Tōkyō bijutsu, 1986.

———. *Nihon no kinsei, 5, Shōnin no katsudō*. Tokyo: Chūō kōronsha, 1992.

Hayashiya Tatsusaburō. *Chūsei bunka no kichō*. Tokyo: Tōkyō daigaku shuppankai, 1953.

Hiraga Gennai. "Nenashigusa." 1763. In *Nihon koten bungaku taikei, 55, Furaisan jinshū*, ed. and annot. Nakamura Yukihiko, pp. 33–94. Tokyo: Iwanami shoten, 1961.

Hirai Naofusa. "Saisen." In *Kokushi dai jiten*, vol. 6, s.v. Tokyo: Yoshikawa kōbunkan, 1986.

Hiranuma Yoshirō. *Kinsei jiin monzen machi no kenkyū*. Tokyo: Waseda daigaku shuppanbu, 1957.

Hirota Masaki. "Kinsei no seijuku to kindai." In *Nihon no kinsei, 16, Minshū no kokoro*, ed. Hirota Masaki, pp. 295–330. Tokyo: Chūō kōronsha, 1994.

———. "Kinsei no seiritsu to minshū." In *Nihon no kinsei, 16, Minshū no kokoro*, ed. Hirota Masaki, pp. 7–32. Tokyo: Chūō kōronsha, 1994.

———. "Yonaoshi ni miru minshū no sekaijō." In *Nihon no shakaishi, 7, Shakaikan to sekaizō*, ed. Asao Naohiro, pp. 261–98. Tokyo: Iwanami shoten, 1987.

Hiruma Hisashi. *Edo no kaichō*. Tokyo: Yoshikawa kōbunkan, 1980.

———. "Edo no kaichō." In *Edo chōnin no kenkyū*, ed. Nishiyama Matsunosuke, 2: 273–472. Tokyo: Yoshikawa kōbunkan, 1973.

———. "Keidai no yose." In *Edo Asakusa o kataru*, ed. Sensōji hinamiki kenkyūkai, pp. 234–39. Tokyo: Tōkyō bijutsu, 1990.

———. "Samazama na kōdō bunka." In *Nihon no kinsei, 14, Bunka no taishūka*, ed. Takeuchi Makoto, pp. 319–50. Tokyo: Chūō kōronsha, 1993.

Houser, William B. *Economic Institutional Change in Tokugawa Japan: Osaka and the Kinai Cotton Trade*. Cambridge, Eng.: Cambridge University Press, 1974.

Howell, David L. "Hard Times in the Kantō: Economic Change and Village Life in Late Tokugawa Japan." *Modern Asian Studies* 23, no. 2 (1989): 349–71.

Hsu, Francis L. K. *Iemoto: The Heart of Japan*. Cambridge, Mass.: Schenckman, 1975.

Hurvitz, Leon, trans. *Scripture of the Lotus Blossom of the Fine Dharma*. New York: Columbia University Press, 1976.

Ikegami Akihiko. "Azuma bashi." In *Edo Asakusa o kataru*, ed. Sensōji hinamiki kenkyūkai, pp. 122–27. Tokyo: Tōkyō bijutsu, 1990.

———. "Hinoetora no Edo taika." In *Edo Asakusa o kataru*, ed. Sensōji hinamiki kenkyūkai, pp. 141–45. Tokyo: Tōkyō bijutsu, 1990.

———. "Meiwa no kasai to Kinryūsan rinji renjū." In *Kaminarimon Edo banashi*, ed. Sensōji hinamiki kenkyūkai, pp. 23–28. Tokyo: Tōkyō bijutsu, 1986.

Ikegami, Eiko. *The Taming of the Samurai: Honorific Individualism and the Making of Modern Japan*. Cambridge, Mass.: Harvard University Press, 1995.

Imada Yōzō. "Asakusa no meibutsu otoko: Fukai Shidōken." In *Kaminarimon Edo banashi*, ed. Sensōji hinamiki kenkyūkai, pp. 126–30. Tokyo: Tōkyō bijutsu, 1986.

Ishimori Shūzō. "Tabi kara ryokō e: Edo jidai no tabi." In *Gendai Nihon bunka ni okeru dentō to henyō, 6*, ed. Moriya Takeshi, pp. 76–91. Tokyo: Domesu shuppan, 1989.

Ishioka Hisao. "Yōkyū." In *Kokushi dai jiten*, vol. 14, s.v. Tokyo: Yoshikawa kōbunkan, 1993.

Itō Tasaburō. "The Book Banning Policy of the Tokugawa Shōgunate." *Acta Asiatica* 22 (1972): 36–61.

Itō Yuishin. "Bukkyō no minkan juyō." In *Nihon minzoku bunka taikei*, 4, *Kami to Hotoke—Minzoku shūkyō no shosō*, ed. Miyata Noboru, pp. 173–226. Tokyo: Shōgakkan, 1983.

Iwahashi Masaru. *Kinsei Nihon bukka shi no kenkyū*. Tokyo: Ōhara shinseisha, 1981.

Iwata Kōtarō. "Toshi keizai no tenkan." In *Nihon no kinsei*, 9, *Toshi no jidai*, ed. Yoshida Nobuyuki, pp. 263–302. Tokyo: Chūō kōronsha, 1992.

———. "Uchikowashi to minshū sekai." In *Nihon toshishi nyūmon*, 2, *Machi*, ed. Takahashi Yasuo and Yoshida Nobuyuki, pp. 79–104. Tokyo: Tōkyō daigaku shuppankai, 1991.

Jannettam, Ann Bowman. *Epidemics and Mortality in Early Modern Japan*. Princeton: Princeton University Press, 1987.

Jansen, Marius B. "Japan in the Early Nineteenth Century." In *The Cambridge History of Japan*, vol. 5, *The Nineteenth Century*, ed. Marius B. Jansen, pp. 50–115. Cambridge, Eng.: Cambridge University Press, 1989.

Jinbo Kazuya. "Yūya." In *Edogaku jiten*, pp. 247–48. Tokyo: Kōbundō, 1994.

Jinnai Hidenobu. "The Spatial Structure of Edo." In *Tokugawa Japan: The Social and Economic Antecedents of Modern Japan*, ed. Chie Nakane and Shinzaburō Ōishi, pp. 124–46. Tokyo: Tokyo University Press, 1990.

———. *Tokyo: A Spatial Anthropology*. Trans. Kimiko Nishimura. Berkeley: University of California Press, 1995.

Kagawa Takayuki. *Nihon no rekishi*, 14, *Kuzure yuku sakoku*. Tokyo: Shūeisha, 1992.

———. "Toshi shōgyō no hatten." In *Kōza Nihon rekishi*, 6, *Kinsei* 2, ed. Rekishigaku kenkyūkai and Nihonshi kenkyūkai, pp. 195–228. Tokyo: Tōkyō daigaku shuppankai, 1985.

Kamiya Takehiro. "Fukujin to yakujin." In *Fukujin shinkō*, ed. Miyamoto Kesao, pp. 59–75. Tokyo: Yūzankaku, 1987.

Kashiwahara Yūsen. "Gohō shisō to shomin bunka." In *Nihon shisō taikei*, 57, *Kinsei Bukkyō no shisō*, ed. Kashiwahara Yūsen and Fujii Manabu, pp. 533–56. Tokyo: Iwanami shoten, 1973.

———. "Kinsei Shinshū to genze riyaku." In *Nihon shūkyō no genze riyaku*, ed. Nihon Bukkyō kenkyūkai, pp. 238–52. Tokyo: Daizō shuppan, 1970.

———. *Nihon Bukkyōshi: Kindai*. Tokyo: Yoshikawa kōbunkan, 1990.

Kasuya Hiroki, ed. *Shinhen senryū dai jiten*. Tokyo: Tōkyōdō shuppan, 1995.

Kelly, William W. "Incendiary Actions: Fires and Firefighting in the Shogun's Capital and the People's City." In *Edo and Paris: Urban Life and the State in the*

Early Modern Era, ed. James L. McClain, John M. Merriman, and Ugawa Kaoru, pp. 310–31. Ithaca, N.Y.: Cornell University Press, 1994.

Ketelaar, James Edward. *On Heretics and Martyrs in Meiji Japan: Buddhism and Its Persecution*. Princeton: Princeton University Press, 1990.

Kimura Motoi, ed. *Kyūdaka kyūryō torishirabe chō: Kantō hen*. Tokyo: Tōkyōdō shuppan, 1995.

Kinsei shiryō kenkyūkai, ed. *Shōhō jiroku*. 3 vols. Tokyo: Nihon gakujutsu shinkōkai, 1964–66.

Kitagawa, Joseph M. *On Understanding Japanese Religion*. Princeton: Princeton University Press, 1987.

Kitahara Akio. "Toki kenjō." In *Kokushi dai jiten*, s.v. Tokyo: Yoshikawa kōbunkan, 1989.

Kitahara Susumu. "Jiryō to nengu." In *Edo Asakusa o kataru*, ed. Sensōji hinamiki kenkyūkai, pp. 87–93. Tokyo: Tōkyō bijutsu, 1990.

———. "Kaminari monzen no meishu." In *Edo Asakusa o kataru*, ed. Sensōji hinamiki kenkyūkai, pp. 115–21. Tokyo: Tōkyō bijutsu, 1990.

———. "Rōkakko to Edokko." In *Nihon no kinsei, 17, Higashi to nishi Edo to Kamigata*, ed. Aoki Michio, pp. 159–92. Tokyo: Chūō kōronsha, 1994.

———. "Saikō sareta Sanja matsuri." In *Edo Asakusa o kataru*, ed. Sensōji hinamiki kenkyūkai, pp. 265–71. Tokyo: Tōkyō bijutsu, 1990.

———. "Sanja matsuri to Ōmori Mura gyoshi no funehiki yaku." In *Kaminarimon Edo banashi*, ed. Sensōji hinamiki kenkyūkai, pp. 156–61. Tokyo: Tōkyō bijutsu, 1986.

Kitami Toshio. *Ichi no gyōshō no minzoku*. Tokyo: Iwazaki bijutsusha, 1970.

Kitamura Gyōon. *Kinsei kaichō no kenkyū*. Tokyo: Meicho shuppan, 1989.

Kobayashi Shigefumi. "Kodai no ichi no keikan: Ryūtsū gai no kinō o chūshin ni." *Waseda daigaku daigakuin bungaku kenkyūka kiyō bessatsu* 8 (1981): 181–89.

Kominz, Laurence R. *Avatars of Vengeance: Japanese Drama and the Soga Literary Tradition*. Ann Arbor: University of Michigan Press, 1995.

———. "Ichikawa Danjūrō V and Kabuki's Golden Age." In *The Floating World Revisited*, ed. Donald Jenkins, pp. 63–83. Honolulu: University of Hawaii Press, 1993.

———. "*Ya no Ne*: The Genesis of a Kabuki Aragoto Classic." *Monumenta Nipponica* 38, no. 4 (1983): 387–407.

Komori Takayoshi. *Edo Asakusa machina no kenkyū*. Tokyo: Sōbunsha, 1984.

———. "Kakushibaita." In *Edogaku jiten*, s.v. Tokyo: Kōbundō, 1994.

Konta Yōzō. "Jūkyū seiki no medeia jijō." In *Nihon no kinsei, 14, Bunka no taishūka*, ed. Takeuchi Makoto, pp. 269–318. Tokyo: Chūō kōronsha, 1993.

Kumakura Isao. "Kinsei ni okeru geinō no tenkai." In *Nihon no kinsei, 11, Dentō geinō no tenkai*, pp. 9–66. Tokyo: Chūō kōronsha, 1993.

———. "Yūjo to yūkaku." In *Gendai Nihon bunka ni okeru dentō to henyō, 6, Nihonjin to asobi*, ed. Moriya Takeshi, pp. 198–215. Tokyo: Domesu shuppan, 1989.

Kurachi Katsunao. "Sei no bunka." In *Iwanami kōza Nihon tsūshi, 14, Kinsei 4*, ed. Asao Naohiro, Amino Yoshihiko, and Ishii Susumu, pp. 355–72. Tokyo: Iwanami shoten, 1995.

Kurimoto Shin'ichirō. *Hikari no toshi, yami no toshi*. Tokyo: Seidosha, 1981.

Kurushima Hiroshi. "Sairei no kūkan kōzō." In *Nihon toshishi nyūmon, 1, Kūkan*, ed. Takahashi Yasuo and Yoshida Nobuyuki, pp. 107–30. Tokyo: Tōkyō daigaku shuppankai, 1989.

Kyū bakufu hikitsugi sho: Edo machikata kakiage—Asakusa. 1825. 2 vols. Ed. and annot. Hayashi Rokurō, Hasegawa Masatsugu, and Asakura Haruhiko. Tokyo: Shin jinbutsu ōraisha, 1987.

LaFleur, William R. *The Karma of Words: Buddhism and the Literary Arts in Medieval Japan*. Berkeley: University of California Press, 1983.

———. *Liquid Life: Abortion and Buddhism in Japan*. Princeton: Princeton University Press, 1992.

Leupp, Gary P. *Servants, Shophands, and Laborers in the Cities of Tokugawa Japan*. Princeton: Princeton University Press, 1992.

Leutner, Robert W. *Shikitei Sanba and the Comic Tradition in Edo Fiction*. Cambridge, Mass.: Harvard University, Council on East Asian Studies, 1985.

Lidin, Olof G. "Ogyū Sorai's Civil Society (*Seidan*)." *Nichibunken Japan Review* 5 (1994): 3–13.

Maki Fumihiko. "Oku no shisō." In *Miegakuresuru toshi: Edo kara Tōkyō e*, ed. Maki Fumihiko, pp. 197–230. Tokyo: Kashima shuppankai, 1980.

Markus, Andrew L. "The Carnival of Edo: Misemono Spectacles from Contemporary Accounts." *Harvard Journal of Asiatic Studies* 45, no. 2 (1985): 499–541.

———. *The Willow in Autumn: Ryūtei Tanehiko, 1783–1842*. Cambridge, Mass.: Harvard University, Council on East Asian Studies, 1992.

Maruyama Masao. "Rekishi gishiki no kosō." In *Nihon no shisō, 6, Rekishi shisō shū*, ed. Maruyama Masao, pp. 3–46. Tokyo: Chikuma shobō, 1972.

Matsudaira Kanzan. *Sensōji shi*. 1813. Reprinted in 2 vols. Tokyo: Sensōji shuppankai, 1939, 1942.

Matsumae Takeshi. "Early Kami Worship." Trans. Janet Goodwin. In *The Cambridge History of Japan*, vol. 1, *Ancient Japan*, ed. Delmer M. Brown, pp. 317–58. Cambridge, Eng.: Cambridge University Press, 1993.

Misumi Haruo. *Geinōshi no minzoku teki kenkyū*. Tokyo: Tōkyōdō shuppan, 1976.

Mitamura Engyō, ed. *Mikan zuihitsu hyakushū, 6, Jijiroku.* Reprinted—Kyoto: Rinkawa shoten, 1927.

Miyamoto Yukiko. "Yūri no seiritsu to taishūka." In *Nihon no kinsei, 14, Bunka no taishūka,* ed. Takeuchi Makoto, pp. 169–218. Tokyo: Chūō kōronsha, 1993.

Miyata Noboru. "Edo chōnin no shinkō." In *Edo chōnin no kenkyū 2,* ed. Nishiyama Matsunosuke, pp. 227–71. Tokyo: Yoshikawa kōbunkan, 1973.

———. *Edo no chiisana kamigami.* Tokyo: Seidosha, 1989.

———. *Edo saiji ki: Toshi minzokushi no kokoromi.* Tokyo: Yoshikawa kōbunkan, 1981.

———. *Ikigami shinkō: Hito o kami ni matsuru fūzoku.* Tokyo: Hanawa shobō, 1970.

———. "Kumagai Anzaemon Inari." In *Kaminarimon Edo banashi,* ed. Sensōji hinamiki kenkyūkai, pp. 167–70. Tokyo: Tōkyō bijutsu, 1986.

———. "Matsuri sute no ronri." *Rekishi kōron* 3, no. 9 (Sept. 1977): 65–72.

———. *Nihonjin no kōdō to shisō, 17, Kinsei no hayarigami.* Tokyo: Hyōronsha, 1976.

———. "Onna no dairiki to misemono." In *Misemono no jinruigaku,* ed. Victor Turner and Yamaguchi Masao, pp. 362–75. Tokyo: Sanseidō, 1983.

———. *Onna no reiryoku to ie no kami: Nihon no minzoku shūkyō.* Tokyo: Jinbun shoin, 1983.

———. "Sensōji ganbaru: Keidai no seichisei." In *Kaminarimon Edo banashi,* ed. Sensōji hinamiki kenkyūkai, pp. 207–12. Tokyo: Tōkyō bijutsu, 1986.

———. "Shomin shinkō no shoson." In *Bukkyō bunka dai jiten,* s.v. Tokyo: Kōsei shuppansha, 1989.

———. *Shūmatsukan no minzokugaku.* Tokyo: Kōbundō, 1987.

———. *Toshi minzokuron no kadai.* Tokyo: Miraisha, 1982.

———. "Toshi to minzoku bunka." In *Nihon minzoku bunka taikei, 11, Toshi to inaka—Machi no seikatsu bunka,* ed. Miyata Noboru, pp. 5–42. Tokyo: Shōgakkan, 1985.

———. *Yōkai no minzokugaku: Nihon no mienai kūkan.* Tokyo: Iwanami shoten, 1985.

Mizue Renko. "Meibutsu no ryūkōsei." In *Kaminarimon Edo banashi,* ed. Sensōji hinamiki kenkyūkai, pp. 66–71. Tokyo: Tōkyō bijutsu, 1986.

———. "Yone manjū to so no hayari." In *Kaminarimon Edo banashi,* ed. Sensōji hinamiki kenkyūkai, pp. 72–78. Tokyo: Tōkyō bijutsu, 1986.

Mizuno Tamenaga. *Zuihitsu hyakkaen, 8–9, Yoshi no sōshi.* 2 vols. Tokyo: Chūō kōronsha, 1981.

Momokawa Takahito. "Ko no fuan na nikutai: Sei no kinsei." In Momokawa Takahito et al., *Edo bunka no henyō: Jūhachi seiki Nihon no keiken*, pp. 7–38. Tokyo: Heibonsha, 1994.

Morioka, Heinz, and Miyoko Sasaki. *Rakugo: The Popular Narrative Art of Japan*. Cambridge, Mass.: Harvard University, Council on East Asian Studies, 1990.

Moriya Takeshi. *Kinsei geinō kōgyōshi no kenkyū*. Tokyo: Kōbundō, 1985.

———. "Kinsei no toshi seikatsu to furyū no tenkai." *Kokuritsu rekishi minzoku hakubutsukan kenkyū hōkoku* 15 (1987): 141–56.

———. "*Misemono kenkyū* kaidai." Appended to Asakura Kamezō, *Misemono kenkyū*, pp. 337–54. Kyoto: Shimonkaku shuppan, 1977.

———. "Toshi sairei to furyū: So no rekishi teki tenbō." In *Nihon minzoku bunka taikei, 11, Toshi to inaka—Machi no seikatsu bunka*, ed. Miyata Noboru, pp. 387–458. Tokyo: Shōgakkan, 1985.

Morris, Mark. "Buson and Shiki: Part One." *Harvard Journal of Asiatic Studies* 44, no. 2 (Dec. 1984): 381–425.

———. "Group Portrait with Artist: Yosa Buson and His Patrons." In *18th Century Japan: Culture and Society*, ed. C. Andrew Gerstle, pp. 87–105. Sydney: Allen & Unwin, 1989.

Naitō Akira. "Edo no toshi kōzō." In *Edo to wa nani ka: Edo-Tokyogaku*, ed. Ogi Shinzō, pp. 32–54. Tokyo: Shibundō, 1986.

———. *Edo to Edojō*. Tokyo: Kashima kenkyūjo, 1966.

Naitō Akira and Hozumi Kazuo. *Edo no machi*. 2 vols. Tokyo: Sōshisha, 1982.

Naitō Masatoshi. "Toshi no sei kūkan to takai: Edo no ju teki kosumoroji." In *Bukkyō minzokugaku taikei, 3, Seichi to takaikan*, ed. Sakurai Tokutarō, pp. 79–106. Tokyo: Meicho shuppan, 1987.

Najita, Tetsuo. "Political Economism in the Thought of Dazai Shundai, 1680–1747." *Journal of Asian Studies* 31, no. 4 (1972): 821–39.

Nakai Nobuhiko. "Commercial Change and Urban Growth in Early Modern Japan." Trans. James L. McClain. In *The Cambridge History of Japan*, vol. 4, *Early Modern Japan*, ed. John Whitney Hall, pp. 519–95. Cambridge, Eng.: Cambridge University Press, 1991.

Nakajima Yōichirō. *Byōki Nihonshi*. Tokyo: Yūzankaku, 1982.

Nakamura Yukihiko. "Kinsei bunjin gishiki no seiritsu." In *Nakamura Yukihiko chojutsu shū*, 11: 375–407. Tokyo: Chūō kōronsha, 1982.

Nakayama Tarō. *Baishō sanzennen shi*. Tokyo: Sunbikai, 1906.

Nakazawa Masaaki. "Shūshōe Shūnie to mochi hana." In *Bukkyō minzokugaku taikei, 6, Bukkyō nenjū gyōji*, ed. Itō Yuishin, pp. 45–64. Tokyo: Meicho shuppan, 1988.

Nishiyama Matsunosuke. "Asakusa hakkei." In *Edo Asakusa o kataru*, ed. Sensōji hinamiki kenkyūkai, pp. 15–19. Tokyo: Tōkyō bijutsu, 1990.

———. "Dai-Ei Hakubutsukan no Asakusa eken." In *Edo Asakusa o kataru*, ed. Sensōji hinamiki kenkyūkai, pp. 2–7. Tokyo: Tōkyō bijutsu, 1990.

———. *Edo Culture: Daily Life and Diversions in Urban Japan, 1600–1868*. Trans. Gerald Groemer. Honolulu: University of Hawaii Press, 1997.

———. *Edogaku nyūmon*. Tokyo: Chikuma shobō, 1981.

———. *Edokko*. Tokyo: Yoshikawa kōbunkan, 1980.

———. "Edo no machi nanushi Saitō Gesshin." In *Edo chōnin no kenkyū*, 4, ed. Nishiyama Matsunosuke, pp. 395–517. Tokyo: Yoshikawa kōbunkan, 1975.

———. *Edo no seikatsu bunka: Nishiyama Matsunosuke chosakushū*, vol. 3. Tokyo: Yoshikawa kōbunkan, 1983.

———. "Ichiritsusai Hiroshige ga: Asakusa Kanzeon sennihyaku nen kaichō." In *Kaminarimon Edo banashi*, ed. Sensōji hinamiki kenkyūkai, pp. 192–99. Tokyo: Tōkyō bijutsu, 1986.

———. *Iemotosei no tenkai: Nishiyama Matsunosuke chosakushū*, vol. 2. Tokyo: Yoshikawa kōbunkan, 1983.

———. "Kannon junrei ni miru shomin shinkō." In *Chichibu Bandō Kannon reijō*, ed. Nishiyama Matsunosuke, pp. 1–6. Tokyo: Shin jinbutsu ōraisha, 1984.

Nishizaka Yasushi. "Kinsei toshi to ōdana." In *Nihon no kinsei*, 9, *Toshi no jidai*, ed. Yoshida Nobuyuki, pp. 173–220. Tokyo: Chūō kōronsha, 1992.

Noma Kōshin, ed. *Ganpon shikidō ōkagami*. Kyoto: Yūzan bunko, 1961.

Nomura Kentarō. *Edo*. Tokyo: Shibundō, 1958.

Okabe Ribee. "Furyū Shidōken den." 1763. In *Nihon koten bungaku taikei*, 55, *Furaisan jinshū*, ed. and annot. Nakamura Yukihiko, pp. 153–224. Tokyo: Iwanami shoten, 1961.

Okamoto Kidō. *Edo ni tsuite no hanashi*. Ed. Kishii Yoshie. Tokyo: Hikari no tomo sha, 1955.

Ono Sokyō. *Jinja Shintō no kiso chishiki to kiso mondai*. Tokyo: Jinja shinpōsha, 1963.

Ono Takeo, ed. *Misemono fūzoku zushi*. Tokyo: Tenbōsha, 1977.

Ooms, Herman. *Charismatic Bureaucrat: A Political Biography of Matsudaira Sadanobu, 1758–1828*. Chicago: University of Chicago Press, 1975.

———. *Tokugawa Ideology: Early Constructs, 1570–1680*. Princeton: Princeton University Press, 1985.

Orikuchi Shinobu. "Hige kago no hanashi." 1915. In *Orikuchi Shinobu zenshū*, 2: 182–211. Tokyo: Chūō kōronsha, 1954.

———. "Nenjū gyōji: Minkan gyōji denshō no kenkyū." 1930. In *Orikuchi Shinobu zenshū*, 15: 47–124. Tokyo: Chūō kōronsha, 1954.

Ōshima Tatehiko. "Yakujin to fukujin." In *Fukujin shinkō*, ed. Miyamoto Kesao, pp. 49–57. Tokyo: Yūzankaku, 1987.

Ōsumi Kazuo. "Buddhism in the Kamakura Period." Trans. James C. Dobbins. In *The Cambridge History of Japan*, vol. 3, *Medieval Japan*, ed. Kozo Yamamura, pp. 544–82. Cambridge, Eng.: Cambridge University Press, 1990.

Plutschow, Herbert E. *Chaos and Cosmos: Ritual in Early and Medieval Japanese Literature*. Leiden: Brill, 1990.

Rai Kiichi. "Koyū bunka no seijuku." In *Kōza Nihon rekishi, 6, Kinsei 2*, ed. Rekishigaku kenkyūkai and Nihonshi kenkyūkai, pp. 151–94. Tokyo: Tōkyō daigaku shuppankai, 1985.

———. "Kusazōshi ni arawareta shomin no sekaizō: Kibyōshi ni miru Edo no chōnin ishiki." In *Nihon no shakaishi, 7, Shakaikan to sekaizō*, ed. Asao Naohiro, pp. 225–60. Tokyo: Iwanami shoten, 1987.

Reader, Ian. *Religion in Contemporary Japan*. Honolulu: University of Hawaii Press, 1991.

Rogers, Lawrence. "She Loves Me, She Loves Me Not: Shinjū and *Shikidō ōkagami*." *Monumenta Nipponica* 49, no. 1 (Spring 1994): 31–60.

Rozman, Gilbert. "Edo's Importance in the Changing Tokugawa Society." *Journal of Japanese Studies* 1, no. 1 (Autumn 1974): 91–112.

Ruch, Barbara. "The Other Side of Culture in Medieval Japan." In *The Cambridge History of Japan*, vol. 3, *Medieval Japan*, ed. Kozo Yamamura, pp. 500–543. Cambridge, Eng.: Cambridge University Press, 1990.

Ryūtei Tanehiko. "Shunjō gidan mizuage chō." In *Hiseki Edo bungaku sen*, 5, annot. Irie Tomohide, pp. 15–143. Tokyo: Shōbunsha, 1975.

Saeki Junko. *Yūjo no bunkashi: Hare no onna tachi*. Tokyo: Chūō kōronsha, 1987.

Saigō Nobutsuna. "Ichi to utagaki." *Bungaku* 48, no. 4 (1980): 34–49.

Saitō Akitoshi. "Sanjūsan ka sho junrei to Kannon shinkō." In *Chichibu Bandō Kannon reijō*, ed. Nishiyama Matsunosuke, pp. 48–52. Tokyo: Shin jinbutsu ōraisha, 1984.

Saitō Gesshin. *Bukō nenpyō*. 1850. Reprinted in 2 vols., ed. Kaneko Mitsuharu. Tokyo: Heibonsha, 1968.

———. *Edo meisho zue*. 1834–36. Reprinted—Tokyo: Jinbutsu ōraisha, 1967.

———. *Saitō Gesshin nikki*. 1830–36. Ed. Tōkyō daigaku shiryō hensanjo. Tokyo: Iwanami shoten, 1997.

———. *Tōto saijiki*. 1838. Reprinted in 3 vols., annot. Asakura Haruhiko. Tōyō bunko, 159. Tokyo: Heibonsha, 1970.

Sakudō Yōtarō. "The Management Practices of Family Business." In *Tokugawa Japan: The Social and Economic Antecedents of Modern Japan*, ed. Chie Nakane and Shinzaburō Ōishi, pp. 147–66. Tokyo: Tokyo University Press, 1990.

Satō Toyozō. "Shōgun-ke onari ni tsuite, 1: Muromachi shōgun-ke no onari." *Kinkō sōsho* 1 (1974): 457–70.

———. "Shōgun-ke onari ni tsuite, 4: Ashikaga shōgun-ke no jike e no onari to kenbutsu." *Kinkō sōsho* 4 (1977): 559–76.

———. "Shōgun-ke onari ni tsuite, 6: Tokugawa shōgun-ke no onari so no ichi." *Kinkō sōsho* 7 (1980): 537–74.

———. "Shōgun-ke onari ni tsuite, 7: Tokugawa shōgun-ke no onari so no ni." *Kinkō sōsho* 8 (1981): 565–626.

Satō Yōjin. "Chaya." In *Edogaku jiten*, s.v. Tokyo: Kōbundō, 1994.

———. *Ehon mizuchaya fūzoku kō*. Tokyo: Yūkō shoten, 1977.

———. "Okabasho." In *Edogaku jiten*, s.v. Tokyo: Kōbundō, 1994.

Seigle, Cecilia Segawa. *Yoshiwara: The Glittering World of the Japanese Courtesan*. Honolulu: University of Hawaii Press, 1993.

Sekiyama Naotarō. *Kinsei Nihon no jinkō kōzō*. Tokyo: Yoshikawa kōbunkan, 1957.

Sensōji hinamiki kenkyūkai, ed. *Sensōji nikki*. 18 vols. Tokyo: Kinryūsan Sensōji, 1978–96.

Shibundō henshūbu, ed. *Senryū Edo meisho zue*. Tokyo: Shibundō, 1970.

Shikitei Sanba. *Ukiyo buro*. 1809–13. Ed. Nakamura Michio. *Nihon koten bungaku taikei*, 63. Tokyo: Iwanami shoten, 1957.

Shimizutani Kōshō. *Junrei no kokoro*. Tokyo: Okura shuppan, 1986.

———. *Kannon junrei no susume*. Osaka: Toki shobō, 1983.

———. "Sensōji to fudasho." In *Kaminarimon Edo banashi*, ed. Sensōji hinamiki kenkyūkai, pp. 3–9. Tokyo: Tōkyō bijutsu, 1986.

———. "Sōsō engi to reigen." In *Edo Asakusa o kataru*, ed. Sensōji hinamiki kenkyūkai, pp. 28–33. Tokyo: Tōkyō bijutsu, 1990.

Shinjō Tsunezō. *Shinkō jisha sangei no shakai keizaishi teki kenkyū*. Tokyo: Hanawa shobō, 1982.

Shintei zōho kokushi taikei: Tokugawa jikki, vols. 38, 39, 42. Reprinted—Tokyo: Yoshikawa kōbunkan, 1964.

Shioiri Nobukazu. "Sensōji no bōsha okuri: Shōgatsu gyōji no kanten kara." In *Bukkyō minzokugaku taikei, 6, Bukkyō nenjū gyōji*, ed. Itō Yuishin, pp. 321–52. Tokyo: Meicho shuppan, 1988.

Shirato Waka. "Inherent Enlightenment (*hongaku shisō*) and Saichō's Acceptance of the Bodhisattva Precepts." *Japanese Journal of Religious Studies* 14, nos. 2–3 (June-Sept. 1987): 113–27.

Shively, Donald H. "Popular Culture." In *The Cambridge History of Japan*, vol. 4, *Early Modern Japan*, ed. John Whitney Hall, pp. 706–69. Cambridge, Eng.: Cambridge University Press, 1991.

———. "The Social Environment of Tokugawa Kabuki." In *Studies in Kabuki: Its Acting, Music, and Historical Context*, ed. James R. Brandon, William P. Malm, and Donald H. Shively, pp. 5–18. Honolulu: University of Hawaii Press, 1978.

———. "Sumptuary Regulation and Status in Early Tokugawa Japan." *Harvard Journal of Asiatic Studies* 25 (1964–65): 123–64.

Smith, Henry D., II. "The Edo-Tokyo Transition: In Search of Common Ground." In *Japan in Transition: From Tokugawa to Meiji*, ed. Marius B. Jansen and Gilbert Rozman, pp. 347–74. Princeton: Princeton University Press, 1986.

———. "The Floating World in Its Edo Locale, 1750–1850." In *The Floating World Revisited*, ed. Donald Jenkins, pp. 25–45. Honolulu: University of Hawaii Press, 1993.

Smith, Henry D., II, ed. *Ukiyoe ni miru Edo meisho*. Tokyo: Iwanami shoten, 1993.

Soranaka, Isao. "The Kansei Reforms—Success or Failure?" *Monumenta Nipponica* 33, no. 1 (1978): 151–64.

Sueki Fumihiko. "Kami to Hotoke." In *Zusetsu Nihon no Bukkyō, 6, Shin-Butsu shūgo to Shugen*, ed. Tanabe Saburosuke, pp. 33–48. Tokyo: Shinchōsha, 1989.

Sutton-Smith, Brian. *The Ambiguity of Play*. Cambridge, Mass.: Harvard University Press, 1997.

Taishō shinshū daizōkyō. Tokyo: Daizō, 1924–32.

Taitō-ku kyōiku iinkai, ed. *Tomi kōgyō ikken ki*, 1. Tokyo: Taitō-ku kyōiku iinkai, 1991.

Takano Toshihiko. *Kinsei Nihon no kokka kenryoku to shūkyō*. Tokyo: Tōkyō daigaku shuppankai, 1989.

———. *Nihon no rekishi, 13, Genroku Kyōhō no jidai*. Tokyo: Shūeisha, 1992.

Takatori Masao. *Bukkyō dochaku*. Tokyo: Nihon hōsō shuppan kyōkai, 1973.

Takeuchi Makoto. "Festivals and Fights: The Law and the People of Edo." In *Edo and Paris: Urban Life and the State in the Early Modern Era*, ed. James L. McClain, John M. Merriman, and Ugawa Kaoru, pp. 384–406. Ithaca: Cornell University Press, 1994.

———. "Shomin bunka no naka no Edo." In *Nihon no kinsei, 14, Bunka no taishūka*, ed. Takeuchi Makoto, pp. 7–54. Tokyo: Chūō kōronsha, 1993.

———. "Tenmei kikin to Kaminarimon no saiken." In *Kaminarimon Edo banashi*, ed. Sensōji hinamiki kenkyūkai, pp. 162–66. Tokyo: Tōkyō bijutsu, 1986.

———. "Uchikowashi." In *Edogaku jiten*, s.v. Tokyo: Kōbundō, 1994.

———. "Yanagisawa Nobutoki to Sensōji." In *Kaminarimon Edo banashi*, ed. Sensōji hinamiki kenkyūkai, pp. 99–104. Tokyo: Tōkyō bijutsu, 1986.

Takigawa Masajirō. *Yūko no rekishi*. Tokyo: Shibundō, 1965.

Takizawa Bakin. *Bakin nikki*. 4 vols. Tokyo: Chūō kōronsha, 1973.

Tamamuro Fumio. "Bakuhan taiseika no Bukkyō." In *Ajia Bukkyō shi Nihon hen, 7, Edo Bukkyō—Taisei Bukkyō to chika shinkō*, ed. Nakamura Hajime and Kasahara Ichio, pp. 7–70. Tokyo: Kōsei shuppansha, 1972.

———. *Nihon Bukkyō shi: Kinsei*. Tokyo: Yoshikawa kōbunkan, 1987.

———. *Shin-Butsu bunri*. Tokyo: Kyōikusha, 1977.

Tanabe, Willa Jane. "The Lotus Lectures: Hokke Hakkō in the Heian Period." *Monumenta Nipponica* 39, no. 4 (Winter 1984): 393–407.

Tani Seigo. *Saishi to shisō: Shintō no inori*. Tokyo: Kokusho kankōkai, 1985.

Tanigawa Akio. "Edo no bochi no hakkutsu: Mibun kaisō no hyōchō toshite no haka." In *Yomigaeru Edo*, ed. Edo iseki kenkyūkai, pp. 79–111. Tokyo: Shin jinbutsu ōraisha, 1991.

Taniyama Masamichi. "Kamigata keizai to Edo jimawari keizai." In *Nihon no kinsei, 17, Higashi to nishi, Edo to Kamigata*, ed. Aoki Michio, pp. 113–58. Tokyo: Chūō kōronsha, 1994.

Terakado Seiken. *Edo hanjō ki*. 1832–36. 3 vols. Annot. and trans. Asakura Haruhiko and Andō Kikuji. Tōyō bunko, 259. Tokyo: Heibonsha, 1974.

Tokoro Rikio. "Edo no machi to monzen machi." In *Edo Asakusa o kataru*, ed. Sensōji hinamiki kenkyūkai, pp. 100–107. Tokyo: Tōkyō bijutsu, 1990.

———. "Go-shuinjō." In *Edo Asakusa o kataru*, ed. Sensōji hinamiki kenkyūkai, pp. 80–86. Tokyo: Tōkyō bijutsu, 1990.

———. "Jōkyō ni nen Sensōji bettō tsuihō jiken ni tsuite." In *Kaminarimon Edo banashi*, ed. Sensōji hinamiki kenkyūkai, pp. 200–206. Tokyo: Tōkyō bijutsu, 1986.

———. "Monzen machi no shihai." In *Edo Asakusa o kataru*, ed. Sensōji hinamiki kenkyūkai, pp. 94–99. Tokyo: Tōkyō bijutsu, 1990.

———. "Sensōji Sanfudai ni tsuite." In *Kaminarimon Edo banashi*, ed. Sensōji hinamiki kenkyūkai, pp. 224–28. Tokyo: Tōkyō bijutsu, 1986.

Totman, Conrad. *Early Modern Japan*. Berkeley: University of California Press, 1993.

Tsuji Tatsuya. "Politics in the Eighteenth Century." Trans. Harold Bolitho. In *The Cambridge History of Japan*, vol. 4, *Early Modern Japan*, ed. John Whitney Hall, pp. 425–77. Cambridge, Eng.: Cambridge University Press, 1991.

Tsuji Zennosuke. *Nihon Bukkyōshi: Kinsei hen no yon*. Tokyo: Iwanami shoten, 1955.

Tsukada Takashi. "Kasōmin no sekai: Mibun teki shūen no shiten kara." In *Nihon no kinsei, 7, Mibun to kakushiki*, ed. Asao Naohiro, pp. 225–68. Tokyo: Chūō kōronsha, 1992.

Tsukamoto Akira. "Toshi kōzō no tenkan." In *Iwanami kōza Nihon tsūshi, 14, Kinsei 4*, ed. Asao Naohiro, pp. 67–106. Tokyo: Iwanami shoten, 1995.

Turner, Victor. *From Ritual to Theater: The Human Seriousness of Play*. New York: Performing Arts Journal Publications, 1982.

Umeda Yoshihiko. *Nihon shūkyō seidoshi: kinsei hen*. Rev. ed. Tokyo: Tōsen shuppan, 1972.

Unno Hiroshi. *Edo no sakariba*. Tokyo: Seidosha, 1995.

Vaporis, Constantine Nomikos. *Breaking Barriers: Travel and the State in Early Modern Japan*. Cambridge, Mass.: Harvard University, Council on East Asian Studies, 1994.

Varley, Paul. *Japanese Culture*. 3d ed. Honolulu: University of Hawaii Press, 1984.

Wakabayashi, Bob Tadashi. *Japanese Loyalism Reconstrued: Yamagata Daini's "Ryūshi shinron" of 1759*. Honolulu: University of Hawaii Press, 1995.

Wakita Haruko. *Nihon chūsei toshi ron*. Tokyo: Tōkyō daigaku shuppankai, 1981.

Walthall, Anne. "Edo Riots." In *Edo and Paris: Urban Life and the State in the Early Modern Era*, ed. James L. McClain, John M. Merriman, and Ugawa Kaoru, pp. 407–28. Ithaca: Cornell University Press, 1994.

———. "Peripheries: Rural Culture in Tokugawa Japan." *Monumenta Nipponica* 39, no. 4 (Winter 1984): 371–92.

Watanabe Chikako. "Yakudoshi toshiiwai." In *Kōza Nihon no minzoku shūkyō, 1*, ed. Gorai Shigeru, pp. 325–40. Tokyo: Kōbundō, 1979.

Watt, Paul B. "Jiun Sonja, 1718–1804: A Response to Confucianism Within the Context of Buddhist Reform." In *Confucianism and Tokugawa Culture*, ed. Peter Nosco, pp. 188–214. Princeton: Princeton University Press, 1984.

White, James W. *The Demography of Sociopolitical Conflict in Japan, 1721–1846*. Berkeley: University of California Press, 1992.

Yabe Zenzō. *Shinsatsu kō*. Tokyo: Shiroutosha, 1934.

Yamaguchi Masao. "Sumō ni okeru girei to uchūkan." *Kokuritsu rekishi minzoku hakubutsukan kenkyū hōkoku* 15 (1987): 99–130.

Yamamura, Kozo. "The Increasing Poverty of the Samurai in Tokugawa Japan." *Journal of Economic History* 31 (June 1971): 378–406.

———. *A Study of Samurai Income and Entrepreneurship: Quantitative Analyses of Economic and Social Aspects of the Samurai in Tokugawa and Meiji Japan.* Cambridge, Mass.: Harvard University Press, 1978.

Yanagawa Keiichi. *Matsuri to girei no shūkyōgaku.* Tokyo: Chikuma shobō, 1987.

Yanagisawa Nobutoki. *Nihon shomin bunka shiryō shūsei,* vol. 13, *Enyū nikki.* Ed. Geinōshi kenkyūkai. Tokyo: Sanichi shobō, 1977.

Yanagita Kunio. "Ishi-gami mondō." In *Teihon Yanagita Kunio shū,* 12: 1–161. Tokyo: Chikuma shobō, 1963.

———. "Itaka oyobi sanka." In *Teihon Yanagita Kunio shū,* 4: 473–92. Tokyo: Chikuma shobō, 1963.

———. "Nihon no matsuri." In *Teihon Yanagita Kunio shū,* 10: 153–314. Tokyo: Chikuma shobō, 1962.

———. "Shinju hen." In *Teihon Yanagita Kunio shū,* 11: 1–180. Tokyo: Chikuma shobō, 1963.

———. "Toshi to nōson." In *Teihon Yanagita Kunio shū,* 16: 237–391. Tokyo: Chikuma shobō, 1962.

———. "Yama no jinsei." In *Teihon Yanagita Kunio shū,* 4: 55–186. Tokyo: Chikuma shobō, 1963.

Yasumaru Yoshio. *Nihon no kindaika to minshū shisō.* Tokyo: Aoki shoten, 1974.

Yoritomo Motohiro. *Mikkyō to mandara: So no mangekyō teki sekai.* Tokyo: Nihon hōsō shuppan kyōkai, 1990.

———. "Mikkyō to shuhō." In *Zusetsu Nihon no Bukkyō, 2, Mikkyō,* ed. Sekiguchi Masayuki, pp. 47–103. Tokyo: Shinchōsha, 1988.

Yoshida Nobuyuki. "Chōnin to machi." In *Kōza Nihon rekishi, 5, Kinsei 1,* ed. Rekishigaku kenkyūkai and Nihonshi kenkyūkai, pp. 151–88. Tokyo: Tōkyō daigaku shuppankai, 1985.

———. "Kyodai jōkamachi: Edo." In *Iwanami kōza Nihon tsūshi, 15, Kinsei 5,* pp. 149–88. Tokyo: Iwanami shoten, 1995.

———. "Omotedana to uradana: Shōnin no shakai, minshū no sekai." In *Nihon no kinsei, 9, Toshi no jidai,* ed. Yoshida Nobuyuki, pp. 303–58. Tokyo: Chūō kōronsha, 1992.

Yoshiwara Ken'ichirō. "Hirokōji." In *Edogaku jiten,* s.v. Tokyo: Kōbundō, 1994.

———. "Kaji." In *Edogaku jiten,* s.v. Tokyo: Kōbundō, 1994.

Yukawa Takashi. "Kinsei teki kaichō no seiritsu to bakufu no so no seisaku ito ni tsuite." *Shikan* 90 (1975): 25–37.

Character List

Adachi Morinaga 安達盛長
Akiba Daigongen 秋葉大権現
akubasho 悪場所
akujin 悪神
akutai shibai 悪態芝居
Anzaemon Inari 安左衛門稲荷
aragoto 荒事
Asai Ryōi 浅井了意
Asakusa hakkei 浅草八景
Asakusa hitotsuya 浅草一つ家
Asakusa Kannon 浅草観音
Asakusa Kannon reijō 浅草観音霊場
asobi 遊び
asobi-be 遊部
asobi-me 遊女
asobu 遊ぶ
Atago 愛宕
Awashima 淡島
ayatori 綾取

Baba Bunkō 馬場文耕
bakasawagi 馬鹿騒ぎ
bakufu 幕府
bakuhan 幕藩

Bandō Kannon reijō 坂東観音霊場
Bandō Kannon reijō ki 坂東観音霊場記
Batō Kannon 馬頭観音
Benzaiten 弁才天, 弁財天
bettō 別当
bettōdai 別当代
Bishamon 毘沙門
Bon 盆
Bon'ichi 盆市
Bonmōkyō 梵網経
botefuri 棒手振り
buke 武家
Bukō nenpyō 武江年表
bunjin 文人
Buyō Inshi 武陽隠士

chakumi onna 茶汲女
Chichibu Kannon reijō 秩父観音霊場
Ch'ien-shou ch'ien-yen Kuan-shih-yin p'u-sa ta-pei-hsin t'o-lo-ni ching 千手千眼観世音菩薩悲心陀羅尼経

chigari 地借
chihō fudasho 地方札所
Chikamatsu Monzaemon 近松門左衛門
chingo kokka 鎮護国家
chōgin 丁銀
Chōju-in 長寿院
chōnin 町人
Chu Hsi 朱熹
Chūkai 忠海
chūshin 中心
Chūun 忠運

daidōgei 大道芸
Dai-Hannya 大般若
Daijingū 大神宮
daijō hi-Butsu setsu 大乗非仏説
daikan 代官
Daikoku 大黒
daitsū 大通
danna 檀那
dannaji 檀那寺
daraku Bukkyō 堕落仏教
Darani-kō 陀羅尼講
Dazai Shundai 太宰春台
deai chaya 出合茶屋
de-gaichō 出開帳
dekasegi 出稼ぎ
Denbō-in 伝法院
dengaku 田楽
Dengyō Daishi Saichō 伝教大師最澄
deshi 弟子
dōban 堂番
dohyō 土俵
dōraku 道楽

Ebisu 恵比須
Echizen Matsudaira 越前松平
Echū 恵中
Edo hanjōki 江戸繁昌記
Edo kaimono hitori annai 江戸買物独案内
Edo Kannon fudasho 江戸観音札所
Edokko 江戸っ子
Edo meisho zue 江戸名所図会
Edo sō kanoko meisho taizen 江戸惣鹿子名所大全
ekō 回向
ekō girei 回向儀礼
Ekō-in 回向院
ema 絵馬
engi 縁起
Enma 閻魔
Enmei-in 延命院
Enmyōji 延命寺
ennichi 縁日
Ennin 円仁
Enyū nikki 宴遊日記
Erin 慧琳
Etchū Tsugaru 越中津軽
Fan wang ching 梵網経
fuda 札
fudasashi 札差し
Fudō 不動
Fugen 普賢
Fujimoto Kizan 藤本箕山
Fukai Shidōken 深井志道軒
Fumonbon 普門品
furegashira 触頭
furiuri 振売
furoya 風呂屋
furyū 風流
Fushimi Inari 伏見稲荷
fushin 普請

gakugyō 学業
gei 芸
geinō 芸能
Genroku 元禄
genze riyaku 現世利益
goeika 御詠歌
gojōmoku shūmon danna ukeai no okite 御条目宗門檀那請合之掟
gōkan 合巻
gokenin 御家人
Gokokuji 護国寺
goma 護摩
Gomamoku-kō 護摩木講
gōmune 乞胸
go'nin-gumi 五人組
gōnō 豪農
Goō kaji 牛王加持
goyō 御用
gozen 御前
Gozen-kō 御膳講
gunki monogatari 軍記物語
gusokukai 具足戒
gyaku kawase 逆為替

hachinin-gei 八人芸
Haji no Nakatomo 土師中知
hakai 破戒
hanada bōshi 縹帽子
hanazumō 花相撲
hare ハレ
hare no ba ハレの場
hari はり
Haruyama Utanosuke 春山歌之助
Hashimoto Yakushi 橋本薬師
hatamoto 旗本
hatsuuma 初午
Hayakawa Toraichi 早川虎市
hayarigami 流行神
hayarigami shinkō 流行神信仰
Hayashi Shihei 林子平
Hayatake Torakichi 早竹虎吉
Heishin kikō 丙辰紀行
heiwa 平和
hi-Butsu 秘仏
Hieizan hatto 比叡山法度
Higaki kaisen 菱垣廻船
Higaki kaisen zumi toiya nakama 菱垣廻船積問屋仲間
hihō (hidden treasures) 秘宝
hihō (secret dharma) 秘法
hikari no toshi 光の都市
hikyaku 飛脚
hinin 非人
Hinokuma Hamanari 檜前浜成
Hinokuma Takenari 檜前竹成
Hiraga Gennai 平賀源内
hitotsuya 一つ家
hiyoke-chi 火除地
hōe 法会
hōji zazen 法事座禅
hōjōe 放生会
Hokekyō 法華経
Hokkei 北渓
honden 本殿
hongaku shisō 本覚思想
honji suijaku 本地垂迹
honmatsu seido 本末制度
honne 本音
hōsō 疱瘡
Hossō 法相
hōtoku 報徳
Hōzen-in 法善院

hyō 俵

Ichide Shōshichirō 一出正七郎
ichigami 市神
Ichikawa Danjūrō 市川団十郎
ichimi 一味
iemochi 家持
iemoto 家元
igaku no kin 異学の禁
igyō 易行
Ihara Saikaku 井原西鶴
Ikeda Sadatsune 池田定常
iki いき
ikigami 生神
ikioi 勢い
Ikuta Yorozu 生田万
imi 忌
Ina Tadataka 伊那忠尊
Inari 稲荷
ingei 印契
inori 祈り
inzō 印相
Iō-in 医王院
Ise okagemairi 伊勢御陰参り
ishimakura 石枕
itsukime イツキ女
Iwaki Takayoshi 岩城隆恭

jigoku meguri 地獄巡り
Jijiroku 事々録
jinku okuri 神供送り
jinme 神馬
jinsei 仁政
Jippensha Ikku 十返舎一九
jiryō 寺領
jiryoku kōsei undō 自力更生運動
jisha bugyō 寺社奉行
jisha-chi 寺社地
jisha mōde 寺社詣
jishin-ge 自信偈
Jissō-in 実相院
Jitō 慈等
Jiun Sonja 慈雲尊者
jiyū 自由
Jizō 地蔵
jōmen 定免
Jōon-in 常音院
jōruri 浄瑠璃
Jūmannin-kō 十万人講
junrei 巡礼
junrei fuda 巡礼札
ju teki 呪的
jūzenkai 十善戒

kabuki mono かぶき者
kabu nakama 株仲間
kagura 神楽
Kaibara Ekken 貝原益軒
kaichō 開帳
kaihōku 解放区
Kaijō monogatari 海上物語
Kaikoku zakki 廻国雑記
kaisho 会所
Kaitokudō 懐徳堂
kakae yashiki 抱屋敷
kakemise 掛見世
kakuryoku 角力
kakushi baita 隠売女
Kameido Tenjin 亀戸天神
Kameido Tenmangū 亀戸天満宮
kami asobi 神遊び
Kamigata 上方
Kaminarimon 雷門
kamishimo 上下
kanameishi 要石
kan-Butsu 潅仏

Kanchi-in 観智院
Kanda matsuri 神田祭
Kan'eiji 寛永寺
kange 勧化
kani musume 蟹娘
kanjin 勧進
kanjin kōgyō 勧進興行
kanmon 貫文
Kannon Bosatsu 観音菩薩
Kannon-hō 観音法
Kannonkyō 観音経
Kannon myōō shū 観音冥応集
Kantō jimawari 関東地廻り
karakuri ningyō 絡繰人形
karitaku 仮宅
karuwaza 軽業
kasegi 稼ぎ
Kasei bunka 化政文化
kaseide asobu 稼いで遊ぶ
kashihonya 貸本屋
Kashima Daimyōjin 鹿島大明神
katabira 帷子
katsurame 桂女
Katsushika Hokusai 葛飾北斎
kau 買う
kawase tegata 為替手形
Kawashima Kayū 川島歌遊
keidai 境内
Keidai sō mise unjō chō 境内惣見世運上帳
Keizai roku 経済録
ken 間
kenchi 検地
Keshinosuke 芥子の介
kibyōshi 黄表紙
kichiji 吉事
kido 木戸
kienrei 棄損令
kigan 祈願
Kikukawa Kunimaru 菊川国丸
kimon 鬼門
kinen 祈念
Kinryūsan 金竜山
Kirinnosuke 麒麟之助
kiriotoshi 切落
Kishibo 鬼子母
kishō 祈請
Kitagawa Utamaro 喜多川歌麿
kitō 祈祷
kitō danna 祈祷檀那
kitō girei 祈祷儀礼
kitōji 祈祷寺
kizewa 生世話
kō (artisan) 工
kō (confraternity) 講
koban 小判
kōdō bunka 行動文化
kōgi 公儀
Kōgi roku 孝義録
kōgyō 興行
Kōjin 荒神
kokkeibon 滑稽本
kokoro 心
koku 石
Komakata 駒形
komori 篭り
Kongō-in 金剛院
Kongō rikishi 金剛力士
Konkōmyōkyō 金光明経
konpon Bukkyō 根本仏教
konyoku 混浴
Konzō-in 金蔵院
kōshaku 講釈
kōshin 庚申
koto 琴

kouta 小唄
Koyasu no Ishi 子安の石
Kuchō 公澄
kudarimono 下り物
kudoku nichi 功徳日
kugai 公界
kugutsu 傀儡
Kumagai Anzaemon 熊谷安左衛門
Kumagai Inari 熊谷稲荷
Kumano 熊野
Kume 久米
Kume Heinaibee 久米平内兵衛
kumiai 組合
kumotsu 供物
Kunen 公然
Kuruma Zenshichi 車善七
kusazōshi 草双紙
kusō 供僧
kyōdōtai ishiki 共同体意識
kyōka 狂歌
kyokugoma 曲独楽
kyokumari 曲鞠

machi 町
machi bugyō 町奉行
mai 枚
Masukagami 増鏡
Matsudaira Kanzan 松平冠山
Matsudaira Sadanobu 松平定信
Matsui Gensui 松井源水
matsuri 祭
matsuri age 祭り上げ
matsuri sute 祭り棄て
Meguro Fudō 目黒不動
meibutsu 名物
meisho meguri 名所廻り
michi 道
miko kigensetsu 巫女起源説
mikoshi 神輿
Mimeguri Inari 三囲稲荷
Minato 湊
minshū 民衆
miru 見る
mise 店
misemono 見世物
misemono-gei 見世物芸
Mitsui Echigoya 三井越後屋
miuchi 身内
miyage 土産
Miyako meisho zue 京名所図絵
miyasama onari 宮様お成り
mizuchaya 水茶屋
Mizuno Tadakuni 水野忠邦
Momijiyama Tōshōgū 紅葉山東照宮
Monju 文珠
monme 匁
monomane 物真似
monomi yusan 物見遊山
monoyomi 物読
monzeki 門跡
monzen 門前
monzen machi 門前町
Morita-za 森田座
morohaku 諸白
muen 無縁
Murayama-za 村山座
mure no shūkyō 群れの宗教
musō no megusuri 夢想の目薬
myōgakin 冥加金
Myōon-in 妙音院
Myōtoku-in 妙徳院

Nagato Hosokawa 長門細川
nagaya kurashi 長屋暮らし
Nakai Chikuzan 中井竹山

nakamise 仲見世
Nakamura-za 中村座
Namiki 並木
nanga 南画
Naniwa 難波
Naniwa-kō 浪花講
Nankei 南渓
Nansō Satomi Hakken den 南総里見八犬伝
nanushi 名主
Nara chaya 奈良茶屋
narimono 鳴物
nehan 涅槃
Nenashigusa 根南志具佐
nenbutsu 念仏
nenjū gyōji 年中行事
Nezu Gongen 根津権現
Nichion-in 日音院
nigu 二求
Nijikken chaya 二十軒茶屋
nikujiki 肉食
ninjōbon 人情本
Ninnōkyō 仁王経
Ninomiya Sontoku 二宮尊徳
ninsoku yoseba 人足寄場
Niōmon 仁王門
Nishi Takamori-kō 西高盛講
Nishinomiya Ebisu 西宮恵比須
Nishizawa Ippō 西沢一鳳
nori 海苔
noshime 熨斗目
nozoki 覗
nyobon 女犯

ofumi お文
Ogyū Sorai 荻生徂徠
Ōhara Yūgaku 大原幽学
oie sōdō 御家騒動
okabasho 岡場所
Okashi-kō 御菓子講
Okita おきた
okite 掟
oku 奥
Okuyama 奥山
omaetate no honzon お前立ての本尊
omote 表
onando 御納戸
onna jōruri 女浄瑠璃
Onza darani 温座陀羅尼
ōoku 大奥
Oroku お六
Ōshio Heihachirō 大塩平八郎
Otatami-kō 御畳講

paekchŏng 白丁

reigenki 霊験記
reijō 霊場
Rikugien 六義園
Rinnōji 輪王寺
Rōjo Benzaiten 老女弁財天
Rokkakudō 六角堂
rokudō-bakku 六道抜苦
rōnin 浪人
Rōsoku-kō 蝋燭講
ryō 両
Ryōgoku 両国
ryōnai 領内
Ryūtei Tanehiko 柳亭種彦

Sado Rokugō 佐渡六郷
Saichō 最澄
Saigoku Kannon reijō 西国観音霊場
saijitsu 祭日
saiku 細工

sainan 災難
sairei 祭礼
saisen 賽銭
Saitō-bō 斎頭坊
Saitō Gesshin 斎藤月岑
saiyaku 災厄
sajiki 桟敷
Sakai-ya 堺屋
sakariba 盛り場
Sakurazuna Komaju 桜綱駒寿
sandoku 三毒
Sanfudai 三譜代
Sanja Daigongen 三社大権現
sanki 三季
sankin kōtai 参勤交代
Sankyō kaisho 三橋会所
sannai 山内
Sannō Gongen 山王権現
Sannō-sai 山王祭
Santo-kō 三都講
Santō Kyōden 山東京伝
Sanzu-no-Kawa 三途の川
saru (monkey) 猿
saru (remove) 去る
sarugaku 猿楽
saruwaka 猿若
Seidan 政談
seii tai shōgun 征夷大将軍
seikai 誓戒
Seishi 勢至
Seji kenbun roku 世事見聞録
sekihan 赤飯
sekkyō 説経
Sendō-bō 専堂坊
senju darani 千手陀羅尼
senki 疝気
senryū 川柳
Sensōji 浅草寺
Sensōji nikki 浅草寺日記
Sensōji shi 浅草寺志
Sen'yō eikyū roku 撰要永久録
Senzō-in 泉蔵院
Senzoku 千束
shaku (measurement) 尺
shaku (sharp pain) 癪
sharebon 酒落本
shasō 社僧
shibai 芝居
Shibaraku しばらく
shichibu tsumikin 七分積金
shichinan 七難
shidōkin 祠堂金
shigoto 仕事
shikidō 色道
Shikidō ōkagami 色道大鏡
shiki kanjin sumō 四季勧進相撲
shikimoku 式目
Shikitei Sanba 式亭三馬
Shiman rokusen nichi 四万六千日
Shingaku 心学
shingon 真言
shinkō 信仰
Shinobazu Benzaiten 不忍弁財天
shintai 神体
Shiroki-ya 白木屋
Shitennōji 四天王寺
shō 商
Shōchi-in 正智院
shogan 諸願
Shōgo-in 聖護院
shōgun onari 将軍お成り
shōji 承仕
Sho-jiin jōmoku 諸寺院条目
Shōji Jin'emon 庄司甚衛門
shōjin otoshi 精進落とし

Shō Kannon 聖観音
shōrui awaremi no rei 生類憐みの令
shōshimin 小市民
shoshū sōryo hatto 諸宗僧侶法度
shudō girei 修道儀礼
Shugendō 修験道
Shugen Honzan 修験本山
shugenja 修験者
shukkesha 出家者
shūmon ninbetsu chō 宗門人別帳
shunga 春画
shūshō 修正
Sō Yoshiari 宗義藩
Soga monogatari 曾我物語
sokushin jō-Butsu 即身成仏
somekosode 染小袖
sōshiki Bukkyō 葬式仏教
Sūden 崇伝
Sugimoto Mojūrō 杉本茂十郎
sui 粋
sun 寸
Suō Mōri 周防毛利
susuhaki 煤掃
susu harai 煤払
sutego 捨子
Sutejirō 捨次郎

taberu 食べる
Taiheiki 太平記
Takizawa Bakin 滝沢馬琴
tako-age 凧揚げ
Tamenaga Shunsui 為長春水
tanagari 店借
Tanigawa Sadakichi 谷川定吉
Tanuma Okitsugu 田沼意次
tatemae 建前
tayū 太夫
Tendai 天台
Tenkai 天海
tenka matsuri 天下祭
Tenmangū 天満宮
tenryō 天領
Terakado Seiken 寺門靜軒
terakoya 寺子屋
terauke 寺請
Tōba-kō 塔婆講
tobi 鳶
Tōei 東叡
Tōkaidōchū hizakurige 東海道中膝栗毛
Tōkaidō Yotsuya kaidan 東海道四谷怪談
toku 徳
Tokugawa Nariaki 徳川斉昭
Tokumi toiya 十組問屋
Tokuō-in 徳応院
tokuri 徳利
Tokuryū 徳竜
tomitsuki 富突
tosei 渡世
toshi-no-ichi 年の市
Tōshō Daigongen 東照大権現
Tōshōgū 東照宮
Tōto saijiki 東都歳時記
Tōyama Kagemoto 遠山景元
tsū 通
tsubazeriai 鍔迫合
tsubo 坪
tsubone 局
tsuina 追儺
tsuizen kuyō 追善供養
tsujibansho 辻番所
tsuji hōge 辻放下
Tsuruya Nanboku 鶴屋南北

Tsutaya Jūzaburō 蔦屋重三郎
tsutsushimi 慎み
tsūzoku dōtoku 通俗道徳

uchikowashi 打毀
ujiko 氏子
ukiyo 浮世
Ukiyo buro 浮世風呂
unjōkin 運上金
ura 裏
uradana 裏店
utagaki 歌垣
Utagawa Hiroshige 歌川広重
Utagawa Kuniyoshi 歌川国芳
Utagawa Toyokuni 歌川豊国

yaba onna 矢場女
yabo 野暮
yabusame 流鏑馬
yaku 役
yakudoshi 厄年
yakuryō 役料
yakusha 役者
Yakushi 薬師
Yamagata Daini 山県大弐
Yamamoto Kojima 山本小島
Yamanashi Inakawa 山梨稲川
yami no toshi 闇の都市
yamori 家守
Yanagawa Itchōsai 柳川一蝶斎
Yanagisawa Nobutoki 柳沢信鴻
yashi 香具師
yashiki 屋敷
yasuuri 安売り
yatori onna 矢取女
Yin-Yang 陰陽
yōkyū 楊弓
yonaoshi 世直し
yorishiro 依代
yose 寄席
Yoshida Oikaze 吉田追風
Yoshida Zenzaemon 吉田善左衛門
Yoshiwara 吉原
Yoshiwara saiken 吉原細見
yoshizubari 葦簀張
yūgei 遊芸
yukidaore 行倒れ
yuna 湯女
yūraku 遊楽
yusan 遊山
Yushima Tenjin 湯島天神

zashiki jōruri 座敷浄瑠璃
Zōjōji 増上寺
Zōka-kō 造花講
Zon'ō 存応
Zuijinmon 随身門

Index

Harvard East Asian Monographs

(* out-of-print)

*1. Liang Fang-chung, *The Single-Whip Method of Taxation in China*

*2. Harold C. Hinton, *The Grain Tribute System of China, 1845–1911*

3. Ellsworth C. Carlson, *The Kaiping Mines, 1877–1912*

*4. Chao Kuo-chün, *Agrarian Policies of Mainland China: A Documentary Study, 1949–1956*

*5. Edgar Snow, *Random Notes on Red China, 1936–1945*

*6. Edwin George Beal, Jr., *The Origin of Likin, 1835–1864*

7. Chao Kuo-chün, *Economic Planning and Organization in Mainland China: A Documentary Study, 1949–1957*

*8. John K. Fairbank, *Ching Documents: An Introductory Syllabus*

*9. Helen Yin and Yi-chang Yin, *Economic Statistics of Mainland China, 1949–1957*

*10. Wolfgang Franke, *The Reform and Abolition of the Traditional Chinese Examination System*

11. Albert Feuerwerker and S. Cheng, *Chinese Communist Studies of Modern Chinese History*

12. C. John Stanley, *Late Ching Finance: Hu Kuang-yung as an Innovator*

13. S. M. Meng, *The Tsungli Yamen: Its Organization and Functions*

*14. Ssu-yü Teng, *Historiography of the Taiping Rebellion*

15. Chun-Jo Liu, *Controversies in Modern Chinese Intellectual History: An Analytic Bibliography of Periodical Articles, Mainly of the May Fourth and Post–May Fourth Era*

*16. Edward J. M. Rhoads, *The Chinese Red Army, 1927–1963: An Annotated Bibliography*

17. Andrew J. Nathan, *A History of the China International Famine Relief Commission*

HARVARD EAST ASIAN MONOGRAPHS

*18. Frank H. H. King (ed.) and Prescott Clarke, *A Research Guide to China-Coast Newspapers, 1822–1911*

19. Ellis Joffe, *Party and Army: Professionalism and Political Control in the Chinese Officer Corps, 1949–1964*

*20. Toshio G. Tsukahira, *Feudal Control in Tokugawa Japan: The Sankin Kōtai System*

21. Kwang-Ching Liu, ed., *American Missionaries in China: Papers from Harvard Seminars*

22. George Moseley, *A Sino-Soviet Cultural Frontier: The Ili Kazakh Autonomous Chou*

23. Carl F. Nathan, *Plague Prevention and Politics in Manchuria, 1910–1931*

*24. Adrian Arthur Bennett, *John Fryer: The Introduction of Western Science and Technology into Nineteenth-Century China*

25. Donald J. Friedman, *The Road from Isolation: The Campaign of the American Committee for Non-Participation in Japanese Aggression, 1938–1941*

26. Edward LeFevour, *Western Enterprise in Late Ching China: A Selective Survey of Jardine, Matheson and Company's Operations, 1842–1895*

27. Charles Neuhauser, *Third World Politics: China and the Afro-Asian People's Solidarity Organization, 1957–1967*

28. Kungtu C. Sun, assisted by Ralph W. Huenemann, *The Economic Development of Manchuria in the First Half of the Twentieth Century*

*29. Shahid Javed Burki, *A Study of Chinese Communes, 1965*

30. John Carter Vincent, *The Extraterritorial System in China: Final Phase*

31. Madeleine Chi, *China Diplomacy, 1914–1918*

*32. Clifton Jackson Phillips, *Protestant America and the Pagan World: The First Half Century of the American Board of Commissioners for Foreign Missions, 1810–1860*

33. James Pusey, *Wu Han: Attacking the Present through the Past*

34. Ying-wan Cheng, *Postal Communication in China and Its Modernization, 1860–1896*

35. Tuvia Blumenthal, *Saving in Postwar Japan*

36. Peter Frost, *The Bakumatsu Currency Crisis*

37. Stephen C. Lockwood, *Augustine Heard and Company, 1858–1862*

38. Robert R. Campbell, *James Duncan Campbell: A Memoir by His Son*

39. Jerome Alan Cohen, ed., *The Dynamics of China's Foreign Relations*

40. V. V. Vishnyakova-Akimova, *Two Years in Revolutionary China, 1925–1927*, tr. Steven L. Levine

*41. Meron Medzini, *French Policy in Japan during the Closing Years of the Tokugawa Regime*
42. Ezra Vogel, Margie Sargent, Vivienne B. Shue, Thomas Jay Mathews, and Deborah S. Davis, *The Cultural Revolution in the Provinces*
*43. Sidney A. Forsythe, *An American Missionary Community in China, 1895–1905*
*44. Benjamin I. Schwartz, ed., *Reflections on the May Fourth Movement.: A Symposium*
*45. Ching Young Choe, *The Rule of the Taewŏngun, 1864–1873: Restoration in Yi Korea*
46. W. P. J. Hall, *A Bibliographical Guide to Japanese Research on the Chinese Economy, 1958–1970*
47. Jack J. Gerson, *Horatio Nelson Lay and Sino-British Relations, 1854–1864*
48. Paul Richard Bohr, *Famine and the Missionary: Timothy Richard as Relief Administrator and Advocate of National Reform*
49. Endymion Wilkinson, *The History of Imperial China: A Research Guide*
50. Britten Dean, *China and Great Britain: The Diplomacy of Commercial Relations, 1860–1864*
51. Ellsworth C. Carlson, *The Foochow Missionaries, 1847–1880*
52. Yeh-chien Wang, *An Estimate of the Land-Tax Collection in China, 1753 and 1908*
53. Richard M. Pfeffer, *Understanding Business Contracts in China, 1949–1963*
54. Han-sheng Chuan and Richard Kraus, *Mid-Ching Rice Markets and Trade: An Essay in Price History*
55. Ranbir Vohra, *Lao She and the Chinese Revolution*
56. Liang-lin Hsiao, *China's Foreign Trade Statistics, 1864–1949*
*57. Lee-hsia Hsu Ting, *Government Control of the Press in Modern China, 1900–1949*
58. Edward W. Wagner, *The Literati Purges: Political Conflict in Early Yi Korea*
*59. Joungwon A. Kim, *Divided Korea: The Politics of Development, 1945–1972*
*60. Noriko Kamachi, John K. Fairbank, and Chūzō Ichiko, *Japanese Studies of Modern China Since 1953: A Bibliographical Guide to Historical and Social-Science Research on the Nineteenth and Twentieth Centuries, Supplementary Volume for 1953–1969*
61. Donald A. Gibbs and Yun-chen Li, *A Bibliography of Studies and Translations of Modern Chinese Literature, 1918–1942*
62. Robert H. Silin, *Leadership and Values: The Organization of Large-Scale Taiwanese Enterprises*
63. David Pong, *A Critical Guide to the Kwangtung Provincial Archives Deposited at the Public Record Office of London*

HARVARD EAST ASIAN MONOGRAPHS

*64. Fred W. Drake, *China Charts the World: Hsu Chi-yü and His Geography of 1848*

*65. William A. Brown and Urgrunge Onon, translators and annotators, *History of the Mongolian People's Republic*

66. Edward L. Farmer, *Early Ming Government: The Evolution of Dual Capitals*

*67. Ralph C. Croizier, *Koxinga and Chinese Nationalism: History, Myth, and the Hero*

*68. William J. Tyler, tr., *The Psychological World of Natsume Sōseki*, by Doi Takeo

69. Eric Widmer, *The Russian Ecclesiastical Mission in Peking during the Eighteenth Century*

*70. Charlton M. Lewis, *Prologue to the Chinese Revolution: The Transformation of Ideas and Institutions in Hunan Province, 1891–1907*

71. Preston Torbert, *The Ch'ing Imperial Household Department: A Study of Its Organization and Principal Functions, 1662–1796*

72. Paul A. Cohen and John E. Schrecker, eds., *Reform in Nineteenth-Century China*

73. Jon Sigurdson, *Rural Industrialism in China*

74. Kang Chao, *The Development of Cotton Textile Production in China*

75. Valentin Rabe, *The Home Base of American China Missions, 1880–1920*

*76. Sarasin Viraphol, *Tribute and Profit: Sino-Siamese Trade, 1652–1853*

77. Ch'i-ch'ing Hsiao, *The Military Establishment of the Yuan Dynasty*

78. Meishi Tsai, *Contemporary Chinese Novels and Short Stories, 1949–1974: An Annotated Bibliography*

*79. Wellington K. K. Chan, *Merchants, Mandarins and Modern Enterprise in Late Ch'ing China*

80. Endymion Wilkinson, *Landlord and Labor in Late Imperial China: Case Studies from Shandong by Jing Su and Luo Lun*

*81. Barry Keenan, *The Dewey Experiment in China: Educational Reform and Political Power in the Early Republic*

*82. George A. Hayden, *Crime and Punishment in Medieval Chinese Drama: Three Judge Pao Plays*

*83. Sang-Chul Suh, *Growth and Structural Changes in the Korean Economy, 1910–1940*

84. J. W. Dower, *Empire and Aftermath: Yoshida Shigeru and the Japanese Experience, 1878–1954*

85. Martin Collcutt, *Five Mountains: The Rinzai Zen Monastic Institution in Medieval Japan*

86. Kwang Suk Kim and Michael Roemer, *Growth and Structural Transformation*

87. Anne O. Krueger, *The Developmental Role of the Foreign Sector and Aid*

*88. Edwin S. Mills and Byung-Nak Song, *Urbanization and Urban Problems*
89. Sung Hwan Ban, Pal Yong Moon, and Dwight H. Perkins, *Rural Development*
*90. Noel F. McGinn, Donald R. Snodgrass, Yung Bong Kim, Shin-Bok Kim, and Quee-Young Kim, *Education and Development in Korea*
91. Leroy P. Jones and Il SaKong, *Government, Business, and Entrepreneurship in Economic Development: The Korean Case*
92. Edward S. Mason, Dwight H. Perkins, Kwang Suk Kim, David C. Cole, Mahn Je Kim et al., *The Economic and Social Modernization of the Republic of Korea*
93. Robert Repetto, Tai Hwan Kwon, Son-Ung Kim, Dae Young Kim, John E. Sloboda, and Peter J. Donaldson, *Economic Development, Population Policy, and Demographic Transition in the Republic of Korea*
94. Parks M. Coble, Jr., *The Shanghai Capitalists and the Nationalist Government, 1927–1937*
95. Noriko Kamachi, *Reform in China: Huang Tsun-hsien and the Japanese Model*
96. Richard Wich, *Sino-Soviet Crisis Politics: A Study of Political Change and Communication*
97. Lillian M. Li, *China's Silk Trade: Traditional Industry in the Modern World, 1842–1937*
98. R. David Arkush, *Fei Xiaotong and Sociology in Revolutionary China*
*99. Kenneth Alan Grossberg, *Japan's Renaissance: The Politics of the Muromachi Bakufu*
100. James Reeve Pusey, *China and Charles Darwin*
101. Hoyt Cleveland Tillman, *Utilitarian Confucianism: Chen Liang's Challenge to Chu Hsi*
102. Thomas A. Stanley, *Ōsugi Sakae, Anarchist in Taishō Japan: The Creativity of the Ego*
103. Jonathan K. Ocko, *Bureaucratic Reform in Provincial China: Ting Jih-ch'ang in Restoration Kiangsu, 1867–1870*
104. James Reed, *The Missionary Mind and American East Asia Policy, 1911–1915*
105. Neil L. Waters, *Japan's Local Pragmatists: The Transition from Bakumatsu to Meiji in the Kawasaki Region*
106. David C. Cole and Yung Chul Park, *Financial Development in Korea, 1945–1978*
107. Roy Bahl, Chuk Kyo Kim, and Chong Kee Park, *Public Finances during the Korean Modernization Process*
108. William D. Wray, *Mitsubishi and the N.Y.K, 1870–1914: Business Strategy in the Japanese Shipping Industry*

109. Ralph William Huenemann, *The Dragon and the Iron Horse: The Economics of Railroads in China, 1876–1937*
110. Benjamin A. Elman, *From Philosophy to Philology: Intellectual and Social Aspects of Change in Late Imperial China*
111. Jane Kate Leonard, *Wei Yüan and China's Rediscovery of the Maritime World*
112. Luke S. K. Kwong, *A Mosaic of the Hundred Days:. Personalities, Politics, and Ideas of 1898*
113. John E. Wills, Jr., *Embassies and Illusions: Dutch and Portuguese Envoys to K'ang-hsi, 1666–1687*
114. Joshua A. Fogel, *Politics and Sinology: The Case of Naitō Konan (1866–1934)*
*115. Jeffrey C. Kinkley, ed., *After Mao: Chinese Literature and Society, 1978– 1981*
116. C. Andrew Gerstle, *Circles of Fantasy: Convention in the Plays of Chikamatsu*
117. Andrew Gordon, *The Evolution of Labor Relations in Japan: Heavy Industry, 1853–1955*
*118. Daniel K. Gardner, *Chu Hsi and the "Ta Hsueh": Neo-Confucian Reflection on the Confucian Canon*
119. Christine Guth Kanda, *Shinzō: Hachiman Imagery and Its Development*
*120. Robert Borgen, *Sugawara no Michizane and the Early Heian Court*
121. Chang-tai Hung, *Going to the People: Chinese Intellectual and Folk Literature, 1918–1937*
*122. Michael A. Cusumano, *The Japanese Automobile Industry: Technology and Management at Nissan and Toyota*
123. Richard von Glahn, *The Country of Streams and Grottoes: Expansion, Settlement, and the Civilizing of the Sichuan Frontier in Song Times*
124. Steven D. Carter, *The Road to Komatsubara: A Classical Reading of the Renga Hyakuin*
125. Katherine F. Bruner, John K. Fairbank, and Richard T. Smith, *Entering China's Service: Robert Hart's Journals, 1854–1863*
126. Bob Tadashi Wakabayashi, *Anti-Foreignism and Western Learning in Early-Modern Japan: The "New Theses" of 1825*
127. Atsuko Hirai, *Individualism and Socialism: The Life and Thought of Kawai Eijirō (1891–1944)*
128. Ellen Widmer, *The Margins of Utopia: "Shui-hu hou-chuan" and the Literature of Ming Loyalism*
129. R. Kent Guy, *The Emperor's Four Treasuries: Scholars and the State in the Late Chien-lung Era*
130. Peter C. Perdue, *Exhausting the Earth: State and Peasant in Hunan, 1500–1850*

131. Susan Chan Egan, *A Latterday Confucian: Reminiscences of William Hung (1893–1980)*
132. James T. C. Liu, *China Turning Inward: Intellectual-Political Changes in the Early Twelfth Century*
133. Paul A. Cohen, *Between Tradition and Modernity: Wang T'ao and Reform in Late Ching China*
134. Kate Wildman Nakai, *Shogunal Politics: Arai Hakuseki and the Premises of Tokugawa Rule*
135. Parks M. Coble, *Facing Japan: Chinese Politics and Japanese Imperialism, 1931–1937*
136. Jon L. Saari, *Legacies of Childhood: Growing Up Chinese in a Time of Crisis, 1890–1920*
137. Susan Downing Videen, *Tales of Heichū*
138. Heinz Morioka and Miyoko Sasaki, *Rakugo: The Popular Narrative Art of Japan*
139. Joshua A. Fogel, *Nakae Ushikichi in China: The Mourning of Spirit*
140. Alexander Barton Woodside, *Vietnam and the Chinese Model.: A Comparative Study of Vietnamese and Chinese Government in the First Half of the Nineteenth Century*
141. George Elision, *Deus Destroyed: The Image of Christianity in Early Modern Japan*
142. William D. Wray, ed., *Managing Industrial Enterprise: Cases from Japan's Prewar Experience*
143. T'ung-tsu Ch'ü, *Local Government in China under the Ching*
144. Marie Anchordoguy, *Computers, Inc.: Japan's Challenge to IBM*
145. Barbara Molony, *Technology and Investment: The Prewar Japanese Chemical Industry*
146. Mary Elizabeth Berry, *Hideyoshi*
147. Laura E. Hein, *Fueling Growth: The Energy Revolution and Economic Policy in Postwar Japan*
148. Wen-hsin Yeh, *The Alienated Academy: Culture and Politics in Republican China, 1919–1937*
149. Dru C. Gladney, *Muslim Chinese: Ethnic Nationalism in the People's Republic*
150. Merle Goldman and Paul A. Cohen, eds., *Ideas Across Cultures: Essays on Chinese Thought in Honor of Benjamin L Schwartz*
151. James Polachek, *The Inner Opium War*
152. Gail Lee Bernstein, *Japanese Marxist: A Portrait of Kawakami Hajime, 1879–1946*

HARVARD EAST ASIAN MONOGRAPHS

153. Lloyd E. Eastman, *The Abortive Revolution: China under Nationalist Rule, 1927–1937*
154. Mark Mason, *American Multinationals and Japan: The Political Economy of Japanese Capital Controls, 1899–1980*
155. Richard J. Smith, John K. Fairbank, and Katherine F. Bruner, *Robert Hart and China's Early Modernization: His Journals, 1863–1866*
156. George J. Tanabe, Jr., *Myōe the Dreamkeeper: Fantasy and Knowledge in Kamakura Buddhism*
157. William Wayne Farris, *Heavenly Warriors: The Evolution of Japan's Military, 500–1300*
158. Yu-ming Shaw, *An American Missionary in China: John Leighton Stuart and Chinese-American Relations*
159. James B. Palais, *Politics and Policy in Traditional Korea*
160. Douglas Reynolds, *China, 1898–1912: The Xinzheng Revolution and Japan*
161. Roger Thompson, *China's Local Councils in the Age of Constitutional Reform*
162. William Johnston, *The Modern Epidemic: History of Tuberculosis in Japan*
163. Constantine Nomikos Vaporis, *Breaking Barriers: Travel and the State in Early Modern Japan*
164. Irmela Hijiya-Kirschnereit, *Rituals of Self-Revelation: Shishōsetsu as Literary Genre and Socio-Cultural Phenomenon*
165. James C. Baxter, *The Meiji Unification through the Lens of Ishikawa Prefecture*
166. Thomas R. H. Havens, *Architects of Affluence: The Tsutsumi Family and the Seibu-Saison Enterprises in Twentieth-Century Japan*
167. Anthony Hood Chambers, *The Secret Window: Ideal Worlds in Tanizaki's Fiction*
168. Steven J. Ericson, *The Sound of the Whistle: Railroads and the State in Meiji Japan*
169. Andrew Edmund Goble, *Kenmu: Go-Daigo's Revolution*
170. Denise Potrzeba Lett, *In Pursuit of Status: The Making of South Korea's "New" Urban Middle Class*
171. Mimi Hall Yiengpruksawan, *Hiraizumi: Buddhist Art and Regional Politics in Twelfth-Century Japan*
172. Charles Shirō Inouye, *The Similitude of Blossoms: A Critical Biography of Izumi Kyōka (1873–1939), Japanese Novelist and Playwright*
173. Aviad E. Raz, *Riding the Black Ship: Japan and Tokyo Disneyland*
174. Deborah J. Milly, *Poverty, Equality, and Growth: The Politics of Economic Need in Postwar Japan*

175. See Heng Teow, *Japan's Cultural Policy Toward China, 1918–1931: A Comparative Perspective*
176. Michael A. Fuller, *An Introduction to Literary Chinese*
177. Frederick R. Dickinson, *War and National Reinvention: Japan in the Great War, 1914–1919*
178. John Solt, *Shredding the Tapestry of Meaning: The Poetry and Poetics of Kitasono Katue (1902–1978)*
179. Edward Pratt, *Japan's Protoindustrial Elite: The Economic Foundations of the Gōnō*
180. Atsuko Sakaki, *Recontextualizing Texts: Narrative Performance in Modern Japanese Fiction*
181. Soon-Won Park, *Colonial Industrialization and Labor in Korea: The Onoda Cement Factory*
182. JaHyun Kim Haboush and Martina Deuchler, *Culture and the State in Late Chosŏn Korea*
183. John W. Chaffee, *Branches of Heaven: A History of the Imperial Clan of Sung China*
184. Gi-Wook Shin and Michael Robinson, eds., *Colonial Modernity in Korea*
185. Nam-lin Hur, *Prayer and Play in Late Tokugawa Japan: Asakusa Sensōji and Edo Society*